D0200828

SYDNEY SMITH

By the same author

The Church in an Age of Negligence

SYDNEY SMITH

PETER VIRGIN

HarperCollins*Publishers*

HarperCollins*Publishers*
77–85 Fulham Palace Road,
Hammersmith, London W6 8 J B

Published by HarperCollins*Publishers* 1994
1 3 5 7 9 8 6 4 2

A catalogue record for this book is
available from the British Library

ISBN 0 00215890 6

Set in Linotron Sabon at
The Spartan Press Ltd
Lymington, Hants

Printed in Great Britain by
HarperCollinsManufacturing Glasgow

For Rachel and Talitha in love and gratitude

CONTENTS

PREFACE

Sydney Smith (1771–1845) deserves to be more widely known. His contemporaries would be mystified by his relative obscurity. 'You can't say too much about Sydney' was the verdict of Sir Walter Scott; Macaulay, the great Whig historian, spoke of 'The Smith of Smiths'; Abraham Lincoln was an avid admirer; and Queen Victoria found Sydney's jokes so amusing that they invariably threw her into fits of laughter. Few of those who met Sydney doubted that he had a touch of comic genius. He has been described as 'the greatest English wit of the nineteenth century', a century which, of course, includes Oscar Wilde.

Sydney deserves recognition apart from his humour. He is, as G. K. Chesterton rightly pointed out, 'one of the most remarkable of the makers of the great modern mood of liberty'. Sydney's record on this score is impressive: he argued passionately for removal of civil disabilities from the backs of religious minorities, for freedom in the expression of political opinions, and for compassionate government in Ireland. A robust and effective social commentator, he was a firm friend of the oppressed, the mentally ill and the poor, and he championed the rights of women.

I have tried in this biography to paint a portrait of Sydney 'warts and all', giving as much weight to his flaws as to his virtues. Beneath the brilliant surface of Sydney's life lurked deep and troubled waters. Effervescent in society, he was often morose when alone. 'You say', he once told a friend, 'I have many comic ideas rising in my mind; this may be true; but the champagne bottle is no better for holding the champagne.' There were also other tensions. A person driven by high principle, he was very ambitious for himself and could be money-grubbing. Complete lack of vanity coexisted with enormous pride.

Somewhere among the voluminous papers of the diarist A. C. Benson is a brief sketch of the ideal subject for biography. 'Such men and women', writes Benson, 'have inspired deep emotions, have loved intensely, have cast a glow upon the lives of a wide circle, have said delicate, sympathetic, perceptive and suggestive things, have given meaning and joy to life, have radiated interest and charm' (David Newsome, *On the Edge of Paradise*, John Murray, 1980, p. 12). Sydney fully meets this ideal.

There is one qualification in a subject for biography which Benson does not mention; although one man or woman necessarily holds centre-stage, it is vital to have a lively supporting cast. Sydney's family and friends do not let the audience down. His father was a larger-than-life character, a strange mixture of Scrooge and Count Casanova, while his mother was beautiful, fragile and artistic. Among Sydney's intimate friends were numerous fascinating men and women: Henry, third Baron Holland, full of sparkling anecdote and conspicuous affability; his wife Elizabeth, the famous hostess, a woman who was both imperious and superstitious, a scheming person who could be very generous, a sensuous beauty laid low by persistent attacks of hypochondria; Earl Grey, prime minister, who frequently had Sydney to stay at his home in Northumberland; Samuel Rogers, the leading society poet, a gentle man with a cadaverous appearance and an acerbic wit. You will meet all these and many more.

Sydney was very informal, treating prime ministers in much the same way as he treated his own servants. Everyone who met him noted how approachable he was: he was known throughout society as 'Dear Sydney'. I have maintained this tradition, calling him by his Christian name. I am sure he would not have wished me to have done otherwise.

Sydney once wrote: 'Great men hallow a whole people, and lift up all who live in their time.' Without knowing it, he had written his own epitaph.

Peter Virgin
London
May 1993

ACKNOWLEDGEMENTS

My first and deepest debt of gratitude is to Alan Bell, Librarian of the London Library. Alan made available to me the transcripts of Sydney's unpublished letters, which he is editing for the Oxford University Press. (Nowell C. Smith edited *The Collected Letters of Sydney Smith*, 2 vols, 1953; it is a tribute to Alan Bell's bibliographical skills that he has managed more or less to double the corpus, including a very great number of letters that are vital to an understanding of Sydney's personal and family life.) It is not too much to say that, without Alan's generosity, this biography could not have been written. I have also learned from the insights in Alan's own biography, *Sydney Smith*, published by OUP in 1980.

My second debt of gratitude is to David Holland. David has a link with the Smith family; he is a descendant of the first marriage of Sir Henry Holland, physician in ordinary to Queen Victoria, who subsequently married Sydney's elder daughter, Saba. David has been unstinting of help and hospitality. He owns valuable family documents, which he unselfishly allowed me to take away for study.

Numerous other people have assisted me along the way. D. A. Armstrong, formerly keeper of archives at the Church of England Record Office, found material relating to one of Sydney's frequent controversies. Clare Brown of the Victoria and Albert Museum, expert in eighteenth-century embroidery, gave me valuable advice on Georgian fashion. Roger Custance, archivist of Winchester College, provided me with background information on life at Winchester in the 1780s; he also kindly read the chapter on Sydney's schooldays. Caroline Dalton, archivist of New College, Oxford, opened up several avenues of research into Sydney's life at New College in the 1790s. Tim Faun, who lives at Bishop's Lydeard House – the final resting-place of Sydney's peripatetic father – was extremely hospitable; he also did some thorough research into the history of Bishop's Lydeard House. John Field, archivist of Westminster School, helped me find my way around the records in his keeping. Eeyan Hartley, keeper of the archives at Castle Howard, found several items for me which I would not have been able to find myself. Hedley Marten, Wykehamist, kindly showed me around Winchester College. Vernon Pheasant, scholar and country gentleman, gave me much information about the social background of Yorkshire gentry. Frederick and Anne Procopé entertained me regally – I remember with especial affection a massive *filet de boeuf* – while I was researching in Yorkshire. Captain Read, who lives at Sydney's rectory at Combe Florey, gave me a sparkling tour of that beloved place. Tessa Reitman, who is the great-great-great-granddaughter of Sydney's elder brother Bobus, made some interesting remarks about the life of the traveller and conservationist Charles Waterton. Anne Richards ferreted out some material relating to Sydney which I had missed. James and Margaret Thomas, and their family, looked after me splendidly while I was doing some research in Edinburgh. John Walsh pointed me in the direction of useful background studies into eighteenth-century English wit. Inspection of the rectory at Foston-le-Clay in Yorkshire, an amiable house built by Sydney himself, was carried out under the wise guidance of Mrs Wormald, who now lives there. And Dr Christopher Wright of the British Library kindly loaned me a copy of his collation of the Holland House Dinner Books.

Many friends have read this book in typescript. The finished version has benefited enormously from their interest and advice. Gerry Aherne saved me from several serious howlers. Peter Beer has an unerring eye for obstacles to fluency in style; he also alerted me to some trenchant comments about Sydney made by the painter Benjamin Haydon. Nicholas Brown accurately identified the inadequacies of an early draft of the Introduction; he was also useful on Talleyrand. Some perceptive remarks by Richard Crossley deepened my understanding of the social mores of Georgian Yorkshire gentry. Caroline Dawnay was immensely helpful, showing me how to redraft early versions of several chapters. Maggie Dillon was quick to spot several egregious errors in my grammar. David Grant offered valuable insights into Sydney's famous speech at Taunton in favour of the Reform Bill. Peter Holland, as infuriatingly efficient as ever, sent me several pages of incisive comment. Caroline Hillyard eliminated three or four bad blunders and Nicholas Hillyard made numerous helpful suggestions; I benefited especially from his assessment of the character of Sydney's father. Tony Hogg made me aware of fresh material to do with the late-eighteenth-century Scottish Enlightenment. Matthew Stemp pointed out some confusions in my presentation of Sydney's finances. And, finally, Francesca Taylor provoked me into rethinking my view of key aspects of the emotional interaction between Sydney and his wife, Catharine. The weaknesses and errors that remain in the book are, I must stress, my own.

I have been fortunate in having HarperCollins as my publisher. Stuart Proffitt has been an enthusiastic supporter of the project from its inception; I have always found his advice percipient and well considered. Alison Hobson took infinite pains with my first submitted draft; her suggestions for improvement ran to many pages. Finally, Rebecca Wilson did a very thorough job in tidying up the final version.

I beg to acknowledge the gracious permission of Her Majesty the Queen to make use of papers in the Royal Archives at Windsor. Permission has also been kindly granted by the following institutions: Bodleian Library, Oxford; Borthwick Institute of Historical Research; British Library; Church of England Record Office; Derbyshire Record Office; Durham University Library; Fondren Library, Rice University, Houston, Texas; Greater London Record Office; Haverford College Library, Haverford, Pennsylvania; Hertfordshire Record Office; Houghton Library, Harvard University; Henry E. Huntington Library, San Marino, California; India Office Library; Iowa University Library; Keele University Library; National Library of Wales; National Library of Scotland; Warden and Scholars of New College, Oxford; James M. and Marie-Louise Osborn Collection, Yale University Library; St Paul's Cathedral Library; Pierpont Morgan Library, New York; Public Record Office, Kew; Staffordshire Record Office; Trinity College, Cambridge; Trustees of the Chatsworth Settlement; Trustees of the Wedgwood Museum, Barlaston, Stoke-on-Trent; University College London; North Yorkshire County Record Office; West Yorkshire Archive Service; and York Reference Library. A number of individuals have been equally generous: A. S. Bell, D. R. Bentham, Lord Cobbold, P. R. Glazebrook, Earl of Harewood, D. C. L. Holland, Hon. Simon Howard, Lord St Aldwyn and Major Christopher York.

It would not be appropriate to end without mentioning my two daughters, Rachel and Talitha. They both read the book in typescript, and have been a powerful source of support and encouragement. My thanks to them are expressed in the dedication.

SYDNEY SMITH

INTRODUCTION

'I sat next to Sydney Smith, who was delightful . . . I don't remember a more agreeable party.' BENJAMIN DISRAELI

'As coarse as hemp.' THOMAS CARLYLE, of Sydney Smith

'His great delight was to produce a succession of ludicrous images . . . It may be averred for certain that in this style he has never been equalled, and I do not suppose he will ever be surpassed.'   LORD JOHN RUSSELL, of Sydney Smith

'I am a very ignorant, frivolous, half-inch person.'
                                              SYDNEY SMITH

The year is 1803. It is spring and the scene is set in Edinburgh. Two men are huddled together, discussing avidly deep into the night, one of them a thirty-one-year-old Englishman with more than a few drops of French blood. A little above medium height, he is of burly build and swarthy complexion; 'doomed to external copper' is how he put it himself. His face has one weakness – the mouth; small and a little pursed, it was once unkindly likened to an oyster. Otherwise, his features convey a sense of strength. He has a well-developed chin, his nose is long and slightly aquiline, and he has a high, pale, 'intellectual' forehead. Much power comes from the eyes: they are deep and dark, almost black, always full of light and, when he is angry, can pierce a man to the soul. Black eyebrows give these eyes an added force. Nature has given him an actor's voice: light, musical and resonant, but very strong. He has a military bearing, never failing to carry himself erect.

   In other regards, however, he is thoroughly Bohemian. His hair, abundant and fine, is brushed upwards after the contemporary French fashion: it is not easy to keep tidy, and he does not often make the effort. He dresses casually, to say the least. 'His neckcloth always looked like a pudding tied round his throat, and the arrangement of his garments seemed more the result of accident than design.' Careless of dress, he is also clumsy in movement. A college friend said of him, puckishly, that he resembled an Athenian carter. Sydney Smith, being Sydney Smith, both enjoyed and preserved the joke.[1]

Few of Sydney's friends were as remarkable as his companion on this spring night in Edinburgh. Henry Brougham, although only twenty-four, was already making his mark. He was one of the most able men of his generation: a rousing speaker, a good mathematician, a fine writer, a fluent linguist, a formidable lawyer. Prominent in politics, he ended his career as Lord Chancellor. Unfortunately, Brougham's intellectual stature was not matched by moral worth; he was arrogant, rude and treacherous. Sydney was impressed by Brougham's brilliant capacities but was not blind to his damning faults of character. 'Catiline, Borgia, Guy Faux Brougham returns this week' runs part of one of Sydney's letters.

On this night in Edinburgh, Sydney and Brougham were putting the finishing touches to a review of a book on vegetarianism by Joseph Ritson, a little-known antiquarian. As Sydney later admitted, they had pored over the pages of Ritson's text, searching for a chink in their opponent's armour 'through which we could drop one more drop of verjuice'. Ritson's inconsistencies – he was a vegetarian on moral grounds – were ruthlessly exposed: 'Is not the devouring of eggs, the causing of acute misery to a tender mother, and the procuring of abortions?'[2]

The attack appeared in the third issue of the *Edinburgh Review*. The idea for this literary periodical did not come from Henry Brougham, the future Lord Chancellor, but from Sydney. At first the notion of setting up the *Review* was no more than a prank, suggested at a tea party in the early winter of 1801–2. Youthful enthusiasm swept away obstacles and the first issue appeared in October 1802. It was an immediate success. Everyone, not least those who took part in the project, was taken by surprise. 'The truth is', wrote Brougham sixty years later, 'the most sanguine among us, even Smith himself, could not have foreseen the greatness of the first triumph.'

The *Edinburgh Review* was the first literary periodical to be taken seriously, the first to receive critical acclaim. Within a decade it was transcending the 'greatness of the first triumph'. Sales in September 1814 were close on 13,000. Putting this figure in perspective, the print-run of *The Times* two years later was 8,000 copies a day.

Founding the *Edinburgh Review* was one of Sydney's main achievements. He also played a leading role in establishing its reputation. Sydney was a born journalist: his prose reads like overheard conversation. He was well aware that he was the best communicator among the reviewers, that his pieces were the lightest, the most widely read. 'Too much I admit would not do of my style', he once wrote, 'but the proportion in which it exists enlivens the Review . . . I am a very ignorant, frivolous, half-inch person; but, such as I am, I am sure I have done [the] Review good, and contributed to bring it into notice'.[3] Sydney's carefree approach to writing served him well. He wrote quickly, almost casually, putting ideas down as they came into his head. This gives his prose immediacy and, at times, exceptional directness and power.

Sydney could be amusing but he could also be satirical: friends claimed that his pen was more to be feared than that of any writer since Swift. Like Swift, Sydney was a political pamphleteer. His most famous production is the anonymously published *Letters of Peter Plymley*, ten short pamphlets which came out in 1807–8. In these *Letters* he savaged the reputations of two future prime ministers: George Canning and Spencer Perceval. *Peter Plymley* caused a stir in the political world, the playwright Richard Brinsley Sheridan declaring that it was 'the most argumentative, logical, ingenious, and by far the wittiest performance I ever met with'.

Sydney used his satirical gifts to promote social and educational reform. He inveighed against the inhumanity of employing young boys to sweep chimneys – 'What is a toasted child, compared to the agonies of the mistress of the house with a deranged dinner?' – and was at his facetious best when discussing the barbarous practice of using man-traps to catch poachers. He sometimes amazes with his modernity. He publicized the work of a small experimental asylum which, standing out against the medical orthodoxy of the day, recommended humane treatment of the mentally ill. Among the methods used was the earliest form of occupational therapy. He also advocated novel ways of teaching languages, and wanted to broaden the curriculum in both schools and universities.

The most interesting aspect of Sydney's educational thinking is his attitude towards the education of women. In an article in the *Edinburgh Review* in 1810, Sydney put forward the scandalous suggestion that men were not intellectually superior; such differences as did exist between the sexes could be put down to the influence of training and social expectation, not to innate ability. He drove his argument to its logical conclusion, arguing that a scholarly education – serious literature, history, philosophy – should be available to women. The economy suffered from the failure to realize female potential: 'Half the talent in the universe runs to waste, and is totally unprofitable'; and women would be much happier if they had the chance to acquire, through education, the habit of drawing their resources from themselves. Pessimists among men said that such a revolutionary scheme would never work. But, Sydney reminded his readers, there was an excellent precedent: 'A century ago, who would have believed that country gentlemen could be brought to read and spell with the ease and accuracy which we now so frequently remark?'

The stereotype of the satirist is of a crusty character, embittered by life, a stereotype which Sydney does not fit: he was outgoing and immensely charming, especially to women. He was once with a young woman who was admiring, from a respectable distance, a sweet pea. The woman turned to Sydney and said: 'Oh, Mr Smith! this pea will never come to perfection.' Sydney was silent for a moment and then replied: 'Permit me, then, to lead perfection to the pea.' And without more ado, he took the young woman gently by the hand and led her slowly towards the plant. Sydney also had an affectionate innocence which never left him. Towards the end of his life, he went for a walk around his garden on a wintry morning. Noticing a single crocus struggling up through the frost-bound lawn, he touched it with his crutch-stick and exclaimed: 'See! The resurrection of the world!'

Sydney, said one of his friends, was 'an irresistibly amusing companion'. He had a sense of the ludicrous which anticipates the wit of the famous English humorist Edward Lear. A young Scot was proposing to marry an Irish woman twice his age and more than twice his size. 'Going to marry her!' exclaimed Sydney; 'going to marry her! Impossible! You mean a part of her; he could not marry her all himself. It would be a case, not of bigamy, but trigamy . . . There is enough of her to furnish wives for a whole parish . . . I once was rash enough to try walking round her before breakfast, but only got half-way and gave it up exhausted.'[4]

Sydney startles us, and he startled those who knew him. The men and women of aristocratic society who listened to his bawdy jokes found it hard to believe that he was a clergyman. On the other hand, those who heard him preach – he was eloquent, passionate and often rather grave – did not always readily acknowledge that he was, under a different guise, a fashionable wit. The variety of functions might seem odd to us, but it did not seem odd to him. Sydney was able to change roles with great ease: he saw no contradiction in being a satirist and a social campaigner, a tutor and a farmer, a celebrity and a parish priest. He even spent some time building his own house.

1

FABER MEAE FORTUNAE

'Mankind are always happy for having been happy, so that
if you make them happy now, you make them happy twenty
years hence by the memory of it.'

SYDNEY SMITH,
Elementary Sketches of Moral Philosophy

In April 1826, Sydney went on holiday to Paris, the first time he had
been abroad for thirty-eight years. He returned with plenty of presents
for the family – three bonnets, twenty-four handkerchiefs, a pelisse, a
silk garment – but only bought one thing for himself: a massive seal,
purchased for six shillings and bearing the coat of arms of a peer of
France. When he got back Sydney turned the heraldic emblem into a
seal for his letters, a style of gently self-mocking buffoonery that is
typical of the man.

Sydney, as this pleasantly mischievous story shows, took a jaunty
view of social distinctions. He did not at all mind coming, as he put it,
from 'a long line of Tinkers and Taylors'; indeed, he was proud of the
fact. Sydney judged people by what they were in themselves, not by the
power or privileges they had managed to accumulate. As to the
circumstances of his own relatively modest upbringing, he made a
virtue of necessity, taking as his personal motto a Latin aphorism:
Faber meae fortunae ('the smith of my own fortune').

This was jocular but it was also, to quite a marked degree, a motto
born of bitterness. Sydney, once he was famous, was fond of telling his
friends that he had achieved everything through his own efforts: his
father, Robert, had never given him a penny. Not only did Sydney
resent Robert Smith, he was also embarrassed by him, describing him
on one occasion as 'a good kind of man, who disappeared about the
time of the assizes & we asked no questions'. No man who cares for his
father besmirches his name, even in jest; Sydney's strong implication
about imprisonment was, moreover, untrue.

Equally revealing is the account of Robert Smith's marriage given by Sydney's elder daughter, Saba, in the *Memoir* which she wrote of her father. The wedding took place on 8 August 1768 and was held at the fashionable church of St George's, Bloomsbury, a few hundred paces south of the British Museum. Repeating an oral tradition of long standing in Sydney's household, Saba says with scarcely disguised malice that the bridegroom left the bride at the 'church-door' and went off to America.

Character assassination by innuendo is the best way to describe this remark. It was not as Saba describes it at all. Robert Smith's bride, Maria Olier, was a minor when he was courting her. He needed to go on business to America, but he also wanted to marry Maria. Faced with a choice between elopement and marriage with parental permission, Robert decided to stick to the rules. He approached Mrs Olier, explaining the reasons for his American trip and asking for the assurance of Maria's hand on his return. Mrs Olier was adamant in her refusal: 'Either party might change their minds, and then the promise so much wished for would prove painful. Both should be free. If on his return he continued in the same mind, and her daughter also, she should cheerfully consent to the Marriage.'[1] Faced by this unpromising stance on Ellen Olier's part, Robert decided to marry first and go to America shortly afterwards.

These marital negotiations reveal the essence of Robert Smith: he was a man of indomitable will who ruled his children with an iron hand. It was not a form of treatment to which Sydney responded. Towards the end of his life he said, with a sad wisdom born of experience, 'Attend to the happiness of children. Mankind are always happier for having been happy, and a happy childhood is the last remembrance which clings to us in old age. I have always regretted that I had no such recollections.' One of the worst things about Sydney's early years was the clamp put by his father upon freedom. Sydney often told his own children about his wasted youth; his father dined at three o'clock in the afternoon and would expect his family to sit quietly with him afterwards, often for hours. To an active boy such as Sydney, imposition of this kind of prolonged and unproductive idleness did no good at all.

Robert Smith was also irresponsible. He might have been less wanton if fewer burdens had been put on his shoulders early on. He was the eldest of five children – there was also another son, John, and three daughters – and his father died at a relatively young age. This meant that the family merchanting business, based in the City of London at East Cheap, was left in Robert's immature hands. Soon tiring of the tedium of commercial routine, he let his brother take over while he went to America for three or four years.

It was a fateful, indeed fatal, decision. At the time, soon after 1760, there was already tension between England and America but this did not deter Robert, a born speculator, from setting up a number of commercial ventures. These did not get off to a good start – hence the need for a second visit soon after his marriage to Maria in 1768 – and they did even worse once war was declared in 1776. By 1781, Robert Smith's American investments were virtually worthless.

Failure in America did not stop him from trying elsewhere. The record is extremely patchy (there are only a few family papers relating to this early period, all of which have been unearthed in recent years), but there are occasional references to commercial dealings as far afield as Europe, India and the West Indies. In no instance did Robert Smith's plans bear fruit. He was a hopelessly incompetent business-man, unable even to grasp the fact that, in the England of the eighteenth century, it was impossible to manage far-flung commercial interests on his own, from a country house in Sussex or Surrey. Whenever one of his schemes went wrong, someone else was always blamed. Robert Smith's agents certainly let him down, but their untrustworthiness is less surprising than his gullibility in expecting that things would turn out otherwise.

Robert Smith did not permit his financial failures to blunt his social aspirations. Throughout his career he sought to make contact with people of importance in society, and was always socially confident, having a high opinion of himself. Late in life he became a rural magistrate, a position of considerable prestige. He earlier managed to befriend, among others, the Duke of Northumberland. Robert also got on well with Michael and Henrietta Hicks Beach. Michael Hicks Beach was MP for Cirencester from 1794 until 1818. His main residence was Williamstrip Park in Gloucestershire and, being an MP, he was a man of some influence.

Robert Smith's financial imprudence was in stark contrast with his younger brother's rectitude. John Smith reaped due reward for his consistent effort: his riches accumulated steadily, in the way that riches sometimes do. When he died, he left behind him an estate which has been variously estimated at 'above £100,000' and 'upwards of £150,000'.[2] Either was a huge sum. Using the standard inflation indices, an estate of £100,000 in 1790 was equivalent to one of over £4,100,000 by 1990. One of Robert's three sisters also became wealthy, marrying into the Trower family, who were successful stockbrokers.

The burgeoning wealth of his brother did nothing to help Robert Smith be at peace in his world. He married Maria Olier when he was twenty-nine. After his return from the notorious second American trip, which followed the marriage ceremony with such undue celerity, the children came with disconcerting regularity. First, in 1770, was Robert Percy; early in life his father called him 'Bobus', and it is by this name that, from school onwards, he was always known. Sydney, who was second, was born at Woodford in Essex on 3 June 1771. The next year there was Cecil; and the fourth and final boy, Courtney, was born in 1773. The Smiths' only daughter, Maria, was born in 1774: five children in five years. All were healthy except Maria; according to Saba, she was attacked by 'an affection [*sic*] of the spine when she was about 15' which left her permanently deformed.

Even when he had a young and growing family, Robert Smith still would not settle down; he was always away to France, Italy or Spain. When he was not travelling abroad he was moving house. He would buy a property, alter it, and then sell it for less than he had paid. Sydney recollected that he did this nineteen times: almost certainly an exaggeration but still showing how restless and financially irresponsible his father was. Sydney's peripatetic childhood, living in houses dotted about the country – Essex, Herefordshire, Hampshire – rivals that of Dickens. Living a roving life did not help Sydney to feel secure. It also left ugly scars on Robert Smith. When he reached late middle age, he came to want a farm on which he could pass his declining years. The failure to get what he desired was to lead to a breach with Sydney.

How did Robert Smith manage? What did he live on? His few surviving letters contain only one allusion to the overall state of his finances. Writing to his American agent, William Burrows, in April 1781 he admits that times are hard: 'I am entirely out of business and thank God and the assistance of my family live independent with a fair prospect of seeing my five children provided for after me'.[3] The 'assistance' which he received from his family probably took the form of an arrangement for sharing the profits of the merchanting business in East Cheap which he had briefly run when he was young. In other regards the letter is conspicuously disingenuous. A miser to his fingertips, Robert Smith never had the slightest intention of providing for his children; his hope was that they would become rich as quickly as possible and provide for him. His expectations for his own financial independence were less fanciful. Although 'entirely out of business', he had enough money in the 1780s to send all four of his sons to public schools. Robert Smith lived well into his eighties and died a rich man, but kept up the pretence of poverty, dressing with the drab simplicity of a Quaker and wearing a large flap hat resembling the headgear used by a coal-heaver, miserly affectations which deceived nobody except himself.

Living under the shadow of his father's financial mismanagement seared Sydney's soul. In adult life he had an almost pathological fear of debt; he would spend his evenings sifting through business papers, examining them 'with as much plodding method as an attorney's clerk'. Creditors were always paid on time and 'dead' bills were kept meticulously in parcels of a hundred. Not a single one was ever thrown away.

When there is conflict between father and son, the son will often take delight in growing up to be everything his father wishes he were not. Robert Smith was keen on commerce and his moods went up and down with the Stock Exchange: Sydney had no commercial bent and showed little interest in the price fluctuations of Consols. Robert thought that the father should be a benevolent despot within the family: Sydney was, in domestic matters, a constitutional monarch who consulted his 'subjects' – his children – well before they were fully grown up. It was the same with views on politics: Robert's unyielding Toryism was met by Sydney's liberal Whiggery.

Sydney's mother, *neé* Maria Olier, came from a family of French Protestants. Since she was born around 1750 it was probably her grandfather – not, as is commonly thought, her father Isaac – who was expelled from his native land of Languedoc after Louis XIV, determined to rid France of all its Protestants, revoked the Edict of Nantes in 1685. To be forced into exile is not a pleasant experience in the modern world but in the late seventeenth century it was incomparably worse.

Sydney believed that his Gallic blood accounted for his gaiety of spirit. More significant is whether the persecution of the Olier family played any part in the development of Sydney's political beliefs. The parallel with Cardinal Newman is instructive. Newman's mother, like Sydney's, was from Huguenot stock: Newman became in his maturity a great advocate of the primacy of the individual conscience, while

Sydney earlier in the nineteenth century was the leading apologist for religious liberty. It would be natural to conclude that the history of his mother's family was a source of inspiration in Sydney's quest to protect the interests of the disadvantaged and the dispossessed. Unfortunately, however, no direct link can be established. Neither in public nor in private did Sydney at any time present himself as the descendant of an exiled Huguenot; nor did he ever point up the irony in the fact that, coming from a family which had been thrown out of France by a Catholic king, he was in the vanguard of the campaign to secure, in England, political rights for those who held to the same religious faith as his family's tormentor. The flight from France is a backdrop in Sydney's life.

Sydney was extremely fond of his mother, a woman of ravishing beauty. Those who met her noted the facial resemblance to the famous contemporary tragic actress Mrs Siddons. Add to this that she was physically delicate, and that she had great natural goodness, and it will be no surprise to learn that she was revered by all her sons.

Around the time of Sydney's birth, there was deep unhappiness in the Smith household: Mrs Smith began to suffer from epileptic fits. Once they started they grew steadily worse.[4] It did not help that she had to bear the strain of bringing up four boys, or that her husband was often away from home. For the children, living with Maria's illness must have been a horrific experience. The symptoms of epileptic attacks – muscular spasms, discolouration of the face – often make adults panic, but at least they can rationalize what is happening. Children are differently placed; with them, fear feeds upon incomprehension. With his father often away, and his mother in such poor health, it is little wonder that Sydney, when a grown man, had a tendency to melancholy and felt shy and insecure.

Sydney never wrote about the traumas of his childhood: there is not, for instance, a single reference in his letters to his beloved mother's epilepsy. More remarkable still, he hardly ever mentions the depth of his affection for her. Only once is he known to have given an indication of the pulse of his heart, in a letter to the novelist E. L. Bulwer: 'I lov'd my own Mother intensely' are Sydney's simple words.

Sydney's sensitivity over his feelings towards his mother shows up in surprising ways. He once explained why he liked going to the theatre to see comedies but could not bear to watch tragedies. 'My heart is too soft. There is too much real misery in life.' He then goes straight on, not even pausing for a breath, seemingly unaware of the discontinuity in his own thought. 'But what a face she had! The gods do not bestow such a face as Mrs Siddons' on the stage more than once in a century.' Who was it that Maria Olier looked like? Sarah Siddons!

Watching his mother's fits taught Sydney to admire beyond measure female fortitude. 'Women', he writes in an early letter, 'have infinitely more philosophical endurance than men.' Ask a wife 'to drink a cup of poison for some good which would accrue from it to her husband and Children and she will swallow it like green tea'. This is what Maria Olier had done throughout her life, enduring all things and suffering all things on behalf of her family. His parents' marriage was also, in Sydney's view, a matter of pitting his father's toughness against his mother's fragility. It had not been an even battle; Sydney grew up believing strongly that women were the psychologically weaker sex. The heart of a man, he once wrote, is 'all flesh and blood' whereas that of a woman is a 'strange composition of tears, sighs, sorrows, ecstasies, fears, smiles'.

Sydney's unhappy childhood – his father's dictatorial behaviour and frequent absences from home, his mother's epilepsy, the constant moving around – is an important ingredient in the composition of his special brand of humour. Outwardly strong, Sydney was inwardly vulnerable. Jesting, for him, was a salve, a balm, a way of dealing with a hard and bitter world.

The Smith household was never dull. Robert Smith might have been an impossible character but he was also good company, having, according to Sydney's wife, a vivid and retentive memory, a good store of anecdotes and, most of all, *'wonderful natural eloquence'*.[5] His wife had intelligence and charm. When Sydney went away to school, her letters to him were so enthralling that his schoolfellows begged him to read them aloud.

Sydney's elder brother was also quite exceptional. He had an intellect of rare power, inherited his father's phenomenal memory and had a dry sense of humour. Sydney held him in the highest esteem, describing him as a 'very capital personage, full of sense, genius, dignity, virtue and wit'. Bobus was much loved by his friends, but he adopted a combative stance towards the world; there were complaints that his conversation had 'smartness and point and sarcasm'. His main weakness of character was an uncontrollable temper. Arguing with him could be a nerve-racking experience. Cecil once had a disagreement over the role of juries, soon regretting that he had raised the subject. The violence of the quarrel shook Cecil. Writing to Maria, he explained that Bobus had begun with 'egregious absurdity' and had ended with 'brutal rudeness'.[6]

It was characteristic of Cecil that he should have been bruised by Bobus's wrath. He was the most brittle of the four boys and the most easily hurt. Cecil stood out in other ways. He had a good mind but, unlike his three brothers, was not in the least bookish. He was also the only male member of the household who took any interest in fashion. Cecil was a man about town: lively to be with, keen on excitement, fond of gambling and hopeless with money. Although not at all shrewd he was, thought Bobus, 'very goodhearted'.

Goodhearted is the last term that could ever be used to describe Courtney. Courtney was very clever, indeed he was almost as clever as Bobus and Sydney, but he was thoroughly disagreeable. He was abusive about everyone (he called Sydney, for instance, a 'mountebank' and a 'buffoon'), quite as miserly as Robert Smith and extremely misanthropic. There is a brief character sketch of him by Bobus. His elder brother conceded that he was hard-working, and that he was 'plain' in his ideas of right and wrong. However, on the debit side, there was 'a want of measure in his language and a disposition to treat his superiors as few people would think it right to treat their footmen', not ideal qualities in a younger brother.

Maria was the polar opposite of Courtney; Bobus complained that she had 'usurped all the good sense as well as good temper of the whole family'.[7] Her spinal deformity was a savage handicap; she never married and never left home. Looking after her father was a severe test of her equanimity. On one occasion he required her to make written answers to three questions, the first of which was, 'Whether I can charge you with ever treating me harshly or brutally'. Her reply to this brutal question is taut in its pain. 'For God's sake therefore if you don't wish to see me die at your feet, let this be the last time I ever have to answer such dreadful questions as you have put me. Let this be the last time I shall ever be necessitated but by my actions to avow my love & respect for you & to declare to you that nothing can ever lessen it.' She died, much lamented by her brothers, at the age of forty-one. Sydney thought that she had 'run through all the stamina of constitution Nature had allotted her, and died of old-age. The loss of a person whom I would have cultivated as a friend, if Nature had not given her to me as a relation, is a serious evil.'

The peripatetic Smith home was an intense intellectual academy. Cecil went out to play whenever he could, but the other three boys would lie together for hours on the floor, discussing and arguing about books. Sydney later came to agree with his father's judgement; they were, Sydney admitted, 'the most intolerable and overbearing set of boys that can well be imagined'. This precocity was hard to deal with, but it was good for mental development: Bobus, Sydney and Courtney all learned, at a young age, to give no quarter in debate.

Sydney made a good start at school. When he was six he was sent to King Edward VI's Grammar School, Southampton. (The Smiths were living at South Stoneham nearby, having long since left Woodford where Sydney had been born.) The master of King Edward's was Richard Mant; in his early thirties, he was a scholar of repute and a good teacher.[8] Sydney always spoke of King Edward's with pleasure and enjoyed his time there. It was scant preparation for the cruelties that were to come.

2

JOSEPH WARTON AND THE BIBLING ROD

'Schoolmasters encouraged pupils to love . . . not the filbert but the shell, not what may be read in Greek but Greek itself.'

SYDNEY SMITH

Winchester College has one of the most attractive settings of any school in the world. Founded by William of Wykeham towards the close of the fourteenth century, it is the oldest public school in England and its medieval buildings are still intact. Next to it is the spectacular Perpendicular cathedral and under its walls a branch of the Itchen, a river famous for its trout.

In 1782, recently turned eleven, Sydney entered Winchester as a scholar. That success does not imply any outstanding achievement on his part. The annual election of Winchester scholars, held in July, had long been a matter of form. Candidates had to translate a simple sentence from Latin into English. They were also asked, 'Well, boy, can you sing?' 'Yes, sir,' came the reply. 'Well then, let us hear you.' The candidates then recited, in a normal tone of voice, the first line of the hymn 'All people that on earth do dwell'. (The explanation of this odd routine is that all scholars, according to the statutes of the school, had to be capable of singing plain chant.) But if the method of Sydney's entry to Winchester says nothing about his intellectual ability at this early age, it does give a hint of his father's social influence. Six men elected Winchester scholars; three of them, including the Warden, came from the school, and the other three represented the sister foundation of New College, Oxford. Robert Smith must have pulled someone's sleeve, but it is not known whose it was.

Sydney, while at public school, was separated from two of his three brothers. In a rare act of wisdom, Robert Smith realized that it would be a mistake not to split up his sons: they were, with the exception of

Cecil, far too competitive. So Bobus went off to Eton and Sydney to Winchester, with Cecil following Bobus and Courtney following Sydney. This arrangement favoured Bobus more than it favoured Sydney. Apart from having to cope with a constant flow of abusive language and a consistently disrespectful attitude towards those in authority, there were other drawbacks to being with Courtney: he was 'an uncouth quarrelsome little Boy of strange fancies, dirty habits, always in scrapes'.[1] Looking after his wayward brother created problems for Sydney, but these were insignificant when placed against the difficulty he had in accustoming himself to life in his new surroundings.

Winchester was beautiful but it was also monastic. Some of those who were not scholars (they were called commoners) lived at home in the town and therefore avoided the full rigours of the educational system. For Sydney, however, there was no escape. The seventy scholars of Winchester lived apart from those commoners who were boarders, being housed in seven communal rooms, known as chambers. These chambers varied in size; the largest took thirteen boys and the smallest only seven. All the rooms were situated on three sides of Chamber Court, an enclosed medieval quadrangle which was the inner sanctum of the school. Each chamber was home to a number of juniors, or 'inferiors', and at least two of the eighteen prefects; there were no commoner-prefects. The living conditions of inferiors in chambers were spartan. Their beds, given to the school in 1540, were made of solid oak two or three inches thick and were blackened with age; oak planks did duty as springs. Each boy had a wooden chest in which to keep his clothes. When doing private academic work, this chest doubled as a seat. The work itself was done at what was called a 'toys', a small desk with a cupboard on top. The boys did at least have the consolation of knowing that they could keep themselves warm: each chamber had a massive fireplace in which faggots four feet long were burned. Supervision by masters was perfunctory. The most that could be hoped for was a brief visit at night to check that candles had been snuffed, and that all was quiet. The heavy, iron-clad chamber door was kept locked during the hours when scholars were, supposedly, asleep.

Sydney's day began at 5.30 AM. His first duty, to wash himself, was more easily said than done. Prefects had their own washing-bowls, and water was brought to them by junior boys: inferiors had to tiptoe across the cobblestones of Chamber Court, drawing water from a conduit hard up against the wall. If Sydney ever felt in need of refreshment at this unearthly hour of the morning, he would have drunk water out of the same silver goblet, fastened to the conduit by a chain, which is still in use today. Before returning to his chamber he may well have made use of an earth closet, which was without a door.

Morning chapel was at 6.30 A M. Prayers were read by one of the three chaplains, who all held posts at the cathedral. In conformity with the religious spirit of the age, there was little show of devotion; chaplains quite often set the boys a bad example by gabbling the prayers. Morning school started early, at 7.30 A M. On Tuesdays and Thursdays this first session of lessons was relatively short. For on these days the boys, under the supervision of the senior prefect, the Prefect of Hall, marched out of the school to play on St Catherine's Hill, a piece of isolated downland near the village of St Cross. On other days morning playtime was less vigorous, with the boys going into the meadows near the school.

At 10 A M, having already been up for four and a half hours, the boys were given breakfast. There was an hour's school from eleven until noon, followed by a further hour's play and then lunch. Afternoons were largely taken up with lessons, although on Tuesdays and Thursdays there was another visit to St Catherine's Hill. Dinner was at six. From seven until eight the boys worked in chambers – 'toytime'. This period of private study was organized unconventionally at Winchester. Every inferior had as his 'tutor' one of the eighteen prefects. Tutors were encouraged to give academic assistance during toytime, correcting simple errors; they were also charged with the duty of protecting the younger boys from bullying. Well-intentioned though the tutorial system was, it was open to abuse. A clever young scholar could find himself doing two sets of work: his own and his tutor's. Short evening prayers were read in the ante-chapel at 8.30 P M. Boys were expected to be in bed by nine.

The daily routine at Winchester did not suit Sydney. In reaction to its harshness a strong streak of laziness developed in him, which he never subsequently managed to eradicate. His unsuccessful efforts to overcome the failing are recorded in a journal: 'lost two hours in bed from dawdling and doubting'; 'I must get up at last, it will be as difficult then as now'; 'lost a day by indolence; the only method is to spring up at once'.[2]

Meals were taken by the scholars in Hall, a building scarcely distinguishable from a monastic refectory; there were six long, narrow tables, three on each side, and a dais at one end. The eighteen prefects sat at two tables on their own, while the fifty-two inferiors were crammed around the other four. Prefects had knives and forks and were also provided with plates, but inferiors had to cut their meat with their own penknives and ate off wooden platters about nine inches square and an inch thick. (Wooden platters of the same size are still in use today, but for bread not for meat.) All meals were presided over by the Prefect of Hall; no master so much as put his head around the door.

Sydney did not enjoy going to Hall. Eating conditions were appalling; the wooden platters, he later remembered, were 'rarely or ever clean'd or even *scraped*'.[3] Sydney also found the diet grossly inadequate. Beer was available in virtually unlimited quantities at every meal (boys were not permitted to drink tea or coffee because neither beverage was mentioned in the school's statutes!) but otherwise the fare had little to be said for it. For breakfast there was only bread and butter: a plea for cheese had been made in 1766, but it seems not to have been granted. Sunday lunch was roast beef, a rare treat; but on the four succeeding days the beef was boiled. This was less popular, being described by one old Wykehamist as 'sodden'. On Fridays and Saturdays, being fast days, there was by way of variation baked plum pudding. This, once again, did not merit praise; the same old Wykehamist said that the 'lumps of suet appeared to be nearly equal in number to the raisins'.

Dinner was predictable: always mutton, either roast or boiled, and potatoes. Ancient custom was rigidly adhered to. The boys were always given a sheep and a half, no more and no less. Prefects were supplied with meat dressed to their own orders, but the other scholars had to engage in what amounted to a lottery, the rules of which did not favour those who were young and small. Joints for non-Prefects were always cut up in the same way: portions varied both in quality and in size. Dividing these variable spoils was the responsibility of the senior boy on each table. The temptation to give himself the best cut was not always resisted. Quite often those who had recently joined the school did not get any mutton at all. Sydney said that this happened to him on 'many occasions'. He also did not forget that his breakfast of bread and butter was 'commonly purloin'd' by older boys.

Lessons – in Wykehamist slang, times when the boys were 'up to books' – were taken in the 'new' school, an elegant building completed in 1687. Anything less like a classroom in a modern school would be hard to imagine. New school was big, indeed it was very big: no less than seventy-seven feet long and thirty-five feet wide. The pupils, both scholars and commoners, occupied the body of the room, sitting on tiered seats. The headmaster's wooden rostrum was in one corner, up against the wall. (The rostrum is still there, a relic of a former age; new school is now a library.) The rostrums used by the other masters were also against the wall.

It was not a lay-out calculated to maximize contact between those teaching and those taught. Twenty years after Sydney had left Winchester, he let his views become known. Boys in public schools, he complained, were largely self-taught. The most able thrived on this system but those of average ability came off badly. Although this criticism is fairly obvious, Sydney gives it freshness by using a vivid natural analogy. 'In a forest, or public school for oaks and elms, the trees are left to themselves; the strong plants live, and the weak ones die: the towering oak that remains is admired; the saplings that perish around it are cast into the flames.'

It is interesting that Sydney should have thought of fire when writing about new school. Heating a room of close on 2,700 square feet is difficult. Prior to the 1780s the authorities at Winchester did not even try: it was during Sydney's schooldays that a fireplace was built in new school. Even so, Sydney many years later could still remember several winters of bitter cold.[4]

What, then, did Sydney and Courtney learn as they sat on their tiered seats, often feeling numb from the cold, in new school? A little basic arithmetic, possibly; some English almost certainly (prizes for English Verse and English Essay were introduced in 1782, the year Sydney entered the school); a smattering of history and geography; rudimentary religious instruction – all boys were taught the Church Catechism; probably no French, with even less chance of any German; and, finally, no science at all. It is a formidable list of weaknesses and omissions. The gaps, as at Eton and Westminster, were filled up with classics: an enormous amount of Latin and, higher up the school, a great deal of Greek. There was translation from the original languages into English, grammatical analysis, learning by rote and, most of all, verse composition. It was this last part of the syllabus which made the heaviest demands. Speed and dexterity were the qualities that were striven for. When boys reached the top of the school, the headmaster would give out a theme – 'Courage', 'The Joys of Spring', or suchlike – and the scholars would be expected to produce epigrammatic Latin verses after only a few minutes of reflection.

In his maturity, Sydney became a passionate opponent of the curriculum at Winchester. In 1809 he launched a savage attack upon it in the *Edinburgh Review*, sparking off a fierce controversy. He mischievously points out that some of the knowledge the boys gained from their classical education might be put to uses of which their parents thoroughly disapproved. Was it necessary for English schoolboys to know 'with whom Pan slept? – with whom Jupiter? – whom Apollo ravished?' At the centre of Sydney's case was the thoroughly modern notion that education should serve the needs of society, something which Georgian public schools singularly failed to do. 'There are few boys who remain to the age of eighteen or nineteen at a public school, without making above ten thousand Latin verses', acquiring a vast expertise which was quite useless in later life.

Monastic mornings, hunger, bitter cold and hard and tedious work did not exhaust the inventory of complaint; there was also the cane. Most offences were dealt with by 'scourgings', also known as 'scrubbings'. These were dispensed by one of the masters at the end of a period of school. Scourgings were given for very light offences, such as being late for chapel, and were part of everyday life. On a typical day, a quarter of the boys, or even more, would be flogged. The cane which the masters used was not strikingly practical, consisting of a long wooden handle to which were attached four apple twigs spaced far apart. (The apple twigs came from Herefordshire, and were sent down to Winchester in bundles.) Recipients had to kneel down, baring about two inches of their backs. This added a degree of speculative excitement to the proceedings: there was a reasonable chance that all four of the twigs would fail to make contact with the bare flesh. By tradition, masters gave four cuts for a scourging. The blows came thick and fast – after all, there were always many boys to get through – a speed of activity which did not make for accuracy. When he had finished the beatings the master took off his academic cocked hat, a strange three-cornered contraption, rather like the hats worn by coachmen on state occasions, flung down his scourging rod, and strode out of new school.

Moral offences, happily quite rare, were rewarded with a 'bibling'. Biblings were the prerogative of the headmaster, and were carried out in new school immediately before supper. The offender came forward to the headmaster's rostrum and knelt. Two senior boys stood beside the reluctant hero and bared three or four inches of his back – a lot more than for a scourging, greatly reducing the speculative element.

Six of these potentially much more painful lashings had to be endured. As with scourgings, the cameo of public theatre was completed by the headmaster taking off his academic hat, throwing his instrument of chastisement on the floor and sweeping out of the room.

What boys most feared was not scourgings or even biblings, but 'tundings'. These, astonishing to relate, were in the patronage of Prefect of Hall. After supper the scholars were invited to gather on the dais at the end of Hall. Prefect of Hall then deputed one of the other prefects to deal out the tunding. The thrashing was given with a pliant ground-ash stick, a much more lethal weapon than a scourging rod, and there was no limit to the number of strokes. Tundings were rarer than biblings (there might be no more than one or two in the course of a year) and were only given for conduct 'unbecoming the character of a Wykehamist and a gentleman'.

The practice of tunding furnishes spectacular proof of the power of boy-government at Winchester. Prefect of Hall enjoyed a range of privileges not available to any other boy at an English public school. He sat next to the headmaster in new school; he was in sole charge of meals in Hall; his accommodation in seventh chamber was more spacious than that of the other boys; he received gratuities from his fellow scholars (as did four other prefects as well as the headmaster); he decided who should receive a tunding; and he was responsible for the behaviour of the whole school whenever the boys went to play in the water meadows beside the Itchen or on St Catherine's Hill. Successive Prefects of Hall zealously guarded their pre-eminent position, and the other prefects were also very defensive of what they called their 'ancient liberties'. Chief among these was the right to get inferiors to 'fag' for them, that is, to brush their clothes, clean their shoes, make their beds and run errands. Boy-government reached the peak of its power at night. It was unthinkable that a boy would report an incident to a master. And it was equally unthinkable that a master would try to find anything out. If he did, he had 'as much chance of success as a Protestant JP would have of probing the secrets of the confessional'.

The school suffered from massive built-in inertia. Senior boys had all suffered as inferiors themselves, they had survived the experience, and there was a strong tendency, once they were ensconced in a position of power, to perpetuate indignities. Every boy, reminisced Sydney, started out as a slave and ended up as a tyrant. One historian of the school has asserted that the 1770s and 1780s, a period covering

Sydney's schooldays, witnessed the worst bullying in Winchester's long history.

Winchester did have its compensations. The scholars were very hard on any of their number who tried to pull rank. They lived according to the code of behaviour set out in the school's statutes; scholars were 'to esteem no man's person and [to] hold all distinction of birth and wealth amongst themselves to be merged in the grand fraternity of letters'. Sydney, with his undistinguished background, was an obvious beneficiary of this enactment. He also enjoyed the considerable freedom that the boys had whenever they went to St Catherine's Hill. There were no organized games, which was just as well because Sydney hated cricket and football. Favourite pastimes included roaming over the countryside, hunting badgers and digging up field mice (which were taken back to chambers and kept in cages).[5]

Sydney's ill-fortune in being sent to Winchester was balanced by his luck in having as his headmaster one of the most remarkable teachers there has ever been in England. Joseph Warton had a glittering list of friends: David Garrick, Samuel Johnson, Edmund Gibbon, Horace Walpole. These relationships came about because of Warton's literary renown. He was a poet from a family of poets; both his father and his brother Thomas were Professor of Poetry at Oxford. Joseph began his own poetical career at a young age, writing sonnets at Winchester with the help of his great friend, the brilliant William Collins, a boy whose melancholy was later to drive him insane. Warton's approach to poetry was unconventional. He had the temerity to challenge the ascendancy of classicism in his *Essay on the Writings and Genius of Pope*; and he was, in his own work, a precursor of the Romantic revival. With his emphasis upon the power and importance of imagination, he had great influence on his pupils. One of them, W. L. Bowles, established a reputation for himself as a minor poet; and Bowles, in his turn, helped to form the poetic genius of Coleridge. When Sydney attacked the education he received at Winchester, he forgot Warton's flair. The headmaster's tuition left its mark: Sydney, in later life, was capable of brilliant flights of fancy.

The headmaster may have also influenced Sydney's political ideas. Warton, according to his biographer, was a 'decided enemy to bigotry and intolerance'.[6] This remark, when shorn of its eighteenth-century code, means that he was a Whig, not a Tory. Sydney never spoke of the time when he rejected his father's rigid Toryism, from which it is reasonable to infer that the rebellion was already well under way by the time he left Winchester.

Warton was an extrovert. Fanny Burney met him in 1783 and found him delightful. Fanny herself was already a celebrity; her first novel, *Evelina*, published anonymously in 1778, had been a phenomenal success. Being self-taught, Fanny was somewhat in awe of Warton's wide-ranging culture. 'He is', she noted in her diary, 'a very communicative, gay, and pleasant converser, and enlivened the whole day by his readiness upon all subjects.' Samuel Johnson was less impressed. Where Fanny saw a fascinating ebullience of spirit, he saw an irritating eccentricity. When in his cups the Doctor would amuse his friends by parodying Warton, describing him as an 'enthusiast' – definitely not a compliment. He was especially taken aback by Warton's curious habit of hugging his guests while showing them a picture or admiring a view.[7]

Schoolboys tend to love eccentric teachers, especially when, as in Warton's case, they are also famous. Warton won affection but he did not gain respect. Eccentrics rarely if ever make good disciplinarians, a rule to which he was no exception. He had a fine feeling for Latin words, but his grasp of the nuances of Latin grammar was uncertain. Whenever Warton came across a passage which he found difficult, he would try to distract the boys' attention, a ploy that rarely worked. So lax was his control that a boy, on one occasion, threw a Latin dictionary at his head. Keeping order became more difficult as he grew older. By the time Sydney entered the school, Warton was already sixty and had been headmaster for sixteen years. The new pupil joined in the fun of being badly behaved. Spurred on by hunger, Sydney masterminded the construction of a catapult factory, where he was caught one night red-handed. Instead of punishing him, Warton gave a persuasive demonstration of the force of the argument in favour of his own immediate retirement by praising him for his ingenuity. Sydney had had in his sights a plump turkey.

It is a pity that Sydney was not at Winchester while Warton was at the height of his powers. The school, from the late 1770s, was in a state of precipitous decline. The number of scholars was kept at the statutory level of seventy, but figures for commoners slumped catastrophically. In 1779 there was a reduction from 116 to 105; in 1780 there were 77; and by 1788, the year in which Sydney left the school, the figure had sunk to 38 – a third as many as there had been a decade earlier.

Sydney was not exposed solely to liberal ideas at Winchester; the Tory case was put by George Huntingford, an assistant master since 1770 or so. Early in his career, Huntingford formed a close relationship with Henry Addington, who was one of his pupils. Addington was prime minister in 1802–3, and was created Viscount Sidmouth in 1805. The friendship was broken only by death; Huntingford wrote several hundred long letters to Sidmouth over a period of some sixty years. Only nine years older than his pupil, the young teacher showed towards the future prime minister neither discretion nor reserve: 'I verily believe,' he told him in 1780, 'I could die for you with even a degree of pleasure.' Huntingford had a strong personality and has been charged with a share of the responsibility for the ultra-conservative cast of Addington's mind.[8] Sydney did not think much of the future prime minister. When Addington was in power, he wrote of him: 'It moves every particle of bile in my composition to see the country under the influence of such Goosocracy.' Believing Addington to be a goose, it is unlikely that he thought Huntingford a swan.

Sydney hated Winchester, as did his brother. Courtney ran away twice, and Sydney was still disturbed by mention of the place even after he had reached old age. But although the brothers were unhappy, they both did very well. For four years in succession, Courtney won one of the two gold medals given by the Crown for compositions in Latin verse and prose. Sydney also carried off a number of prizes and rose, in his last year, to a position of pre-eminence in the school: he was Prefect of Hall. Sydney came to feel that it was unwise to vest so much power in a schoolboy. In a judgement fairly safe from contradiction, he put forward the opinion that 'the *head* of a public school is generally a very conceited young man.'[9]

Being Prefect of Hall did not wipe away Sydney's earlier tears. The most enduring legacy of his years at Winchester was passionate resentment against the pointlessness and inefficiency of the system of education he had been forced to undergo. Day after day spent studying Latin and Greek texts, using lexicons and grammar books, was drudgery. Learning, Sydney thought, should be fun. As for his life in chambers, he came to feel that his sufferings had not only been severe, they had also been valueless. In no situation in his adult life had he ever been called upon to accept privations remotely as painful as those he had endured at Winchester. Sydney held those who sent their sons to public schools in contempt. In one of his commonplace books he lists a number of popular fallacies. The first of these runs: '*Because I have gone through it, my son shall go through it also.*' He then illustrates this general principle with a poignant example. A man 'has his eye nearly knocked out' at a public school and then decides, twenty years later, that he is 'determined to act a manly part in life' so he sends his progeny off to face the same treatment. In an article in the *Edinburgh Review* in 1810, Sydney argued that the education at public schools was bad for the formation of character. Enjoying himself richly, he drew up a list of Englishmen – Thomas Wolsey and Sir Thomas More, Spenser and Shakespeare, Ben Jonson and Samuel Johnson, Francis Bacon and Isaac Newton, Oliver Cromwell and the duke of Marlborough, William Pitt the Younger and Edmund Burke – who had all become great men after being taught elsewhere. The best education was one which mingled domestic and school life. Where this was not possible, parents should choose a small private school with twenty or thirty pupils.[10]

Sydney made few friends at Winchester; all his important long-term relationships date from later years. Not only was he starved of emotional satisfaction, he also failed to get to know those who might be useful to him in later life. Opportunities of laying the basis for future self-advancement were mostly missing; the abilities of nearly all Sydney's contemporaries at Winchester were mediocre. Only two boys later rose to positions of prominence. William Howley, elected a scholar in 1779, was already a prefect when Sydney entered the school. Howley later scaled every rung in the ecclesiastical ladder, becoming archbishop of Canterbury in 1828. Sydney and Howley were not close while they were at school, and they saw little of each other in adult life. In the late 1830s, during the course of one of his controversies, Sydney embarrassed the primate by publishing details about a supposed incident that had taken place at Winchester way back in 1784. Howley, as a prefect, had required Sydney to play a game of chess. The future archbishop had lost and had then flown into a rage, knocking Sydney down with the chessboard. Such intemperance is not the kind of behaviour of which ecclesiastical dignitaries like to be reminded. Howley hotly denied Sydney's interpretation of events and may well have been right: Sydney was rarely averse to adding a little embroidery to the unfinished cloth of a good story.[11]

The other boy among Sydney's contemporaries at Winchester who later distinguished himself was Edward Maltby. The son of a weaver, he was one of the very few men from lowly backgrounds who managed to become a bishop, holding the see of Durham for twenty years. Bobus became one of Maltby's closest friends. Sydney was on reasonably good terms with him, but never had a high opinion of Maltby's mind; an 'excellent man and a great fool' is how he summed him up. For reasons that will later become apparent, Maltby's success in becoming bishop of Chichester in 1831 aggravated Sydney enormously.

Sydney's experience at Winchester contrasts vividly with that of his elder brother at Eton. England's premier school offered Bobus glorious opportunities, of which he took full advantage. He knew how well he was placed. 'Nobody ever passed through *this world*', he wrote while he was at Eton, 'without being the richer for it.'[12] The list of Bobus's friends reads like a roll call of the great and the good. Wellington, the 'Iron Duke', was fond of telling the story of how he had beaten Bobus in a fight. They did not share each other's company much in adult life, but Bobus did form lifelong friendships with George Canning, most witty of prime ministers, with George Howard, Viscount Morpeth, son of the fifth earl of Carlisle, and with Henry Fox, third Baron Holland, partly brought up by his famous uncle, Charles James. These relationships, particularly those with Canning and Fox, were to influence the direction taken by Bobus's life. Friendship with Henry Fox was to become even more important to Sydney.

Bobus would not have been befriended by influential aristocrats unless he had first earned their respect. Placed in brilliant company at Eton, he more than held his own. He was fortunate in that his greatest strength lay in making Latin verses, the expertise which was prized above all others and which brought the most sought-after accolades. Bobus was the most able versifier among his contemporaries at Eton; indeed, he was later considered by some expert judges to be the best maker of Latin verses in England. A reputation in this field was a ready passport to political or other fame. Apart from his Latin verses, Bobus shone at Eton in other ways. His chief exploit dates from 1786, when he was sixteen. He was one of four boys who started the *Microcosm*, a weekly satirical magazine. Two of the others were Canning and Canning's great friend John Hookham Frere, a whimsical and absent-minded boy of great talent who was later to dissipate his energies in a life of occasional diplomacy and indolent intellectualism.[13]

The *Microcosm* was launched on 6 November 1786 and ran for forty numbers. Its last issue was on 30 July 1787 and it was then sold to a publisher for £50, an event without precedent for a school magazine. The co-founders achieved considerable notoriety, Canning telling his mother after ten numbers that the periodical was received at Eton with 'great applause and encouragement'. Later royalty joined in the praise. The *Microcosm* was not bulky – each issue consisted of a single brief essay – but the quality of the writing was high. Bobus submitted nine pieces, all of them on historical or philosophical subjects. His prose is self-assured, and he reveals a maturity of judgement well beyond his years. On the darker side, there is also evidence of an élitism and arrogance which were frequently noted in Bobus later on, and from which Sydney was mercifully free. A boy of sixteen should still be optimistic about mankind, but Bobus's soul was already corroded by cynicism. 'The vulgar herd of Mortals', he told readers of the *Microcosm*, 'are blinded by Ambition, elated by Hope, depressed by Fear, melted by Love, tortured by Jealousy.'[14]

The pattern of the relationship between Sydney and Bobus was already set. Sydney did not feel that he was on a par with his elder brother. Although he did not resent Bobus's achievements, he was none the less conscious of walking in his shadow. It was a position from which he took a long time to escape. In old age, when his own fame was secure, Sydney still treated Bobus with deference, the natural respect that a younger has for an elder brother strengthened by conviction of superior attainment in early life. Nothing could persuade Sydney that being Prefect of Hall was as impressive as gaining the respect of Canning, Morpeth and Holland.

3

A PRETTY FEATURE IN A PLAIN FACE

'Poverty is no disgrace to a man, but it is confoundedly inconvenient.'
SYDNEY SMITH

Sydney's progress in his academic career was never slowed down by the need to vault the hurdle of stiff exams. He had won a scholarship to Winchester on the back of being able to recite the first line of the hymn 'All people that on earth do dwell'. The method of entry to Winchester's sister foundation at Oxford was less strenuous. Scholars of Winchester entered New College by dint of precedence, so Sydney, being Prefect of Hall, did not have to exert himself beyond taking the first vacancy. He did this early in 1789, turning up at New College on 6 February. Effortless ease of entry was not Sydney's only privilege. Scholars of Winchester did not go to New College as students in the normal way; they started off as probationary fellows, members of the college who would, after two years, become full fellows and thus part of the teaching staff. Once a man obtained a full fellowship, he had freehold tenure; only gross immorality justified deprivation. Sydney had won for himself more than a university education; he had gained, if he wanted it, a job for life.

New College was not only an academic society, it was also a clerical one. The second rubric in the college statutes stated that all fellows should be fit to be ordained. In the early centuries of the college's life the rubric had been strictly enforced, but by the time of Sydney's arrival the fellows were allowed discretion as to timing, although they were still expected to take orders at a reasonably early stage in their careers.

Life at New College was safe, but it was not stimulating. Although there were seventy fellows (the same number as for scholars at Winchester) most of them had curacies or lived elsewhere. If teachers were few, students were fewer still. For 1789, the year of Sydney's entry to the college, there are only five names in the Admissions Book. In fact that was rather a good year; in 1790 there were only three admissions. It was a similar story in 1791 and 1792: three admissions in the former year and four in the latter. This adds up to a paltry total of fifteen admissions over four years.[1]

Not only were Sydney's contemporaries at New College few, they were also undistinguished. Thomas Scutt is typical. He went up to New College as a probationary fellow in the same year as Sydney, eventually getting a rural living. The comment about him in the college records is sparse: 'He married a widow (Mrs Sergison) and during her life time assumed her name, but after her death resumed his own name.' John Stubbs, another Winchester scholar, became a probationary fellow in 1793 and also ended up as a rural cleric: 'He died in consequence of being thrown from his Gigg [*sic*].'[2] Only William Howley, who had been at Winchester with Sydney, was destined for high office.

If New College was comatose, so was the rest of the university. Eighteenth-century Oxford lacked the vigour it had had during the previous century: entrants averaged 460 a year in the 1660s, only 200 a year in the 1750s. With the reduction in numbers had come a narrowing in social focus. Gone were those intending to be diplomats, gentlemen of leisure and military men; it was mostly prospective clergy who now took degrees. Uniformity also extended to politics. That the university should have a Tory as its MP was accepted as axiomatic. In the parliamentary election for 1780, the Whigs had the rare temerity to put up a candidate. They chose well: Sir William Jones of University College, known as 'Oriental' Jones, a very lively character and an outstanding scholar, the father of modern comparative linguistics. Despite impressive credentials, Jones quickly withdrew. 'A Whig', he declared, 'has as little chance *in* the University as a single bee would have in a wasp's nest.'[3] When Louis XVI was beheaded in January 1793 there was a period of official mourning, and undergraduates took to wearing 'loyal flannel'. It was not an atmosphere which Sydney found congenial.

When it was built in the last quarter of the fourteenth century, New College was planned around an innovative design, enclosing everything that was essential – chapel, library, fellows' quarters, muniment tower, bursary, warden's lodgings – within a single quadrangle. This layout was neat and simple but also cramped; the fellows lived in twenty chambers (ten chambers each with four men, the other ten each with three) on two floors around the cloisters. In the late seventeenth century the cloisters were extended by adding a third storey and the garden triangle, containing eleven more chambers, was built. Spaciousness was still further improved by the non-residence of most of the fellows. Food was plentiful and good. Some of the Dinner Books – not, unfortunately, covering the period of Sydney's residence – have survived. The fellows, it seems, were bon viveurs. One night in October 1772, for example, George Huntingford, devoted friend of Henry Addington and assistant master at Winchester, dined on '2 fowl frigasced [*sic*]' for which he paid 4s 6d, scollop oysters at 3s 4d and, as a sweet, apple pie at 1s 6d.

There was only one respect in which life at New College could not be commended. It was necessary to pay periodic visits to the Long Room, reached from the main quadrangle by walking along an L-shaped covered corridor. The first floor of the Long Room housed the latrines; beneath was a massive cesspit. It was a means of sanitation inspiring in some of its users appreciation bordering upon awe, an author of 1677 describing it as a 'Stupendous Piece of *Building*, it being so large and deep, that it has never been emptied since the Foundation of the College, which was above 300 years since, nor is it ever like to want it.' It was not, in fact, quite as 'stupendous' as the author thought; cleanings, for instance in 1485, were thought necessary from time to time. Earth closets were put in on the ground floor of the Long Room in 1830.[4]

Sydney's life at New College was civilized, not to say indolent. Morning chapel was at seven or eight o'clock. Attendance was compulsory, but was not enforced. A piece of paper, scrawled on by a New Collge chorister, has recently come to light. It bears the date 26 April 1796, a time when Sydney had already been a full fellow for five years. Given the contents, it is just as well that Sydney's name is not mentioned:

Yeates just gone out of chapel, making as if he was ill, to go to Botleigh with Miss Watson. Mr Prickett reads prayers. Mr Lardner is now reading the second lesson. Mr Jenks reads the first. Slatter (master of New College school) shams a bad Eye because he does not know the English of the theme and could not do it. A whole holiday yesterday being St Mark. Only the Subwarden of the Seniors at Prayers.

31

After morning chapel, supposing he went, Sydney was expected to dedicate himself to academic work. He was, yet again, fortunate with examinations. It had become customary for New College men to be exempted from exams set by the university, a strange relaxation of academic discipline which was not put right until 1834. The supervision of Sydney's studies, in his early years, would have been under the sole control of his tutor at New College. College records are so defective that it is not even known who Sydney's tutor was. The curriculum was the same as that at other Oxford colleges: a vast amount of construing of Greek and Latin texts (work which Sydney was already heartily sick of, having done such a lot of it at Winchester), with some philosophy and history. Mathematics and science were conspicuous by their absence. The university also put on optional lecture courses. The only one that Sydney is known to have attended is a series on anatomy, one of his abiding interests, given by the Regius Professor of Medicine, Sir Christopher Pegge.

All his life, Sydney was a zealous supporter of university reform. One of his strongest attacks upon the prevailing system was published in the *Edinburgh Review* in 1809. Sydney argued for an expansion of the curriculum to include economics and politics, but without any lively hope of success. 'A genuine Oxford tutor would shudder to hear his young men disputing upon moral and political truth, forming and pulling down theories, and indulging in all the boldness of youthful discussion. He would augur nothing from it, but impiety to God, and treason to kings.'[5] It was not easy being an Oxford Whig.

Dinner was taken at three o'clock in the afternoon; in March 1791 the time was moved back an hour to four. It was a formal occasion, a daily reminder to Sydney that he was living in an exceptionally rigid society. His hair must be dressed and powdered, and he had to wear a black or dark suit as well as silk stockings. Seating arrangements in Hall were laid down in the statutes. It was all a matter of status and of seniority; probationary fellows, for instance, were in the middle of the dining area. After dinner there was more 'compulsory' chapel. Supper, taken around 9.30 PM, was sometimes enjoyed in a local coffee house (men from New College mostly went to Bagg's, at the corner of Holywell), or it could be shared with someone else in his rooms, or it could be taken alone.

Sydney did not socialize much. Not that he lacked the inclination: he was without the means. Although New College was one of the richest Oxford colleges, the junior fellows, those who had not yet become Masters of Arts, which took seven years, were not paid well. Sydney had to live off £50 or so a year, which was not easy. He had to furnish his rooms, pay his servant's wages, purchase clothes, meet his bills at Bagg's and find enough for a coach home. On top of all these, there was the cost of books; a later letter suggests that expenditure on this front drove Sydney into debt. Oxford was an expensive place to live: an aristocrat's son had no difficulty in getting through £300 a year. It did not help that Sydney also met a debt, of upwards of £30, which Courtney had run up while he was at Winchester; the younger brother was too scared to go to his father, and Sydney relented in the face of Courtney's importunings. He came to regret his kindness later. Although it had taken over half a year's income to bail Courtney out, the debt was never acknowledged, let alone paid off.[6]

New College did little for Sydney, and Sydney did little for New College; there is only one trace of his activity in the college records. For a three-week period in the spring of 1793, he was made steward of the Junior Common Room. The finances of the JCR were in a mess and Sydney was asked to sort them out, drawing up a set of rules. He shows a zest for financial detail that was characteristic of him in his later years. There must be a complete record of income and expenditure so that it 'may immediately be discovered whether the Common room be in a losing or gaining stage; & how far it may be necessary to lower or increase the price of wine'. Care should be taken to avoid financial error or fraud. With this in mind the butler must monitor closely business done with tradesmen who were given credit, comparing their bills with the sums in his own accounts. Nothing was left to chance; Sydney even stipulated that coal ought in future to be bought in the summer months, in order to take advantage of seasonally low prices. These prudent measures show how long and dark was the shadow cast over Sydney's life by his father's financial fecklessness.

By the time Sydney had reached twenty-three and had been at New College for five years, it was time to start thinking about an alternative career. Cecil and Courtney had gone straight from school to jobs in India, getting writerships, the most menial post in the Indian Civil Service, from which they had to work their way up. Bobus, as eldest son, was more fortunate. He went as scholar to King's College, Cambridge, and then Robert Smith financed him while he worked for his Bar exams.

Sydney wanted to follow in his elder brother's footsteps, but was prevented from doing so: Robert Smith would support one son but not two. His father's tight-fistedness was a major source of resentment to Sydney. Robert Smith should not, however, be judged too harshly. As a fellow of New College, Sydney was already set on a natural career path. He would become ordained, obtain a curacy somewhere, keeping his fellowship meanwhile, and wait for a college living to fall vacant. This is what his contemporaries Thomas Scutt and John Stubbs did, and it is what Sydney had, at any rate for a period, to do as well.

So it was that Sydney left Oxford in the summer of 1794, moving to a curacy at Netheravon on Salisbury Plain. His father probably gave a helping hand, for Sydney obtained the position through the patronage of Robert Smith's friend Michael Hicks Beach, who was squire of Netheravon as well as of Williamstrip.[7] The Hicks Beach family – Michael, his wife Henrietta, and several children – were not often at Netheravon, but Sydney liked it when they were there. They stayed at Netheravon House, a secluded four-storey building on a small knoll a hundred yards from the church. A yew tree walk, now alas done away with, led down from the house to the church porch.

Looking after the parish was hard. Netheravon was a small place of less than fifty families; it was so backward that there was not even a village schoolmaster. Apart from a few farmers and a scattering of artisans, everyone was a labourer. Living in such a tiny, isolated community did not suit Sydney. 'Nothing', he told Michael Hicks Beach after he had been there nine months, 'can equal the profound, the unmeasurable, the awful dullness of this place.' Netheravon itself was pleasant enough, one of a string of villages – Upavon, Enford, Fittleton, Netheravon, Figheldean, Bulford – lying in the valley of the River Avon. The problem, as Sydney put it himself, was that Netheravon was no more than 'a pretty feature in a plain face'. Salisbury Plain was plain indeed. The best description of it I know is by John Aubrey, the great seventeenth-century antiquarian. Salisbury Plain, said Aubrey, represents 'the remains of the smooth primitive world when it lay all under water'. Stand in the middle of the plain, look about in every direction and you will see exactly what Aubrey means. Some of the bleakest parts of Salisbury Plain are near Netheravon. To the west is Enford Down and to the east Haxton Down. Walk over these great tracts of treeless chalk downs on a cold December day, imagine the loneliness of the eighteenth-century shepherd with his flock, and you will share the desolation that Sydney felt.

Because there were few landmarks, and no roads to speak of, journeys across Salisbury Plain in winter-time were hazardous. In her *Memoir*, Saba recalls an occasion when Sydney was caught by a sudden snowstorm. 'Having lost all means of tracing his way, there being no trees or vestige of human habitation for miles around, it was by mere chance that he arrived, late at night, and fearfully exhausted, at his own home.'

Life was lonely. The vicar being non-resident, Sydney had use of the parsonage. It was a building that singularly failed to impress. When Sydney had been at Netheravon a few weeks, he wrote to Michael Hicks Beach in his best laconic tone: 'You may assure yourself Sr that the Parsonage house, owing to the uncommon heat of the Summer is perfectly dry. I have suffered a little from the smell of paint, but that is entirely gone off at present.' A butcher's cart drove over from Salisbury once a week, the only chance that Sydney had to obtain any meat. Quite often he made do with a plate of potatoes, smothered in mushroom ketchup. Although he bore these deprivations reasonably well, he never accepted his curacy as his lot in life. 'Poverty', he once said, 'is no disgrace to a man, but it is confoundedly inconvenient.'

Sydney was appalled by the sordid living conditions, the paltry diet and the threadbare clothing of the people of his parish. Soon after his arrival, he laid plans to start a Sunday school. The children, gathered together, were a pitiful sight. 'On Sunday last', Sydney told Henrietta Hicks Beach, 'there were 3 or 4 children with their feet upon the cold stones without any shoes, and one came a perfect *Sans culottes* – or at least only with some grinning remnants of that useful garment, just sufficient to shew that he was so clad from necessity, and not from any ingenious Theory he had taken up against such a useful invention. If the Sunday School had begun, I should have imagined that the poor boy thought it his duty to come ready for whipping, as a fowl is sent from the poulterers, trussed and ready for roasting.'[8]

This vivid description of a group of children is quite a rarity. Records of the lives of the poor in Georgian England are scanty. For most places, there is nothing except statistics of births, marriages and deaths, sometimes supplemented by information gathered by those responsible for management of the local poorhouse. Neveravon is different. Nine months before Sydney took over as curate, Mr Verrey, steward to Michael Hicks Beach, carried out a comprehensive social survey, to which Sydney later added his own comments. Verrey tells a tale of shocking poverty. His report covers forty-two families, virtually the whole parish. In twelve instances, comment was encouraging: 'decent and tolerably comfortable', 'house and children kept clean', 'very comfortable cottage', 'industrious family', and so on; but the other thirty families were all in varying stages of destitution and neglect.

Worst of all were those who could not look after themselves and therefore had to be cared for in the poorhouse. James Clark lived there with his crippled wife and four children, the eldest of whom was nine. The family, Sydney told Michael Hicks Beach, was 'aliment for Newgate, food for the halter, a ragged, wretched, savage, stubborn race'. Some of the other inmates were in equally bad shape. Daniel Sutton, aged seventy-two, was subject to fits and Daniel Hiscocks, twelve years younger, had a 'leprous disorder'. Hiscocks, said Sydney, was 'perfectly wretched & helpless'. Then there was W. Powell, a forty-five-year-old widower with two daughters, aged fourteen and fifteen. Powell's spirits could not be roused; he was 'quite dejected having lately lost his mistress'. Henry Cozens, a fifty-year-old musician, and his wife fared little better: 'She complains of her eyesight & he complains of her frailty.'

Many couples outside the poorhouse were also in dire straits. Some could not cope because they had too many children. John Thomas had five girls, the eldest being twenty-three. His wife had recently been ill. Thomas's eldest daughter 'applied to the Vestry on Sunday' for relief; the overseers 'directed one shilling to be given her with a strict caution to make the most of it'. James Draper already had four children; his wife, adding to the burden, had given birth 'a week ago'. Draper had a bad leg and 'receives victuals for his work'. Since his wife's confinement, the parish had allowed the family 6s 6d a week in relief. Three women, Mary Carter, Pheobe Sheppard and Sarah Mastlin, brought up children born out of wedlock. Only one of the three, Pheobe Sheppard, was given any help; she received one shilling a week for the younger of her two offspring, who was five.

Others had to struggle just to get by. Some had physical disabilities. William Kill was blind; he lived with his two daughters, both of whom had 'tarnished their character'. John Russell, aged fifty-five, was an even sadder case. Russell worked for farmer Lee, receiving hopelessly inadequate wages of 4s a week. The low pay did not protect him against ill-treatment. 'Young farmer Lee has beat this poor old man several times; last week he beat him with a large stick and nearly crippled him.' Charles Slade lived with his wife and three children.

Sydney says of this family: 'wretched from their Irish extraction, from numbers, from disease, from habits of idleness'. Isaac Wansbury had a wife and two children, aged five and a half and three and a half. 'The house is in a most shattered condition both within and without; there is no chamber, & they are obliged to sleep on the Ground Floor.' John Head had a wife and four children, aged from four years to four months. The Heads had 'neither sheet nor blanket, & only a miserable straw bed for the children'. Sydney adds: 'weak witless people, totally wretched, without sense to extricate themselves from their wretchedness'. William Piper, with a wife and three children, was almost as poverty-stricken: 'they were forced to cut up an old stool for firing.'

Very few people at Netheravon were able to rise above their poverty, win relatively easily in the fight for existence and have enough emotional and spiritual energy left over to care for others. Mr Verrey had complimentary things to say about the Spratts, who looked after a five-year-old orphan boy. 'The parish allows 2s per week for him, & Spratt's wife pays 2d out of it for his schooling; she is very kind to this child.' The Wheelers did even better. Robert Wheeler was fifty-four, his wife, an epileptic, the same age. Like several other people in the parish, Wheeler worked for farmer Gibbs. Despite Mrs Wheeler's epilepsy, this couple performed heroic deeds. Even though they had two children of their own, they still took in other people's. There was an orphan girl of thirteen: 'she spins very well, but work is scarce & she is principally supported by the Wheelers.' The household was completed by the two small daughters of William Kite, carter to farmer Gibbs. Kite was paid 7s a week, out of which he gave the Wheelers 4s towards the upkeep of his children. No one in Verrey's survey could hold a candle to Robert Wheeler and his wife.

Confronted by the terrifying poverty of his parishioners, Sydney did what he could. His plans for a Sunday school came to fruition. The children met in the shop of Harry Cozens, the local tailor. Sydney gives several reasons for choosing Cozens in preference to other candidates. He was a 'sensible' man; he was literate himself, and had a literate household – 'his wife reads, his Brother reads, and his apprentice reads'; and his mother, who lived next door, had a good kitchen which could be used to cope with any overspill. Henrietta Hicks Beach helped out, sending twenty spelling books and the same number of New Testaments and Prayer Books. Early in 1796, Sydney also started a School of Industry, selecting twenty poor girls and setting them to darn, sew and knit in the forge of Bendall the blacksmith. The girls' first project was to make a coarse canvas bag to hold their belongings.[9] These were small initiatives, but Sydney lacked the financial resources to do anything more substantial or imaginative.

In the summer of 1796, two years into his curacy, Sydney moved back to Oxford, where he was priested. He was weary of Netheravon and had hopes, which were not fulfilled, of getting a tutorship at New College. His first surviving letter to his father is dated 26 June and was written from Oxford. Although, over the past year, Sydney's fellowship had been worth £50 'clear of all deductions', and although the curacy at Netheravon brought in a further £50, he had still required a subsidy of £40 from his father. He asked for rather more, £65, to help him through the next twelve months. Moving back to Oxford had cost £10; his furniture at Netheravon, purchased for £35, had only realized £27 at sale; he had budgeted £18 for the upkeep of his horse, but found that he had overspent by £6; there were certain 'necessary repairs' that had to be carried out to his rooms in New College; and he also mentions a string of exceptional expenses, among them £1 5s 6d for payment of Priest's Orders.

Despite his curacy and his fellowship, at the age of twenty-five Sydney was still dependent. It was not a situation he liked. 'A College Tutorship is exactly £50 per annum. If I could get one I should in that case exonerate you.' Sydney's desire for financial independence stemmed partly from pride and partly from a wish to remove a source of friction with his father. Relations with Robert Smith were not good. Sydney ends his letter on a plaintive note: 'I hope my dear Father you will do me the favour of writing to me, as it will be a proof that you begin to feel a returning regard for me . . . Adieu my dearest Father, give my best love to Maria and my Mother.' Estrangement from Robert Smith was nothing new. Father and son were already at loggerheads in 1786, when Sydney was in his fourth year at Winchester.

Sydney's movements over the next two years are unclear. He spent some time back at Netheravon, he visited his parents on several occasions, and he went at least once to Williamstrip. Mostly, though, he was at New College. Sydney had a fresh academic occupation: learning thoroughly both German and French. The eldest Hicks Beach boy, Michael, would soon leave Eton, and the plan was for Sydney to accompany him as a private tutor, while Michael undertook a course of study at a reputable European university. The prospect of prolonged absence on the Continent encouraged Sydney to make renewed efforts to mend fences with his father, a difficult task, as a letter written in early November 1797 aptly testifies:

> Once again my dear Father give me leave to express a hope, that you will soften your resolution and permit me to stay a longer time with you and the family than you limited me to at my departure. If you wish me to stay away to prevent the fatal consequences of a rupture between us, I have only this garantie [*sic*] to give you that you never had before: upon a serious review of my conduct I have allow'd myself to have been principally in the wrong which, till that time, I never even dreamt of. If you meant it as a rebuke for my conduct upon the particular occasion you mention'd, remember I shall see no more of you for 2 or 3 years, and if in the interval I lose you which *may* be the case – or my Mother which I very much fear *will* be the case – the punishment you inflict will be much more severe than you meant it to be. Whichever you decide, I acknowledge you have been much provok'd and I submit. Adieu my dearest Father, and believe me with every sentiment of respect and regard.
>
> Yours,
>
> Sydney Smith[10]

Robert Smith treated Sydney quite in the same way as he treated Bobus, Cecil and Courtney. Unpredictable and irritable, he sought to impose his will and made heavy emotional demands. The sons reacted to harassment in different ways. Bobus confronted his father head on, in explosive encounters; Courtney retreated into surliness; and Cecil could not cope at all. Sydney's method of dealing with parental hostility was complex. He started by fighting his own corner. Finding he was getting nowhere, he retreated; and, once he was going backwards, he lost the will to continue the struggle, suffering the indignity, as is indicated in the letter above, of abject defeat. It was not a strategy that increased Sydney's sense of self-respect, nor did it help him to become emotionally mature. Sydney was purchasing peace at a high price, paid by himself. His anger was being driven inwards; and he was constantly having to convince himself that he was in the wrong when he knew, deep within himself, that he was not.

In December 1797 Sydney was invited to stay for two weeks or so at Bowood, the great Lansdowne house near Calne in Wiltshire. He was there as the guest of William Petty, earl of Shelburne, briefly prime minister from July 1782 until February of the next year but now retired from politics and in charge of England's leading literary salon. It was Sydney's first taste of avant-garde society. It suited him well. After he had been at Bowood a few days he wrote a letter to Michael Hicks Beach, apologizing for its brevity: 'I would write to you more at large, but it is dinner time and this Aristocrat or rather Democrat gives such good dinners, that they are by no means to be neglected, and especially not by such an Epicure as me.'

Sydney's stay at Bowood was not entirely given over to self-indulgence; he was there to 'be the Imam' at Bobus's marriage. His bride, Caroline Vernon, was thirty-six, nine years older than Bobus, and the bloom of youth had long since gone. One of her male friends, exhibiting a vindictiveness often held to be the preserve of the opposite sex, described her as 'scraggy'. The loss of Caroline's looks did not matter to Sydney; he wrote his father, pointedly not invited to the wedding by Bobus, a glowing report: 'Her figure and appearance are commanding, her manners very affable, her temper sweet, her understanding very superior, all solid, effective, fit for sterling practice, in short just the woman to win Bobus's heart, and to govern him with the greatest possible advantage.'[11] Sydney, worried by Bobus's turbulent passions, his fits of uncontrollable anger, was right in thinking that an older woman, with a strong mind, would be good for his elder brother.

The forthcoming marriage was important for Sydney as well as Bobus. Through a series of dynastic alliances, Caroline Vernon was linked to the Russells, the Foxes and the Lansdownes, three of the foremost Whig families in the land. An aunt had married John Russell, fourth duke of Bedford; one half-sister, Mary, wedded Stephen Fox, second Baron Holland; and another half-sister, Louisa, became the second wife of Shelburne. Hence the choice of Bowood as the venue for the match. A marital alliance between the Smiths and the Vernons would dramatically improve the social prospects of the whole Smith family.

Already, there were signs of what might lie in store; while he was at Bowood, Sydney was able to renew his acquaintance with Bobus's great schoolfriend Henry Fox, third Baron Holland – they had already met some years before, at Cambridge. Bobus's own position *vis-à-vis* Fox would be soon be somewhat peculiar: his bride-to-be was the half-sister of Holland's father! (Stephen Fox, the second baron, had died young, leaving his only son to inherit the baronetcy at a year old.)

The marriage of Bobus and Caroline took place on 9 December in the great library at Bowood. Sydney conducted the ceremony at what was, for him, the unsuitable hour of 5.30 A M. This was in order to fit in with honeymoon plans; soon after six, Mr and Mrs Robert Smith set off in a chaise for Wycombe, a Lansdowne family home. Sydney was sad to see them go. Writing to his mother soon afterwards, he sums up the occasion in a few words: 'he cried, she cried, and I cried.'[12]

It was not long before the social significance of Bobus's marriage became apparent. Lord Holland's spinster sister Caroline met Maria early in 1798 and liked her very much; a 'charming little creature' was Caroline's verdict. Sydney had to face a far harsher social baptism; he was introduced to Lord Holland's formidable wife, who did not take to him at all. In a letter to her sister-in-law, she launched into an attack upon Sydney's character that was so peppered with 'violent invective' that Caroline Fox felt compelled to come to his defence: 'As to Sydney Smith it is impossible to conceive any thing much more disagreeable than his first manner, & I always told you that you would not find it prepossing [*sic*]. However, I am persuaded much good sense, some humour & very great good nature lie behind so that I hope you will see him again & endeavour to penetrate below the surface.'[13]

Caroline Fox's comments are the earliest assessment that we have of Sydney. When she said that she did not find his 'first manner' prepossessing, she was referring to his gaucheness, a problem that he had to live with for many more years. Her order of priorities is revealing. '. . . much good sense, some humour & very great good nature': a thumbnail sketch of an affable merchant, not of a famous wit.

Both before and after 'being the Imam' at Bobus's marriage, Sydney visited his parents who were now living at Bath. The first stay was in October, and the second can be dated from a letter which Sydney wrote to Michael Hicks Beach from a temporary residence at 3 Edgar Buildings on 19 January 1798.

Timing is important. The Austen family, including Jane, were in Bath throughout November and right up to Christmas, and may well have remained into the New Year. They lodged at 1 Paragon Buildings, no more than a minute's walk away from where Sydney wrote his letter. Added credence to a possible meeting between Sydney and Jane is given by the fact that Jane knew Michael and Henrietta Hicks Beach, and moved among families who were part of the Hicks Beaches' social circle.

Jane may have had Sydney in mind when, a few months later, she came to sketch the portrait of Henry Tilney, also a clergyman, in the novel that was later to be published as *Northanger Abbey*. There is similarity in bearing. Henry Tilney, we are told, 'seemed to be about four or five and twenty [Sydney was twenty-six at the time], was rather tall, had a pleasing countenance, a very intelligent and lively eye, and, if not quite handsome, was very near to it.' There is also similarity in conversational style. Tilney's talk, says Jane, was full of 'fluency and spirit', and his manner had 'archness and pleasantry'. One example of such 'archness' is especially interesting. 'No one', says Tilney, 'can think more highly of the understanding of women than I do. In my opinion, nature has given them so much that they never find it necessary to use more than half.' This is the sort of parody of Sydney's conversation that might be written by someone who did not know him well. Sydney loved making remarks with a twist in the tail. He would not, however, have phrased the statement in the way used by Henry Tilney: Sydney had a high view of women's intelligence and never indulged in belittling them.

In the spring of 1798, Sydney abandoned the plan to go abroad with young Michael Hicks Beach. The deteriorating political situation in Europe (France had invaded Switzerland in February) was the reason for the abrupt about-turn. Sydney, unusually, was being timid. Going to Europe was difficult but by no means impossible: two young English poets, Wordsworth and Coleridge, set off for Germany in the autumn of 1798. Once the Continent was ruled out, Sydney decided to travel north. Since the middle of the eighteenth century, English aristocrats had been sending their sons to Scottish universities either before or after doing degrees at Oxford and Cambridge. The fame of David Hume and Adam Smith, pioneers of the Scottish Enlightenment, was the magnet. After hostilities broke out in Europe, the attractions of the northern kingdom were magnified. A good number of young English aristocrats found their way to Edinburgh or Glasgow around the turn of the nineteenth century. For instance William Lamb, later second Viscount Melbourne, confidant, as prime minister, to the young Queen Victoria, was sent to Glasgow; and Shelburne's heir, Lord Henry Petty, went to Edinburgh.

Edinburgh stood in higher esteem than its rival and was the popular choice; it was therefore Edinburgh that was chosen. A date for departure was set of 1 June. Before Sydney and Michael set out, the ticklish matter of remuneration had to be settled. Sydney was uneasy, feeling that it was the responsibility of his patron to make the first move. Robert Smith tried to resolve the impasse by interposing himself between Sydney and his patron, but Sydney rebuffed him. Mr Hicks Beach left things until the last moment and then made a handsome offer. Sydney would receive £500 a year for two years, with the first £500 being paid immediately and a second instalment of £500 at the end of the two-year period. Sydney later calculated that, after expenses, his two years with young Michael Hicks Beach enabled him to save the very useful sum of £730.[14] The fellow of New College and curate of Netheravon left England knowing that his financial prospects had been transformed.

4

THE ATHENS OF THE NORTH

'Friendships grow in youthful Soils; their progress is much slower in ground that has been much stirr'd about & cultivated'

SYDNEY SMITH TO RICHARD HEBER,
March 1819

Sydney and young Michael Hicks Beach did not set out for Edinburgh alone; they took with them a German courier-valet called Mithoeffer, a companion thrust upon them by their over-confident preparations for a continental tour. Sydney, keen on puns, gave the valet the nickname of Metaphor. An early port of call was Warwick castle, where Lord Warwick gave them a 'most hospitable reception'. This was an important visit: Lord Warwick's second wife was Henrietta Vernon, the sister of Bobus's wife. Sydney knew that keeping on the right side of the aristocracy was vital if he was to further his clerical career.

After Warwick the party moved on to Birmingham, Sydney's first encounter with an industrial town. His summary is succinct; Birmingham, he told Henrietta Hicks Beach, was a place of 'loud noises, and bad Smells'. They went next to Lichfield and Matlock; the latter stopping-place Sydney found 'enchanting'. After Matlock the roads deteriorated, being especially bad between Bakewell and Disley: 'I doubted very much at first . . . whether I should put myself to death, or go to sleep, but during the debate I insensibly adopted the latter and so the matter was settled.' Sydney found Manchester ugly but was impressed by Liverpool, a scene of commercial activity 'equal to any thing I have seen in London'.

From Liverpool the party travelled through Lancashire into the Lake District, passing through Preston, Lancaster and Kendal, before making a detour to Keswick. The main excitement in this part of the journey was an ascent of Skiddaw. The long and sometimes arduous journey had not sapped Sydney's energy; he was in excellent form:

Off we set, Michael, the guide and myself at one in the morning . . . I who find it rather difficult to stick upon my horse on the plainest of roads, did not find that facility increased by the darkness of the morning, or the precipitous paths we had to ascend. I made no manner of doubt, but that I should roll down into the Town of Keswick the next morning and be picked up by the Town Beadle dead in a gutter. Moreover I was moved a little for my reputation, for as I had a bottle of brandy in my pocket, placed there by the special exhortations of the Guide and Landlord, The Keswick Coroner and jury would infallibly have brought me in 'a Parson as died of drinking'.[1]

Once they reached the summit, they found themselves in thick cloud; their sense of enjoyment was not increased by the fact that they were being whipped by a keen wind in bitter cold. The brandy Sydney had been pressed to bring with him helped to allay their discomfort. As dawn turned to morning, Sydney gave the Romantic side of his nature full rein:

The wind the complaisant wind now pulled away the vapours at intervals and gave us a hasty view in different quarters of the magnificent Scene which surrounded us. When the clearance was to the East, we looked over the level county of Northumberland, and saw the light of day rising from the German Ocean; beneath us was Keswick, all quiet and the solemn tranquil lake of Derwent; beyond these the Westmorcland mountains began to be tinged with the golden morning, or we caught the Isle of Man, the Northern Coast of Ireland, the Firth of Solway, or the hills of Cheviot well known to Song and history. Above us was the blue heaven, and all under were the Sons of men scattered in fair cities, and upon hills and down in the dales, and over the whole face of the Earth.

After a 'monstrous breakfast' it was time to set out for Penrith. After Penrith the fun of the journey ended. Going through the Scottish Borders and across the Lowlands was not pleasant: 'the Country was abominable, the Inns bad, the Post chaises dirty, Everything indicative of Vermin, and want.'

Sydney was relieved to reach Edinburgh. His deprecatory remarks about his new environment – Scotland was 'that knuckle-end of

England, that land of Calvin, oat-cakes, and sulphur' – are not to be taken seriously. From the start he liked the country. Even in old age, the sights and sounds of Edinburgh were still vivid in Sydney's memory: 'Ah! what charming walks I had about Arthur's Seat, with the clear mountain air blowing in one's face. I often think of that glorious scene.' Sydney felt especially exhilarated whenever a strong wind blew off the sea: 'even the experienced Scotch fowls did not venture to cross the streets, but sidled along, tails aloft, without venturing to encounter the gale.'

He liked the people whom he met in the streets, in markets, and at other public places. The Scots were, of course, made the butt of his jests – 'It requires a surgical operation to get a joke well into a Scotch understanding. Their only idea of wit . . . is laughing immoderately at stated intervals' – but this does not represent his real sentiments; he found local people generous, warm and friendly. Sydney only had one complaint to make about Edinburgh: the 'total want of all faecal propriety and excremental delicacy'. He did not exaggerate. Edinburgh Old Town is built upon a French pattern. The High Street and Canongate run along the spine of a ridge joining the Castle to Holyrood House. Down both slopes of the ridge are numerous high buildings divided from each other by narrow closes. Late in the evening it was the custom, in the eighteenth century, to discharge the collected filth of the day into these closes. When about to throw excrement out of the window, it was considered good manners to call out 'Gardy-loo' (*gardez l'eau*); and if anyone was unfortunate enough to be walking underneath at the time, there was the certainty, unless the passer-by was stone deaf, of receiving the reply 'Haud yer han.' In the mornings, except on Sundays, the streets were cleaned by the City Guard. Before its abolition in 1817, the Guard was one of the sights of Edinburgh. A guardsman's uniform was more military than it was civil: red coat, red breeches, black gaiters, white belt and a large cocked hat. The guardsmen carried muskets and bayonets but hardly ever used them.[2]

Sydney settled in the New Town, still under construction to the north of the Old Town and being built according to a plan drawn up by James Craig and accepted by the city council in 1767. Craig chose a chequerboard, or gridiron, design: wide and straight streets, with low houses built in a Classical style. A greater contrast with the Old Town would be difficult to imagine. The architecture of the New Town epitomizes the rationality, common sense and careful balance of the

eighteenth-century Scottish mind. Sydney took lodgings at 38 South
Hanover Street, where he and his two companions had a whole floor
to themselves. Sydney was pleased with his surroundings, telling
Henrietta Hicks Beach that 'Our Situation is in the centre of the finest
Street I have yet seen in Great Britain.' There was a living-in servant
and Sydney also employed a cook, whom he paid the princely sum of
sixpence a day. Mithoeffer was given the task of doing the shopping,
but his command of English was very poor and the local Scots accent
completely defeated him. What he returned with was initially a source
of merriment, but his skill did gradually improve after he was given
some coaching by Sydney. Sydney also helped out from time to time
with other domestic chores, being part of the team (Mithoeffer and the
cook were the others) that tried to make a pie. The culinary
experiment did not work out: the crust was as hard as a biscuit.
Sydney relished his new life. 'There is always some beef in the Salt tub,'
he assured Mrs Beach, 'and I look into the family affairs like a fat old
lady of 40.'

Teaching Michael was hard work. Sydney's pupil was fond of
horses and even fonder of dancing, but he was no academic. Reading
between the lines of the letters that Sydney wrote to the boy's parents,
it is clear that there was a personality conflict: Sydney made Michael, a
boy of average ability, feel mediocre, and Michael responded by being
deliberately irritating. He went to bed early when Sydney wanted him
to stay up late, was unpunctual – a failing which infuriated Sydney –
made desultory efforts at learning and spent an inordinate amount of
time in front of the mirror. Academic progress was slow and Sydney
was forced to lower his sights, admitting after six months that 'I am
now decidedly convinced that whatever share of knowledge Michael
may gain by reading with me, it is quite out of my power to give him a
taste for books, in that degree which I think useful and ornamental in
his situation in life.'

A little later, when tutor and pupil were separated for a while,
Sydney wrote Michael a heavily ironic letter. 'I hope', Sydney began,
'you sometimes take a book in hand. As I have often told you, to enjoy
the pleasures of doing nothing you must do something. Idle people
know nothing of the pleasures of idleness; it is a very difficult
accomplishment to acquire in perfection.' It is doubtful whether this
letter made much impression. Michael kept to his side of the bargain,
staying with Sydney for the full two years; while Sydney suffered at his
pupil's hands nothing worse than a few insults and, on one occasion, a

'tremendous blow on the nose' when he was trying, with Mithoeffer's help, to put Michael to bed after a drinking bout with friends.[3]

Sydney did not go to Edinburgh empty-handed; he carried with him in his pocket a sheaf of social introductions given him by Michael's father. Sydney used his patron's influence to gain a toe-hold in Edinburgh society, dining soon after his arival with Baron Norton, a Baron of the Scotch Exchequer, and meeting Charles Hope, a 'man of eminence at the Scotch Bar'. (Hope later became President of the Court of Session and was given an English baronetcy.) Sydney also made contacts further afield, setting off on a brief tour of the Highlands within two weeks of arriving at Edinburgh. Michael and he 'toiled six miles to the top of Ben Lomond' and then made their way to the castle of the duke of Buccleuch, where they met the French king's brother and his suite. The company may have been exalted but it did not enthral Sydney; 'We were,' he told Mrs Beach, 'not much pleased with our day.' There simply was not enough electricity around. 'Her Grace is a most excellent woman, but a very stately piece of ancient life as I ever saw – the Duke seems to be one of those kind of men who baffle all attempts to hate, praise or blame them.'

Another place of call was Dunkeld, the seat of the duke of Atholl, where they sat down to eat with their host and his 'beautiful' wife as well as the 'most imprudent Duchess of Gordon'. (This was Jane Maxwell, wife of the fourth duke; one of the leaders in both Edinburgh and London society, she was a confidante of William Pitt the Younger and a patroness of Burns, and was unconventional in her behaviour, a fact to which Sydney's use of the word 'imprudent' makes delicate reference.) The next day the duchess was flung out of her chaise when the horse took fright. Travel proved to be more traumatic than arrival: she had the good fortune to land 'upon her bum a part upon which she might certainly descend from much greater heights with equal impunity'. Sydney was not a man who stood upon ceremony; nor, at any rate on this occasion, did the duchess.

After his return to Edinburgh, Sydney did not see much of Baron Norton and Charles Hope. Many of the men and women in Edinburgh society were too conventional for Sydney's taste. A lot of them automatically distanced themselves by moving in the social circle of a man whom Sydney profoundly disliked: Henry Dundas, the local Tory MP. Sydney later wrote that Dundas exercised 'supreme power over the northern division of the island'. This judgement is not swelled by hyperbole. In the latest parliamentary election, that for 1796,

Dundas had seen to it that 36 seats out of 45 were occupied by sycophants or friends. Of the remaining nine, it is probable that four were in the hands of allies, and it is possible that a further three were so. Edinburgh was Dundas's citadel. The city council was under his thumb, he made sure that Whig lawyers made little progress in their careers, and the local press was either loyal or quiescent. One contemporary described him as the 'Pharos of Scotland. Who steered upon him was safe; who disregarded his light was wrecked.'[4]

Sydney soon started to build up his own social network. One of his first and best friends was Dugald Stewart, Professor of Moral Philosophy at Edinburgh University since 1785. Sydney attended Stewart's lectures, and these became a formative influence. Stewart was not an original thinker (he relied heavily upon the system of Scottish rationalism developed by Thomas Reid) and, being asthmatic, his delivery was weak. He nevertheless had great capacity to exalt and to inspire. Part of his secret was command of language; there was, one of his hearers said, 'eloquence in his very spitting'. More important was loftiness of character. In his lectures, Stewart passed quickly over the details of philosophic debate, turning his discourses into a kind of sermon: he spoke of the intimate connection between virtue and enjoyment, of the satisfaction that was to be derived from the study of science and literature, and of the evidence for the immortality of the human soul. Sydney, while at Oxford, had been intellectually and morally starved; now he was getting sustenance.

Sydney also benefited from the company of men of his own age and interests. These contacts were made at Stewart's lectures; and also at clubs, most of which met in oyster cellars and taverns. From the most prestigious club, the Speculative Society, founded in 1764 and still in existence, Sydney was debarred; membership was restricted to members of Edinburgh University. There was no shortage of other places to go. Eighteenth-century Edinburgh probably had more private clubs than any other town of comparable size anywhere in the world. Every taste was catered for and every eccentricity was pandered to. At the Jacobite Club the members talked in Latin. The distinctive feature of the Cape Club was that it parodied Masonic ritual; every member of the Cape was given a mock knighthood – Sir Thumb, Sir Carpet, Sir Handle and so on. Dourness, a central element in the traditional stereotype of the Scottish character, is not a quality that can readily be associated with the more lively young men in late eighteenth-century Edinburgh. The most debauched among them joined the Beggar's Benison, where they went in for obscene practices comparable to those of the English Hellfire Club. '18 assembled, and Frigged upon the Test Platter' runs the minutes of one meeting. The Prince Regent was an enthusiastic supporter of the Beggar's Benison, making a point of attending meetings whenever he was in Edinburgh.[5]

Sydney was to meet the Prince Regent later, but not at the Beggar's Benison; sexual impropriety, in any form, was anathema to him. What he most enjoyed was talking and drinking with friends. When he was in a serious mood, he went to meetings of the Academy of Physics, an offshoot of the university Literary Society. This gave him an opportunity to get to know a number of remarkably able young Scots. Most able of all was the Academy's founder, Henry Brougham. When Sydney arrived in Edinburgh, Brougham was not quite twenty but had already taken his degree at Edinburgh University, which he entered when he was fourteen. Sydney's new friend showed precocious talent. When only seventeen a paper on optics by Brougham had been accepted and read at the Royal Society. Modesty was not one of his faults; he claimed that his paper made an 'addition to the Newtonian doctrine' and wrote, seventy years later, that omission of certain sections of it from the subsequent printing held back for decades the discovery of photography. In later life, one of Brougham's friends said of him that his 'power of attainment' was 'almost miraculous'. There seemed to be nothing that Brougham could not do. It was said only half-jestingly that if a new language were to be invented, Brougham would be sure to have learnt it by the same evening.

There was to come a time, in the mid-1830s, when occupation of 10 Downing Street was within Brougham's grasp. The opportunity passed him by. Appearances, in his case, were not deceptive: he looked shifty and was shifty. His physical movements were extremely awkward, creating a poor impression which was reinforced by his thinness and his height; he had, thought Sydney, a 'Gristly face'; and it did not help that there was a nervous twitch to the mouth. A graphic account of Brougham showing off at a dinner table comes from the pen of the popular writer Harriet Martineau. What especially struck her was Brougham's extraordinary capacity for speed: he thought excessively fast, spoke excessively fast and ate excessively fast. He also had a voracious appetite, stretching out his long arms for any dish he fancied. The largest spoons, Harriet noted mischievously, seemed to have a strange habit of finding their way into Brougham's gnarled hands. His speech was liberally sprinkled with swear-words, and was occasionally indecent. He played up incessantly to women. Harriet thought him insane.

Sydney was fully conscious of his friend's deviousness. 'I really like Brougham', he once wrote, 'and regret most heartily that he will not walk thro' life in a straight path.' Duplicity was the air that Brougham breathed, intrigue the food he lived upon. His buffoonery angered the solemn, and his overweeningly high opinion of himself angered the diffident. He is perhaps best known to posterity for inventing the curious carriage, much like a garden chair, that bears his name. It was typical of its owner that the carriage should have, emblazoned on its outside, a large B surmounted by a coronet. 'There goes a carriage', said Sydney, 'with a *B* outside and a wasp within.'

Francis Horner was the same age as Brougham and had grown up with him: they played together as infants in front of Horner's house, they both went to Edinburgh High School, they had then gone on to Edinburgh University, and they both wanted to be lawyers. There, however, the resemblance ends. Horner lacked Brougham's intellectual capacity but had a much finer heart. Childhood somehow seems to have passed him by. Even at an early age he was always courteous, deferential to his elders, honourable and kind. Sydney made friends with him very soon after he set foot in Edinburgh. Some of those to whom Sydney was given letters of introduction spoke out against Horner, describing him as a 'person of violent' – that is, Whig – 'political opinions'. This was enough to ensure that Sydney sought the young man out. Despite the age gap, it was not long before they were close. Temperamentally they were very dissimilar: Horner's seriousness contrasted with Sydney's joviality, his conscientiousness with Sydney's laziness, his ponderousness with Sydney's quickness. What attracted Sydney to Horner was his moral power. As friendship developed, he grew to feel a degree of respect for the 'Knight of the Shaggy Eyebrows' (his pet name for Horner) which did not fall far short of reverence.[6]

The other member of the Academy who became an inseparable *convive* was Francis Jeffrey. Five years older than Brougham and Horner, he was, like them, a native of Edinburgh. He had learnt his letters in a small school 'in the abyss of Bailie Fyfe's Close', one of the numerous alleyways that led off the High Street. After attending Edinburgh High School, Jeffrey left the city, going to Glasgow University. There was also a spell at Queen's College, Oxford, which he hated. His sojourn there left him with a strange semi-English accent, at once both high-keyed and modulating, both cooing and metallic. Whenever he was henceforth south of the Border, he 'pined hourly' to hear the 'Doric sounds' of his native tongue. When Sydney met him, Jeffrey had been back in Edinburgh some years, struggling to make his way, as would Brougham and Horner, at the Scottish Bar.

Everything about Jeffrey spoke of activity. A short man (he was about five feet six inches tall), he was physically striking, with a red face, jet black eyes and a mass of stiff black hair. He moved quickly but erratically – his limbs, said one of his friends, looked as though they were being 'jerked about with a wire' – and he spoke quickly too. He was without the slightest trace of artifice or affectation, and was charming to women. The essence of Jeffrey was paradox: stoutness in body but lightness in step, volubility in speech but fluency in thought, optimism in character but pessimism about prospects for any endeavour he was engaged in. Jeffrey's mind was immensely sharp and analytic, he had deft manners and, in conversation, he moved with the greatest rapidity from subject to subject. He was also a superb mimic. He once kept Jane and Thomas Carlyle in fits of laughter for several hours, impersonating people he had known. Jeffrey hit off their characteristic gesticulations, accents and facial expressions, all at the same time. The Carlyles were mesmerized by his virtuoso performance.

As with his other friends, Sydney loved to tease. Jeffrey's shortness was a constant source of merriment: 'One buck rabbit will clothe him to the heels.' Sydney also made fun of Jeffrey's obsession with severe intellectual analysis. 'If you could be alarmed into the semblance of modesty, you would charm everybody; but remember my joke against you about the Moon and the Solar System; – "Damn the solar system! bad light – planets too distant – pestered with comets – feeble contrivance; – could make a better with great ease".' This was a neat parody of Jeffrey's sten-gun sentences.

At a deeper level, Jeffrey helped to satisfy one of Sydney's most pressing emotional needs: the requirement to form lasting ties with men whom he could look up to. His lack of inner self-confidence is evident in a letter which he wrote to Jeffrey in August 1801, after they had known each other three years. 'Many thanks, my dear Jeffrey, for the pleasant expressions of good-will your letter contains. The friendship of worthy, sensible men I look upon as the greatest blessing of life. I have always felt myself flattered that you did not consider my society beneath your attention.'[7] Given Sydney's glittering and varied gifts, the last sentence reads oddly. It makes more sense when one calls to mind Sydney's insecurity, deeply rooted in his nature and the product of his turbulent childhood. He needed, with part of himself, to feel inferior. Hence the strength of the link with others apart from Jeffrey: Horner is a good example, as is Bobus.

The meetings of the Academy of Physics are important. Held weekly, they enabled Sydney to consolidate his friendships with Brougham, Horner and Jeffrey. They also broadened his mind. The Academy was, in a sense, an extension of Dugald Stewart's lectures: all the regular members were devotees of the Professor of Moral Philosophy, and had gone to his courses at some time in their careers. The Academy was also a training ground for the later launching of the *Edinburgh Review*. Each week a paper was read, either an original contribution to learning or a book review. There might be something on mathematics one week and something else on metaphysics the next; other subjects covered included history, jurisprudence, politics, economics and geology. Sydney, always something of an intellectual magpie, was in his element.

Teaching, socializing and debating were Sydney's three main activities in Edinburgh: the fourth was preaching. He spoke from the pulpit at the Charlotte Chapel in Rose Street, whose minister, Archibald Alison, was among the most cultivated of the Scottish Episcopalian clergy. Sydney started preaching soon after he settled in Edinburgh: the first mention of his work at Charlotte Chapel is in a letter to Henrietta Hicks Beach in September 1798. It was not long before preaching began to loom large in Sydney's future plans. Always a restless man, he had not been in Edinburgh as long as six months before he began thinking about what he might do when his two years with Michael were up. He took the unusual step of confiding in his father. 'It is', he told him, 'my wish at present to push myself as a preacher either in Bath or London.'

Preaching at Charlotte Chapel was a voyage of self-discovery for Sydney: he found that he had eloquence, that he could move and manipulate an audience. The power of his words was the greater for being naturally and easily expressed. There is a pertinent entry in the journal of Henry Cockburn, one of Sydney's Scottish friends. In the entry, which dates from 1849, Cockburn muses to himself about extempore preaching, and his thoughts go back to a sermon on death preached by Sydney at the Charlotte Chapel half a century earlier:

He held the manuscript in his hand, and read it exactly as an ordinary reader holds and reads from a printed book; but the thoughts had been so well considered, the composition was so proper, and the reading so quiet and impressive, that I doubt if there were a dozen dry eyes or unpalpitating hearts in the church; and every sentiment, and many of the expressions, and the whole scope and pathos of the discourse, are still fresh upon my mind at the distance of many years.

This sermon on death was probably one of Sydney's early efforts. He had learnt how to use voice modulations to good effect, but had not yet broken with the paralysing contemporary convention which required Anglican preachers to be statuesque. To use flamboyant gestures was to invite comparison with Methodists, an analogy which would not bode well for one's ecclesiastical career. Sydney was nevertheless determined to strike out on his own. His acting ability, and his sense of theatre, could not be suppressed. During these Edinburgh years he bravely became more and more like a Methodist in his preaching style, making ample use of a wide range of histrionic tricks. Encouraged by the praise of the congregation at Charlotte Chapel, he became an author for the first time: a slim volume of six sermons in a private printing of 100 copies was published in the spring of 1800. The next year he sent off to the press a much-enlarged second edition, extending to two volumes and containing a further eight discourses.

The preface to this second edition shows that Sydney, after three years in Edinburgh, felt confident enough of his popularity to be publicly provocative. Fewer people, he argued, were going to church: they found services long and tedious, and sermons lacked eloquence as well as being packed with biblical allusions which passed over the congregation's heads. Not only content was criticized, but also delivery:

A clergyman clings to his velvet cushion with either hand, keeps his eye riveted upon his book, speaks of the ecstasies of joy, and fear, with a voice and a face which indicate neither, and pinions his body and soul into the same attitude of limb, and thought, for fear of being called theatrical and affected . . . Is it wonder, then, that every semi-delirious sectary who pours forth his animated nonsense with the genuine look, and voice of passion, should gesticulate away the congregation of the most profound and learned divine of the established church, and in two Sundays preach him bare to the very sexton. Why are we natural everywhere but in the pulpit?[8]

Sydney had a rebellious spirit but he was also very ambitious and was fully aware that his life would be much easier if he could bring himself to conform. But the iconoclast within him could not be held down. In adopting a florid preaching style, he was not being exhibitionist: he was being himself.

In the letter which Sydney wrote his father towards the close of 1798, stating his future intention of becoming a preacher in Bath or London, he disclosed a further piece of more pressing news. As befitted the nature of the information he was about to give, his tone is more determined than in previous correspondence. No doubt his father would have preferred a warning in advance. Failure to give it was defended on general grounds.

> . . . you my dear Father must know how these things are carried on. Nobody sets out with a systematic intention of making himself fond of any woman – but he thinks himself quite safe and free at first, but assiduity is added to assiduity and kindness heaped upon kindness on both sides, till affection which has gathered by slow and unperceived degrees is at last so great that the option is taken away, and all consultation and advice is a mockery. At the proper time of asking it, nobody means to marry – at the usual time of asking it, nobody means to follow advice, unless it agrees with his previous determination. I hope therefore you will attribute my conduct in this respect to the ordinary tenor and impulse of men's actions and thoughts, and not to any want of respect and affection.

The woman in question, who was about to become Sydney's fiancée, was Catharine Pybus, a close friend of Maria's since childhood. She had therefore known Sydney a long time, a circumstance which helped affection to gather by 'slow and unperceived degrees'. There still was a crossing of the Rubicon from firm friendship to lifelong commitment, a journey which seems to have taken place a short while before Sydney set out for Edinburgh in June 1798. There is certainly no inkling of any intended match in a letter he wrote to his father the previous Christmas: 'I shall be very glad to see Miss Pybus, pray remember me kindly to her.' This is the first mention of Sydney's future wife. It established a precedent for future discretion. In Sydney's correspondence there is only one assessment of Catharine, in a letter written to a friend in October 1799, just under a year after the start of the official engagement: 'As for the lady, she is three years younger than me, a very old friend of mine – a good figure, and *to me* an interesting countenance, of excellent disposition, extremely good sense, very fond of music, and me – a wise, amiable woman such as without imposing, specious qualities will quietly for years and years make the happiness of her husband's life.'[9] This is not the language of Romantic love. It is, however, suggestive of a man who recognized his own insecurity and consequent requirement of emotional support; and who was confident that he had found a partner stable and sensible enough, as well as sensitive enough, to help him to make a contented home.

First, though, Sydney and Catharine had to reach the altar. Difficulties arose because Sydney, like Bobus, was marrying into a higher social class. The connections of the Pybuses could not compare with those of the Vernons, but the family was still a cut above the Smiths. Catharine's father, John, was by now dead. In his youth he had accumulated considerable wealth in India, becoming a member of the Council of Madras and being the first English ambassador to Ceylon. After he returned home he joined a partnership of Bond Street bankers. Catharine's elder brother, Charles, was a typical second generation *nouveau riche*. He employed his father's wealth to get himself into Parliament as MP for Dover, and had risen to become a Lord of the Treasury in the government of the Younger Pitt. Charles Pybus's reaction to the proposed match was vitriolic. His uncompromising stance led to an irreparable breach between brother and sister. Catharine found it hard to cope with the abrupt and destructive change in her brother's feelings towards herself: 'I believe he once loved me almost to adoration . . . I believe he now abhors me as much as he once idolized me.'

Catharine's mother, Martha, proved more tractable. She was not immune from snobbery but she did not want to lose her daughter. In a letter more notable for honesty than for tact, Catharine describes her mother's hesitations and uncertainties to her prospective father-in-law. 'I doubt not but what she might have felt a desire to see me what the world would call *well married provided it had been compatible with my happiness*; thus far I am sure you must admit a Parent's anxiety for the future establishment of a child to be *laudable*. Beyond that it never reached, for from the moment she felt convinced that my comfort could only be ensured by my marriage with Sydney (& the short space of one day was sufficient to persuade her of this) every other consideration instantly vanished from her mind, and she became as warm an advocate for it as we could be ourselves.'[10]

By the time this letter was dispatched (which was not until March 1800) the damage had already been done. Martha Pybus's initial letter to Robert Smith, written in January 1799, was lukewarm. 'If my opinion were to be taken', she told Sydney's father, 'I should recommend their deferring their union till more favourable times.' There were two ostensible reasons for postponement: Sydney was not sure of promotion and, in any case, the couple would find it hard to make ends meet. 'You . . . must feel the different expense now to what it was a few years ago', Martha told Robert Smith. This was not invention on her part. England in the late 1790s faced severe economic difficulties. The greatest agricultural boom in the nation's history was already well under way, land prices were soaring, and the annual inflation rate would soon exceed 30 per cent.

Robert Smith was nevertheless justified in taking umbrage at Martha Pybus's letter. Since the two families had, through the friendship between Maria and Catharine, long been linked, a more positive response was called for. Robert Smith was right to conclude that the letter strongly implied that Sydney was not good enough for her daughter. The reference to 'different expense' was particularly galling. Robert Smith desperately wanted to buy a farm in order to benefit from rising land values. Whatever his capital may have been worth, and almost certainly he was a lot richer than he made out, he could not lay his hands on enough cash to finance the purchase. Frequent begging letters to Cecil and Courtney in India had not got him anywhere. No one likes to be reminded of things that are causing them acute frustration, least of all a man as selfish as Robert Smith.

It was the terms of the proposed marriage settlement that really riled Sydney's father. When he wrote to announce his betrothal, Sydney said that his future wife's fortune amounted to £8000. Negotiations with the executors of Catharine's father's will did not go well. After more than a year, Sydney became so exasperated that he 'saw nothing left but a suit in Chancery'. This was a counsel of despair: the dilatoriness of the Georgian Court of Chancery was legendary. Delay in reaching a settlement was not Sydney's fault. Anxious to counter any charge of being motivated by mercenary considerations, he argued that the money should belong solely to Catharine; only in the event of her death would he have the use of it, and even then he would be restricted to a life interest. Nor was Martha Pybus to blame: she thought that Sydney was being too hard on himself. It looks as if it was Charles Pybus who was creating difficulties. If he was, he did not have his own way. The terms, as finally hammered out, included Martha Pybus's proposal for £1000 to be put in joint names and set aside for emergencies. It was a prescient move: the jointure, slowly built up over a good many years, helped to bail Sydney out at a critical point in his future career.

Sydney was happy at the way things were turning out. The jointure obviously pleased him. Another aspect of the proposed settlement pleased him even more. Throughout the negotiations, he had a hidden agenda. Catharine admits as much in her brief family history, given the name of 'Narrative', written a few years after Sydney's death. 'Sydney', she states, 'had often said that he had other reasons for the strictness with which he desired to have my money placed out of his power than merely to shew my relations and friends that he wished not for the smallest control over it, and these were, that had it remain'd in our hands, his Father would have been *sure* to have required it to have been lent to him, to invest in land of which he was to have the management.'[11] Thwarted by Cecil and Courtney, Robert Smith was determined not to be thwarted also by Sydney and Catharine.

Sydney was equally determined that he would. He thought, quite rightly, that his father was being thoroughly unreasonable, he wanted to placate the Pybus family, and he was also keen to settle a score. At the time of his engagement to Catharine, he had come to his father with a request for money. 'Will it', Sydney wondered, 'be in your power to afford me any assistance?' Considering how well he was being paid by Michael Hicks Beach, and bearing in mind the size of his future wife's fortune, this pleading of poverty was impudent. It was also remarkably stupid; Sydney ought to have learned that it was ill-advised to approach Robert Smith on such matters. His father's answer was predictably curt. 'Not one penny. If you would have remain'd unmarried your fellowship would have been your provision by giving you a Living.' Sydney now had an ideal opportunity to get his own back. This was easily achieved; he simply ensured that his father was excluded from negotiations over Catharine's settlement.

Although the broad outlines of an agreement had been set with the executors, tying up the loose ends proved surprisingly difficult. The unexpected delay made Catharine very uneasy. Writing to her future father-in-law on 30 May 1800, she lays bare both her concerns and her resolute intentions: 'considerable tho' mysterious difficulties seem to be started now . . . I do assure you I shall not marry until I see them clear'd away, & until I am perfectly certain of what my pecuniary circumstances are to be.'

A few days later the clouds suddenly cleared. A further letter from Catharine to Robert Smith, written on 9 June, is quite altered in its tone. 'I am', she told him, 'on the tiptoe of expectation for the answer of the Executors as to their final arrangement of the business.' It was not a false alarm. Catharine and Sydney were married at Cheam in Surrey, the location of her family home, on 2 July 1800. Very little is known about the ceremony, apart from the poignant fact that Sydney followed the lead given by Bobus in not inviting his parents. Robert Smith, already smouldering with anger over Sydney's success in making sure that he did not get his hands on Catharine's dowry, was furious.

Despite this sad start to Sydney and Catharine's marriage, happiness was in store for both parties. Catharine wrote what she thought of her husband in her 'Narrative'. 'There never before *was*, and never again *will be* another Sydney!!'[12] She loved his original and lively mind, and his fierce gentleness with her. Living with Sydney was exciting. Like many women, Catharine fell completely for his charm. He knew how to flatter women, how to make them feel important, how to please. He once wrote to Mrs Sarah Austin, later the editor of some of his letters, asking about the times when steamboats sailed from Boulogne. 'Pray excuse this trouble. I have always compunctions in asking you to do anything useful; it is as if one were to use blonde lace for a napkin, or to drink toast and water out of a ruby cup.' There was, from a woman's point of view, always a hint of danger in Sydney: his talk was peppered with delicate sexual innuendoes. At an evening conversation party an old friend entered the room, dressed in a crimson velvet gown. Sydney rose and greeted her: 'Exactly the colour of my preaching cushion!' He then led her forward to the light, pretending to be lost in admiration, and exclaimed: 'I really can hardly keep my hands off you; I shall be preaching on you, I fear.'

Sydney also held Catharine in high esteem. He was someone who had a great regard for the opposite sex, a quality in a man which a woman is never slow to sense. There is a revealing comment in one of Sydney's letters: 'I hardly know *any man* who deserves *any woman*.'[13] Moral superiority was bolstered by intellectual equality: he thought that women were quite as clever as men and ought to have, wherever possible, a scholarly education. Increasing the educational qualifications of women would benefit the economy, and women themselves would be happier if they could draw upon the inner resources that a good education would give them. Catharine was lucky to have him; very few of Sydney's male contemporaries were as egalitarian.

Partly as a reaction against his father's selfishness, Sydney became a model family man: sexually faithful, relaxed and happy in the company of his wife, and fond of children. Paternal feeling was met and embraced by maternal feeling; Catharine, like Sydney, hated being away from home. The emotional dynamics between the couple also worked well. Sydney was fun to be with but he could also be emotionally demanding. He had a strong melancholic streak; he tended to worry, especially about money; and the life of the household revolved around his work routine. He would sit down at his desk in the morning and write for an hour or two at great speed. After he had finished, he would want to be amused. Catharine, fortunately, fitted easily into a supportive role.

After a short tour together the newly-weds visited Sydney's parents. Given the failure to ask them to the wedding, the atmosphere was always likely to be tense, but Catharine was still quite unprepared for her father-in-law's extraordinary behaviour. They had not been in the house more than a few days when Robert Smith lost his temper completely. His verbal violence was etched for ever on Catharine's memory. Nearly half a century later, she was still able to remember the words with which he abused her husband. 'You *knew* I wished to purchase a farm, your *Father* should have been first thought of! What right had *you*, where you had it in your power to benefit *me*, to indulge in such silly romantic notions of securing to her her property?'[14] Her mother-in-law was also taken aback. Sydney was less surprised; he was beginning to understand the irrational elements in his father's personality.

Robert Smith's posturings were absurd. The Pybus family, Tory in its politics and snobbish in its social inclinations, would not have accepted any marriage settlement which gave Sydney a share in his wife's wealth beyond the agreed jointure; the notion that Charles Pybus would have sat idly by while Robert Smith sequestered Catharine's money to his own use, cannot be rationally countenanced. Sydney acted shrewdly in keeping his father out of the pre-marital negotiations. He also saw to it that Robert Smith was not made a trustee, choosing Bobus instead. Being passed over rankled. Sydney explains his decision in a later letter: 'I asked my brother to be trustee because he was a younger man and a lawyer and resident in London.' All of this was true but beside the point. They both knew the real reason for the exclusion: Sydney thought that his father was not to be trusted. Such an attitude, on the part of one of his sons, was more than Robert Smith could take. From now on, father and son were scarcely on speaking terms.

Sydney and Catharine journeyed on to Williamstrip, and then set out for Edinburgh, accompanied by Michael and Henrietta Hicks Beach as well as their son William; it had been decided that Sydney would continue his tutorial duties with the Hicks Beach family. For a day during the trip north Sydney sulked, saying not a single word. He attempted to justify his behaviour in a letter to Mrs Hicks Beach, written from Edinburgh after the Hicks Beaches and the Smiths had parted company. Sydney began by giving her, in rotund phrases, a lecture on *noblesse oblige*. 'When people of good breeding and education travel together they share equally the pleasures and inconveniences of the journey, amongst the rest in the article of sleeping rooms.' It was a standard of aristocratic refinement that Henrietta herself had recently failed, by a wide margin, to attain. 'You uniformly through the whole of our tour put Mrs Smith in the worst room and took the best for yourself, without the smallest apology or any one softening expression whatsoever. Is not this to say in language *too plain to be mistaken*, I do not think this woman worthy of being treated with the common forms of politeness.'[15]

To write to his patroness in this manner was foolhardy, to say the least. There are several possible explanations of Sydney's ill-temper. There is, to begin with, what might be termed the bull factor: the pride of young husbands is, quite notoriously, easily bruised. Mrs Hicks Beach was a firm believer in the conspiracy theory; she thought that Sydney had been egged on by Catharine. This incident is also illustrative of the underlying tensions that are a permanent feature of Sydney's relations with the aristocracy. He enjoyed being with them, courted them, flattered them and used them to further his ecclesiastical career, but at the same time, being an intensely proud man, he chafed at his dependence upon them. Being made to feel socially inferior was something he could not bear. His self-assertion on these occasions was excessive. He ends his letter to Mrs Hicks Beach by coming close to challenging her to a rupture. 'Farewell, my dear Madam. You are little accustomed to such plain truths as this Letter contains; and yet I do not think you will hate me for telling them to you.'

Henrietta Hicks Beach was thrown completely off balance. The idea of offering Catharine a choice of rooms had never entered her head. Her dignity, however, prevented her from admitting this humbling fact. Catharine's room, she told Sydney, had been 'sometimes equal to mine and sometimes better'. This could be construed as subtle – the statement did not preclude the possibility that Catharine's room had usually been worse – but such was not Henrietta's intention. It was no part of her plan to be intellectually sophisticated; she simply wanted the discussion to be closed as quickly as possible. To this end she included in her letter the results of a general examination of conscience, intended both as self-exculpation and as a chilling rebuke. 'I must do myself the justice to say my good Sir that after a strict re-view of my past behaviour from the commencement of our acquaint-ance, I can fairly acquit myself of having at any time treated you or Mrs Smith with negligence or disrespect.'

The asperities dragged on; there was another letter from Henrietta and two more from Sydney. The most surprising thing about this correspondence is that Mrs Hicks Beach allowed Sydney to have the last word. 'It is some little pity that Mrs Smith, in conformity with established usages, was never *once offered* to choose her own accommodation first – and that you never in any instance appealed to her own ideas of best and worst – this would have settled and sweetened every thing in a moment.'[16] It says much for Henrietta's goodness of heart that she did not bring her husband into the fray; a really vindictive woman would have gone much further, taking William away from Sydney's tutorial care. Although Sydney had the better of the exchange, he achieved little apart from bolstering his own *amour propre*. He had shown himself capable of being tetchy and unpredictable, and he had revealed that, when roused to anger, he was conspicuously lacking in charm. Sydney, when in a tight corner, was his father's son.

5

BEYOND THE FRINGE

'. . . this journal, the genius of which seems to consist in stroking the animal the contrary way to which the hair lies.'
SYDNEY SMITH, of the *Edinburgh Review*

The tiff with Henrietta Hicks Beach added to Sydney's sense of uncertainty. Late in 1798, he had told his father that he intended to 'push' himself as a preacher either in Bath or London, announcing at the same time his engagement to Catharine. During 1799 he altered his future plans; he now wanted to obtain a curacy between twenty and forty miles from the metropolis, taking pupils to add to his income. In October, he wrote to a friend as though everything had already been settled: 'I shall quit Scotland in May and be married soon after.' Despite Sydney's apparent confidence, the proposal to search for a curacy near London was, in fact, discarded. Early in 1800 Sydney wrote to his father, telling him that he had decided to move to Bath, where he would both preach and take pupils. By April, Bath had been abandoned for Edinburgh. 'There cannot possibly be any Spot in England where young men can be so advantageously educated as here', he told Mrs Hicks Beach.[1]

There were no further twists or turns. The newly married couple settled in lodgings in Queen Street (Sydney had left South Hanover Street in May 1799). Also in the household was the Hicks Beaches' younger son, William. Sydney was delighted with his new pupil. Superlatives abound: 'He is, without any exception, the very best and most gentlemanly young man I ever saw'; 'nothing can possibly exceed the excellence of his behaviour in every respect'; 'he is universally admired in this place by everybody who knows him and it is impossible to admire him too much'; William is 'without exception the most amiable and conciliating young man I ever was acquainted with'.

Despite his great liking for the boy, Sydney was not happy with the arrangement. The problem was one of finance. Sydney had done well out of teaching William's elder brother; he was set to do much less well out of his new charge. There had been correspondence with William's father on the matter of payment prior to Sydney's marriage. The point was never clearly spelt out, but it would seem that Sydney's patron felt that there ought to be new terms because Sydney was only prepared to commit himself for one year. Michael Hicks Beach, in these changed circumstances, offered £200. Sydney was not amused but felt that he lacked bargaining power. In a letter to Mr Hicks Beach on 24 June 1800, he submitted to the pay cut with good grace. 'I promise to be perfectly satisfied with your decision on the Subject, and on my part if I find that £100 per Annum will do instead of two I shall not draw one farthing more.'[2]

It was just as well for Sydney that this unequivocal undertaking was not used against him in subsequent negotiations. Sydney had not been long back in Edinburgh before he was putting in for a pay rise. The ostensible reason was yet another change to future plans. Writing to Mrs Hicks Beach on 9 November 1800, he indicated that any move to Bath or London had been postponed; he would now stay in Edinburgh for '2 or 3 years'. On this basis he wondered whether he had 'any further remuneration of any kind to expect from Mr Beach' above and beyond the £200 he was receiving for the current year. Henrietta wrote back, suggesting that Sydney put forward his own proposals. His reply to her letter is dated 3 December: Sydney asked for £500 for the second year and the same amount for a third year, if there was one. What he was requesting was, in effect, that the level of payment made for William's elder brother be restored. Henrietta then countered this proposal, suggesting £400 for both years as a compromise.

Sydney dug in his heels. His next letter, written on 28 December, was determined. 'I confess I had great objections to propose terms myself, because I thought it unprecedented and incorrect, but having done so in compliance with your desire, I cannot allow myself even to think of accepting any others.' He would resign his tutorship with William in the spring and had given notice at his lodgings.[3]

Despite appearances the door was not quite closed. Sydney agreed to find an alternative tutor for William. Dugald Stewart and Archibald Alison, the obvious candidates, were full up. This left Daniel Sandford, later bishop of Edinburgh, who had a vacancy in the autumn of 1801. Unfortunately, his establishment could not be recommended. Sandford took in eight or nine pupils and William would not have a room of his own until he was third or fourth in seniority. Judging from the tone of this letter, it looks as if Sydney, his anger abated, was looking for an excuse to back down. Writing to Mrs Hicks Beach on 2 February 1801, he as good as threw in the towel. 'If you feel uneasy at leaving your son [at Sandford's], I will return here with pleasure and resume his education upon your own terms – or upon any others whatever you choose to dictate.'

At this point, Robert Smith became involved. He had for once a valid excuse for interference: he knew the Hicks Beaches socially and rightly felt that Sydney's prideful petulance was unacceptable. In his letter to Mrs Hicks Beach, written on 7 February, he told her that she was not alone in being badly treated by Sydney. 'I had not the most distant information of the business . . . till last week . . . and it is with grief I confess myself very much hurt from this pointed neglect, so recent after his marriage of which and all its arrangements I am equally an utter stranger.'

It is doubtful whether this exhibition of self-pity carried much sway with Mrs Hicks Beach: what she wanted was support for her own stance in the dispute with Sydney. Robert Smith was only too happy to supply it. His son, he explained, was a rash young man and his character was vitiated by false pride, but his heart was in the right place. 'I am convinced he is a good man, holding you and Mr Beach in the highest esteem and attached to your son William warmly . . . He has mistaken the point of honour, of which he thinks improperly, and fearful of sinking in your opinion, had not courage to recede from a point to which he never should have committed himself.' This hit the right note. Sydney had 'mistaken the point of honour'; he had, in other words, acted wrongly according to the aristocratic code. The figure of £500 a year ought to have been put forward as a tentative suggestion, not a resolute ultimatum. This was hard to argue against. Robert Smith was doing no more than point out that Sydney should have continued to follow his own previous practice of not wresting the initiative, despite the fact that Henrietta Hicks Beach had invited him to make a proposal.

Sydney's emollient letter of 2 February, combined with Robert Smith's suggestion that his son's actions were not to be taken too seriously, tipped the balance. Henrietta, who was mature enough to resist the temptation to indulge in recriminations, took Sydney back as William's tutor. On her terms, of course; payment would in future be at a rate of £400 a year. Sydney, grateful that the row was over, wrote to her on 21 February, saying that he would take a house in Edinburgh for the next two years.[4]

He did manage to wring one concession out of Mrs Hicks Beach: permission to take in other pupils. This new departure did not work out quite as he hoped. Initial indications were good. The son of Thomas Orde-Powlett, who had been created Baron Bolton in 1797, arrived several months later, in October 1801. The boy's father was prepared to pay £400 a year, the same as the recently revised tuition fee for William Hicks Beach, a piece of news which perked Sydney up no end: he would be coming out of the dispute with Mrs Hicks Beach a richer man than he went in. Sydney also liked the look of Lord Bolton's arithmetic. Orde-Powlett would be joining half-way through the academic year, and half a year's fees were, according to Lord Bolton, £300.

There was, from Sydney's point of view, the added attraction that teaching this new pupil might also turn out to be a good investment. The Boltons had excellent ecclesiastical connections and young Orde-Powlett might be able to help Sydney in his future career. Expectations on this front proved premature. Sydney made immediate enquiries and was not pleased by what he found out. The results of his investigation were reported to Robert Smith on 7 November: 'I have already discovered three clergymen his relations who are hanging upon him – so that you see my chance of any advantage beyond my salary is not very brilliant.'

Sydney was usually a good judge of character, but he made a hideous mistake with Orde-Powlett. The new pupil, according to Sydney, was 'mild and ductile'. William Hicks Beach was much shrewder, quickly becoming aware of Orde-Powlett's worrying eccentricities. Writing to his mother on 30 October, he notes with amusement that his new companion managed to combine, without any apparent sense of self-irony, considerable ugliness with even greater vanity: Orde-Powlett was 'excessively awkward in all his motions & very far from handsome in his face, but withal so vain of his person that I believe he usually spends the morning in viewing'. When he did eventually arrive at lessons, his attention span was minimal: he fell asleep at the least opportunity, frequently compounding the offence by snoring.

Early in the New Year, Orde-Powlett's behaviour went beyond the pale. With eight shillings in his pocket, he left Edinburgh with the laudable, if somewhat optimistic, intention of walking to England. His financial resources showed signs of depletion well before the soles of his shoes had a chance to wear out: the old woman in charge of the inn where he stayed the first night relieved him of more than half his money. Sydney, in a dire panic, alerted the sheriff's officers, arranged for handbills to be prepared and sent a servant in hot pursuit. The young man was quickly overtaken, and Sydney's servant managed to hoodwink him into believing that he was taking him by coach to England.[5] Sydney wrote to Lord Bolton, saying that he thought his son would be safer somewhere else.

He soon found a replacement: 'Mr Gordon' (later of Ellon), who was a natural son of the third earl of Aberdeen, the grandfather of the famous statesman. Like Orde-Powlett, Gordon was willing to pay £400 a year, doubling Sydney's tutorial income. The new charge was easy both to teach and to get on with. He became a friend in later life, as indeed did William.[6] Sydney liked people who were straightforward, friendly and reliable. William was all three.

The autumn of 1801 was a trying time for Sydney. His mother's health had always been precarious, and her death had long been expected. In November 1797, when preparing for his abortive European tour, Sydney had given as a major reason for seeking a reconciliation with his father the fact that he 'very much' feared that 'Jona', as her husband called her, would not live long enough to welcome him home.

Now the time for her deliverance from pain had come. Bobus describes the excruciating finale in a letter written to Lady Holland on 30 October. His sister Maria, Bobus explains, 'had been my mother's constant companion and nurse & she died in her sight after six hours attack of [illegible] dreadful fits during which she did not recover her understanding for one moment'. Sydney, as was his custom, hid his feelings. Writing to Henrietta Hicks Beach in mid-November, he adopts a stance of Stoic resignation. 'Many thanks, my dear Madam, for your friendly message. Every one must go to his grave with his heart scarred like a soldier's body, – sometimes a parent, sometimes a child, a friend, a husband, or a wife. Thus the bands of this life are gradually loosed, and death at last is more welcome than the comfortless solitude of the world.' This is the letter of an elderly man striving to penetrate the mystery of suffering, not that of someone just turned thirty who has recently lost his mother, a mother whom he was later to declare that he 'loved intensely'.

If his mother's death was expected, his father's reaction to it was not. Sydney hoped that bereavement would bring the family closer together. As soon as he heard the news, he wrote spontaneously and affectionately to Robert Smith, now living near Trowbridge in Wiltshire. 'What can I say or do. On such occasions as this, what nonsense and folly are all the common topics of conversation . . . God Almighty bless and defend you all. I would give a thousand worlds if I were within reach.' A week later Sydney wrote again, inviting his father and Maria to come and stay for a while in Edinburgh. Robert Smith's reply, which has not survived, caught Sydney unawares. He gives a résumé of it in a further letter written on 24 November:

I have received an answer to my invitation in which you call me Rascal, Villain, Fool, Scoundrel, Pedant, etc. All these opprobrious epithets, as well as your animadversions upon my wife, I do now as I have often *done* before very sincerely forgive. Any condemnation of my conduct by you founded upon facts, and expressed with moderation and dignity I should very seriously regret. But after an experience of fifteen years, this very energetic language produces no other effect upon me than to make me regret the unhappy state of mind which must have given birth to it.[7]

Robert Smith's outburst was totally unjustified. Sydney had not given him any fresh cause for complaint, nor was he overcome by grief at his wife's death. His behaviour is remarkably revealing of his personality. In her 'Narrative', Catharine paraphrases the reasons for his extraordinary insensitivity. 'So long as poor Jona lived I have borne patiently with you because I knew that if I had quarrel'd with you it would have broken her heart; but now that she is gone, I never *will* see you more; for I never will forgive and never shall forget your selfishness in so tying up your Wife's fortune, as to put it out of your power to assist your *Father*!!!' All of Robert Smith's frustrations, all of his destructive bile, come pouring out in these sentences. Rage overwhelmed him.

More letters passed between father and son. Robert Smith was resolute and would not be reconciled. Sydney, grieving for his mother, understandably felt betrayed. He did not actually cut himself off completely from his father but came close to doing so. In a letter inappropriately dated Christmas Day 1801, Robert Smith was made the unwilling recipient of a moral reprimand. 'I can only wish that by moderating your anger . . . by respecting the feelings even of your children, and by putting the most favorable interpretation on their actions, you may experience that increase of happiness which always results from the exercise of benevolent affections.' This was an attempt at role reversal, with Sydney treating his father as though he were an erring son. The advice was not well received.

In the wake of his mother's death, and while he was coping with his father's treachery as well as Orde-Powlett's highly eccentric behaviour, Sydney had the inspired notion of starting the *Edinburgh Review*. The seed was sown at a tea-party with Horner and Jeffrey, held in Jeffrey's house in Buccleuch Place, sometime before Christmas 1801. It did not take long for the seed to germinate. By 13 January 1802, Sydney was already soliciting support outside Edinburgh, writing to a London friend that if he knew of any people who had 'a mind to barbeque a poet or two, or strangle a metaphysician, or do any other act of cruelty to the dull men of the earth, we are in hopes they will make our journal the receptacle of their exploits.'

In the same letter, Sydney outlines the progress that had been made so far. The proposed review would come out quarterly and would cost five shillings. Contributions would be anonymous. There were two reasons for this decision. Reviewing was held in low esteem, being regarded as mere hack writing, and it was imperative to have some shield behind which reviewers could protect themselves from the wrath of Dundas. Sydney and his companions had also decided to take no notice of the 'refuse' of the press; the proposed review would concentrate exclusively upon 'works of merit'. This was courageous but risky. Publishing at the turn of the nineteenth century was, in modern parlance, vertically integrated – there were no publishers as such, all books being both produced and sold by booksellers. Literary periodicals were few and far between; most of them, moreover, were financed by booksellers and were used, quite unashamedly, to promote their own lists. To review only works of merit would involve overturning current practice by establishing editorial independence. Finding a bookseller in Edinburgh who would accept such terms was tricky. Tricky but not impossible. Archibald Constable had already come forward. Although he was not very experienced – on the eve of his twenty-eighth birthday, he had been a bookseller in the city for six years – he did have one superb qualification: he was an impulsive risk-taker, prepared to pay authors hitherto unheard-of prices for manuscripts.

Including Sydney, there were seven men on the planning committee; the other six were all young Scots. Horner (now twenty-three) and Jeffrey (who had reached twenty-eight) were the two other main luminaries; Horner would write on politics and economics while Jeffrey would take on literary subjects. There was a third lawyer, John Murray. Still only twenty-two, he came from a Tory background but had been converted to Whiggery by Horner. Murray later had a successful career (he became a Scottish judge in 1839) and was, like Horner and Jeffrey, one of Sydney's lifelong friends.

John Allen, at thirty, was virtually a greybeard. An impecunious Edinburgh doctor of fine intellect, his private lectures on physiology enthralled all who attended them. A bachelor, he was much loved. Allen's appearance amused Sydney immensely. Extremely short-sighted, he always wore an over-large pair of round silver spectacles, perched precariously on the end of his nose. His face was broad and his head very big. Allen was imposing but he was also ludicrous: the column of his portly frame rested upon a massive, tubular base. 'Allen's legs are enormous – they are clerical', declared Sydney. In later years he was to see more of Allen than he did of Murray, and more, indeed, than he did of Horner or Jeffrey.

The sixth member of the editorial committee also had medical expertise; this was Anthony Todd ('Tim') Thomson. Like many Scots he later made his way south, becoming a professor at the University of London. Finally, there was Alexander Hamilton, an expert in oriental languages. He was, in one regard, quite exceptional: he was the only one of the seven who had published any literary reviews.[8]

There was one glaring omission from the membership of the planning committee: Henry Brougham. He could, Sydney insisted, write as much as he liked so long as he had no influence on policy. Sydney took this decision because he thought that Brougham was 'violent and unmanageable'. When he did not trust someone (his own father, for instance) he always had a good reason. Rejection from the inner circle, although wise, did nothing to attach Brougham to the proposed review. Early in April 1802, Jeffrey suggested some books he might like to 'barbecue' for the first issue. 'He answered', Jeffrey told Horner, 'with perfect good humour, that he had changed his view of our plan a little, and rather thought now that he should decline to have any connection with it.' He came back into the fold in late summer but, a little later on, justified Sydney's lack of faith in him by scheming with the proprietors of a rival journal.[9]

Although the planning committee made a strong start, by the early summer of 1802 they were having to face up to fears that their hopes might be dashed. It is not possible to launch a new periodical or newspaper without encountering setbacks and difficulties, a rule to which the *Edinburgh Review* was no exception.[10] The plan was to have the first issue out by 25 June, a schedule which proved too tight. Jeffrey was uneasy at the delay, writing to a friend in May: 'Our Review has been postponed till September and I am afraid will not go on with much spirit even then. Perhaps we have omitted the tide that was in our favour . . . I foresee the likelihood of our being all scattered before another year shall be over, and, of course, the impossibility of going on on the footing upon which we have begun.'

Jeffrey's pessimism was well founded. The restlessness, bred of frustration, which provided the energy propelling the scheme forward also threatened, at the same time, to tear it apart. Jeffrey, earning less than £100 a year at the Scottish Bar and recently married, was looking around for an alternative career; Horner was disconsolate ('I am creeping into a little business, which gives me the shadow and fancy of occupation', he had written in his diary the previous year) and was thinking about moving to Lincoln's Inn; Brougham took such a dull view of his legal prospects that he was toying with the idea of joining the army; and Sydney was once again becoming restive, wondering what he would do when his two years with William Hicks Beach ran out in the spring of 1803.

John Allen went a step further, leaving Edinburgh altogether. Sydney, as it happens, was responsible for his departure. Bobus's friend Lord Holland was on the point of setting out on a three-year European tour. He wrote to Sydney, asking if he knew of a Scottish doctor who would be suitable to go with the family. Sydney unhesitatingly recommended Allen, Lord Holland went along with the proposal, and Allen, faced by a choice between penury in Edinburgh and the comfort which was the enviable concomitant of aristocratic patronage, did not have to think for too long before deciding to set off for London on 15 June.[11]

The six remaining members of the planning committee faced heavy odds. There was likely to be fierce opposition from Henry Dundas, the 'Pharos of Scotland'. Dundas was already making his influence felt: it was his policy of keeping Whig lawyers in their place which was responsible for the acute frustration felt by Jeffrey, Horner and Brougham. Sydney feared direct intervention. On his insistence, meetings were held in secret. John Murray, Tim Thomson and the rest were instructed to make their way singly through the bowel-like wynds of the Old Town, eventually meeting up in a small shop in Craig's Close, an alley (now demolished) nearly opposite St Giles' cathedral in Edinburgh High Street. The shop was a safe haven: it belonged to Bailie Willison, printer, who was Archibald Constable's father-in-law. Sydney's precautions were not silly. The political atmosphere in Edinburgh was tense and Dundas went to great lengths to keep the city under his control. A few years earlier he had seen to it that Henry Erskine, leader of the Scottish Whigs, was voted out of office as Dean of the Faculty of Advocates.

Even if Dundas failed to round up the 'confederates' (Sydney's own word), success was far from assured. A previous literary review, also called the *Edinburgh* and with the famous economist Adam Smith among its editors, had been an abject failure; the first issue had been for July 1755, the second, and last, for January 1756. Sydney, Jeffrey and Horner nevertheless won through. Constable's commitment was, in the end, the decisive factor. Showing typical panache, he agreed to fund the first three issues. As a quid pro quo, contributors would have initially to write for glory, not for pay. The new deadline, set for September, was not quite met. The first issue came out on 10 October 1802.

Initially, editorial duties were shared between Sydney, Jeffrey and Horner. They knew they had to tread carefully; if they allowed a single article into the *Edinburgh Review* sympathizing with what were then considered extremist ideas – manhood suffrage, free-thinking relig-ious views, and the like – Constable could well face prosecution by the government, and the periodical would certainly be doomed. Articles to do with religious controversy were therefore excluded, and care was also taken to avoid being blatantly partisan in politics. The reader was nevertheless left in no doubt that the *Review*, although independent, sided with the Whigs. This was made clear by the blue and buff cover, colours taken from the coat and waistcoat of Charles James Fox. A stand was made, in the first issue, for Whig causes. Reviewing a book on England's West Indian sugar colonies, Brougham pleaded for legislative prohibition of the slave trade and condemned, in the strongest terms, any expansion of the nefarious traffic. There was also emphatic support from Sydney for another pet Whig scheme: the granting of political rights to Catholics. Using a bantering style that he was to develop in years to come, he insinuated that opponents of the measure were living in cloud-cuckoo-land. 'We should as soon dream, that the wars of York and Lancaster would break out afresh, as that the Protestant religion in England has any thing to apprehend from the machinations of Catholics.'

Moderate in political opinion, the *Review* was fearless in its personal attacks: fifteen of the twenty-nine articles in the first issue were uncomplimentary. Sydney showed more alacrity for abuse than any of the other contributors, even Brougham. In the first issue he wrote an extremely bitter piece on Archdeacon Nares, editor of the *British Critic*, the leading High Church journal. In one of his sermons the archdeacon had trespassed on to the secular ground of economics, accusing farmers of being responsible for the currently high price of cereals. Sydney, who had imbibed the free-trade economics of Adam Smith from Dugald Stewart's lectures, would have none of it. 'This style of reasoning is pardonable enough in those who argue from the belly rather than the brains; but in a well fed and well educated clergyman, who has never been disturbed by hunger from the free exercise of cultivated talents, it merits the severest reprehension.'

Apprehension would be a better word with which to describe Jeffrey's response. He wrote to Sydney prior to publication, asking him to tone the article down. In his defence Sydney told Jeffrey that Nares had been 'hangman for these ten years to all the poor authors in England, is generally considered to be hired by government, and has talked about social order till he has talked himself into £6 or £700 a year'. Sydney liked to fight his battles upon what he was convinced was firm moral ground. He may also have had a more disreputable motive. In an article in the *British Critic*, Nares had severely criticized the preface to the second edition of Sydney's *Sermons*.[12] Even though Sydney may have been driven, at least in part, by personal animus, he managed to stand up successfully to Jeffrey.

The *Edinburgh Review* was often rude but never dull. A good example of its sprightly style, again from the first issue, is the opening of Sydney's short review of the Revd Dr Langford's *Anniversary Sermon of the Royal Humane Society*:

An incident which happened to the gentleman engaged in reviewing this Sermon, proves, in the most striking manner, the importance of this charity for restoring to life persons in whom the vital power is suspended. He was discovered, with Dr Langford's discourse lying open before him, in the state of the most profound sleep; from which he could not, by any means, be awakened for a great length of time. By attending, however, to the rules prescribed by the Humane Society, flinging in the smoke of tobacco, applying hot flannels, and carefully removing the discourse itself to a great distance, the critic was restored to his disconsolate brothers.

Around three-quarters of the articles in the first issue were written by four men: Horner, Brougham, Jeffrey and Sydney. How strange is that historical chemistry which produces a profusion of exceptional talent in the same place at the same time. Horner became one of the best economists of his generation; Brougham's intellectual range was quite exceptional – science and economics, mathematics and history, educational theory and legal practice were all within his grasp; and Jeffrey was the leading literary critic of the first quarter of the nineteenth century. It was chance which brought them together, just as it had been chance which had brought Sydney to Edinburgh.

Thanks to Constable's entrepreneurial flair, the *Edinburgh Review* was safe for the first three issues. Sydney and Constable then sat down together and worked out a permanent scheme. The two crucial proposals came from Sydney. Jeffrey was appointed editor on a salaried basis. This was an excellent choice; Jeffrey had persistence and an eye for detail, qualities which Sydney lacked. Sydney's second suggestion was equally astute; he persuaded Constable to agree that contributors would, in future, be paid a minimum of ten guineas a sheet, equivalent to sixteen printed pages, with discretion to Jeffrey as editor to pay some reviewers (Sydney's name was included in the privileged list) considerably more. Although the force in this novel notion was somewhat weakened by the transparency of Sydney's self-interest, his instincts are hard to fault. For the *Edinburgh Review* to flourish, it was necessary to turn reviewing into an honourable, well paid profession.

The *Review* caught on immediately in Edinburgh. The initial print run of 750 sold out in less than a month, and a second edition of 750 was ordered. These also went as, indeed, did a further 650. All in all, 2150 were sold within a year. These figures are more impressive than they look. It was not a literate age: the reading public was reckoned by contemporaries to make up less than 1 per cent of the population. Constable had managed to sell the first issue of the *Edinburgh*

Review to around 2 per cent of whose who lived in the city and its neighbourhood.

Getting established in the London market was much harder. The metropolis was the hub of British cultural life. Those who lived there, conveniently unaware of much of what went on in the rest of the country because of poor communications, were not initially impressed by a literary periodical produced elsewhere. There were also pro-longed difficulties over distribution. The first issue was handled by Joseph Mawman, a well-known bookseller, but a satisfactory arrangement could not be worked out and Mawman promptly resigned. His place was taken by Thomas Longman; he showed his commitment by purchasing a half share but, despite this, the agreement with Constable only lasted a few years. In 1807, Longman sold the London rights to John Murray, then of Fleet Street, for £1000. Two years later Constable opened a London office, taking over management himself, but it closed within a year. The next bookseller to try its hand was White Cochrane and Co. Continuity was not established until 1814, when Constable and Longman got together again. Despite all these problems at the London end, sales still grew apace. In September 1814 the print run was close on 13,000. Putting this figure in perspective, *The Times* two years later was selling 8,000 copies a day.[13]

Sydney made a major contribution to the first four issues of the *Edinburgh Review*, writing 19 articles out of 101; only Brougham, credited with 21, wrote a greater number. Sydney did not specialize: there are six articles on travel narratives, four on sermons, two on politics, one each on philosophy, drama, humour, theology and the state of the church, a review of a novel, and a brief squib. His style is sharp, witty and dry; there is economy in the use of language and exactness in the expression of thought. His ideas are surprisingly free of youthful excess. In one of these articles he discusses the possibility of re-establishing a republic in France. It was, thought Sydney, an experiment which could not be adopted 'without the greatest peril'. Praising the evolutionary nature of English political development, he contrasts it favourably with the French penchant for revolutionary change. 'A nation grown free in a single day is a child born with the limbs and the vigour of a man, who would take a drawn sword for his rattle, and set the house in a blaze, that he might chuckle over the splendour.' These are vivid and incisive images, showing the sort of grasp we might look for in a great novelist.

Sydney shows, in one of these early articles, that he had already thought deeply about the nature of his own special art. Wit, Sydney insists, is a special form of playfulness, a kind of delightful intellectual gymnastics. Repeating what he had written in one of his early notebooks, he explains that its essence is surprise. He illustrates his point with an anecdote, already well known by Sydney's time. Louis XIV, harassed by a veteran officer who constantly importuned him for promotion, said one day, loud enough to be heard: 'That gentleman is the most troublesome officer I have in my service.' 'That is precisely the charge', replied the old officer, 'which your Majesty's enemies bring against me.'[14]

What is especially impressive about these nineteen articles is Sydney's confidence and assuredness, revealed in his lightness of touch. At the outset of his literary career, he already had the great gift of being able to suffuse the commonplace with life. There is a good example in his review of a travel book, Robert Percival's *Account of the Island of Ceylon*. Sydney is describing the local fauna. What could have been humdrum is transformed by brilliant use of personification. 'We were struck,' writes Sydney, 'with Mr Percival's account of the honey-bird, into whose body the soul of a common informer appears to have migrated. It makes a loud and shrill noise, to attract the attention of anybody whom it may perceive; and thus inducing him to follow the course it points out, leads him to the tree where the bees have concealed their treasure; after the apiary has been robbed, this feathered scoundrel gleans his reward from the hive.'

How powerful, and yet how effortless, Sydney's writing is. His was a rare talent: his natural literary ability was so great that he never had to work hard in order to develop a style or find a voice. The methods that served him in these articles in the early issues of the *Edinburgh Review* also served him in his maturity. It is instructive to compare his review of Percival's *Account* with a much later piece of work, also published in the *Edinburgh Review* and written in 1826. Once again, Sydney was reviewing a travel book, the best-selling *Wanderings in South America* by Charles Waterton, a highly eccentric Catholic squire. Waterton was a shabbily dressed ascetic of religious temperament: he looked, it was said, like 'a spider after a long winter'; he was also a man of many parts: an intrepid explorer, a leading taxidermist and an important early conservationist. Waterton's boyish flamboyance was grist to Sydney's literary mill. There is a delightful passage in *Wanderings* in which he describes how he caught a young boa constrictor, ten feet long, which he wanted to take back to England for stuffing. Waterton judged that the snake was 'not thick enough to break my arm in case he got twisted round it', so he grabbed it by the tail, punched it on the nose, allowed it to coil itself around him and, thus encumbered, 'marched off with him as my prize'. Waterton's antics with snakes greatly amused Sydney.

> . . . the snake, though high-spirited, is not quarrelsome; he considers his fangs to be given for defence, and not for annoyance, and never inflicts a wound but to defend existence. If you tread upon him, he puts you to death for your clumsiness, merely because he does not understand what your clumsiness means; and certainly a snake, who feels fourteen or fifteen stone stamping upon his tail, has little time for reflection, and may be allowed to be poisonous and peevish.

Sydney's fascination with bird-life, evident in his earlier review of Percival's *Account*, did not lessen with the years. He was especially taken with Waterton's description of the campanero:

> . . . how far does the gentle reader imagine the campanero may be heard, whose size is that of a jay? Perhaps 300 yards. Poor innocent, ignorant reader! unconscious of what Nature has done in the forests of Cayenne, and measuring the force of tropical intonation by the sounds of a Scotch duck! The campanero may be heard three miles! – this single little bird being more powerful than the belfry of a cathedral, ringing for a new dean – just appointed on account of shabby politics, small understanding, and good family!

It is the reference to the dean's politics, added as an apparent afterthought, which gives this passage its power.

Sydney honed his main literary weapons of clarity, directness, personification and simile very early on. They never let him down. I will quote just one more paragraph from his review of Waterton's *Wanderings*, one of the funniest articles he ever wrote. Here is Sydney on the strange behaviour of the sloth:

> The sloth, in its wild state, spends its life in trees, and never leaves them but from force or accident. The eagle to the sky, the mole to

the ground, the sloth to the tree; but what is most extraordinary, he lives not upon the branches, but under them. He moves suspended, rests suspended, sleeps suspended, and passes his life in suspense – like a young clergyman distantly related to a bishop.[15]

Some of the mischief in this passage is lost to us. Waterton was the first European to see the sloth in its habitat. When he wrote his *Wanderings*, he was able to confound conventional opinion by pointing out that the sloth was well adapted to its surroundings; those who had only seen the animal in captivity had uniformly concluded that it was hopelessly ungainly and good for nothing, no one having considered the possibility that the sloth might be able to function quite adequately upside down. Sydney, in his own eulogium on the physical prowess of the sloth, was poking fun at the unimaginative ignorance of the scientific establishment as well as making amusing reference to the nepotistic tendency of his brother clergy. Capacity to puncture pomposity was one reason for Sydney's enormous popular appeal.

The most remarkable thing about Sydney's seven articles in the first issue of the *Edinburgh Review* is that he managed to write them at all. His life prior to publication was dominated by upheaval. In 1801 he had moved once more, quitting 19 Queen Street for 46 George Street. It was at George Street, in February 1802, that his first child, Saba, was born. The name, which Sydney thought 'pretty', was chosen in humorous allusion to an obscure verse in the Psalms: 'The kings of Sheba and Seba will offer gifts'. Saba was healthy and strong, but Catharine was very weak. Ten days after the birth she reached a low point, from which she was slow to recover. After six weeks or so, she was still so poorly that she had to give up breastfeeding. Sydney appointed himself 'head nurse', attending to all her wants. Since he also had to teach William Hicks Beach and Mr Gordon, he had little time to write reviews.

The pressure of the spring did not let up in early summer. On 31 May, Sydney told Michael Hicks Beach that Catharine's health remained 'extremely precarious'; on doctor's orders, he was going to take her on holiday to Burntisland, across the Forth, as from 10 June. The holiday, timed to coincide with the completion of the tutorial year, lasted nearly three months. Sydney, Catharine and Saba lived in a small rented cottage. Apart from a 'severe attack' of croup, Saba continued to do well. Catharine also reaped immediate benefit from the sea air. She was, Sydney told Henrietta Hicks Beach in July, 'as cheerful and as happy as it is possible for a woman to be who is suffering from great bodily weakness'. In the same letter, Sydney describes the contrivances he had rigged up in order to make their 'cabin' comfortable. The meat larder was a hamper hung to a beam, a herring barrel did service as Catharine's dressing table, and her bell was a pair of tongs tied to a rope passed through the door.

Sydney was still 'head nurse' but he was also reading and writing. There is a sly reference to his literary activities in a letter to Henrietta. 'The books', he writes, 'are kept in the corner cupboard with the yellow pickles.'[16] It is not known how many of Sydney's seven pieces were written on Burntisland; probably the majority were. It was, in the circumstances, an exceptional achievement.

Before returning to Edinburgh, Sydney and Catharine went on a brief tour, visiting Loch Lomond, Glasgow and the Falls of Clyde. Catharine's health was now fully restored. Sydney was relaxed and in fine form, able to derive maximum amusement from the behaviour of the landlady at Luss. Mrs Smith, he told Henrietta Hicks Beach, received 'severe censure . . . for asking for a clean towel in preference to a dirty one – a preference the good hostess seemed to attribute entirely to caprice'. The couple were back in Edinburgh in good time for publication of the first issue of the *Edinburgh Review* on 10 October, but were not able to bask in the sun of this success for long. On 8 November 1802 news was received of the death of Mrs Pybus. This was a heavy blow for Catharine. Her father and sister were long since dead, and her brother had cut her off because she had married Sydney; now her mother, a source of strong emotional support, was dead as well.

Soon there was another upset. On 24 November, Bobus was elected Advocate General of Bengal. Leaving his legal career in England, which was not going well, he would now become the senior law officer of the East India Company, which ruled India. He would have an income of £5000 a year, and it would also be possible to make at least as much again from private practice. Bobus calculated that, after ten years or so, he would be able to return to England a rich man.[17]

Bobus left England in April 1803. Caroline Fox and 'Aunt Ebey', Bobus's unmarried sister-in-law Elizabeth, travelled to the Isle of Wight to see him off. It was a tense and difficult parting. Not the smallest gift that Bobus placed on the steps of the altar of easy money was exercise of his fatherhood. Bobus's eldest son, Leveson, was to go with him but his two other children, Caroline and Vernon, were to be left behind. Aunt Ebey was furious. Being put in a position where she would 'supplant' her sister in the affections of Caroline and Vernon 'is what really hurts & vexes her more than she is able to express', Caroline Fox told her brother, the third baron. Bobus, the brother whom Sydney loved, was at bottom even more of a careerist than Cecil or Courtney.[18]

Bobus and his father did not part on amicable terms. One evening quite soon before he set out for Southampton, Bobus lost his temper. He apologized for his 'want of command' over himself and pleaded for a reconciliation, but his efforts were in vain. Robert Smith's obstinacy drove Bobus's wife to distraction. She wrote her father-in-law a pleading letter. 'If', began Caroline, 'you wish for my perfect good opinion, for my happiness – if either are worth your notice – forgiveness is the Virtue I call upon you for. Forgive one, forgive both your sons. If we are doomed to cross the sea with your curses instead of your blessing, receive at least the son that is left behind.'

Forgiveness was a word that rarely made an appearance in Robert Smith's vocabulary. Bobus had to leave England without a reconciliation. Sydney was fully aware of the consequences of the breach. Since the death of his mother in October 1801, his relationship with his father had been hanging by a thread. That thread now broke. Robert Smith followed up his fulminations against Bobus with further recriminatory letters to Sydney, accusing him of being dominated by his wife. The notorious marriage settlement had, 'in great part', been Catharine's idea, and the row with Henrietta Hicks Beach over payment for William was also put down to the '*pride and folly*' of Mrs Sydney.[19]

Sydney categorically denied both charges. He realized, at the same time, that there was no longer any hope of achieving a rapprochement with his father. His final letter, written in April 1803, was blunt. 'I have ever enjoyed so small a portion of your affection that I had no hope of preventing what has happened *myself*. My only dependance was upon the influence of my brother and Mrs Robert Smith. The moment I learnt what has happened with respect to them I lost all thought of reconciliation because I knew that every hope of it was at an end.' The closing paragraph is extremely sad:

> I am hurt I confess to find myself an outcast – but it will be a great consolation to me if you will notice my children as they grow up,

and if anything happens to me, show some countenance to my wife – who has never meant harm to any human creature, and who has lost all her friends on my account. Accept my dear father my fervent thanks for all the kindness I have ever experienced from you, and may God Almighty bless and protect you.[20]

Bobus's voluntary exile, and the separation from his father, were not Sydney's only family problems. His brother Cecil – or rather Cecil's wife Eliza – was also causing anxiety. Cecil had married in India in 1793; the couple had only one child, a boy bearing his father's name.[21] The happiness of the marriage had been undermined by Cecil's inability to manage his financial affairs. His extravagance followed a predictable course, increasing in line with each advance in his career in the Indian Civil Service. He was an avid supporter of the principle, popular among the financially incautious, that expenditure can safely be allowed to rise until it meets every source of income plus all means of available credit. Eliza thought likewise; she was a flighty woman, fond of diamonds. In April 1800 she sailed for England with young Cecil, giving as her reason the 'long & severe returns of her nervous attacks'.[22] She returned to Madras early in 1802, leaving her son with Robert Smith and Maria, who were to look after him while he was being educated in England. Finding herself alone on the boat, Eliza, a woman of gregarious temperament, sought company. Much of her time was spent with the ship's second officer. The crew was soon hoisting the sails to a new tune: 'the lady in the black gown, the second officer does —'. By the time the ship reached the Cape, Eliza was far advanced in pregnancy. She resolved this emergency by retiring to her cabin, where she took a prodigious quantity of vinegar, and was seen soon afterwards, throwing overboard a bundle of linen. Later in the voyage she had a second miscarriage, and made sure this time that she kept a memento of her sexual exploits – the foetus was lovingly preserved in a bottle.[23]

After berthing at Madras the second officer was dismissed for misconduct. Cecil wilted under the strain of having to live with the social stigma which was the inevitable consequence of his wife's much-publicized adultery. He wrote to Robert Smith towards the end of 1802, saying that he would send Eliza back to England. A further letter, dated 22 January 1803, gives his reasons. 'I have no hesitation in pronouncing her as unfit company for any part of my family & shall feel hurt if they do not immediately cease all intercourse with her

. . . Such has been the horror of her conduct that God only knows if the child is mine or not.'

Sexual sensations are rarely kept secret within families. If Sydney was alerted to Eliza's egregious infidelities, which he almost certainly was, he kept what he knew to himself. Writing to Lord Holland's sister, he gives a heavily bowdlerized version of recent events. 'Mrs Cecil', he told Caroline Fox in April, 'is to be reshipped in July. Government I suppose allow a bounty upon such reexportations; her imprudence however is not a subject to joke about. I am afraid she has done herself irreparable mischief at Madras by such a petulant and abrupt departure from her husband about some absurd nonsense or another'.[24] Why the need for the cover-up? He was worried that Eliza's 'imprudence', which was 'not a subject to joke about', would in some way sully the reputation of the whole Smith family. Sydney liked to project an image of himself as frank and honest, but he was quite prepared to be devious whenever he perceived that concealment was the best means of protecting his own vital interests.

There were also other partings. Jeffrey's prediction that many of those responsible for the success of the *Edinburgh Review* would soon head south proved to be correct. John Allen had already set off for the Continent with Lord Holland in June 1801. Horner migrated to Lincoln's Inn in March 1803 and Brougham followed a year later.

Sydney was wondering what he should do. In November 1802, he told a friend that he was 'coming to live in London in the Spring'. His resolution, however, was not as firm as it appeared. He liked living in Edinburgh and Bobus's imminent departure for Bengal removed one of the prime reasons for moving south. Early in the New Year, an excellent excuse for further prevarication presented itself: William Hicks Beach asked Sydney if he would stay on as tutor for another year. It was Catharine who cut off Sydney's line of retreat. When she came to write her 'Narrative', she praised herself for having pushed her husband in the right direction. 'Now, dear Children, this is the *only* decision of my whole life (except that of my *Marriage*) of which I am *really proud*!! I *strongly opposed* his remaining permanently in Edinburgh: where as an Episcopalian Clergyman he was only tolerated (and considered but as a Dissenter); he could hope *there* for no professional advancement; Pupils, as well as health to attend to them, were both uncertain, I *earnestly exhorted* him to settle in London where I felt sure of his success.'

Catharine's presence can be sensed in Sydney's answer to

Mrs Hicks Beach: 'I could not hold myself justified to my wife and family if I were to sacrifice, any longer, to the love of present ease, those exertions which every man is bound to make for the improvement of his situation.' The details of leave-taking still had to be worked out. Catharine was expecting another baby. The hope was that she would go and stay with an aunt for her lying-in, but the aunt died and so it was decided to take lodgings in Edinburgh until 1 September. Sydney wrote to Mrs Hicks Beach, asking if William wanted to remain with them until their departure. This, however, did not suit: William left Edinburgh in May 1803.[25] Sydney and Catharine stayed a few more months; but once their second child, a boy whom they named Noel, had been born they set their sights on London.

6

THE SACRED PARALLELOGRAM

'I believe the parallelogram between Oxford Street, Piccadilly, Regent Street, and Hyde Park, encloses more intelligence and human ability, to say nothing of wealth and beauty, than the world has ever collected in such a space before.'

SYDNEY SMITH

Sydney did not wait for his rental agreement in Edinburgh to run out, setting off for the metropolis on 8 August 1803. It was a difficult journey of twelve or fourteen days, made easier by the kindness of Mr and Mrs Hicks Beach who lent him their chaise. Catharine, in a poor state of health after her confinement, breastfed Noel all the way. Saba, just turned eighteen months, was lively and hard to contain. Sydney was melancholy, thinking of the friends he had left behind and of the uncertainty that lay ahead; he felt 'like a full-grown tree transplanted – deadly sick at first, with bare and ragged sinews, shorn of many a root'. This nervous insecurity was characteristic of Sydney, and explains why Catharine was proud of her success in getting him to make the move in the first place. It would have been less of a wrench if Bobus had still been around. The nearer Sydney got to London, the more he became aware of his aloneness: his mother was dead, his three brothers were in India, and he and his father were not on speaking terms. It was hard, too, for Catharine. Her mother had died the previous year, she did not wish to be reconciled to her brother, and she had lost contact with her aristocratic Tory friends.

The first few months in London were unsettled. The Smiths spent six weeks or so in a house in Grosvenor Square, lent to them by the Noel family – Sydney had got to know Mrs Noel, as well as her two sons, Charles and Gerard, while he was in Edinburgh. By early October, Sydney and Catharine were occupying their London home: 8 Doughty Street. It was a pleasant setting (when Charles Dickens moved into number 48 in 1837, Doughty Street was a private road boasting a gateway and a porter at each end) just to the west of Gray's Inn Road. The Smiths were not in Doughty Street for long: a letter to Jeffrey, written on 30 November, was sent from temporary lodgings at 77 Upper Guildford Street, which was nearby. Sydney's surviving letters, which are irregular during these months, give no clue to the reason for the sudden move. The new home may have been damp or in need of repair; or, alternatively, Sydney and Catharine may have been unable to resist an itch for improvement. Given their behaviour on later occasions, zeal for architectural innovation cannot be ruled out. They certainly had the means; Catharine's mother had left her a valuable set of pearls, which she had sold for £500. The proceeds may have been used to buy new windows and doors at Doughty Street.

There was domestic upheaval and there was also domestic pain. Saba lost her hair – Sydney describes her as being in 'dim Eclipse'; more disconcertingly Noel, still scarcely a few months old, began coughing up blood and then started to have fits. Sydney thought that his son was on the point of death. The fits had no clear pattern but were very frequent and extremely violent: there were forty of them within the space of two weeks. Once the fits subsided, whooping cough set in. Noel recovered, but then had a relapse and died around mid-November. 'Children are horribly insecure,' Sydney told Jeffrey; 'the life of a parent is the life of a gambler.'

The loss of Noel affected Sydney less than Catharine; she felt the shock strongly, he coped by throwing himself into activity. Sydney, in these first months in London, quickly built up a social circle. He had chosen to live in Doughty Street because it was in a district where there were several of Bobus's friends. (Bobus himself, prior to his departure for Bengal, had lived in Guildford Street which intersects Doughty Street from east to west.) Sydney's most important contact was James Mackintosh. Six years older than Sydney, Mackintosh had precocious talent and had long been well-known. His reputation was founded on a book published in 1791, when he was twenty-six; under the title of *Vindiciae Gallicae*, it was one of the most effective Whig replies to Edmund Burke's deprecatory *Reflections on the Revolution in France*. A native of the Highlands, Mackintosh had been educated at Edinburgh University but had left the city in 1788. Like Horner and Brougham after him, he had sought to make his fortune at the English Bar. Sydney already knew Mackintosh a little (they had first met in the summer of 1801, and were probably introduced by Bobus), but after the move to London the relationship between the two men blossomed.

In some ways, Mackintosh was not an obvious friend. He was immensely learned – Jeffrey thought that his range of study was 'nearly as large' as that of Francis Bacon – and he was also grave and a trifle ponderous. Sydney liked men who carried their learning lightly and who gave off electricity. But he was also always quick to respond to goodness, and he found this quality in Mackintosh in abundance. What Sydney especially liked was the way in which his new friend had his passions under control. Mackintosh, said Sydney after his death, 'could not hate – he did not know how to set about it. The gall-bladder was omitted in his composition.' It is not hard to see why such a person made a deep impression upon Sydney. He, after all, had Robert Smith as his father.

There was much boisterousness, and a lot of fun, in the vicinity of Doughty Street. Mackintosh held twice-weekly supper parties for twenty to thirty people, and the same social set met once a week at Sydney's. Mackintosh looked back on these months as 'one of the happiest' periods of his life. Horner felt the same. 'At Sydney Smith's,' runs his diary entry for 22 January 1804; 'the happiest day I remember to have spent.'[1] This mutual sense of liveliness was partly youthful exuberance, partly the pleasure that comes from a meeting of minds (Sydney, Horner and Mackintosh were all ardent Whigs), and partly the excitement generated by making new friends. Sydney, in these evening parties at Mackintosh's house and at his own home, came to know a number of men who were to become lifelong companions. There was Samuel Rogers, the best-known society poet of the age: his major work, *The Pleasures of Memory*, had come out in 1792. A retired banker, Rogers had recently moved to a house in St James's Place, overlooking Green Park, where he lived a bachelor life of fastidious elegance. Then there was Rogers's best friend, Richard 'Conversation' Sharp. Like Rogers he had a commercial background – he was a hat manufacturer – and, again like Rogers, had repute as a wit. One of his best *bons mots* is preserved by Saba in her *Memoir*. 'Many in this world', said Sharp, 'run after felicity like an absent man hunting for his hat, while all the time it is on his head', sentiments of which the Buddha would have approved. Sydney liked making jokes at Sharp's expense; he was, Sydney declared, 'as wise and ugly as the Serpent, and as innocent and as amorous as the dove'.

Quite a lot of the regulars at these evening parties were lawyers. One of them, John Whishaw, had rooms next to Francis Horner in New Square. Whishaw was short, stout and lame; he had a cork leg. Slow to express his opinions, he was decisive when he did so, a characteristic which earned him the nicknames of 'The Mufti' and 'The Pope'. Another lawyer was James Scarlett, later created Baron Abinger. Now coming into prominence, he later became the most successful advocate of the day. Scarlett brought with him his closest friend, the lawyer Samuel Romilly, who lived nearby in Russell Square. Largely self-taught, Romilly had been taken up by the avant-garde Whigs who met at Lord Shelburne's mansion at Bowood. A friend of William Wilberforce, Romilly dedicated much of his life to the anti-slavery movement; he also grew into one of the greatest parliamentary law reformers of the nineteenth century. He and Sydney had something important in common: Romilly's grandfather Etienne, a Huguenot, had fled from France in 1701. Romilly, like Sydney, was an impassioned champion of religious liberty.

The circle of relaxed conviviality was broken in January 1804 when Mackintosh, who had earlier withdrawn as a candidate for Advocate General against Bobus, went off to be Recorder of Bengal. Sydney was lucky to have another social venue to fall back on. On 17 December 1803 he had been elected a member of the King of Clubs, a small and prestigious dining club which met monthly at the Crown and Anchor in the Strand. As with much else in Sydney's life at this period, Bobus had a part to play. The King of Clubs had originated at a dinner party held at Mackintosh's house in 1798. Present had been Bobus, Rogers, Sharp and Scarlett: the name was Bobus's idea. Romilly was elected on 26 March 1802 and Horner on 25 June 1803. The dinners that Mackintosh held at his house were, in a sense, the King of Clubs in exile. Sydney was elected partly because he knew most of the members, partly because of his reputation as founder of the *Edinburgh Review*, and partly because he took Bobus's place.

Dining clubs were pivotal in late Georgian social and political life. They were places where careers were advanced, allegiances were formed and relationships were cemented. The King of Clubs was more important than most. Its members were all young, nearly all of them had fine futures in front of them, and they were all Whigs. Sydney and Horner were fortunate in being elected before the other prominent Edinburgh reviewers; Brougham was not admitted until 1805, and Jeffrey had to wait until 1811. Sydney made many new friends and quickly established himself, being elected treasurer in 1805. One of the attractions of the club, in Sydney's eyes, was that it had strong representation both of Scots and of Englishmen who had spent some time in Scotland. Mackintosh, Horner, Jeffrey and Brougham come into the former category; in the latter, membership included Shelburne's son and heir, Lord Henry Petty, as well as William Lamb who, as Lord Melbourne, would later be prime minister. Scots resident in London are notoriously clannish and this partly explains the success of the club; in 1808 it was resolved to admit no more than thirty members, all of whom must live in either England or Scotland. Sydney thoroughly enjoyed these dinners and remained a member of the club until it was dissolved in June 1823.[2]

Life was not all play. Sydney's pride held him back from relying on Catharine's private wealth. Bobus helped out, giving Sydney an annual gift of £100 'for a few years'. This was kind but only a stop-gap; Sydney wanted to develop his own sources of income. He made a modest start through the good offices of the Noel family. Colonel Noel was auditor of the New River company, one of those jobs involving some pay in return for virtually nominal duties which could always be picked up, provided one had the right contacts. Sydney first became Noel's deputy and then took on the post himself. This job, which was worth £70 a year, is a fine illustration of one of Sydney's own sardonic sayings: 'In this world the salary or reward is always in the inverse ratio of the duties performed.'[3]

It was as a preacher, building on his success in Edinburgh, that Sydney hoped to establish his financial independence. He knew that he had ability and, now that the *Edinburgh Review* had been launched, he was also well-known. There were many opportunities for employment. Fashionable parish churches – St George's, Hanover Square, St James's, Piccadilly, and so on – were full to overflowing. The overspill was accommodated in chapels, run on capitalist lines; the lessees, who were often clergy, charged worshippers an annual fee, known as a pew rent, for seats. Tenants of chapels were always on the look-out for fresh preaching talent in order to increase the size of the congregation. A number of hospitals and charities also had places of worship attached to them, and those who ran these institutions sought to attract wealthy patrons by providing church services where the sermon was delivered by a well-known preacher.

Although there was plenty of work about, Sydney initially found the going hard. Finding a place to preach in, he wrote in this winter of 1803–4, was 'more difficult than I had imagined. Two or three random sermons I have discharged, and thought I perceived that the greater part of the congregation thought me mad. The clerk was as pale as death in helping me off with my gown, for fear I should bite him.' Despite some restlessness in the pews, it was not long before Sydney was appointed alternate morning preacher at two places: the Berkeley Chapel in John Street, Berkeley Square, and the Fitzroy Chapel, further north in the parish of St Pancras. Sydney's fee at John Street was £90 a year, but he made only £50 a year out of the Fitzroy. Catharine, with typical enthusiasm, made much (probably too much) of Sydney's impact at the Berkeley Chapel. 'The chapel, in spite of its advantageous position, was nearly deserted . . . In a few months, not a seat to be had! Ladies & Gentlemen often standing in the aisles during the whole Service.'[4]

Sydney added a third preachership, in the evening this time, in March 1805: Sir Thomas Bernard, a wealthy philanthropist, used his influence as treasurer of the Foundling Hospital to get Sydney in. The Foundling, occupying a site adjacent to that now taken up by Great Ormond Street Hospital, was the flagship charity of the eighteenth century, specializing in the care of unwanted children. Getting a preachership there was quite a coup.

A few months later an even better position was within Sydney's grasp. He had Mackintosh to thank for this new opportunity. Soon after he moved into Doughty Street, Mackintosh had introduced him to his brother-in-law Josiah Wedgwood, second son of the founder of the celebrated pottery works. Josiah liked to encourage literary talent (for many years he gave an annuity to Coleridge) and wanted to do something for Sydney. The Wedgwoods had a warehouse on the corner of St James's Square, within a stone's throw of Piccadilly. Backing on to the warehouse was a chapel, formerly Catholic but now in the possession of some Swedenborgians. The lease of the chapel would soon come up for renewal. In July 1805, Sydney wrote to Josiah, asking him if he could have first refusal. Wedgwood was only too happy to oblige, telling Sydney that the rent would be 'trifling'. Here was the breakthrough that Sydney badly needed. York Street Chapel had a seating capacity, excluding servants, of around 350. If Sydney could fill the pews, he would be able to make at least £400 a year.

There was just one snag. As the law then stood Dissenting ministers were free to lease or open chapels wherever they liked, but Anglican clergy had first to get the permission of both the incumbent and the patron of the parish in which the chapel was situated. York Street was in the parish of St James's, Piccadilly; indeed, it was only a few yards from the mother church. The proximity could create a difficulty; it was not at all clear that Sydney's keenness to occupy York Street would be matched by the keenness of the rector of St James's to have such an able man preaching on his doorstep. Sydney was nevertheless confident that his presence in York Street would be preferred to that of the Swedenborgians. If the fact that he was a fellow Anglican was not enough to see him through, he felt he could rely on more mundane considerations. The rector of St James's, Dr Gerrard Andrewes, was one of Sydney's predecessors as evening preacher at the Foundling Hospital, and was 'well acquainted with Mr Smith as also with his connections'.

There was an exchange of correspondence with Andrewes in December 1805: three letters from Sydney and two in reply. The only thing that Sydney managed to get out of the rector was one of those elaborate commendatory remarks in which the age delighted, but which all aspirants for office learned to dread: 'It is no compliment for me to say, Sir, that your superior talents and abilities, with the happy gift you so eminently possess of rendering them useful, must ever make you regarded as a great treasure by those who have the happiness to receive your instructions.' Sydney was hoping for something better than to be called a great treasure, even by a fellow clergyman.

Catharine was outraged. Here was a really attractive opening, for which Sydney was eminently qualified but which he had been forced to relinquish because of the specious opposition of another clergyman whom, rubbing salt in the wound, he knew quite well. Forty years later the volcano of her wrath was still emitting lava. 'A prohibition so timid, so mean, so heartless, was perhaps under all similar circumstances never before pronounced!', she wrote in the manuscript of her 'Second Narrative'.[5] Sydney's wife was never knowingly guilty of understatement.

One day in the 1860s the Victorian author Augustus Hare called upon a pair of garrulous old sisters, both of them spinsters, living at Mainsforth near Bishop Middleham in Durham. The ladies described to Hare one of the sermons that Sydney had preached in London more than half a century earlier. 'I remember the sermon as if it were today', said one of the sisters. The climax had been a fiery passage in which Sydney had spoken of the portals of mortality. Over them, he had said, were written four words: 'Death! Plague! Famine! Pestilence!' At this point in the sermon the Misses Robinson became solicitous for the safety of the chapel clerk, whose job it was to read the service. The clerk was sitting immediately below the pulpit and Sydney was indulging himself in his favourite pastime of pounding the preacher's cushion. He 'thumped' it, said one of the Misses Robinson, until it 'almost touched' the clerk's head. A lady further along the pew, fumbling for an explanation of the preacher's behaviour, was heard to whisper: 'This is Sir Sydney Smith, who has been so long in the wars, and that is what makes him so violent.' It was not the only time that Sydney was to be confused with his namesake, the hero of Acre.

On another occasion, Sydney's forthrightness provoked a rare argument with Catharine. She followed her usual practice of reading his sermon through, and then sat down to discuss it with him a few minutes before he was due to set off to preach it at the Foundling. Catharine said that the Fazakerlys, firm family friends, were likely to be at the chapel and would heartily dislike the tone of Sydney's sermon, which they would think (quite wrongly) was directed at themselves. She pleaded with Sydney to preach one of his old sermons in preference to the new one, but her efforts were in vain. Sydney put an end to the discussion with a rhetorical flourish: 'Kate, do you think, if I feel it my duty to preach such a sermon at all, that I can refrain from doing so from the fear of giving offence?' Sydney, as was usual when a moral issue was at stake, was being thoroughly stubborn. Catharine's gloomy prognostications were fulfilled: the Fazakerlys, incensed by the sermon, refused to have anything to do with the Smiths. But Sydney held fast to his friends. The ice separating the families slowly melted and the Fazakerlys, a quarter of a century later, were welcome guests at Sydney's Somerset rectory of Combe Florey.

There was in Sydney a strain of severity which was never revealed in the dining-room but was sometimes evident when he was in the pulpit. His advice on the best way to spend Sundays is unlikely to have been well received by his fashionable congregation. Sydney did not tell his hearers anything as anodyne as to refrain from whist and to cut down on their consumption of port. 'On the Sabbath,' he declared, 'every man ought to think of death; not to think of death languidly, but to bring it in bold relief before his eyes; to gaze at it as if he were hereafter to meet it.' These are strange words on the lips of a famous wit; a more obvious place to look for them is in one of Dr Johnson's private diaries.

Sydney never flattered those who sat in the pews. He was especially insistent that the wealthy should not take a condescending attitude towards the disadvantaged and the poor. It was not good enough to read about poverty, 'pure moral misery wrought up into an artful tale'; the rich must put away their parasols, make visits, and be of practical help. Servants must be treated with tact and consideration, and as though they were friends. Every man, even he who is utterly rejected by society, has his sensitivities, his feelings. 'Without one soul in all the earth that harbours a thought of him, without a place where to lay his head, loathsome from disease and shunned by men, the poorest outcast has still . . . some pride in reserve, and you may make his tears more bitter and his heart more heavy.' Sydney believed profoundly in the spiritual equality of man. He would have agreed with the man who said that the easiest way to find out whether an aristocrat was a Christian was to ask his servants.

Despite the melodrama, despite the occasionally discomfiting forthrightness, and despite the severity, people still flocked to hear Sydney preach. His renown as the founder of the *Edinburgh Review* obviously helped, giving him curiosity value, but there was more to his popularity than that. Sydney's persuasive abilities are evident in an appeal for financial assistance made on behalf of the beleaguered Swiss, whose tiny republic had first been invaded and then occupied by the armed might of France. The slaughter was rendered especially terrible by the contrast with the tranquillity of Switzerland's scenery: 'From the depth of sweet retreats echoed the shrieks of murdered men, stabbed in their humble dwellings under the shadow of the high mountains, in the midst of those scenes of nature which make solemn and pure the thoughts of man, and appal him with the majesty of God.' Towards the end of the sermon, Sydney invited the congregation to imagine that they had become lost on a craggy Swiss pass. The Swiss people would have befriended them. 'If any one of you had been wandering in their mountains, they would have treated you kindly and gently; if you had been sick, they would have watched your bed; if you had been weary, they would have sheltered you in their cabins; if you had been hungry, their very children would have come to share their food with you, and their little faces would have been clouded with sorrow, till the countenance of the poor stranger within their gates was turned to joy.' The language is powerful, simple and direct.

Sydney never disturbed men's faith or stirred up theological controversy. This is because he was not theologically minded himself. He had an unquestioning faith in God: disbelief was an intellectual posture that he found profoundly threatening, and which he did not make the slightest effort to understand. One of the worst sins, in Sydney's opinion, was to sow seeds of religious doubt in a child's mind. He would, he said, 'a thousand times prefer that his child should die in the bloom of youth, rather than it should live to disbelieve'. Harsh words indeed. Sydney treated 'infidelity', as he called it, with amused condescension. He was once at a dinner party where a French free-thinker told the assembled company that he was a materialist. Sydney turned to him and asked if he had enjoyed the soufflé. 'Indeed, I did,' replied the Frenchman, suddenly polite. 'And do you', rejoined Sydney, 'doubt the existence of the cook?'[6] This answer was an adaptation of an argument for the existence of God put forward by the contemporary English theologian William Paley in his *Natural Theology*, published in 1802. In a famous analogy, Paley likened the universe to a watch. In both cases, claimed the archdeacon, the mechanism was so intricate, so delicately balanced, that it could not be explained by chance.

Other key elements in Sydney's theology also came from Paley. Sydney liked the way in which the archdeacon always took a plain man's view on complicated theological issues. Paley argued, for instance, that Christ's claim to divinity rested primarily upon his physical Resurrection from the dead, a historical event attested by a mountain of evidence. The archdeacon's argument for the immortality of the soul was equally simple. The certainty of immortality could be derived from the constitution of the human mind. There is an excellent paraphrase of Paley's position in one of Sydney's sermons: 'We cannot believe', said Sydney, 'that He has given us minds capable of forming the notion of immortality, but unworthy of enjoying immortality itself.'

Sydney's religious faith enhanced his natural buoyancy of spirit, his most remarkable quality, bearing in mind the horrors he experienced in childhood. His three brothers were all, in their various ways, wounded men: Bobus craved privacy and had few friends, Cecil found life hard to cope with, Courtney was at odds with almost everyone. Sydney also had his own inner tensions, exacerbated later in life by frustrated ambition, but he always managed to rise above his problems. He was fully aware that the world was a place of much pain and suffering – no one was free of it – but he had within him the constant consolation of God's abiding Presence. No man was a friendless stranger in a friendless land. 'Nothing is overlooked . . .

God knows even the least of all our sufferings . . . if it was not right it would not be . . . there is no wretch in the obscure corner of a desert upon whom the eye of God is not bent, and in whose sorrow the ministering angels are not busy.'

What mattered to Sydney was living a Christian life, slowly building up a Christian character. It was, he acknowledged, a demanding task. 'That charity alone endures which flows from a sense of duty and a hope in God. This is the charity that treads in secret those paths of misery which all but the lowest of human wretches have fled: this is that charity which no labour can weary, no ingratitude detach, no horror disgust; that toils, that pardons, that suffers; that is seen by no man, and honoured by no man, but, like the great laws of nature, does the work of God in silence, and looks to a future and better world for its reward.' Elevating Christian ethics, Sydney played down Christian doctrine. He would have been horrified by the notion that a man could be damned because he did not believe in the Virgin Birth or had doubts about the doctrine of the Trinity.

People liked Sydney's rational tone, and they also liked his ethical emphasis. It was not an age of fervent spirituality; Holy Communion, rarely received more than three or four times a year, was given low priority. Sydney, in this regard, was a man for his own times: it is impossible to imagine him spending hours in prayer in preparation for making an important decision. He once gave a revealing sermon 'on the importance of public worship', taking as his text a verse from the twenty-fourth chapter of St Luke: 'And they were continually in the temple, praising and blessing God'. It was not a spiritual challenge that Sydney was prepared to take up. 'I do not', he began, 'purpose to recommend, after the model of apostolical righteousness, a devotion so fervid, and so incessant, as that mentioned in my text.'[7] This assurance was doubtless met by an audible sigh of relief emanating from the pews.

Sydney's faith was real and important to him, but his understanding of Christianity was nevertheless very defective. His belief was simple and rational but it was also complacent and comfortable. He was, with part of himself, a humanist, a reductionist, someone who speaks of Christ as though he were an Athenian philosopher with the added lustre, the extra polish, of an eighteenth-century English country gentleman. Hence Sydney's popularity as a fashionable preacher. Despite his eccentricities, he told people what they wanted to hear.

Getting preacherships at the Berkeley and Fitzroy chapels was not the only success that Sydney had in 1804: on 10 November he lectured for the first time at the Royal Institution in Albemarle Street, a break which, like his later appointment as preacher at the Foundling Hospital, he owed to the patronage of Sir Thomas Bernard. The Royal Institution had been set up five years earlier. The first set of lectures to attract much attention was a series on chemistry by Humphry Davy. Horner went along in March 1802, noting that the audience was '300 or more'. Sydney outshone Davy. He was initially signed up for a single course of ten lectures. By the time these were nearing completion, he was being listened to by between 500 and 600 people a week. A second series of ten, beginning in the spring of 1805, was hurriedly agreed upon. Sydney now learned what it was like to be fêted. Mary Berry, the young friend of the delightful letter-writer Horace Walpole, lived in Curzon Street, a few minutes away from the Royal Institution. She made a point of not missing Sydney's histrionic skills and went to the lengths of writing a poem entitled 'On buying a New Bonnet to go to one of Sydney Smith's Lectures'. Mary was among the audiences of 600 to 800 who flocked to Sydney's second series. She was fortunate that she lived nearby. An eye-witness gives a graphic account of the press of people. 'All Albemarle Street and a part of Grafton Street were rendered impassable by the concourse of carriages . . . There was not sufficient room for the persons assembling: the lobbies were filled, and the doors into them from the lecture room were left open; the steps leading into its area were all occupied; many persons, to obtain seats, came an hour before time.' The ways of fashionable society were still beyond the reach of Sydney's pocket; he walked from Doughty Street, arriving with muddy shoes. Muddy shoes or not, Catharine was made ecstatic by her husband's popularity. '*He was no longer unknown*!! He was *universally* courted! Everyone was *pleased* and *proud* to make his acquaintance!'[8]

Fashion, of course, is fickle. A third course of lectures, given in the early months of 1806, drew much smaller numbers. The main reason for the decline in Sydney's popularity is that he had overreached himself: the first two series are crammed full of ideas but the third is decidedly thin. A second, spiteful, explanation for the comparative failure of the third course is given by the diarist Joseph Farington, who records that Sydney's levity had been ridiculed in the prologue to a play at Westminster School, forcing the lecturer to adopt a 'different manner'. Farington may have been right. Sydney was sensitive to criticism and desperately wanted public recognition. It would nevertheless be entirely wrong to judge these lectures on the basis of their unsatisfactory finale. No one can take from Sydney his achievement in the first two sets, and it is upon these that his fame rests.[9]

Preparing them was very demanding. Sydney had other work to do: sermons for the Berkeley and the Fitzroy and, from March 1805, for the Foundling also. There were, moreover, emotional complications. Within a week of giving his first lecture in the first course, Sydney became involved in yet another familial imbroglio. As if all of this was not enough, there were also domestic troubles to contend with. Catharine was, for the third time, heavily pregnant; Douglas, a replacement for the dead Noel, was born in February 1805. Fortunately, Sydney was good at working under pressure. Articles for the first issue of the *Edinburgh Review* had been written in cramped conditions on Burntisland, and he now produced some of his best lectures at the Royal Institution in similarly trying circumstances.

Sydney alludes to his exhaustion in a letter written to Francis Jeffrey about a week before the birth of Douglas. The letter also shows Sydney's great gift for friendship. Despite feeling rattled and worn, he was able to make time both for gossip and for the loving personal touch. His tone is familiar and bantering; he is frank about himself; and there is some heartfelt praise of Francis Horner, the much admired 'Knight of the Shaggy Eyebrows':

> I thought you had entirely forgotten me, and was pleasing myself with the notion that you were rising in the world, that your income was tripling and quadrupling in value, and that you were going thro' the customary and concomitant process of shedding your old friends and the companions of your obscurity – when, behold! yr. lr. arrived, diminished your income, blunted your fame, and restored your character.
>
> . . . I am sure you will be glad to hear of Mrs S. first. I have been expecting that she would be brought to bed every night for the last eight days, but to the amazement of the obstetric world she is still as pregnant as the Trojan Horse. I will advertise you of her delivery. Saba is quite well: as for me, I am plagued to death with Sermons and Lectures, and am afraid I have rather overloaded myself . . .
>
> Horner is a very happy man; his worth and his talents are acknowledged by the world at a more early period than those of any independent and upright man I ever remember. He verifies an

observation I have often made, that the world do not dislike originality, liberality, and independence so much as the insulting arrogance with which they are almost always accompanied. Now Horner pleases the best judges, and does not offend the worst. He will entirely excel Brougham.

God ever bless you, my dear Jeffrey! – is the prayer of your sincere friend,

SYDNEY SMITH

Sydney made an unlikely choice of subject for his Royal Institution lectures: moral philosophy. His qualifications to lecture to a mixed fashionable audience on this topic were weak. He got around the difficulty in a characteristic way by expanding his brief. 'Moral philosophy', he said breezily, includes 'everything which relates to the human mind.' This nonchalant definition opened the way for him to give two lectures on wit, two more on habit, four on the passions and one on taste. Sydney rightly judged that the audience would not mind. They came to be instructed and amused, not to listen to arcane philosophical disputes. Sydney had nothing original to say about the problem of evil or the nature of the human will. He was, however, extremely entertaining. Francis Horner summed up Sydney's appeal very well. 'Who else,' he wondered, 'could make such a mixture of odd paradox, quaint fun, manly sense, liberal opinion, striking language?' Sydney, in these lectures, shows himself to be one of the foremost communicators of the age. He inspires by his vivacity and charm. His touch is never heavy, always light. Admire, for instance, the ease with which he traverses the minefield of eighteenth-century German philosophy:

To Leibnitz, and his successor Wolfe, succeeded an endless list of German metaphysicians, whose systems I am so far from being acquainted with, that I am too ignorant to pronounce their authors' names – Baumgarten, Meyer, Crousaz, Plouquet, Mendelssohn (the antagonist of Hume), and Eberhard, Platner, and names without any vowels or any end.

This superb list is terminated by Professor Kant, the explanation of whose philosophy I really cannot attempt: first, from some faint doubts whether it is explicable; next, from a pretty strong conviction that this good company would not be much pleased to sit for another half-hour and hear me commenting on his twelve categories . . .

Many in the audience were dazzled by Sydney's way with words. Robert Peel, later prime minister, was present at some of the lectures and wrote to tell Catharine after Sydney's death that he still remembered one of the recitations: testimony, after nearly half a century, to Sydney's superb communication skills. Another of Catharine's correspondents was Jane Marcet, a popular writer on scientific and economic subjects. 'I remember that I was a perfect enthusiast', said Jane. At one moment Sydney 'inspired his hearers with such awe & reverence by the solemn piety of his manner that his discourse seemed converted into a sermon, & at others by the brilliancy of his wit made us die of laughing.'

Sydney had been deeply impressed by the intellectual vibrancy of Edinburgh society and wanted to make the ideas of Scottish thinkers more widely known. The lectures are full of quotations from Adam Smith, Thomas Reid and Dugald Stewart. Sydney's method of propagandizing, although effective, was idiosyncratic. He did not attempt systematic exposition but spoke of Scottish thinkers as though they were interesting gentlemen who might well have important things to say. Sometimes Sydney was a rebellious pupil, taking an opposite side. He found fault with Thomas Reid's understanding of the nature of human desire. Reid claimed that fear, love, hatred and so on were innate. Not so, argued Sydney. Desires develop through the mechanism of association of ideas. A child has no innate fear of a lighted candle; indeed its first thought is to grasp it. It is only through the experience of pain that it learns to associate in its mind lighted candles with disagreeable sensations. By such simple examples did Sydney command attention.

In an important lecture Sydney elaborates on the theme, previously expounded in the *Edinburgh Review*, that incongruity, because it maximizes the element of surprise, is at the heart of humour. He shows, in a manner that can only be called Dickensian, an appreciation of the power of cumulative burlesque:

If a tradesman of a corpulent and respectable appearance, with habiliments somewhat ostentatious, were to slide down gently into the mud, and dedecorate a pea-green coat, I am afraid we should all have the barbarity to laugh. If his hat and wig, like treacherous servants, were to desert their falling master, it certainly would not diminish our propensity to laugh; but if he were to fall into a violent passion, and abuse everybody about him, nobody could possibly resist the incongruity of a pea-green tradesman, very respectable, sitting in the mud, and threatening all the passers-by with the effects of his wrath. Here, every incident heightens the humour of the scene:— the gaiety of his tunic, the general respectability of his appearance, the rills of muddy water which trickle down his cheeks, and the harmless violence of his rage! But if, instead of this, we were to observe a dustman falling into the mud, it would hardly attract any attention, because the opposition of ideas is so trifling, and the incongruity so slight.

There are many acute comments in Sydney's lecture on the evil passions. Sydney fully understood the nature of sulkiness; having Courtney as a brother obviously helped. 'Sulkiness', he told his audience, 'is anger half subdued by fear.' He was especially good on envy, defining it as resentment excited by a sense of inferiority. He then adds a brilliant afterthought: 'A ploughman does not envy a king; but he envies another ploughman who has a shilling a week more than he has.' This notion, known as relative deprivation, is a key element in the analysis of society by modern sociologists.

Many of Sydney's best remarks were based upon self-observation. He had harsh things to say about shyness: 'It looks like a virtue without *being* a virtue.'[10] Often, he said, shyness is the offspring of misplaced pride. 'A young man, in making his first appearance into society, is so ignorant as to imagine he is the object of universal attention; and that every thing he does is subject to the most rigid criticism.' This, Sydney felt, applied to himself with particular force.

Sydney also put forward his own views on life. It was a key feature of his homespun philosophy that a man should keep to his 'own line of talent', that he should strive to be what nature intended him for. It was advice that, alas, people did not often follow. Sydney depicted the human predicament in a famous analogy:

If you choose to represent the various parts in life by holes upon a table, of different shapes – some circular, some triangular, some square, some oblong – and the persons acting these parts by bits of wood of similar shapes, we shall generally find that the triangular person has got into the square hole, the oblong into the triangular, and a square person has squeezed himself into the round hole. The officer and the office, the doer and the thing done, seldom fit so exactly, that we can say they were almost made for each other.

Was Sydney, I wonder, aware that his own life as a clergyman was a perfect example of the truth of what he was saying?

Sydney's method in these lectures is to use common sense, eliciting further support for his side of the question by being amusing. In his seventeenth lecture, 'On the faculties of animals, as compared with those of men', he launches a droll attack upon the well-known seventeenth-century French philosopher René Descartes. Animals, thought Descartes, are machines lacking the rudiments of intelligence. Sydney challenges this claim, asking the audience to call to mind the wiles of a hunted stag. 'The artifices of a gentleman pursued by bailiffs, and the artifices of an animal pursued for his life, are the same thing – call them by what name you will.' There is in an earlier lecture a fine passage on instinct: 'Insects are like Molière's persons of quality – they know every thing (as Molière says) without having learnt anything.' Sydney also had the lawyer's capacity to make a plausible case out of highly implausible material. A good example is his attempt to deny that there is any distinction between utility and beauty. Beauty, according to Sydney, consists in adaptation of means to ends:

> Go to the Duke of Bedford's piggery at Woburn, and you will see a breed of pigs with legs so short, that their stomachs trail upon the ground; a breed of animals entombed in their own fat, overwhelmed with prosperity, success and farina. No animal could possibly be so disgusting if it were not useful; but a breeder, who has accurately attended to the small quantity of food it requires to swell this pig out to such extraordinary dimensions – the astonishing genius it displays for obesity – and the laudable propensity of the flesh to desert the cheap regions of the body, and to agglomerate on those parts which are worth ninepence a pound – such an observer of its utility does not scruple to call these otherwise hideous quadrupeds, a beautiful race of pigs.

This is not convincing, but it is beguiling all the same.[11]

Sydney's family had been causing him pain virtually since delivery of the first lecture at the Royal Institution. His involvement was not of his own making; since the bitter correspondence with his father at the time of Bobus's departure for India in April 1803, Sydney had, as a matter of policy, kept himself to himself. He was drawn in by Cecil, who was expert at exerting emotional pressure. Following discovery of the fact that Eliza had cuckolded him, Cecil had become determined upon divorce, a legal process of great difficulty: a suit had first to be taken through the ecclesiastical courts and then, once that hurdle was cleared, the matter was dealt with by the House of Lords. For a man living in Madras, it was not an inviting prospect.

There would also be substantial expenses, but these were not thought by Cecil to be a problem. Financial considerations had never stopped him from doing anything in the past, and they were not going to stop him now. He had given his father power of attorney in May 1803, sending over some money in order to get things going. Robert Smith made desultory efforts on Cecil's behalf, but these bore no fruit. In June 1804 he wrote to his son, telling him that nothing could be done. The letter was as a red rag to a bull. Cecil wrote to Sydney, pulling as hard as he could at the always-taut strings of his brother's heart. 'I conjure you by all the ties which have ever united us to exert yourself in this business and to see my father upon it . . . Consider that the happiness and salvation of the brother who tenderly loves you is at stake . . . my beloved brother, try all means to relieve me from my misery.'

Against his better judgement, Sydney allowed himself to become embroiled. His first letter to Maria, used as a go-between, was dated 12–16 November 1804. In the eighteen months since Sydney last had anything to do with his father, he had not managed to add to his stock of knowledge about the art of emotional politics. What was needed was a little courtesy on Sydney's part. It was not forthcoming. In this first letter he impugned his father's efforts on Cecil's behalf. 'Sufficient evidence can only be procured by constant and unremitting efforts of a person living in London, by free expenditure of money, and even by bribery – in short by all the arts well known to an active lawyer, and without the employment of which guilt would escape much more frequently than it does.'

The only thing that Robert Smith can have liked about these high-handed remarks is the implication that he was above bribery, whereas Sydney was not. Equally displeasing was Sydney's agenda for future action. 'I will pledge myself before six months are over my head to carry the divorce through the ecclesiastical courts and in a twelvemonth from that date to get it through the House [of Lords], or . . . to convince Cecil it is impossible.' He ended his letter on an especially irritating note, trying to take possession of the moral high ground. 'I hope my father will not imagine that any disagreement which exists between us has induced me to stir in this business. He has treated me and mine with concerted cruelty and injustice but I heartily forgive him and wish him all happiness. I impute to him no blame.'

Faced by these calculated indignities, there was little that Robert Smith could do. If Cecil wanted to send Sydney off on a wild-goose chase, then so be it. He was sure, anyway, that Sydney would come to his senses soon enough. Robert Smith reluctantly acceded to Cecil's proposal, although agreement did not preclude continuing combat. In the last weeks of 1804, there was a fast and furious correspondence between Robert Smith and Sydney. Typical is a letter of Sydney's, written with studied *froideur*. 'You have long treated me as an outcast, and a stranger, merely because I am poor, and therefore I must request that civility to which every stranger is entitled.'[12]

This is not the stuff of which familial intimacy is made. But get on together they must; it was impossible to pursue Cecil's case vigorously without a meeting. Sydney took a tough line, refusing to deal directly with his father unless a reconciliation first took place. Robert Smith refused to budge for several months and then suddenly gave in. Sydney recounted to Jeffrey what happened. 'I am at last reconciled to my father. He was very ill, very much out of spirits, and tired to death with the quarrel the moment he discovered I ceas'd to care a halfpenny about it. I made him a slight apology – just sufficient to save his pride, and have as in duty bound exposed myself for these next 7 or 8 years to all that tyranny, trouble and folly with which I have no manner of doubt at the same age I shall harass my children.' 'Some slight apology' was, of course, the only thing that had been required all along. Robert Smith was constantly quarrelling with all his sons. He forgot the *casus belli* long before they did. So long as they showed him respect, he was always prepared to bury the war hatchet – until next time.

Sydney busied himself with Cecil's matrimonial affairs through the first half of 1805 but, to his father's intense satisfaction, was forced to give up. Cecil's son remained in England, to be brought up by Robert Smith and Maria, and Eliza fades from the picture. Although he had been vindicated, Robert Smith remained in aggressive mood. In September 1805, Cecil wrote to say he had decided to drop divorce proceedings. He also asked his father to be more kind, more gentle: 'profligate, selfish, unfeeling & ungrateful . . . these epithets I do not think I deserve'. He was not alone in being abused; in a recent letter Robert Smith had made 'severe remarks' about Bobus and Courtney, upon which Cecil refused to comment.

The main objection to the irascibility of Sydney's father is that it was effective. He wanted submission and submission is what he got. 'Accept now my dear father as a first tribute from your sons in India, as an addition to whatsoever income you may now enjoy, the sum of £500 per annum for yourself & £100 for Maria to commence from 1 January next.' The words are Cecil's, taken from the same letter of September 1805 in which he announced that he had abandoned his plans for divorce. The £500 was to come from Bobus with the balance of £100 made up by the still-penurious Cecil; Courtney, still a bachelor but by now a judge and fabulously wealthy, did not contribute. Sydney, much to his distaste, was deputed to be paymaster. Anticipating trouble, he wrote a careful note to his father once the money from Bobus had arrived in England. 'I am sorry he has made me the instrument of his offer to you, because I am afraid it will be unpleasant to you; but remember I only do as I am instructed and that if any thing displeases you, the fault is not mine.'

The first payment passed off without incident. Not so the second. On 6 January 1807, Sydney paid into a London bank, for the credit of his father, the sum of £499 7s 6d, a shortfall of 12s 6d. Robert Smith wrote back by return. He had four points to make. Stamp duty was only five shillings; with Cecil's remittance of £100 for Maria the duty was paid by the payer; bankers' receipts were usually exempt; and the instructions of Bobus, the remitter, were precise: '*£500 to be paid into my Father's Bank every first of January*.'[13] What an error it had been to give any financial support to Robert Smith in the first place! Even Courtney, by now, had been dragged in; he had told Bobus in September 1806 that he would, as from 1807, make an annual payment of £250, bringing the total from India to £850 a year. (Courtney, typically, did not pay anything over until April and, even then, made his draft out in rupees.)

What made matters worse was that Robert Smith chose this letter to launch a terrific verbal assault on Sydney. The cause of his anger is obscure; a letter or letters have been lost. In the epistle that survives, Robert Smith recalls an occasion the previous winter when Sydney had told a story about a clergyman who, bringing an action for damages, had been called an idiot by the defending counsel. The judge, in summing up, had sided with the defence, quoting an earlier judgement in which it had been said that a man might be 'a good Parson & yet [a]damn'd fool'. Once this anecdote was out of the way, Robert Smith accelerated into his stride. Maria, as amanuensis, was made to write terrible words. 'How in common sense could you send so serious an attack on my father's peace? . . . My father looking ever to the motive than the fact acquits you of intention to hurt his peace, but insists upon it that you are the most [illegible] and dunderhead [illegible] priest that ever unjustly gluttoned and gorged on the labours of man.'

If there was any 'gluttoning and gorging' going on, it was being done by Robert Smith, not by Sydney. The previous year, Sydney had paid the stamp duty on Bobus's remittance out of his own pocket; now he stood his ground. 'I refuse to pay one halfpenny of this charge; not that the money is any object, but that nothing shall induce me to submit to such indecent and unjust violence.' For once a firm stance was wise. Letters went to and fro for a month until Robert Smith, realizing that he would not have his own way, backed down. His objections to paying stamp duty had, he told Sydney, always been light-hearted. Sydney replied in his best ironic vein. 'I am very glad you were in joke,' he wrote, 'but your letter had as little the air of it as anything I ever saw.'[14]

It would be pleasant to be able to say that the absurd row over payment of stamp duty blew over because Robert Smith felt remorse, but it would not be true. What happened instead was that this lesser matter was swamped by a greater. Cecil was in trouble again. Sydney heard the news from one of Cecil's City friends less than a week after the hostilities over Bobus's gift had broken out. It transpired that Cecil had been in a predicament for over two years but had managed to conceal the fact from his family in England. His difficulties dated from November 1804, when the Presidency at Madras raised a loan. Included in the terms was a decision to accept at banks dollar bills in lieu of gold bullion. Cecil, who was in charge of the Madras treasury, thought the new financial arrangement unfair: European traders dealt in dollars but Indian traders used local currency. Without seeking authorization he changed the rules; rupees would be acceptable as well. There was no suggestion that Cecil had made any personal financial gain, but his enemies at Madras, spurred on by some of the European traders, were determined to destroy his career. Although Cecil had powerful friends, a local committee recommended that he should be removed from office whilst allowing him to remain eligible to apply for an alternative post.[15] Papers were sent to the Court of Directors. It was when these reached London that Sydney discovered what had been going on.

As soon as Sydney became aware of Cecil's plight, he made efforts on his brother's behalf. Anyone who might have influence with the Court of Directors was buttonholed. Sydney called upon George Tierney, a rising Whig politician, and also upon Henry Fox, third Baron Holland. Another contact was Sir Francis Baring, like Lord Holland a fellow member of the King of Clubs. Sir Francis, the founder of Baring Brothers the merchant bank, was one of the richest merchants in Europe; he had been a director of the East India Company since 1779 and was chairman in 1792–3. Sydney also had a meeting with his cousin, the wealthy stockbroker John Trower; and he discussed Cecil's case with John Roberts, a friend of Robert Smith's and, like Francis Baring, a former chairman of the East India Company.[16]

Sydney's rows with his father, although violent, tended to end abruptly; once Robert Smith lost interest in the matter or matters at issue, peace was restored fairly quickly. The current bout of nastiness was no exception. It was a sure sign of improved relations that Robert Smith left the conduct of Cecil's defence in Sydney's hands. Sydney, in return, wrote to his father in March 1807, asking him to be godfather to the most recent addition to the family: a second daughter, Emily. These were important gestures on both sides. Sydney and Robert Smith remained emotionally distant from each other, but they ceased to goad. Cecil eventually escaped from the scrape he was in. He resigned his post as Accountant General in advance of his certain suspension, and was reinstated in the summer of 1808.[17]

7

HOLLAND HOUSE

'How very odd, dear Lady Holl. to ask me to dine with you on Sunday, the 9th, when I am coming to stay with you from the 5th to the 12th. It is like giving a gentleman an assignation for Wednesday when you are going to marry him on the Sunday preceding – an attempt to combine the stimulus of gallantry with the security of connubial relations.'

SYDNEY SMITH TO ELIZABETH, LADY HOLLAND,
23 May 1811

The twelfth of May 1805 was an important day for Sydney: he went to Holland House, the great Jacobean mansion belonging to the Fox family, where he dined as the guest of the third baron, the close friend of his elder brother. Since he had officiated at the celebration of the marital alliance between the 'Tinker and Taylor' Smiths and the aristocratic Foxes, Sydney had gone to Holland House a few times but always with Bobus and Mrs Bobus. Now, as the founder of the *Edinburgh Review*, Sydney commanded a place at this illustrious dinner table in his own right. He would have gone frequently to Holland House in 1803 and 1804, but the Hollands had only just returned from their three-year European tour. The invitation to Sydney on 12 May was the first step in a strategic plan to woo Edinburgh reviewers. Horner made his first appearance at Holland House two weeks later; by the end of June he had dined eight times, sleeping on three occasions. Brougham first came on 15 July; over the next six weeks he dined a further four times, sleeping twice.[1] It was natural that the Hollands should want to draw the main Edinburgh reviewers into their circle. The *Review* was required reading for those who were members of the political world. Not only was it highly influential, it was also, until the launching of the *Quarterly Review* in 1809, without a rival.

Dining at Holland House was a daunting experience. Sydney, who spent nearly all his time in the vicinity of Doughty Street, hired a hackney coach to take him the four miles or so to Holland Park. His probable route was along Kensington High Street until he reached the Holland Arms, then making a right turn into an avenue of trees. The house itself was surrounded by open fields and was, in 1805, quite countrified. Sydney felt embarrassed even before he arrived; most of the other guests came in their own coach and four. The journey was the easy part of the evening. Catharine only had one evening gown and that was trimmed with straw. When, on arrival, the step was let down and Catharine and Sydney appeared, the 'proud, powdered red-plushes grinned . . . and the iron entered into my soul.'

All his life Sydney was sensitive to his surroundings. Holland House overawed him. Grandeur always is a little terrifying. Built upon a palatial scale, Holland House was rich in historical associations. King William III had lived in it for a while and the well-known writer and journalist Joseph Addison had paced up and down its famous library, worrying about his unsuccessful marriage to the countess of Warwick. The library, unhappily, is no more. It ran the whole length of the west wing on the upper floor, and only the east wing still stands. Sydney took coffee in the library when he went to Holland House. It was a magnificent setting. The ceiling was divided into seven vaulted compartments, each set in oak with a blue groundwork; these compartments had, alternately, a skylight and a chandelier. In the middle of the room was a bay window which opened on to a terrace overlooking the Dutch garden, planted by Lord Holland. This garden, with its small box hedges, is still there. Dinner was served in the Gilt Room which led off the library. It was wainscoted throughout and much of its furniture dated from the seventeenth century. The circular table could seat up to fifteen or sixteen, there were two fireplaces and a glittering chandelier. It was not an atmosphere in which Sydney, at least at first, could easily relax. Social life at Holland House was made no easier for him by the realization that he was dining off the best porcelain in France, from the royal factory at Sèvres – collecting Sèvres pieces started to become popular among the English aristocracy in the 1790s.

The nervousness that Caroline Fox had noted in 1798 was still with Sydney in 1805; he would play with his watch-chain and crumble his bread at dinner.[2] Sydney's most humiliating experience was in July 1807, after he had been going to Holland House on a regular basis for more than two years. It was an intrinsically awkward social occasion: Lord and Lady Holland were giving a dinner, for the first time, in honour of that keen member of the Beggar's Benison, the Prince Regent. Sydney was privileged to be among the eleven guests; the duke of Norfolk was also there, as was William Lamb, later Lord Melbourne. Sydney's celebrated gaffe became part of the folklore of Holland House. It was recalled with relish by Lord and Lady Holland for many years and was passed on to their son Charles, who eventually wrote an account of it in the Dinner Books, interesting documents which record the guests at Holland House from day to day, as late as 1872. 'At the dessert on this occasion', Charles Fox began, 'the conversation turned upon wicked men, and the guests named those that they deemed most wicked of remarkable men.' Sydney's mind went back to the period of corruption and turbulence in France following the death of the Sun King, Louis XIV, and to the excesses of the subsequent regency. He could not stop himself from blurting out: 'the wickedest man that ever lived was the Regent Duke of Orleans, and he was a Prince.'

There was a profound silence around the table; as Charles Fox delicately put it, the moral standards of the future king, sitting perilously close to Sydney, were not 'of the highest order'. The Prince Regent was equal to the emergency. Looking straight at Sydney he replied instantly: 'No, the wickedest man that ever lived was Cardinal Dubois, the Regent's Prime Minister, and he was a Priest, Mr Sydney.' Charles Fox adds in conclusion: 'The Prince did not even know or remember that Sydney's name was Smith as well as Sydney.'

It is not surprising that the Prince Regent did not know who Sydney was: the Prince was a habitué of Devonshire House (the main rival establishment to Holland House), a place which Sydney took especial care to steer well clear of. The master of Devonshire House, an ugly Palladian building in Piccadilly, was the fifth duke, a man who had, in full measure, the reserve characteristic of male members of the Cavendish family. Strong emotion of any kind was foreign to him. He had an acute mind (he was a good classical scholar and had a superb knowledge of Shakespeare) but he was singularly averse to making any effort, either physical or mental. His unruffled calm was legendary. The fifth duke was, in short, the very image of the phlegmatic Englishman, precisely the type of character with whom Sydney, with his Gallic blood, found it most difficult to get on.

There was much about Georgiana, the famous duchess of

Devonshire, which Sydney would have liked. She was a woman of quite extraordinary good nature. Innocent and artless, she was without jealousy and without enemies. Although her face was the envy of the fashionable world – 'Your eyes are so bright, my lady', an Irish labourer once told her, 'that I could light my pipe at them' – her beauty was more a matter of presence than of appearance. Georgiana dazzled with her radiance; her movements were unhurried yet vivacious; and she had the rare gift of being able to make other people feel important. The Puritan in Sydney would, however, have been appalled by Georgiana's obsessive gambling, by her showiness (in her youth she had been fond of wearing a towering headdress, adorned with the largest feathers, at least three feet long, ever seen in society) and by her frivolity. Life at Devonshire House was a ceaseless round of receptions, balls, parties and visits to the theatre and opera. Sydney was nervous at receptions and parties, never attended balls, only liked theatrical comedies and hated opera.

The sexual arrangements at Devonshire House would also not have been to Sydney's liking. It was a *ménage à trois*. The third member was Lady Elizabeth Foster, one of the numerous and highly eccentric Hervey clan. Lady Elizabeth's father, Frederick Augustus Hervey, was bishop of Derry and earl of Bristol. The bishop's passionate attachment to the cause of Irish republicanism was matched only by his profanity of speech and sexual licence. He deserted his wife, setting an unhappy precedent which was also followed by his daughter's husband. Lady Elizabeth turned for comfort to the duke, bearing him two illegitimate children.

Georgiana viewed these parturitions with affable equanimity, a stance which was doubtless made easier by her own conduct: a bastard child was born to her in France in 1792. Bess, as Lady Elizabeth Foster was known within the Cavendish household, was Georgiana's best friend. Georgiana was also very close to her younger sister Harriet, who married Lord Bessborough. She was almost as spirited as her sister and was also a sprightly letter writer. On the negative side, she was carefree and impulsive. Like Georgiana and Bess, and like the fifth duke of Devonshire for that matter, she was keen on sexual dalliance, following family tradition by having illegitimate children and numbering among her lovers both the Prince Regent and the playwright Sheridan. The whole ethos of Devonshire House – an ethos of grand extravagance, of whispered conversations on sofas, of sexual promiscuity, of long nights, and of faro, whist and piquet – expressed a set of social priorities and of moral standards which were inimical to Sydney. That is why he stayed away.

Although Sydney had rarely been to Holland House before May 1805, he was still one of the first members of the famous salon; extensive foreign travel by the Hollands had prevented them from establishing the salon on a permanent basis earlier on. Sydney's name appears in the Dinner Books ahead of those of Samuel Rogers and Henry Luttrell, the other two men who, like him, became known as the resident Holland House wits. Rogers, whom Sydney had already met at the King of Clubs and also at Mackintosh's house, first dined on 25 July 1805 and Luttrell nearly four months later, on 17 November.[3]

Rogers was caustic; his remarks 'seemed to cut his lips as he uttered them', thought the actress Fanny Kemble. Known throughout society as 'the Bachelor', he was a stout defender of the advantages of a single life, complaining that marriage was a lottery which he would prefer to avoid: 'It does not much signify whom one marries, for one is sure to find next morning that it was someone else.' Rogers was always on the look-out for refinement in acidity, for the best possible statement of a withering remark. He records with satisfaction in his commonplace book that the English aphorism the 'biter bit' is inferior to its Spanish equivalent: 'He went out to gather wool and came home shorn.' Rogers's humour was enhanced by his speech and his physique. He had a weak, sepulchral voice and a sunken appearance; it has been said of him that his head resembled that of a corpse and that his thin limbs were 'hung together like those of a skeleton in the glass case of a professor of osteology'. Sydney advised him, when sitting for his portrait, to be drawn saying his prayers with his face in his hands.

Rogers's celibate habits were a source of endless amusement to Sydney. 'Damsel-loving Sam' was how he liked to refer to him. He once passed on a message to the poet through the good offices of Lord Holland. 'Pray remember me kindly to S. Rogers. Tell him that his Christian name only is a substantive, that his surname is a verb, and that both together form a proposition and assert a fact which makes him the envy of *one* and the favourite of the *other* sex.'[4] It is surprising to find that 'to roger', as a slang expression for copulation, was already current in the late Georgian period.

Sydney recognized that Rogers's scabrous wit was a style developed for public occasions; it did not express the inner man. He had a full appreciation of Rogers's worth. 'Show me', he once wrote, 'a more kindly and friendly man; 2, one from good manners, knowledge fun taste and observation more agreeable; 3, a man of more strict political integrity, and of better character in private life.' This says as much about Sydney as it does about Rogers. Sydney also loved his friend's fun-loving spirit, the way in which he used to amuse children with conjuring tricks. He was, furthermore, attracted by Rogers's poetic sensibility and by his reverent concern for all living things.[5]

Sydney's high view was shared by Lord and Lady Holland. You can, if you wish, see evidence of their affection for yourself. Go to Holland House and make your way to the west end of the Dutch garden, planted by Lord Holland. You will find there an alcove, constructed out of the fireplace in the harness room of the old stables. This is Rogers's Seat. Above it is still displayed some lines composed in 1812 by Lord Holland as a tribute to his protégé's best-known poem, *The Pleasure of Memory*:

> Here Rogers sat, and here for ever dwell
> With me those Pleasures that he sings so well.

Henry Luttrell, like Rogers a bachelor, considered himself 'the most private of all private men'. He was a natural son of the Colonel Luttrell, later second earl of Carhampton, who fought the famous Middlesex election against the radical John Wilkes. Luttrell had experience of social life in Piccadilly as well as Holland Park: he entered fashionable society under the aegis of Georgiana, duchess of Devonshire. Two leading traits in Luttrell's character were sensitivity and tactfulness, qualities which were so pronounced in him that he bitterly resented their absence in others. There was a touch of effeminacy, and also of Bohemianism, about him. Very much a gourmet, he was fastidious in his habits and took a keen, arguably over-keen, interest in his own health. His letters are full of references to ailments, either real or imagined: 'a violent fever', a bad foot, arthritic fingers, 'a gouty tendency in my constitution', a swollen ankle, 'a troublesome affection [*sic*]) of my lip'.[6] The overwhelming impression with him is of a considerable literary talent which he allowed to go to waste. He kept a diary, which some of his contemporaries regarded highly, but it has not survived. All that he managed to leave behind were a few slim volumes of satirical verse.

When he was at the dinner table, Luttrell conserved his fire-power. He took little part in the general flow of conversation, preferring to slide in his remarks deftly and unobtrusively. Luttrell was an actor as well as a wit, using droll gestures and whimsical facial expressions to reinforce his points. His humour was light and elliptical and lacked the acidity favoured by Rogers. A number of Luttrell's best jokes were on that well-worn subject, the English weather. A fine day in England was 'like looking up a chimney'; a rainy day was 'like looking down it'.

Sydney was fond of Luttrell, although not as much as he was of Rogers. Luttrell, in Sydney's eyes, was overly diffident and reclusive. On the other hand, he liked the way in which Luttrell judged men by what they were, not by the material possessions or political authority they might happen to have. Luttrell's gourmandizing tastes amused Sydney. Full advantage was taken of times when his friend was offered food in country houses that was below par. Luttrell, he wrote to Lady Holland after one of these mournful rural occasions, 'had not his usual soup-and-pattie look; there was a forced smile upon his countenance which seemed to indicate plain roast and boiled and a sort of apple-pudding depression as if he had been staying with a clergyman.' Jokes along similar lines are frequent in Sydney's letters. One of his most famous remarks, 'My idea of heaven is eating *pâté de foie* to the sound of trumpets', is usually misquoted. In the original, this mildly irreverent notion of eternal bliss was not applied by Sydney to himself, but to Luttrell.[7]

Going regularly to Holland House transformed Sydney's social experience. The Hollands held two or three large dinners a week, usually with about twelve guests; and there were also two or three small affairs, with a few people staying the night. 'No strangers' rarely occurs more than once a week in the Dinner Books. Invitations were sent out for any time between five and seven o'clock, usually for six or six-thirty. Lord and Lady Holland followed continental fashion, mixing scientists, artists and politicians in their salon. They were never narrow-minded; although pleased to have Whigs, they were always willing to welcome Tories. Holland House was open to both English and European royalty – George IV, William IV, King Louis Philippe; Talleyrand was a frequent visitor; Byron, Wordsworth and Metternich went there. The Hollands befriended poets, painters and struggling authors of all kinds, and they also kept open house for both French and Spanish political émigrés. The extent of the mingling of intellectual interests, social backgrounds and nationalities sometimes surprised even those who were familiar with Holland House. One day in November 1815, 'the Pope', alias 'the Mufti', alias the lawyer John Whishaw was asked to dine. His fellow guests were such a bizarre collection that he thought it worth while to note them down in his diary. There were two other lawyers, one of whom was Sydney's friend Samuel Romilly; Harriet, Lady Bessborough, and her husband were there, acting as a deputation from the Devonshire House circle; Samuel Rogers represented the world of poetry; there were Spaniards of various parties, 'all of them banished or proscribed'; the great sculptor Canova and his brother; 'a very intelligent deputy from Buenos Aires'; and, finally, an Italian abbot.[8]

Gaucheness is one of the human failings which usually diminishes if we put ourselves in situations where we have to battle against it. With Sydney the struggle was a long one but he emerged victorious. 'I have no shyness with strangers, and care not where, and with whom I dine', he writes in a letter of January 1819. He was forty-seven at the time and had been mixing in Scottish and English society for more than twenty years. He had diagnosed the problem, misplaced pride, in his lectures on moral philosophy. Finding a cure was difficult but he did eventually win through.

Holland House was an ideal place for Sydney: 'alienation', it has been well said, 'was the badge of admission'. Despite his extraordinary abilities, and despite his success in founding the *Edinburgh Review*, Sydney's future prospects were far from secure. He was a member of a family emerging from obscurity: his path in life was not laid out neatly in front of him, he had to make progress as best he could. Moreover he was, as a liberal, a member of a tiny minority within his chosen profession. The bishops and clergy were, with few exceptions, Tories to a man. In an age when advancement for a clergyman depended upon attracting support from a powerful patron or patrons, Sydney's liberal views were a huge handicap. It made all the difference to him that he now had Lord and Lady Holland on his side; provided the Whigs got into power, they would be able to ensure he was promoted despite his liberal opinions.

Holland House also mattered to Sydney for reasons that had nothing to do with his own preferment. Toleration of divergent political views, as well as mixing of nationalities and intellectual interests, was highly congenial to him. He was a man who 'tasted no politics in boiled and roast', who was proud of his French blood and who was eclectic in his pursuits. In Holland House he found a place where he could be himself.

Sydney, like almost everybody else, got on extremely easily with Lord Holland. They had informality in common. They also shared a notable clumsiness in dress: 'in a white waistcoat,' said a contemporary wag, 'Lord Holland looks like a turbot standing on its tail.' The third baron would have laughed heartily at this joke against himself: he was one of the most amiable men of his generation. Samuel Rogers said of him that 'he always comes down to breakfast like a man on whom some sudden good fortune has fallen.'[9] No one ever saw Lord Holland angry and, where his own children were concerned, he was indulgent to a fault. One evening his eldest son, Charles, was allowed into the Gilt Room towards the close of a great banquet given in honour of a number of foreign ministers. In the middle of the table was a large bowl of cream. Charles, who was young enough to be still in petticoats, approached his father with a request: 'Can I play in the cream?' There was a brief discussion between Lord and Lady Holland. Overriding his wife's objections, Lord Holland asked one of the servants to put the bowl of cream on the floor, so that his son could jump in and splash about at his pleasure.

Lord Holland had a keen sense of the ridiculous and was, like Jeffrey, an excellent mimic. After Sydney had been seeing him frequently for a few months, he sang the third baron's praises in a letter to Mackintosh. 'Lord Holland is quite delightful; I hardly know a talent, or a virtue that he has not little or big. The Devil could not put him out of temper. I really never saw such a man.' Something of Holland's easy conviviality comes to us from his statue at Holland House; it is to be found in the middle of a small pond at the end of a gravel path leading northwards away from the house.

Sydney could not bear cold-blooded people; he once said of Lord St Germans that he had 'all the stiffness of a poker without its occasional warmth'. Lord Holland was never cold. The joy that Sydney and Henry Fox took in each other's company was enhanced by a similarity in conversational style. Sydney's daughter Saba loved to see them together. They both had, she thought, great gaiety of spirit. Their conversation was short and varied, and was interspersed with anecdote on both sides: 'the perfection of social intercourse, a sort of *mental dram-drinking*, rare as it was delightful and intoxicating'.[10]

Sydney wrote to Holland with an intimacy which was not vouchsafed to other men. When Holland was ill with gout, Sydney tried to cheer him up with a letter of touching familiarity. 'I hear with great concern of your protracted illness', he begins; 'I would bear the pain for you for a fortnight if I was allowed to roar, for I cannot bear pain in silence, and dignity.' After some pages of garrulous gossip, he ends on a high note. 'God bless you, dear Lord Holland; there is nobody in the world has a greater affection for you than I have, or who hears with greater pain of your illness and confinement.'

The Scottish doctor John Allen was one of Sydney's oldest Edinburgh friends. He had been a member of the committee that planned the *Edinburgh Review*, and it was through Sydney that he had been introduced to the Holland household. With his appearance – the oversized silver spectacles, broad face, large head, more than adequate frame and vast legs – you will already be familiar. He was also remarkable in personality. His most amusing quality, in Sydney's eyes, was the suddenness of his changes in mood: affable at one moment, he was choleric the next. Allen had, in many ways, the temperament of a child. He was, however, a child with an extremely capacious mind. Originally recruited to write for the *Edinburgh Review* on medical subjects, it was not long before he spread his intellectual wings: history, political and constitutional theory and many branches of science all became familiar territory. Renowned for major works on Spanish constitutional history and on the royal prerogative, he was considered by Byron to be one of the best informed and ablest men he knew, and Brougham and Macaulay also had a high opinion of him. Both in physical appearance and in personality, the similarity with Pierre Bezuhov, the hero of *War and Peace*, is quite marked.

Allen was much more than medical adviser at Holland House: he was also librarian, factotum and friend. He carved at dinner, kept the Dinner Books, helped Lord Holland with literary projects, and went with Lady Holland on her drives. In 1811, through the patronage of the Hollands, Allen was made Warden of Dulwich College, becoming Master nine years later; but, following the practice of the day, this lucrative appointment was not permitted to interfere with routine – the occasions when Allen slept away from Holland House were few and far between. His relationship with Lord Holland was easy and friendly, but that with Lady Holland was stormy. Macaulay thought she treated him no better than a negro slave. The diarist Thomas Creevey went to one dinner where he was appalled by her behaviour. She abused Allen, quite unjustly Creevey thought, for his '*horrid temper*', and Allen looked at her with 'eyes of thunder'.[11] He was not always as passive. When annoyed beyond endurance he would throw down his fork at dinner, telling Lady Holland to carve herself.

Allen was a sceptic. He did not believe in God and was not impressed by Christianity, asserting that Jesus was a mythical character. Derisively known in society as 'Lady Holland's Atheist', he could sometimes be seen walking the streets of London muttering to himself, 'No first cause, no first cause.'[12] Sydney made many jests at the expense of Allen's disbelief, never being prepared to treat it seriously. He was 'Upaz Allen', 'generally considered unfavourable to sacerdotal plants'. Compared with a spreading tree in this life, his existence would be less comfortable in the next. 'I never see you', Sydney once told him, 'without thinking of the thousands of years in which you will be boiling in seas of burning Liquid, calling in vain upon the clergy to pull you out.'

Lady Holland was, in Sydney's words, a 'beautiful structure of flesh and blood'; well built, she had long flowing chestnut hair and extremely seductive ruby lips. She used her physical attractions to good effect in her youth, but altered her conduct after her marriage to Henry Fox. She never, however, wavered in her admiration of masculine company. Lady Holland was one of those women who make it abundantly clear that they adore being with men almost as much as they deliberately avoid being with their own sex. A comment made about the household of Odette, the courtesan in Proust's great novel *In Search of Lost Time*, also applies to Holland House during the residence of Lady Holland: 'It is a house which (or so it struck me) is especially attractive to . . . gentlemen. There were several married men there last night, but their wives were all, as it happened, unwell, and so had not come with them.'[13] Lady Holland's dislike of women had a profound effect upon the tone of social life at Holland House. The frivolity, balls, parties and social gossip characteristic of Devonshire House were eschewed. At Holland House it was conversation, an art in which Sydney excelled, which was king.

There was much more to Lady Holland than sexual magnetism; she had an intriguing and paradoxical personality. She was loyal to her friends, treated her servants as though they were part of the family and went out of her way to help poverty-stricken artists. On the other hand, she was a scheming woman, very dictatorial and rude to people she disliked.

She had an imperious will. Naturally strong-minded, her character was toughened by struggles in early life. The daughter of a West Indian planter, she married for the first time at the absurdly young age of fifteen. Her husband, Sir Godfrey Webster, was more than three times her age; he was also a drunkard and a brute. His young wife stood up to him as best she could and when his violence became too much for her, she sought solace in extensive foreign travel. Young Lady Webster also sought solace in other ways. While abroad she had a number of affairs, most notably with Lord Holland to whom she bore a bastard son in November 1796. (It was this son, Charles, whom Lord Holland allowed to wallow in the cream and who, in old age, recorded in the Dinner Books Sydney's celebrated gaffe at the dinner in honour of the Prince Regent.) The divorce from Sir Godfrey, which took place the following year, lived up to its billing as the social scandal of the season. Lord Holland paid dearly for his 'criminal conversation' with Elizabeth Webster: he had to pay Sir Godfrey damages of £6000. The social taint, however, attached itself to his wife. Despite the grandeur of the Fox name, Lady Holland was never accepted at Court, a rejection which hurt her deeply.

Lady Holland was prepared to go to quite extraordinary lengths to get her own way. When, as a teenager, she married Sir Godfrey, she lived with him in a small dower house at Battle in Sussex, while his aunt lived in grandeur at Battle Abbey nearby. It was a position of conspicuous inequality that young Lady Webster was determined to rectify. She was utterly unscrupulous, persuading some friends to dress up as ghosts and go at night to the Abbey, with the aim of frightening her husband's aunt out of the place. This ruse fortunately failed.

Later, Sir Godfrey was on the receiving end of her guile. In 1796 she was travelling around Italy, heavy with Lord Holland's bastard son and depressed about her prospects. Divorce from the brutish Sir Godfrey seemed inevitable, and it was likely that any divorce settlement would deprive her of the custody of all three of her children. Lady Holland was determined to do all in her power to prevent this calamity. When she reached the tiny village of Paullo, on the road to Modena, she stopped for a while, using her leisure time to paint some spots on the arm of her two-year-old daughter Harriet. One of her footmen, accompanied by her two sons, was then sent on to Modena. Harriet had a somewhat longer journey in front of her: disguised as a boy, she was taken by Lady Holland's faithful Italian maid to a pre-arranged meeting place in Hamburg. Having already successfully created the impression of Harriet's supposedly fatal illness, it remained only to fake her death. A guitar case was made to do service as a coffin, the 'body' was several large and smooth stones wrapped in a sheet, and, in order to simulate the face of a small child, she added a miniature waxen mask, placed on a tiny pillow. Her second footman dutifully carried the mournful cargo to the British consul in Leghorn, who followed to the letter her instructions for burial. Sir Godfrey, as comprehensively duped as he had earlier been comprehensively cuckolded, was not told the truth until three years later.

Lady Holland could be extravagant in her contempt for people, but she could also be extravagant in her praise. Like many women of strong personality, she had a compulsive desire to be dominated. Her enthusiasm for the 'Corsican pirate' knew no bounds. Napoleon, she once told her husband's unmarried sister Caroline, was *'my Hero'*. After his ignominious defeat on the field of Waterloo and subsequent exile, guests at Holland House had to listen to the mistress of the house describing the great dictator as 'poor dear Man'. She sent a stream of presents to St Helena: books, gateaux, chocolates. Napoleon's last days were comforted by *'les pruneaux de Madame Holland'*, and he left her a snuff-box in his will. Her memorial to him was somewhat more impressive: she commissioned Canova to model a bust, which was put on display in the Dutch garden.

Lady Holland also had winning vulnerabilities. Thunderstorms threw her into a panic, and fast travel frightened her.[14] She could not bear to be alone and was a severe hypochondriac: at one time she had no fewer than ten doctors. She also had a deep fear of death, exacerbated by lack of religious faith, for although she was not a militant atheist after the manner of John Allen, she shared the agnostic views of her husband and of Henry Luttrell.

There was a sinister side to all this. Lady Holland had a necrological interest that was thoroughly prurient. On one of her early European tours she visited a military encampment near Dunkirk, where she interviewed a certain General Dalton, discussing with him the dead bodies on the battlefield 'with as much Rapture as any Vulture might be supposed to do'. Lady Holland was also very superstitious. She was apprehensive about Fridays, always walked out of performances of *Hamlet* during the funeral scene, and asked the earl of Carlisle to raze his mausoleum at Castle Howard because the sight of it made her sad.

Yet this in many ways strange woman became the leading hostess in Europe. All the intricacies of social planning were in her hands; Lord Holland often came to dinner not even knowing who the guests were going to be. Lady Holland liked to squeeze as many people as she could around the circular table in the Gilt Room. 'Luttrell! make room!' she said on one occasion. 'It must certainly be *made*,' came back the plaintive reply, 'for it does not *exist*.'[15] The aim of the cramped seating arrangement was to make it possible for Lady Holland to control the flow of conversation, coaxing some and silencing others. Everyone who came to Holland House felt her presence. She had wide general reading which she put to good use, and could rapidly change her mood. Her purpose was always to heighten the sense of drama, to give the conversation verve and pace. No one, however distinguished or however famous, was allowed to put a stop to the free flow: 'Now, Macaulay, we have had enough of this; give us something else.'

Any high-profile hostess is both loved and hated: either is preferable to being ignored. Lady Holland stirred up a great deal of conflict. Melbourne, told to change his place, got up and strode out: 'I'll be damned if I dine with you at all.' People left but they always came back. The diarists Charles Greville and Thomas Creevey both went through periods when they would not go to Holland House; indeed, with Creevey, self-imposed exiles occurred quite often. Henry Brougham, angered by Lady Holland's behaviour, cut himself off from Holland House in 1809; a partial truce was agreed seven years later.[16] John Ward, one of Sydney's friends from Edinburgh days, loathed her ladyship: 'She shocks me by the extreme badness of her heart, which she contrives to display in an inconceivable variety of ways.' Ward could not be persuaded to accept a dinner invitation. He nevertheless turned up unexpectedly in March 1832, shortly before his death. Holland House could not be dispensed with. 'Though everybody who goes there finds something to abuse or to ridicule', wrote Charles Greville, 'all continue to go; all like it more or less; and whenever, by the death of either, it shall come to an end, a vacuum will be made in society which nothing will supply. It is the house of all Europe; the world will suffer by the loss.'

Back in 1798, Sydney had got off on the wrong foot with Lady Holland. Now that he was more confident, he found her easier to cope with. In October 1805, after he had been seeing her regularly for five months or so, Sydney told Sir James Macintosh that her ladyship was 'very handsome, very clever, and I think very agreeable'.[17] But in spite of his new-found confidence, he did not enjoy a 'like for like' relationship with Lady Holland. He was always aware that she was his chief patroness, and he was one of her protégés. Also, as is often the case with men when they are in the presence of beautiful women, he felt both exhilarated and insecure. Sydney was too fearful of offending her for Lady Holland to become an absolute and unconditional friend.

About 140 of his letters to her have survived, more than to any other correspondent. With her strange fancies and odd fears Lady Holland was very teasable; yet, remarkable to relate, Sydney, the irrepressible jester, never poked fun at her idiosyncrasies throughout more than forty years of correspondence.

He did, however, mock her when writing to other people. Her lifelong ostracism at Court because of her divorce from Sir Godfrey Webster amused Sydney no end. In 1841 he asked Lord Denman, the Lord Chief Justice, to dinner to meet her ladyship. 'Does Lady Denman know Lady Holland, and, if not, will that deprive us of the pleasure of Lady Denman's company? Lady Holland sinned early in life, with Methuselah and Enoch, but still she is out of the pale of the regular ladies . . . Pray tell me if this will make any difference. Your answer will be received by me in the strictest confidence.'

Lord and Lady Holland, together with John Allen, were once staying at Lilford Hall in Northamptonshire, the home of the Hollands' daughter Mary. At seven one morning a fire started in the drawing-room. John Allen, self-indulgent in creature comfort, was still asleep some time after the blaze had ignited. Sydney, writing to one of his female friends, assumes that it was Lady Holland who roused him: 'When the fire broke out at Lord Lilford's Lady Holland woke up Allen, who hearing the Crackling of the flames, and smelling the Smoke and seeing Lady Hd conceived he had slipt off in the Night to a very serious place at an high Temperature; he attempted to recollect a prayer, but entirely failed, and was fairly pulled out of bed by Lady Hd and the maids.'

Nor did Sydney allow Lady Holland's extreme fear of speed to go unmentioned. About six months before his death, he was told that her ladyship had persuaded the famous engineer Isambard Brunel to give orders that the train they were travelling in should be slowed to less than twenty miles an hour. Sydney makes use of this celebrated incident in order to draw a comic picture of the complexities involved in organizing a proposed visit by Lady Holland:

Lady Holland has not yet signified her intentions under the sign manual; but a thousand rumours reach me, and my firm belief is, she will come. I have spoken to the sheriff, and mentioned it to the magistrates. They have agreed to address her; and she is to be escorted from the station by the yeomanry. The clergy are rather backward; but I think that, after a little bashfulness, they will wait upon her. Brunel, assisted by the ablest philosophers, is to accompany her upon the railroad; and they have been so good as to say that the steam shall be generated from soft water, with a slight infusion of camomile flowers.

Lady Holland's severe hypochondria was also a fit subject for merriment. In 1835 she was examined for heart disease and found to be perfectly healthy. Sydney joked about her good fortune in a letter to another of his female friends: 'I have seen her since, and never saw anyone so crest-fallen and desponding. She did all she could to get me to help her to some fresh complaint, but I was stubborn.'[18]

Although Sydney's friendship with Lady Holland had severe limitations, it was in many ways very positive. As he got to know her better, he learnt to relax in her company and this shows through in his letters. In December 1807 he was at Bath, visiting his father. His letter to Lady Holland contains an entertaining description of a local controversy:

War, my dear Lady Holland, is natural to women, as well as men – at least with their own sex. A dreadful controversy has broken out in Bath, whether tea is most effectually sweetened by lump or pounded sugar; and the worst passions of the human mind are called into action by the pulverists and the lumpists. I have been pressed by ladies on both sides to speak in favour of their respective theories at the Royal Institution – which I have promised to do. In the meantime my mind is agitated by the nicely-balanced force of opposite arguments . . .

A few years later, in 1811, Sydney was anxiously awaiting the return of Bobus from India.

I am looking out daily for the *Diana*. What good omen can there be in a ship with a chaste name? First he chose the Thomas Grenville, then the Diana. Venus sprang from the sea. Fish increase their kind in prodigious numbers. All sea ports are remarkable for their improprieties. Why go to sea in a ship with a chaste name?

The central reality is that Sydney did genuinely love Lady Holland. The depth of his care and concern for her is evident in a letter he wrote her towards the end of his life. He was in pain himself at the time, but rose from his sickbed, setting himself the task of cheering Lady Holland up.

> It is a bore, I admit, to be past seventy, for you are left for execution, and are daily expecting the death-warrant; but, as you say, it is not anything very capital we quit. We are, at the close of life, only hurried away from stomach-aches, pains in the joints, from sleepless nights and unamusing days, from weakness, ugliness, and nervous tremors; but we shall all meet again in another planet, cured of all our defects. Rogers will be less irritable . . . Jeffrey will speak slower; Bobus will be just as he is; I shall be more respectful to the upper clergy; but I shall have as lively a sense as I now have of all your kindness and affection for me.

Sydney was an ideal guest, his style of dinner-table conversation brilliantly suited to the crush at Holland House. He rarely spoke to his neighbour, preferring to fire remarks across the table. He was also careful not to monopolize the conversation; most of his jokes were told in less than half a minute. Often he would pick up and elaborate upon comments other people had made. There was nothing contrived about Sydney's wit; it was spontaneous, varied and dazzling. Its quality is well caught by Samuel Rogers: 'whenever the conversation is getting dull, he throws in some touch which makes it rebound, and rise again as light as ever.'[19] Sydney's talk can still be profitably used as a model. He did not force himself upon his hearers, he never prepared any *bons mots* in advance, and he avoided complicated anecdotes. Sydney, as Hesketh Pearson points out, compares favourably with other famous conversationalists. His wit is without the assertiveness of Samuel Johnson, the discursiveness of Coleridge, the affectation of Oscar Wilde. It was boyish, natural, free.

Sydney's best remarks are succinct. 'Correspondences are like small-clothes before the invention of suspenders; it is impossible to keep them up.' He could, of course, be mischievous. He once said of the bishop of Exeter, Henry Phillpotts, a bellicose High Churchman, that he was 'so like Judas, that I now firmly believe in the apostolical succession'. Sydney's analogies sometimes border upon conceits. He sums up many human relationships with an image drawn from the world of horticulture: 'Marriage resembles a pair of shears, so joined that they cannot be separated; often moving in opposite directions, yet always punishing anyone who comes between them.'

Sydney often reduced the guests at Holland House to tears. His great delight was to produce a succession of ludicrous images. Anything – a chance remark, a report in a newspaper – would set him off. Luttrell said, one evening, that he had once had a musket put in his hands on board a Post Office packet-boat. Sydney immediately produced with a flourish an imaginary 'penny-post cutlass', waving it in front of the other guests, and put a hypothetical telescope to his eye. 'Damn her, she's the "Delight" laden with tallow.'

The cup of Sydney's vivacious spirits quite often overflowed. His changes of mood were as frequent as those of John Allen, but they were also far more pronounced: uproariously funny at one moment, Sydney could be solemn the next. Tom Moore, the Irish poet, thought this was his 'natural character'.[20] During his lectures on moral philosophy, Sydney had manipulated these inner psychological tensions to his own advantage, enthralling his audience by the suddenness with which he moved from a tone of 'reverence' to one of 'brilliancy of wit'. There was, however, a heavy personal cost. It was dangerous for Sydney to let himself go: melancholy was the immediate consequence, a relation of cause and effect which all manic-depressives will recognize.

It is interesting that it was his friend John Ward, a fellow sufferer from severe oscillations in mood, who picked this up. One evening he went to a dinner with Sydney, Luttrell and other guests. During the meal, Sydney had been in 'prodigious glory'. The next morning, Ward received a 'grave epistle' in which Sydney complained that they had both overstepped the mark the previous evening. Sydney said he was worried that their behaviour might 'lead to an interruption of the good humour' which had always been between them, and he then launched into a homily about his clerical character, to which was added a lecture on the importance of prudence, gravity and discretion. Ward was not taken in: 'When the tide is out he takes a gloomy view of things, reproaches himself for the extravagancies of his conversation, and seeks comfort by laying the blame upon somebody else.' He was not biased against Sydney; indeed he paid him one of the best compliments he ever received, telling him in 1809: 'You have been laughing at me constantly, Sydney, for these last seven years, and yet in all that time, you never said a single thing to me that I wished unsaid.'

Sydney was the greatest master of invective – bitter, mordant, pungent – in the age, and yet he went out of his way not to be satirical when he was eating among friends. The gentleness of his humour is the more remarkable in that a cutting style was fashionable. Rogers's wit had a razor's edge to it, as had Bobus's. Sydney's was thoroughly anachronistic in style, reviving the art of innocent raillery practised in the early eighteenth century. Raillery was admirably described by Sir Richard Steele in an article in *The Spectator* in 1713. 'The agreeable Man makes his Friends enjoy themselves, rather than him, while he is in their Company; to say a thing which perplexes the Heart of him you speak to, or brings Blushes into his Face, is a degree of Murder.' Sydney lived out these maxims. When he was at the inner table his geniality, which was the most striking facet of his personality, shone out. Sydney radiated fun. When he was amused, and he was amused all the time, his whole body literally shook. His laughter was infectious without ever being disagreeable or grating; his laugh, said someone, was 'loud but soft', an apt oxymoron. Sydney laughed in anticipation of his own jokes, he laughed while he was making them, and he joined in the laughter which greeted them. He was also good at sustaining amusement. He would pick, affectionately, upon the peculiarities of his friends, dexterously magnifying their foibles and returning to the attack again and again.

One winter Henry Hallam, the historian, was ill in bed with 'flu. Although he was shy and spoke with a slight stutter, Hallam was extremely argumentative. Sydney asked the dinner guests to imagine Hallam lying in bed, tossing and tumbling in his fever. Long after day has turned to night, Hallam's disturbed reverie is interrupted by a watchman passing by and calling out, 'Twelve o'clock and a starlight night.' This was too much for Hallam; he leapt out of bed and thrust his head out of the window. 'I question that; I question that. Starlight. I see a star, I admit, but I doubt whether that constitutes starlight.' Sydney allowed Hallam to return to his bed, only to get him up several more times, disputing commonplace facts with the watchman on each occasion.[21] There is much in this – the light and bantering tone, the visual quality, the repetition – that accurately expresses the nature of Sydney's dinner-table wit.

Sydney loved to play with words. And what better word-play is there than the pun? One evening his friend Mrs Grote entered a drawing-room, wearing a huge rose-coloured turban. Sydney whispered to his companion: 'Now I know the meaning of the word grotesque.' Sydney was once asked how he would set about silencing

Tom Hill, a garrulous book collector and bon vivant. The task, said Sydney, was impossible: 'I know the way to Highgate but not to muzzle [Muswell] Hill.' One of Sydney's best puns had already been coined while he was living in Edinburgh. Walking one day along the foetid streets of the Old Town, he saw two women hurling insults at one another across an alleyway. Sydney turned to his companion and said: 'Those two women will never agree; they are arguing from different premises.'[22]

Sydney did not set out to be original. He never wrote a book of jokes or claimed to have discovered novel insights: his humour was, quite simply, an expression of himself. He was, nevertheless, very innovative. G. K. Chesterton thought that Sydney was the 'real originator of Nonsense'. There are, indeed, similarities between Sydney and Edward Lear. There is the same displacement of the imagination, the same leap into a world that is bizarre one moment and vaguely frightening the next. The difference is that this displacement was habitual with Lear but only occasional with Sydney. One of the passages in Sydney's works that looks forward to Lear is a description of Botany Bay.

> ... in this remote part of the earth, Nature (having made horses, oxen, ducks, geese, oaks, elms, and all regular and useful productions for the rest of the world,) seems determined to have a bit of play, and to amuse herself as she pleases. Accordingly, she makes cherries with the stone on the outside; and a monstrous animal, as tall as a grenadier, with the head of a rabbit, a tail as big as a bed-post, hopping along at the rate of five hops to a mile, with three or four young kangaroos looking out of its false uterus, to see what is passing.

Edward Lear would have loved the chance to draw this scene. There is nothing sinister in Sydney's portrayal of the kangaroo, but it is possible to see how, with the addition of a touch here and a touch there, the passage could become disconcerting or even a trifle menacing. The macabre comes nearer the surface in Sydney's advice to a hostess, who was having two entomologists to dinner. Asked his suggestions for the menu, Sydney flashed back his reply: 'Flea-pâtés, earth worms on toast, caterpillars crawling in cream'. Then there is Sydney's description of the newly-built Brighton Pavilion: 'as if St Paul's had come down and littered'. There is also the unforgettable sketch of Mr Isaac Hawkins Brown. This Englishman, who lived at the Neapolitan court, had a highly eccentric appearance: 'His dress was a volcano silk with lava buttons.' His behaviour was even more odd. Once, at a ball, he danced 'with such inconceivable alacrity and vigour' that the queen of Naples was thrown into convulsions, having a miscarriage which altered the succession. The scene of Isaac Hawkins Brown dancing frantically in front of the indecorous and pregnant queen, as she prostrates herself with mirth, is also made for Edward Lear's pencil.

Sydney also anticipates Oscar Wilde. Like Wilde, he was the master of the quip whose essence lies in the overturning of expected relations. 'I never read a book before reviewing it: it prejudices a man so'; pure Sydney, although one might guess it to be pure Wilde. There is also a further joke at the expense of Mrs Grote, she of the rose-coloured turban. Sydney uses anticlimax, a technique of humour that Wilde was to take up and develop later on. We are led on and then led on some more, until the jaws of the verbal trap are finally snapped shut. 'Go where you will, do what you please, I have the most perfect confidence in your *indiscretion*.'[23]

Sydney lived in an uninhibited age. Adherence to Christian belief did not stand in the way of a down-to-earth attitude towards sex. The 1799 edition of *Public Characters*, a periodical with a good circulation and run in part by clergy, referred delightedly to a 'certain Scotch methodistical lady' who was so fond of Scripture passages that she had some of them emblazoned on her garments. The spiritual message printed on her garter was: '*set your affections on things above*'.[24] English people of all classes were scurrilous in their use of language. I have in front of me the twenty-third edition of Boyer's *Royal Dictionary*, which came out in 1803. Leafing through its pages, there are many examples of unadorned language: 'a short-arse', 'cock-brained', 'a shitten girl', 'he is the crack-fart of the nation', 'a toss-pot', 'a blow job', 'a piss-a-bed', 'turdy', 'they piss through one quill' (act in concert). None of these words or expressions is described as vulgar, none is given a comic meaning, and none was considered to be obsolete.

Sydney was, in respect to language, a man for his own times. Thomas Carlyle describes him as being 'as coarse as hemp'. Coarse is not quite the right word; it brings to mind the aggressive and ill-natured bawdiness of Restoration comedy. Sydney's tone is different: it is playful and amusing. He had a friend called Miss Alcock: 'her

Latin name would be *Domina omnis Penis'*. A (fortunately anonymous) aristocratic woman was once accidentally branded in a sensitive part of the anatomy by a hot stove. 'All London are talking of the Lady who is mark'd *Thomson & Co. Londini*. Weather cold and Petticoats up, she imprudently back'd upon the Stove and is mark'd in the largest Letters. Astley Cooper attended her and, though he never saw her *face*, is quite sure she is a Lady of the highest quality.'[25]

Sydney also spiced his conversation with indelicate biblical allusions. The countryside bored him; when he was there, he felt 'he was in the position of the personage who, when he entered a village, straightway he found an ass', in sly reference to Christ's triumphal entry into Jerusalem as told in the Gospel according to St Mark.[26] When Rogers gave dinners, he went against the convention which decreed that the diners should be bathed in light; instead, he put candles high up on the walls in order to show off his own discriminating art collection. Rogers asked Sydney whether he liked the unusual arrangement. 'Not at all', he replied. 'Above, there is a blaze of light, and below, nothing but darkness and gnashing of teeth.' This brings to mind a verse from the eighth chapter of St Matthew – 'the children of the kingdom shall be cast out into outer darkness: there shall be weeping and gnashing of teeth'.[27]

Sydney thought up a lot of his own quips but he also used, without acknowledgement, witticisms that had been devised by others. One of his best second-hand jokes was taken from J. G. Lockhart, the biographer of Sir Walter Scott. Asked to sit for his portrait by Edwin Landseer, the well-known painter of animals, Lockhart pretended to be scandalized. 'Is', he wondered, 'thy servant a *Dog* that he should do this thing?'[28] Apart from alluding to Landseer's paintings of animals, this amusing reply also contained an echo of the Old Testament: the same words were used by an official of the king of Aram in answer to the prophet Elisha. Sydney did not intend any malice in his literary theft; he would not at all have minded if Lockhart had done the same to him.

8

APOSTLE OF LIBERTY

'When I hear any man talk of an unalterable law, the only effect it produces upon me is to convince me that he is an unalterable fool.'

SYDNEY SMITH,
Letters of Peter Plymley

William Pitt the Younger died on 23 January 1806. He was forty-seven and had been prime minister for half his life. It was the opportunity for which the Whigs had long been waiting. George III, ageing and often ill, could no longer keep his arch-enemy, Charles James Fox, out of office. The premiership went to Lord Grenville; he was a convenient bridge between the old regime and the new, having served under Pitt as foreign secretary. The Foxites nevertheless dominated; they held six posts in the new Cabinet, including Fox himself as foreign secretary. The administration also contained a few members of the old guard, most notably George Huntingford's favourite pupil Henry Addington, now Lord Sidmouth, as Lord Privy Seal. Broad-bottomed, Grenville's government has become known to history as the 'Ministry of all the Talents'.

There was a further momentous political event later in 1806; the death of Fox on 13 September. Lady Holland, with a touch of typical exhibitionism, announced Fox's demise to waiting relatives and friends by walking into the room with her apron over her head. For her husband, his uncle's demise held out the hope of political success as well as the threat of emotional sadness. A Whig Cabinet without a Fox in it would be a very strange animal indeed. Lord Holland had been made a privy councillor in August and entered the Cabinet in a reshuffle early in October, taking over from Sidmouth as Lord Privy Seal.

Around the same time as Holland's promotion, Sydney received, quite out of the blue, a letter from Thomas Erskine, Lord Chancellor.

(It was Erskine's elder brother Henry who, on Dundas's instructions, had been voted out as Dean of the Faculty of Advocates in Edinburgh in 1796.) The Lord Chancellor's letter was refreshingly friendly:

Hampstead, Oct. 6th, 1806

My Dear Sir,

... I should be guilty of insincerity, and be taking a merit with you which I have no claim to, if I were not to say that I should have given the living to the nominee of Lord and Lady Holland without any personal consideration; at the same time, I can add very truly that I thought myself most fortunate indeed, that the friend they selected was so deserving, and one that I should have been happy to have been useful to on his own, and his brother's account. I shall feel great pleasure in cultivating your kind acquaintance.

I have the honour to be, dear Sir,

Yours faithfully,

ERSKINE[1]

The living in question was Foston-le-Clay, north of York. Samuel Rogers thought that the appointment was Lady Holland's doing; as soon as Erskine had become Lord Chancellor, she had started to pester him on Sydney's behalf. Rogers gives an amusing description of the interview between Erskine and Sydney: 'Don't thank me, Mr Smith. I gave you the living because Lady Holland insisted on my doing so: and if she had desired me to give it to the *devil*, he must have had it.' This is probably apocryphal. The text of Erskine's letter suggests that Lord Holland also lent a hand; 'the nominee of Lord and Lady Holland' is the expression that Erskine uses. Joseph Farington (admittedly an unreliable source because he disliked Sydney) reports a conversation with one of Sydney's clerical rivals, who told the diarist that the Lord Chancellor, in making his decision, had ignored 'many old and most respectable claimants to His favor'. There is subtle underlying force in the word 'old' and also in 'most respectable.' Had Lord Holland not succeeded to his uncle's political inheritance it is unlikely, despite Lady Holland's formidable charms, that Sydney would have become rector of Foston.

Sydney visited his living as soon as he could. While he was in Yorkshire he was invited by the decrepit archbishop of York, William Markham, to dine at his palace at Bishopthorpe. Sydney created an impression, although not quite the impression that was intended. Another guest later wrote down his recollections. Markham, he felt, was puzzled by the new rector of Foston. 'The old Archbishop, I could see, though struck with his extraordinary abilities, did not half like, or understand, how one of the inferior clergy should be so much in possession of his faculties in the presence of his diocesan.' Despite archiepiscopal unease, Sydney got what he wanted out of Markham and was allowed to be non-resident from Foston on the strength of his preachership at the Foundling Hospital. Church services in his new parish would be taken in Sydney's absence by a curate to whom he would pay a modest sum.

While he was in Yorkshire on this first visit, Sydney also called on James Horner, a local farmer who rented 200 acres of land the income from which would now be coming to Sydney as rector of Foston. Sydney put it to him that the rent should be doubled from £250 a year to £500, and Horner assented. Sydney's action was not unreasonable. The figure of £250 a year had been agreed upon when the previous incumbent took over, and in the interim an unprecedently strong boom had transformed the profitability of English agriculture.

Now that Sydney was rector of Foston, he was in clover. Farmer Horner was paying him £500 a year, and his three London preacherships were bringing in £190. The Royal Institution lectures had also been profitable. Sydney was paid £90 for the first set, terms which were raised to £150 for the second, and his fee for the final course must have been at least as much. Then, of course, there was also Catharine's private income of at least £250 a year. No wonder that, within weeks of his appointment to Foston, Sydney moved house, forsaking the lawyers' quarter near Gray's Inn Road in favour of 18 Orchard Street, just to the north of Oxford Street and thus a few yards outside the 'sacred parallelogram'.[2]

The Talents had not been in office a year before they started to get into difficulties. The problem was a familiar one for English governments: what to do about Ireland. Irish politics, never simple, had been greatly complicated by the outbreak of war between England and France in 1793. In May 1798 there had been a rebellion in Ireland; the French, ominously, took advantage of the disturbance, making three landings along Ireland's west coast in the late summer and autumn. These were easily repulsed, but made the English government nervous. In an attempt to obtain greater control over Ireland, the Irish parliament was abolished in August 1800 and Ireland became politically united with England. The rise to power of Napoleon Bonaparte put English politicians into a panic: for the first time since 1066 there was a serious threat of a successful foreign invasion. The flotilla intended for England was partially disbanded in the summer of 1805, only for Napoleon to strengthen his continental stranglehold. Between October 1805 and November 1806 he demolished the armies of the European powers in three battles, at Ulm, Austerlitz and Jena. These military victories coincided with a resurgence of rural disorder in Ireland, raising once again the spectre of a French landing. In December 1806, George Ponsonby, the Irish Lord Chancellor, told London that there was talk of a union of Catholics and Protestants to welcome a French invasion. Faced with this threat, the Talents decided to try to conciliate Irish opinion by relaxing some of the penal laws against Irish Catholics. The government turned to an Irish Act of 1793, which permitted Catholics to serve as officers in the Irish army although not in the Irish navy. It was decided to broaden this legislation to allow Catholics to serve as officers in the Irish navy and also, more importantly, in the English army and navy.

Getting this measure through the English Parliament was acknowledged to be difficult, but first it was necessary to win the support of the king. Unfortunately, George III's anti-Catholic prejudices reached Olympian proportions. Fearing a royal rebuff the Talents resorted to subterfuge, Grenville telling George III that the proposed new measure was 'perfectly conformable in its principle' to the concession which had already been granted under the Irish Act of 1793. George was not taken in. Although he gave his assent to the proposed legislation, he also began plotting the overthrow of the administration. When the Cabinet got wind of what he was up to, it became hopelessly split; Grenville gave his casting vote in favour of dropping the bill, but it was decided to tell the king that the government reserved the right to reintroduce the measure. George's response was extraordinary and probably unconstitutional; on 17 March 1807 he demanded a written pledge from each member of the Cabinet that they would not propose 'in any case, any further concessions to the Catholics'.[3] This put the government in an impossible position and Grenville surrendered the seals of office on 25 March. The duke of Portland now came into power, with Bobus's great friend George Canning as foreign secretary and Spencer Perceval as chancellor of the exchequer.

The overthrow of the Talents was a political *cause célèbre*. Partly because they were angered by George III's demand for written pledges, the Whigs put Catholic emancipation at the top of their political agenda. The fallen administration had to be defended against the charge of chicanery in its dealings with the king while, at the same time, it was imperative to mount a propaganda offensive. The Protestant establishment had to be out-argued and, if possible, ridiculed.

One man, more than any other, rose to the occasion. Invited to preach at the Temple church, Sydney delivered a broadside against religious intolerance. The sermon was published at the end of July. In the preface, Sydney gave a confident defence of his position:

> Charity towards those who dissent from us on religious opinions is always a proper subject for the pulpit. If such discussions militate against the views of any particular party, the fault is not in him who is thus erroneously said to introduce politics into the Church, but in those who have really brought the Church into politics. It does not cease to be our duty to guard men against religious animosities, because it suits the purpose of others to inflame them; nor are we to consider the great question of religious toleration as a theme fit only for the factions of Parliament, because intolerance has lately been made the road to power.

The sting is in the tail. Portland, Canning and Perceval are accused, by implication, of using religious bigotry to further their careers. Sydney took a moral line on the issues of withholding voting rights from Catholics and of debarring them from taking up posts in the armed forces and elsewhere. 'To a genuine Christian', he told the congregation, 'it is always an hateful task to abridge the natural rights of any human being, to repress his industry, to damp his ambition, and to make him a stranger in the land of his birth.' This comes close to claiming Christian sanction for the Whig cause. If Holland House was on the side of the angels, the Tories were in league with the forces of evil – there is 'nothing less Christian' than to wish that 'deprivations of civil rights should remain, as a sort of degrading badge upon those who differ from the established church'.[4] That they should so remain was the earnest desire of nearly all the bishops, nearly all the clergy, and the great majority of those who sat in Anglican pews. Sydney was embarking on a collision course with his own church.

133

Sydney's sermon on toleration was by way of being an *hors d'oeuvre*. A far bolder idea was beginning to form in his mind. But first of all he wanted to take advantage of his good fortune in gaining, while the Talents were in power, financial security through acquisition of the living of Foston. So, in the summer of 1807, Sydney took his three children on their first holiday, hiring a house at Sonning-on-Thames near Reading. Saba, who was five, greatly enjoyed herself; it was, she remembered many years later, the 'first breath of air, free from carpet-shakings, that we had inhaled'. Sydney also relished this brief taste of rural life, writing to Lady Holland that 'Mrs S. is quite delighted with her Country Box – so am I. I have seen a great number of thrushes hopping before the window this Evening, but their conduct was by no means innocent or decorous.'

A near neighbour was Sir William Scott, later created Lord Stowell. Sydney liked his company and dined with him quite often. By drinking Sir William's claret, Sydney showed that he 'tasted no politics in boiled or roast'. Sir William was the elder brother of Lord Eldon, Lord Chancellor during the whole of the first quarter of the nineteenth century except for Thomas Erskine's short tenure. The Scott brothers were both Tories. Sir William liked to tease Sydney, telling him, 'Ah, Mr Smith, you would have been in a different situation, and a far richer man, if you would have belonged to us.'[5] This was something which Sydney knew only too well.

While at Sonning, Sydney decided to enter the thick of the political fray by writing a defence of the policy of the Talents towards Ireland. He realized he was jeopardizing his future career. The Whigs had just left a brief spell in office after a quarter of a century in the political wilderness and there was no knowing when they would be back. Protestant, anti-Whig, feeling was running high in the summer of 1807, but Sydney was not disconcerted. It was characteristic of him that he should, in these difficult circumstances, decide to fight back. Also characteristic was the weapon he preferred to use. Not for him the dry academic debate, the sort of polemic that held appeal for politicians at Westminster. Sydney's audience was the intelligent generality, the mass of literate mankind, addressed in ten short pamphlets, none of them more than ten pages long. Published as *Peter Plymley's Letters*, the pamphlets started to come out in the late summer of 1807 and the next year all ten were printed in a collection which proved astonishingly popular, quickly running through sixteen editions.

Sydney knew that prosecution was possible if the author could be found. Elaborate precautions were taken to cover his tracks; he even sent spoof letters, signed 'P. Plymley', to his publisher, J. Budd of Pall Mall. His authorship was an open secret, but Sydney was fierce in his public denials. It was not until 1839, when he brought out his *Collected Works*, that he lowered his guard. 'I have', he wrote in the preface, 'printed in this Collection the *Letters of Peter Plymley*. The Government of that day took great pains to find out the author; all that they could find was, that they were brought to Mr Budd, the publisher, by the Earl of Lauderdale. Somehow or another, it came to be conjectured that I was that author: I have always denied it; but finding that I deny it in vain, I have thought it might be as well to include the Letters in this Collection: they had an immense circulation at the time, and I think above 20,000 copies were sold.'[6]

The *Letters* are purportedly written by Peter Plymley to his clerical brother Abraham, who has a rural living. This establishes the provenance. Sydney is addressing the typical country parson, holding typically Tory views, and he is suggesting that the ideas of his audience are a little behind the times. The tone is affectionate but robust. 'Dear Abraham', Sydney begins the first letter, 'a worthier and better man than yourself does not exist; but I have always told you, from the time of your boyhood, that you were a bit of a goose.'

Much of the strength of the *Letters* comes from Sydney's capacity to identify with the Abrahams of his day. He does this in a wholly surprising way. Part of *Peter Plymley* reads as though it was written by a dyed-in-the-wool backwoodsman with ultra-Protestant prejudices. Sydney laughs at the Catholic religion and holds it up to ridicule. Catholics believe in the 'nonsense of the real presence'; they are men who pay 'fulsome compliments to the thumbs and offals of departed saints'; their priests wear 'painted jackets'. These are insensitive points, insensitively put. In one passage Sydney expostulates against the unfairness of forcing Catholic soldiers to attend Anglican church services. 'How would my admirable brother, the Rev. Abraham Plymley, like to be marched to a Catholic chapel, to be sprinkled with the sanctified contents of a pump, to hear a number of false quantities in the Latin tongue, and to see a number of persons occupied in making right angles upon the breast and forehead?'

Nowhere else in his writings does Sydney attack the Catholic religion with such bitter scorn, such undisguised contempt. He uses this populist tone because it serves his purpose, because he knows that he will be listened to if he can show that he is 'one of us', an English Protestant among English Protestants. Sydney used exaggerated language but he did not go to the lengths of disguising his true beliefs. He genuinely disliked Catholic ritual and was all for plainness in the expression of religious faith. He did not alter his position as he grew older, complaining in old age that the leaders of the newly emerging Oxford Movement 'made the Christian religion a religion of postures and ceremonies, of circumflexions and genuflexions, of garments and vestures, of ostentation and parade'. Sydney felt that, in matters of faith, one must be rational and reserved. That was the aristocratic attitude, and Sydney kept to it.

What is truly remarkable about *Peter Plymley* is that Sydney manages to combine Protestant populism, where his tone is thoroughly vulgar, with, of all things, advanced secular liberalism. The state should, according to Sydney, view the religious affiliation of its citizens with benign indifference. Sydney passionately believed in a liberal, pluralist society. And he believed in it for the right reason: every man, thought Sydney, had the right to the free expression of his opinions. Sydney was, to the very depths of his being, a libertarian. Not that he argued his case in *Peter Plymley* in terms of abstract principle. This, Sydney knew, would get him nowhere. Cleverly, he made his appeal in favour of religious liberty on the basis of more immediate, and more pressing, considerations. England, Sydney pointed out, was fighting a desperate war of survival against the military genius of Napoleon. In these dire national straits, the support of every patriot, be his religious creed what it might, was urgently needed; the proposal by the Talents to open up the armed forces to Irish Catholics was not a matter of pandering to party preference, it was a solemn and absolute necessity. Any other policy was 'little short of positive insanity'. Sydney reinforces his argument with a burlesque:

Here is a frigate attacked by a corsair of immense strength and size, rigging cut, masts in danger of coming by the board, four foot of water in the hold, men dropping off very fast; in this dreadful situation how do you think the Captain acts (whose name shall be Perceval)? He calls all hands upon deck; talks to them of King, country, glory, sweethearts, gin, French prison, wooden shoes, Old England, and hearts of oak: they give three cheers, rush to their guns, and, after a tremendous conflict, succeed in beating off the enemy. Not a syllable of all this: this is not the manner in which the honourable Commander goes to work: the first thing he does is to secure 20 or 30 of his prime sailors who happen to be Catholics, to clap them in irons, and set over them a guard of as many Protestants; having taken this admirable method of defending himself against his infidel opponents, he goes upon deck, reminds the sailors, in a very bitter harangue, that they are of different religions; exhorts the Episcopal gunner not to trust to the Presbyterian quarter-master; issues positive orders that the Catholics should be fired at upon the first appearance of discontent; rushes through blood and brains, examining his men in the Catechism and 39 Articles, and positively forbids every one to sponge or ram who has not taken the Sacrament according to the Church of England.

England had ceased to be a constitutional monarchy; it was now an 'anemocracy' – a land governed by the wind. Were it to blow from the south, France would be able to capture Ireland and, were this to happen, the cause of English freedom would inevitably be lost. It is, Sydney reminded his readers, but a short step from Dublin to Holyhead. He was scathing about the preparedness of the English for battle:

As for the spirit of the peasantry in making a gallant defence behind hedge-rows, and through plate-racks and hen-coops, highly as I think of their bravery, I do not know any nation in Europe so likely to be struck with the panic as the English; and this from their total unacquaintance with the science of war. Old wheat and beans blazing for twenty miles round; cart mares shot; sows of Lord Somerville's breed running wild over the country; the minister of the parish wounded sorely in his hinder parts; Mrs Plymley in fits; all these scenes of war an Austrian or a Russian has seen three or four times over; but it is now three centuries since an English pig has fallen in a fair battle upon English ground, or a farm-house been rifled, or a clergyman's wife been subjected to any other proposals of love than the connubial endearments of her sleek and orthodox mate.[7]

Sydney argued that specious reasons were advanced for not con-ciliating Ireland by emancipating the Catholics. George III felt bound by his Coronation Oath, by which he had pledged himself to defend the Protestant faith; and he had tried to tie the hands of the Talents by requiring them to agree not to make future concessions. The king's behaviour was absurd: 'When I hear any man talk of an unalterable law, the only effect it produces upon me is to convince me that he is an unalterable fool.' An appeal was made, quite inappropriately in Sydney's view, to fear. 'I thought that the terror of the Pope had been confined to the limits of the nursery, and merely employed as a means to induce young master to enter into his small-clothes with greater speed.' As most of the countries of Europe were Catholic, it was ridiculous to claim that Catholics were incapable of fulfilling the duties of civil life. Protestants should accept that the main barriers to understanding were put up by themselves. The point was rammed home with a culinary simile. 'No eel in the well-sanded fist of a cook-maid, upon the eve of being skinned, ever twisted and writhed as an orthodox parson does when he is compelled by the grip of reason to admit any thing in favour of a Dissenter.'

Sydney also confronted the argument that the time when he was writing was not a suitable one for change, that, in his own words, a 'period of universal war is not the proper time for dangerous innovations in the constitution'. To argue in this way was 'as much as to say, that the worst time for making friends is the period when you have made many enemies; that it is the greatest of all errors to stop when you are breathless, and to lie down when you are fatigued.' Sydney anticipates the doctrine of Unripe Time, put forward a century later by F. M. Cornford in his famous satirical pamphlet *Microcosmographia Academica*. 'The Principle of Unripe Time is that people should not do at the present moment what they think right at that moment, because the moment at which they think it right has not yet arrived.' Sydney carefully assembled the facts. Catholics were by far the most numerous religious group in Ireland, in the countryside overwhelmingly so; they had just grievances; they would carry on campaigning until their demands were met; and all attempts to frustrate them would, ultimately, be of no avail. The choice, Sydney argued, was not between conciliation and non-conciliation; it was between some concessions now and many more concessions later on. 'The Catholics will hang over you; they will watch for the moment; and compel you hereafter to give them ten times as much, against your will, as they would now be contented with, if it was voluntarily surrendered.'[8]

Sydney showed much less savoir-faire when dealing with domestic

Irish affairs. An initial mistake was greatly to underestimate the determination of Ulstermen. The English government, Sydney felt, had nothing to fear from a Protestant backlash in Ireland. 'The disaffection of the Orangemen will be the Irish rainbow; when I see it, I shall be sure that the storm is over.' It would be hard to be more erroneous than that! He was equally jejune about Irish Catholics. 'If', he wrote, 'they were brought into the daylight of the world, to the high situations of the army, the navy, and the bar, numbers of them would come over to the Established Church, and do as other people do.' Sydney also thought that the opposition of the Catholic priesthood to English rule sprang solely from their poverty. 'Can any thing be more distressing than to see a venerable man pouring forth sublime truths in tattered breeches, and depending for his food upon the little offal he gets from his parishioners?' He wanted them to be paid by the state (a plan mooted by Pitt prior to the Act of Union) and to be paid well.[9] Once they were well off, they would give up political agitation.

Why did Sydney make such massive miscalculations about Irish affairs? Partly it was because he relied too heavily upon his understanding of human nature. Sydney was a social realist who believed in the upwardly mobile pretensions of the dispossessed. His attitudes appear cynical, but are understandable enough in someone who had to learn to live in the maze of Georgian ecclesiastical politics. There is, secondly, what might be termed the Holland House effect. Sydney mixed constantly with aristocratic Whigs and had come to share their political views. His errors are those of Lord Grenville and Lord Holland. Sydney's condescension towards the Irish is also illustrative of a pattern of misapprehension found among English liberals of the twentieth century as much as the eighteenth. The Romantic irrationality of the Celtic temperament was something that Sydney simply could not comprehend. Like other English liberals, both before and since, he kept on believing, despite a mountain of contrary evidence, that Irish political problems were amenable to simple solutions.

Sydney's case in *Peter Plymley* was also damaged by indulgence in personal abuse. He had two main targets, Canning and Perceval. Canning was accused of being a political dilettante; he was, said Sydney woundingly, a 'pert London joker' of whom 'no other good is known than that he makes pretty Latin verses'. Sydney also complained that the foreign secretary was overweeningly vain. His small party of supporters in Parliament was, Sydney thought, beneath contempt. 'Mr Canning', he wrote in a waspish footnote, 'has his parasites; and if you take a large buzzing blue-bottle fly, and look at it in a microscope, you may see 20 or 30 little ugly insects crawling about it, which doubtless think their fly to be the bluest, grandest, merriest, most important animal in the universe, and are convinced the world would be at an end if it ceased to buzz.' This attack on Canning is mystifying; he was, after all, one of Bobus's closest friends. Sydney's motive may have been to please Lady Holland. Canning was one of her special *bêtes noires*; she disliked his political trimming, of which his acceptance of office under Portland was a prime example. 'My stomach', she said, 'will bear hot water, my stomach will bear cold water, but my stomach absolutely rejects lukewarm water, so Mr Canning makes me sick.'

Canning was treated gently compared with Perceval. The chancellor of the exchequer, it has to be said, made himself fair game. He had recently tried to lay his hands on the revenues of the Duchy of Lancaster for life, a financial sleight of hand that had been foiled by the House of Commons; and it was also not long since he had obtained the sinecure post of Registrar of the Court of Admiralty, a post previously held by his brother, Lord Arden. This slice of luck lifted Perceval's income by £21,000 a year. Sydney was well within his rights in not allowing these facts to go unnoticed. He was also justified in attacking government policy. In an effort to deploy economic sanctions against Napoleon, Perceval had put into force the notorious Orders in Council. These prohibited, *inter alia*, the export of certain key products to every country in Europe that was under Napoleon's control. Included in the prohibited list was rhubarb, used as a laxative. Perceval, announced Sydney, was

> ... the statesman who would bring the French to reason by keeping them without rhubarb, and exhibit to mankind the awful spectacle of a nation deprived of neutral salts. This is not the dream of a wild apothecary indulging in his own opium; this is not the distempered fancy of a pounder of drugs, delirious from smallness of profits; but it is the sober, deliberate, and systematic scheme of a man to whom the public safety is intrusted, and whose appointment is considered by many as a masterpiece of political sagacity. What a sublime thought, that no purge can now be taken between the Weser and the Garonne; that the bustling pestle is still, the canorous mortar mute, and the bowels of mankind locked up for fourteen degrees of latitude!

Where Sydney erred was in attacking Perceval's reputation as a zealous Christian and a devoted family man. The paragraph in *Peter Plymley* is pure vitriol:

I cannot describe the horror and disgust which I felt at hearing Mr Perceval call upon the then ministry for measures of vigour in Ireland. If I lived at Hampstead upon stewed meats and claret; if I walked to church every Sunday before eleven young gentlemen of my own begetting, with their faces washed, and their hair pleasingly combed; if the Almighty had blessed me with every earthly comfort – how awfully would I pause before I sent forth the flame and the sword over the cabins of the poor, brave, generous, open-hearted peasants of Ireland!

Perceval and Sydney had never had any personal dealings, nor had Perceval ever held office in Ireland. The only thing that can be said in Sydney's defence is that he did, much later on, express his deep regret that he had written this passage.

Publication of *Peter Plymley* changed Sydney's life. No longer only a clergyman, he was now also a political pamphleteer. Writing *Peter Plymley* gave Sydney a new self-image; he was, he thought, a man who would always speak his mind and was therefore deserving, in due course, of his reward. Writing to Lady Holland, he was open and frank, 'You may', he told her, 'choose to make me a Bishop . . . If you do make me a Bishop I think I shall never do you discredit; for I believe that it is out of the power of lawn and velvet, and the crisp hair of dead men fashioned into a wig, to make me a dishonest man.'

The seed sown by Sydney did not fall upon stony ground. Lord and Lady Holland did everything to encourage Sydney to believe that, once the Whigs were back in power, they would do their utmost to ensure that he was put on the Bench. Already, indeed, Lord Holland was doing what he could. In the autumn of 1809 he visited Lord Grenville, prime minister in the Talents, at Dropmore. The conversation turned to *Peter Plymley*. Grenville was 'warm and enthusiastic' and Lord Holland, seeing his chance, took it. 'I did not', he told Sydney, 'fail to remind him that the only author to whom we both thought he could be compared in English, lost a bishopric for his wittiest performance; and I hoped that if we could discover the author, and had ever a bishopric in our gift, we should prove that Whigs were both more grateful and more liberal than Tories.'

Sydney was pleased to be compared with Swift; he was even more pleased that Lord Holland had as good as promised him his much-coveted bishopric. Another part of Lord Holland's letter did, however, cause Sydney unease. Lord Grenville was currently engaged in a contest with Lord Eldon for the chancellorship of Oxford University. Holland asked Sydney to canvass on Grenville's behalf. Sydney complied but with reluctance. He feared that the chancellorship would throw Grenville into the company of Oxford Tories and reactionary churchmen, stunting the growth of his liberal opinions. Grenville had served under Pitt; there was a danger, thought Sydney, that he might renege on his current political allegiance. Showing marvellous lack of tact, Sydney gave graphic expression to his doubts about the advisability of the canvass at a gathering at Holland House. 'The Whig canvas for Lord Grenville is like the trustees of the Magdalen' (an asylum for 'penitent women') 'applying to place a reclaimed prostitute at a bawdy house.' Whether this remark reached the ears of Lord Grenville is not recorded. It remains only to add that Grenville squeaked home, beating Eldon by 406 votes to 393.[10]

After the move to London in August 1803, Sydney had more or less given up his connection with the *Edinburgh Review*. Editorial duties were left in Jeffrey's hands. Sydney did help out for a while, scouring London bookshops in company with Horner on the look-out for foreign titles that Jeffrey might have missed, but enthusiasm in the role of book-spy did not last long. Sydney assisted little and wrote less: he submitted one article for the issue of October 1803 and two for that of January 1804, but there is then a break of over two and a half years. Even as a reader Sydney was not much use. 'I have just blinked at the Review', he writes guiltily to Jeffrey, discussing the issue for October 1804. He knew that he should take more interest and that he should contribute. With the sole exception of Brougham, Sydney had written more articles than anyone else in the first four issues; the money would be useful; and he was a man who, despite a tendency towards idleness, never baulked at the prospect of hard work.

Sydney was worried that the *Review* might take a wrong turning and that his association with it might damage his clerical career. These concerns surface in a letter to Jeffrey, written in October 1805:

I hear with great sorrow from Elmsley [a clerical contributor,

'I am of the family of Falstaff.'

Francis Jeffrey, editor of the *Edinburgh Review*. Jeffrey was 'all activity'.

Henry Brougham, Lord Chancellor. Brougham looked shifty and *was* shifty.

Francis Horner, economist: 'the knight of the shaggy eyebrows'.

Samuel Rogers, poet.
'Damsel-loving Sam.'

John Allen, doctor,
constitutional theorist
and *Edinburgh Reviewer*.
The Pierre Bezuhov of
his generation.

Henry Fox, the 3rd Baron Holland. 'He always comes down to breakfast like a man on whom some sudden good fortune has fallen.'

Lady Holland, Lord Holland and house-keeper. Lady Holland was a 'beautiful structure of flesh and blood'.

Holland House, the great Jacobean mansion belonging to the Fox family.

Foston Parish Church. 'As a church service was
about to begin, the gaggle of ducks which lived by
the churchyard gate waddled up the path leading
to the church door.'

Foston Rectory, built by Sydney himself. 'A facsimile of its master's mind.'

Foston.

Feby 16. 1820.

CASTLE HOWARD
J14 59

Dear Lady Georgiana

You will scarcely believe it that I have not written to Miss Berry yet. that is I have not sent my Letter for I have written it ...

Sydney's famous letter of
consolation written to
Georgiana Lady Morpeth
in February 1820.

and drink
... — 2ᵈ ...
... small.
... low
... sation of
... books.
... not faster
... be as busy
... as you can
... like you —
... who amuse
...
... fully be
... dignified
... effects
... you —
... of other
... from
... the best —

12 avoid poetry — dramatic representations
(except Comedy) Music — serious novels
melancholy sentimental people — and
every thing likely to excite feeling or
emotion — not ending in active benevolence
13 — do good. endeavour to please every
body of every degree   14. be as much as
you can in the open air without fatigue
15. make the room where you commonly
sit gay & pleasant —   16 Struggle by
little and little against idleness —
17 — dont be too severe upon yourself or
underrate yourself — but do yourself
Justice —   18. keep good blazing fires
19 — be firm and constant in the exercise
of rational religion — 20. believe me dear
Lady Georgiana very truly Yrs
Sydney Smith

Pen and ink sketch of Combe Florey by Sydney's elder daughter, Saba.
'Our little paradise.'

Bishop Lydeard House, the last resting place of the miser Robert Smith.

later Camden Professor of Ancient History at Oxford] that a very antichristian article has crept into the last no. of the E.R., inaccurate in point of history, and dull in execution. I need no other proof that the Review was left in other hands than yrs, because you must be thoroughly aware that the rumor of infidelity decides not only the reputation but the existence of the Review. I am extremely sorry too on my own account because those who wish it to have been written by me, will say it was so.

'Infidelity', to use Sydney's own terminology, touched the rawest of his nerves. Remember his revealing comment that he would 'a thousand times prefer that his child should die in the bloom of youth, rather than it should live to disbelieve'. In the current instance, Sydney was panicking needlessly. There was only one mildly dubious sentence in the whole of the issue of the *Edinburgh Review* for October 1805; a reviewer stated, jocularly, that 'Hume and Voltaire are carefully pointed out as two wicked infidels, who did not believe in the Holy Scriptures.'

Sydney nevertheless had just cause for concern. Most of the leading Edinburgh reviewers were sceptics. John Allen, 'Lady Holland's Atheist', was open about his disbelief but others, aware of the possibly adverse social consequences, tried to be discreet. Tongues still wagged. Brougham found it hard to conceal the fact that he was a thoroughly secular character, who had little time for religious practice. Jeffrey's lack of commitment to Christian belief was well known in Edinburgh society. Horner revealed the need for a cover up in a letter to Jeffrey. Horner had submitted a piece on a religious topic and sent off the following covering note. 'What I am most anxious about, is, that I have kept myself in the safe and honest medium upon these ticklish subjects. I should be sorry to have betrayed any of the scepticism, which is my real sentiment.' Sydney would have been less concerned if there had not been gossip about himself. J. G. Lockhart, the Tory biographer of Sir Walter Scott from whom Sydney 'borrowed' the biblical quip about sitting, dog-like, for his portrait by Landseer, expressed a view which attracted a lot of support when he wrote: 'I fancy the whole set [of Edinburgh Reviewers] were really most thorough infidels and S. [Sydney] Smith at the top of them in that respect as in all others.' This, of course, was nonsense, but there was nothing Sydney could do to quell such tittle-tattle. What especially worried him was that someone with less judgement than Jeffrey or Horner – Brougham is the obvious candidate – would be guilty of a massive indiscretion. Hence his distancing of himself from the *Review* and hence, also, his failure to write for it.

Once Sydney felt secure in his career, he took up his pen again. The letter from Thomas Erskine, telling Sydney that he was now rector of Foston (tenure, of course, was for life) was dated 6 October 1806; the same month an article by Sydney was published in the *Edinburgh Review*. His contributions to the early issues had lacked coherence; it had been a matter of choosing a book here, and a book there, and writing about it. Now that he was a regular contributor once again, he adopted his earlier policy for a year or so and then changed his tactics, starting to concentrate his literary fire-power. Sydney's target was the Evangelicals, dubbed the 'patent Christians of Clapham' in slighting reference to the domicile of their leader, William Wilberforce. Sydney's first anti-Evangelical article appeared in January 1808; three more were to follow during the course of the next two and a half years.

Sydney knew what he was doing. Attacks upon Evangelicals, he told Jeffrey, 'are very popular with steady men of very moderate understandings' – that is, Tories – 'the description of men among whom the bitterest enemies of the E.R. are to be found'. But attempting to broaden the appeal of the *Review* was not Sydney's sole motive. He wrote against Wilberforce because he enjoyed doing so. Sydney hated Evangelicals. One of the few men in power who was a member of the sect was Spencer Perceval; hence Sydney's attack upon him in *Peter Plymley*. Sydney's antipathy towards Evangelicals was fuelled by resentment: he thought that the bishop of London, Beilby Porteus, an Evangelical sympathizer, had been behind Dr Gerrard Andrewes's refusal to allow him to rent the York Street Chapel. That was not the first time Sydney felt that Porteus had treated him unfairly; he had applied for a position within the bishop's patronage in the spring of 1804, only to be turned down.[11]

In these articles against the Evangelicals, Sydney set out to wound and succeeded. He was not scrupulous and he was not fair. The Evangelical movement was not unified: Arminians disputed with Calvinists, and Wilberforce and his supporters stressed their loyalty to the Church of England, whereas the Methodists, following the death of John Wesley, had split away. Sydney put on a patch, making a blind eye. 'We shall', he announced near the start of his first article, 'use the general term Methodism, to designate these three classes of fanatics' (Arminian and Calvinistic Methodists, and the Evangelical clergy of the Church of England) 'not troubling ourselves to point out the finer shades and nicer discriminations of lunacy, but treating them all as in one general conspiracy against common sense, and rational orthodox Christianity'.[12]

Sydney's pieces may have been bad theology but they were good journalism. He displayed his inventiveness to the full, employing a satirical technique that he had first used in the attack on Joseph Ritson. What Sydney did was to quote, very selectively, from two leading Evangelical periodicals, the *Evangelical Magazine* and the *Methodist Magazine*, in order to condemn his opponents out of their own mouths. Sometimes Sydney's contempt is deserved. Few can object to his derision at the expense of 'E.T.', a female correspondent of the *Evangelical Magazine*, who wrote to inform fellow readers that it was planned to sail a 'religious' packet, exclusively for the use of Evangelicals, weekly between London and Margate: 'No profane conversation is to be allowed.' This, however, is not a representative example of Sydney's quotations. It is not sanctimoniousness that is the main target of his humour, but the honest expression of fervently held religious faith. Evangelical exuberance was what he could not stand. There are numerous passages which Sydney quotes derisively. This one, taken from the *Methodist Magazine*, is headed 'Mr Roberts's feelings in the month of May, 1793:

> But, all this time, my soul was stayed upon God: my desires increased, and my mind was kept in a sweet praying frame, a going out of myself, as it were, and taking shelter in Him. Every breath I drew, ended in prayer. I felt myself helpless as an infant, dependent upon God for all things. I was in a constant daily expectation of receiving all I wanted; and, on Friday, May 31st, under Mr Rutherford's sermon, though entirely independent of it (for I could not give any account of what he had been preaching about), I was given to feel that God was waiting to be very gracious to me; the spirit of prayer and supplication was given me, and such an assurance that I was accepted in the Beloved, as I cannot describe, but which I shall never forget.

There is nothing in this that is excessive and nothing, certainly, that is worthy of ridicule.

Sydney also attacked missions to India. Protestant missionaries had been going to the sub-continent since the early eighteenth century, but it was only under the auspices of the Church Missionary Society, founded in 1801, that activity was regularized. Sydney argued that Evangelicalism was fraudulent. 'It is not Christianity which is introduced there, but the debased mummery and nonsense of Methodists, which has little more to do with the Christian religion than it has to do with the religion of China', by any reckoning an outrageous statement. Sydney claimed that the missionaries were a political menace: 'They are quite insane and ungovernable; they would deliberately, piously, and conscientiously expose our whole Eastern empire to destruction, for the sake of converting half a dozen Brahmins, who, after stuffing themselves with rum and rice, and borrowing money from the missionaries, would run away and cover the gospel and its professors with every species of impious ridicule and abuse.' He had no right to speak in this way of Hindu converts to Christianity or of men who risked their lives in the service of their Lord.

He is on much firmer ground in his satire at the expense of the English Society for the Suppression of Vice, formed in 1802 and increasingly dominated by Evangelicals. The society was active in the prosecution of irreligious literature, and was keen on Sabbath observance. Sydney was rightly sceptical of the benefits of compulsory religion. 'You may', he wrote, 'drag men into church by main force, and prosecute them for buying a pot of beer – and cut them off from the enjoyment of a leg of mutton; and you may do all this, till you make the common people hate Sunday, and the clergy, and religion, and every thing that relates to these subjects.' Sydney realized that the Vice Society had a massive social bias; it was, in his words, 'a Society for suppressing the vices of persons whose income does not exceed £500 *per annum*'.[13] Bear-baiting was prosecuted but not fox-hunting. Sydney, more than most of his contemporaries, understood the direction of Evangelical policy. Wilberforce, anxious to build up the strength of the party within the Church of England, was careful not to offend the aristocracy. He deserved Sydney's jibe, that he had 'all the rigour of the ancient Puritans – without a particle of their honesty or their courage'. Sydney was especially devastating in his exposé of one of the Vice Society's publications, which went out under the title of *Prevention of Cruelty to Animals*. In a justly famous passage, he gave five examples of such cruelty:

– Running an iron hook in the intestines of an animal; presenting this first animal to another as his food; and then pulling
this second creature up, and suspending him by the barb in his
stomach.

Riding a horse till he drops, in order to see an innocent
animal torn to pieces by dogs.

Keeping a poor animal upright for many weeks, to communicate a peculiar hardness to his flesh.

Making deep incisions into the flesh of another animal while
living, in order to make the muscles more firm.

Immersing another animal, while living, in hot water.

Now we do fairly admit, that such abominable cruelties as
these are worthy the interference of the law: and that the Society should have punished them, cannot be matter of surprise to
any feeling mind. But stop, gentle reader! these cruelties are the
cruelties of the Suppressing Committee, not of the poor. You
must not think of punishing these. The first of these cruelties
passes under the pretty name of *angling*; and therefore there
can be no harm in it – the more particularly as the President
himself has one of the best preserved trout streams in England.
The next is *hunting*; and as many of the Vice-Presidents and of
the Committee hunt, it is not possible there can be any cruelty
in hunting. The next is, a process for making *brawn* – a dish
never tasted by the poor, and therefore not to be disturbed by
indictment. The fourth is the mode of *crimping* cod; and the
fifth, of boiling lobsters; all high-life cruelties, with which a
justice of the peace has no business to meddle.[14]

This passage would have pleased Sydney's Scottish mentor, Thomas
Reid: Sydney was using humour to lay bare hypocrisy in high
places.

There are several possible explanations for Sydney's vitriolic
attitude towards Wilberforce and his supporters. Sydney had been
educated in a strongly anti-Evangelical culture; the prevailing view
among Wykehamists was that Evangelicals were bigoted prigs.[15]
There were, in addition, social influences upon Sydney: Lord Holland heartily disliked Evangelicals, and the same was true of Bobus.
It is also quite possible that Sydney had fallen a victim, in his own
ecclesiastical career, to Evangelical prejudice. None of this excuses
either the tone or the content of these four articles. They are the

only occasions, throughout his long connection with the *Edinburgh Review*, that Sydney wrote to please his political opponents. It would have been better for his reputation if the temptation to ridicule had, just this once, been resisted.

9

THE PRINT IN THE SAND

'It is very pleasant in these deserts to see the handwriting of an old friend; it is like the print in the sand seen by Robinson Crusoe.'

SYDNEY SMITH TO JOHN ALLEN, March 1814

By the autumn of 1807, Sydney had been in London four years. Now thirty-six, he was an established metropolitan figure: his lectures on moral philosophy had generally been well received, his three preacherships gave him weekly access to the public, and the *Letters of Peter Plymley*, now coming off the press, were a sensational success. He had been rector of Foston for a year, and this gave him security in his career. However, just as he was becoming settled, continuance of his literary life in London came under threat. William Markham, archbishop of York, died in November at the age of eighty-nine. He was succeeded in the New Year by Edward Vernon-Harcourt who, although he had already been bishop of Carlisle for sixteen years, was no more than fifty and was fit and vigorous.

Within a matter of weeks the new archbishop called Sydney for interview, asking him to explain why he was not carrying out his clerical duties at Foston. This seems a quite unsurprising thing to do: Sydney had a good living in Yorkshire, he was neglecting his parishioners, and it was the archbishop's duty to remedy the situation. In fact, Sydney was being singled out. The diocese of York was in a mess and it remained in a mess. When Vernon-Harcourt took over, only four parishes in every ten had incumbents who lived and worked there; the rest were either looked after by curates or were served by incumbents living nearby and riding over on Sundays to take services. Twenty years later there was no improvement at all. Most clergy would have grumbled, but Sydney was stoic and did not complain. He probably, however, appreciated the irony in the situation; Vernon-

149

Harcourt was one of the very few liberal bishops and got on with Sydney at a personal level very well. The archbishop acted as he did because he felt compelled to do so. The rector of Foston was not only Sydney Smith, he was also Peter Plymley.

Harcourt was lenient up to a point, Sydney reporting to his father early in February that the archbishop had given him leave of absence for a further two years: 'He has not made up his mind whether he shall consider my case as a permanent excuse for absence.'[1] By June 1808 everything seemed settled, Sydney writing to Lady Holland that he had been ordered to reside. 'I have no doubt from what you say that the Archbp acted conscientiously. I will do human nature the justice to say that we are all prone to make other people do their duty.' This was the nearest that Sydney, reticent about his deepest emotions, came to expressing anger over his imminent rustication. Everything was decided, or was it? By early October Vernon-Harcourt was having second thoughts, his vacillation fully deserving Sydney's laconic remark, 'I have heard nothing yet of the doubts and scruples of the Archbishop of York, and hope they may be dying away.'

There were two ways in which Sydney could escape from his predicament. He could exchange Foston for a living nearer London (no easy task), or he could find a second benefice. In the leisured days of Georgian England the best explanation that a clergymen could give his bishop for failure to carry out his clerical duties was to say that he was carrying them out at another living which he held somewhere else. Sydney had been trying to exchange Foston since the summer of 1807 and now redoubled his efforts. He also tried to obtain a second living but did not get very far. There was a hare-brained scheme involving William Otter, who knew Lord and Lady Holland and later became a bishop. It was a complex private deal, the sort of thing that the Georgian clergy were much keener on than they ought to have been. Otter would acquire the living of Harefield, a few miles south of Rickmansworth in Hertfordshire, and then assign it over to Sydney, with Sydney agreeing to quit whenever Otter called upon him to do so. The plan came to nothing.

There was an outside chance that Sydney might get a second Chancery living. In June 1808, Lord Holland considered making an approach to Lord Eldon, but Sydney persuaded him against it. It was a unique intervention, the only occasion on which Sydney restrained his main patron from making an effort on his behalf. Although Sydney was on friendly terms with the Lord Chancellor's brother, Sir William

Scott, his sensitive political antennae told him, quite correctly, that the timing of Lord Holland's suggestion was hopelessly inopportune. To beg in this way was, Sydney pointed out to Lord Holland, 'not a pleasant thing to do at any time, much less so of course when the request is made to a man of opposite politics for a person who has taken as decided a part as I have done – and who am the supposed author of a publication in which the Chancellor himself is so frequently laughed at.' Sydney knew that he stood very little chance of further promotion by the Crown so long as the Tories were in power.

In the autumn of 1808 the log-jam was broken. Whether Vernon-Harcourt took the initiative, or Sydney anticipated the inevitable, is not clear. Suffice to say that Sydney made firm plans to leave London by next Lady Day, 25 March. Moving out of his house in Orchard Street caused a further delay and he was not ready to go until June 1809. The journey to York, a distance of over two hundred miles, was difficult and expensive. The Smiths purchased a small phaeton, drawn by a single horse, and it was in this that they travelled north with Saba, Douglas and Emily, the baggage being moved by wagon separately.

Once they arrived, Catharine was in despair. She describes her state of mind in her usual direct and slightly exaggerated way: 'Never shall I forget the heart-sinking pain I felt on arriving in a hot July evening [actually, it was June] at a dirty inn in York! The streets narrow, close, and dusty, no appearance of inhabitants, but a few tired artisans returning from their day's toil, and with the feeling that there was not one human Being within 200 miles who cared whether or not I lived to see the next day's Sun!!'[2]

If she was displeased with York, she can scarcely have liked Foston. Sydney's parish was twelve miles north east of the city and seven miles south-west of Malton. There is an unflattering description of it in the *Yorkshire Weekly Post* of 1906: 'a dreary-looking village, far off the beaten track, with a few straggling cottages and shops, a public-house and a school, and a broad expanse all round of typical wold-country farm land.' If it was ugly and inaccessible then, it was much more so in 1809. The nearest road was three or four miles away, and the track leading to the parish was no better than a series of deep ruts cut in the stiff local clay. The desolation of Foston was succinctly summed up by Sydney; the place, he said, was 'so far out of the way, that it was actually twelve miles from a lemon'. Just 70 people lived in Foston itself although there was a larger population of 150 or so at Thornton, a hamlet which was also within the parish.

Since 1588, when Phatuel Otbie took over, there had been only eight rectors, throughout the eighteenth century no more than three: Walter Walsh (1701), Charles Cowper (1732) and John Preston (1774). None of the three had ever resided, and Thomas and Henry Fysh who preceded them may have been absentees also. The church was in a state of cheerful dilapidation. A small barn-like building, it had a square wooden belfry which was crooked and painted white, giving it the appearance of a dovecot. Inside there were just twelve pews, all of them high-backed. Above each pew was a row of pegs on which the parishioners could put their hats. The pulpit, which was opposite the church door, was a two-decker with a heavy sounding-board. Galleries ran along the west and north walls. That to the west was so low that its floor could be touched by the congregation below, and the steps leading up to it were unsafe. In the gallery itself were several rows of stepped benches, the topmost so close to the ceiling that there was scarcely room to stand up. The cross-beams in the roof of the church had more pegs for hats. Eccentricity was not confined to the church building. Sometimes, just as a church service was about to begin, the gaggle of ducks which lived by the churchyard gate waddled up the path leading to the church door. Restraining their further progress was one of the duties of the parish clerk.[3]

Backing on to the churchyard was the parsonage. Probably repeating what she had been told by her father, Saba states in her *Memoir* that it was virtually unfit for human habitation, describing it as a single 'brick-floored kitchen, with a room above it, which was in so dangerous a condition that the farmer, who had occupied it hitherto, declined living in it'. The refugee from this 'dangerous' habitation was James Horner, the man who rented 200 acres of Sydney's glebe. He may well have moved elsewhere but he did not leave a 'brick-floored kitchen, with a room above it'. A document drawn up in 1777 tells a different story. The parsonage at Foston was a substantial building, although it lacked the elegance which Sydney, along with the rest of the Georgian clergy, demanded. Nineteen yards long and twelve yards wide, it had a slate roof with some thatch. There were two kitchens, not one. The parlour, which was wooden-floored, was seven yards by five. There was also a cellar, a dairy-cum-pantry, and five other rooms. Phatuel Otbie probably thought it excellent. But the clergy had long since ceased to think of themselves as being on the same level as the farming community. Sydney shared the social expectations of his age and of his class.[4]

Farmer Horner did not occupy all the glebe at Foston; there were 110 acres which were not let out. Looking after these was a nightmare. There were no farm-buildings, there was no equipment and the fencing was hopelessly inadequate. Until such time as he could afford to farm this land properly, Sydney had no option but to leave it untended and uncared for.

Within a week of arriving at York, Sydney signed a lease on a house at Heslington, twelve miles from Foston. The distance from his parish meant that Archbishop Vernon-Harcourt was still unsatisfied. Sydney drove over to Foston on Sundays to take services, travelling in the little phaeton he had purchased for the journey from London, but the archbishop wanted him to do more. In other respects the house at Heslington, which still stands today, suited Sydney well. Its main unusual feature is that it has three-sided bay windows on all three floors. Sydney may have been responsible for this architectural addition: he liked altering the houses he lived in, and he was especially fond of a lot of light because he found that being in a sunny room was an antidote to his periodic fits of ennui. Sydney was also pleased by the twelve-acre farm. Heslington was spacious enough to accommodate Lady Holland, who was notoriously hard to satisfy, without undue difficulty. Sydney would be gratified to know that his former home is now used as the Catholic chaplaincy for the university of York. He would like it rather less that his bedroom has been turned into a confessional.

'With Yorkshiremen I have made no acquaintance nor have I had any opportunity to do so'. Sydney is writing to Lady Holland on 20 August 1809, six or seven weeks after moving in. It did not take him long to realize that he had little in common with most of his neighbours among the gentry and clergy. There was, from the start, a clash of temperaments. Sydney was not a snob; on the other hand, he made no effort to conceal the fact that he found most of the gentry and clergy around Foston and Heslington unspeakably boring. He always felt that his French *joie de vivre* did not sit well with English phlegm and reserve:

There is nothing which an Englishman enjoys more than the pleasure of sulkiness – of not being forced to hear a word from anybody which may occasion to him the necessity of replying. It is not so much that Mr Bull disdains to talk, as that Mr Bull has nothing to say. His forefathers have been out of spirits for six or seven hundred years, and seeing nothing but fog and vapour, he is out of spirits too; and when there is no selling or buying, or no business to settle, he prefers being alone and looking at the fire. If any gentleman were in distress, he would willingly lend a helping hand; but he thinks it no part of neighbourhood to talk to a person because he happens to be near him. In short, with many excellent qualities, it must be acknowledged that the English are the most disagreeable of all the nations of Europe – more surly and morose, with less disposition to please, to exert themselves for the good of society, to make small sacrifices, and to put themselves out of their way. They are content with Magna Charta and Trial by Jury; and think they are not bound to excel the rest of the world in small behaviour, if they are superior to them in great institutions.

This passage describes, with remarkable accuracy, what Sydney thought of his Yorkshire neighbours.

There was also social tension. Sydney's clerical brethren shot and rode to hounds: Sydney himself rode very badly and could not shoot at all: 'When I take a gun in my hand, I am sure the safest place for a pheasant is just opposite the muzzle.' There was an ominous dimension to the conflict in life-styles: Sydney had moral objections to the sporting proclivities of local rectors and vicars. 'If anything ever endangers the Church, it will be the strong propensity to shooting for which the clergy are remarkable. Ten thousand good shots dispersed over the country do more harm to the cause of religion than the arguments of Voltaire and Rousseau.' Sydney argued in this way because he had a strong social conscience. Harsh Game Laws, which restricted shooting rights to men of property, meant that it was impossible to be a hunting and shooting parson without antagonizing the local labouring community.

Sydney had another objection to traditional field sports, but this was much less morally sound. When it suited his purpose, he was able to project the puritanical side of his personality, complaining about activities that threatened to undermine his dignity as a clergyman. This, however, was not a consistent point of view; whatever he might say in public, his private opinions were more tolerant. He played out his role as self-appointed guardian of standards of clerical decorum at a gathering of local clergy held at Malton in August. Sydney had been asked to preach. What he had to say would not have been tactful at any time, but for a clergyman who had only been residing in the area a matter of weeks it was positively inflammatory. 'Are there no decencies, and proprieties, which we owe to our situation in society?', he asked the assembled clerical company. 'Is a minister of God to lead the life of a gamekeeper, or a groom?' Rubbing salt in the wound, Sydney had the sermon published in November. As far as local clerical society was concerned he was happy to live on the periphery, socializing with those whom he liked but neglecting everyone else.

He had the consolation of being with his family. The love of his wife and children was very important to him. He was always the first to admit that he had an intense need for other people: he hated solitude and always worked amid domestic bustle. He was also a practical person, fond of ritual. He liked to work with a medley of strange objects around him: a massive ink-stand made of lead, a magnifying glass, a carpenter's rule, several large steel pens which it was treason to touch, a glass bowl full of shot and water, in Sydney's day a common method of cleaning pens. Boredom he could not bear. In order to combat it he would change his activities throughout the day: there would be varied reading – theological and historical works, some light literature, especially Scott's novels of which he was very fond; he would write his letters and compose his articles for the *Edinburgh Review*; and all of this was interspersed with exercise and a great deal of domestic conversation. He read and wrote very fast indeed. As images flickered across his mind the expression on his face kept changing. He rarely corrected anything he had written. As soon as he finished a manuscript he would fling it down – '*There*, it is done; now, Kate, do look it over, and put in dots to the *i*'s and strokes to the *t*'s' – and go out for a brisk walk. Catharine, left at home, had more to do than put 'dots to the i's and strokes to the t's'. Sydney's is an infuriating hand, apparently legible but often well-nigh indecipherable. His manuscripts, he admitted, looked 'as if a swarm of ants, escaping from an ink-bottle, had walked over a sheet of paper without wiping their legs'.[5]

The structure of Sydney's daily life is revealing. He was a man who was, in surprising ways, quite extraordinarily well organized, he did everything vigorously, and he planned out his days. All of this was, so to speak, the open agenda, but there was also a hidden one. Painfully aware of his melancholic tendencies, he did everything that he could to combat them, training his mind to concentrate on present activity in order to stop himself from harping on the past. 'I always live in the

Present and the Future, and look on the Past as so much dirty linen', he once said. There is a fascinating passage on the same theme in Sydney's lectures on moral philosophy, where he contrasts 'contemplative men of a poetical cast' with the 'bustling active men of the world whose face is always turned the way they are going'. Sydney found it easy to state his preference. 'For my part, I must confess myself rather an admirer of the active school.' What is especially interesting is the reason for his choice; the poetic way 'softens and unstrings the mind, and renders it useless for the struggles of life.' Sydney, inwardly unconfident and subject to severe oscillations in mood, worried, quite needlessly, about his own mental stability. He therefore put himself under a rigorous regimen of mental training in order to keep his spirits as buoyant as he could.

Relaxation was another means by which he tried to ward off melancholy. There was, in these Heslington years, plenty of time for gardening, which he grew to love. There was time, too, for games with his three children. Saba was seven in 1809, Douglas four, Emily two. In the evenings he would tell them stories full of absurd images, the comic descriptions coming one after another with great rapidity. Animals enlivened the domestic scene. The family's favourite pet was Bitty, a tame donkey which the children trained to go upstairs, pick pockets and go for walks. Sydney was animated by an intense desire to make the lives of his children more memorable than his own childhood. He also had a countryman's heart; he was a man who reached out to the whole of the natural world, animate and inanimate. At Heslington, fulfilment of his paternal responsibilities and love of nature went hand in hand. Sydney was never happier than when he went on his daily round of the twelve-acre farm, accompanied by his children. These were slow and leisurely walks, with everyone stopping frequently so that all the livestock – cows, calves, horses and pigs – could be patted in turn.

Sydney had deep care for his children. An illuminating story relating to earlier, London days is recorded in Saba's *Memoir*. One of his children (might it not have been Saba herself?) became terror-struck, waking suddenly every evening in a sobbing state, asking gloomy questions about the death of parents. Sydney brought every comfort to the child's bedside: a toy, a picture-book, a bunch of grapes, a joyous tale, the tenderest of caresses, soothing words. Not until the habit was broken did he relax his vigilance. This story speaks of Sydney's impulsiveness and playfulness, and of his deep desire to please. There was, however, also a darker side; there always was a strain of irresponsibility in him. It is an irony which he would not have appreciated that, like his father, he never could quite subdue the part of him that refused to grow up.

Sydney did not employ a private tutor for Douglas but taught the boy himself. Catharine showed Saba and Emily how to read and write, and then Sydney took over. With his advanced views on the intellectual equality of the sexes, he made an ideal tutor for his daughters. In adult life Saba remembered with gratitude the many essays her father had set her. Sydney's plans for his daughters' studies have not survived, but their outline is clear from some 'hints on female education' which he wrote in early manhood. The emphasis is upon systematic training of the mind and upon stimulation: 'We move most quickly to that point where we wish to go.' Variety was strongly favoured, a view reflecting his own preference for a pot-pourri of activities in order to ward off boredom: history and natural philosophy in the mornings, poetry and *belles-lettres* in the afternoons. Sydney thought that girls should read the best authors in both English and French, and in the latter language he recommended Corneille, Racine and Molière. He hoped they would also tackle Italian.

Saba and Emily were fortunate to have their father to teach them languages: his method was inspired. Some years later, he set out his views in an important article in the *Edinburgh Review*. As with so much else that he wrote, the article is a joy to read: effortless, careless even, with the jewels of his mind left strewn about, waiting to be picked up and admired. Sydney built his method of teaching French and Italian upon a base of simple fact, acknowledged by modern linguists: no matter how complex the grammar of a language, it is accurately reflected in speech. Every man you meet is, in Sydney's vivid phrase, a 'living lexicon'. Foreign languages, he rightly concluded, should be learnt in the same way as native tongues: pick up simple structures through speech, and only turn to dictionaries and grammar books once a reasonable level of proficiency has been acquired. All great literature is contemporary and a man of genius, born in another age, can always speak to our own.

Although Sydney was disparaging about most of the local gentry and clergy, he did make new friends and came to know three people in Yorkshire especially well. One of the three, Francis Cholmeley, he knew a little already. Francis was a liberal Catholic squire who lived at

Brandsby, about eight miles north-west of Foston. He married within a few months of Sydney's arrival and a close relationship between the two families was quickly established, cakes and other presents passing back and forth. The tone of easy familiarity is well caught in a letter from Catharine to Francis: 'I thank you very much for your letter and for the details respecting my beloved Angelica . . . If I make love to your gardener, do you think he will at the right time be induced to send me some of the seeds?'[6] Over the years Catharine had picked up some of her husband's characteristic expressions.

Sydney met Francis Wrangham, the scholarly vicar of Hunmanby, after he had been at Heslington a few months. Two years older than the new rector of Foston, Wrangham had been a promising student at Cambridge in the late 1780s and early 1790s but had failed to obtain an academic post, probably because he was suspected of being a radical in politics. Despairing of Cambridge, Wrangham became vicar of Hunmanby in 1795, where he remained until his death forty-seven years later, dedicating himself to building up an extensive library and to writing poetry and minor classical works. Wrangham, who later became an archdeacon, supported Sydney in his crusade in favour of Catholic emancipation. Sydney was relaxed enough in Wrangham's company to tease. Ambition was Sydney's theme: 'Wrangham, Sir, asks for everything. On a distant rumour of a vacancy lately, he asked to be Bey of Algiers.' In every age there are Wranghams in the Church of England: men of great ability, who would make excellent bishops, but who are passed over because they are suspected of having radical ideas.

Sydney's third friend was Richard York, a Tory squire who lived at Wighill Park, two miles or so north of Tadcaster. Sydney's letters give the strong impression that he was a born-and-bred countryman, who had never travelled further south than Leeds: his topics are rural gossip and rural sports. When York's son gets married, Sydney writes to congratulate him: 'I hope that young Mrs Edward rides to hounds – or at least that she is a good kennel lady; I never saw any lady prosper in Yorkshire who had not this turn.' York would have found it difficult to recognize in his pleasantly garrulous friend the moralizer, hot against shooting, of the Malton sermon.

Sydney did not have as much contact with Cholmeley, Wrangham and York as he would have liked. It was the local custom in that large county to make visits lasting two or three days. Catharine, especially in these early days, was not a keen traveller: she was very maternal and quickly became anxious when away from home. For Sydney, an ambitious man, a famous wit and a diner-out, it was, to say the least, a limited existence. He never felt fully himself when he was away from his natural milieu of the 'sacred parallelogram': the lack of social stimulation in Yorkshire involved a sense of loss which closeness to nature and the joy of being with the family could not quite counterbalance.

One of the ways in which he tried to sustain his spirits was by keeping in touch with his wide circle of friends. A spring visit of ten weeks or so to London was part of his annual routine. Lady Holland, like Sydney a person who was easily bored by her own company, quite often asked him to stay at Holland House. She also visited him from time to time in Yorkshire and, needless to say, they kept up a regular correspondence. John Allen and Francis Horner were other London friends who came up to Heslington and who wrote quite often.

Edinburgh was less accessible. Sydney never travelled so far north while he was at Heslington, but he did persuade Jeffrey and Murray to stop off at his 'inn' on their way to town. Sydney also maintained strong links with other people in Edinburgh. He got on especially well with two people, both of them women. Georgiana Pigou was the daughter of one of Francis Jeffrey's close female friends. In 1819 she married Hugo Meynell, a member of a famous fox-hunting family. Sydney's letters to Mrs Meynell are affectionate, witty and familiar. The other female friend was Jane Apreece, a vivacious brunette well known in Edinburgh society. Jane, who was a 'blue-stocking', paid a visit to Heslington in 1810. Sydney liked her because she never let her brains swamp her femininity. 'Jane seems a friendly, goodhearted rational woman', he told Jeffrey, 'and as much under the uterine dominion as is graceful, and pleasing.' She married Sir Humphry Davy, the famous chemist, in 1812, and the Davys joined the regular run of visitors to Sydney's small farm.

Sydney's social life was never static: he kept on expanding his circle of friends throughout his life. During these Yorkshire years, he got to know a number of English people who lived outside the county. Some of these friendships are surprising. Sydney, for instance, came to be on good terms with Sir George Philips ('Philippi'), the son of a Manchester cotton magnate, a man living well outside Sydney's normal social milieu. He also liked the company of beautiful young women. One new friend in this category was Lady Mary Bennet, the younger daughter of the fourth earl of Tankerville. There are numerous amusing passages in Sydney's letters to Lady Mary. He wrote an enchanting letter to her while he was on a visit to Sir George Philips, who lived at Sedgley, a few miles south of Wolverhampton:

> And now, dear Lady Mary, do you want anything in the flowered cotton, or Manchester velvet, or chintz line? Remember, this is not a town where there are only a few shops, but it is the great magazine from which flow all the mercers' shops in the world . . . Here muslin – elementary, rudimental, early, primeval muslin – is meditated; broad and narrow sarsnet first see the light, and narrow and broad edging! Avail yourself, dear lady, of my being here, to prepare your conquering armour for your next campaign.

During the period of his northern rustication, Sydney entertained his friends with lively descriptions of the details of his life: his ups and downs, his small successes, his petty misfortunes. One of his most endearing qualities was an ability to laugh at himself, a trait of character evident in a letter to Lady Holland:

> I have been lame for some time by a fall from my horse. He had behaved so well and so quietly that I doubled his allowance of corn and in return he kicked me over his head in the most ignominious, and contemptuous manner. This should be a warning to you against raising servants' wages. I am recovering fast tho' sorely bruised; fifteen stone weight does not fall from sixteen hands high with impunity.

Sydney called his horse Calamity and it well earned its name.

It did not bother Sydney that he could not ride anything like as well as his Yorkshire neighbours. Typical of local pride was Charles Waterton, author of the best-selling *Wanderings in South America*, whose seat was Walton Hall, fifteen miles south of Leeds. One of the most amusing episodes in *Wanderings* is a passage in which Waterton praises himself for his equestrian skill. The fearless Catholic squire wanted to add a crocodile to his distinguished taxidermical collection. Being a perfectionist, he insisted that the animal, when captured and killed, remain unblemished. The first stage was to set a simple trap: a rope anchored to a tree, with some curved wooden barbs bound with twine attached to the end of the rope and a small rodent for bait. A stick was used to keep the barbs and bait a little above water, close to the foreshore. The trap was an immediate success. Waterton now had to subdue the crocodile, a task which filled his seven native assistants with feelings which fell well short of enthusiasm. Waterton had no option but to take sole responsibility. Approaching the crocodile very slowly until he was within touching distance, he seized his chance, jumping on its back and turning half-round as he did so. Now pointing in the right direction, Waterton's only remaining problem was to avoid falling off. But how on earth could he keep his balance? Quite easily. He gripped the writhing animal with his legs and, more importantly, twisted its forelegs upwards, turning them into makeshift reins. The seven natives then pulled 'horse' and 'rider' ashore. 'Should it be asked, how I managed to keep my seat, I would answer – I hunted some years with Lord Darlington's fox-hounds.' Sydney's comment on Waterton's bravado is crisp. 'The Yorkshire gentlemen have long been famous for their equestrian skill; but Mr Waterton is the first among them of whom it could be said that he has a fine hand upon a crocodile.' Waterton's prize is now on public view at Wakefield Museum.

Sydney had the rare gift of being able to elevate the commonplace. Such was his felicity of word and phrase that he could make rejection of an invitation seem like acceptance. One wonders what Lord Crewe made of the following example of Sydney's epistolary elegance:

I cannot help writing a line to thank you for your obliging note. I hope one day or other (wind and weather permitting) to pay my respects to Lady Crewe and you, at Crewe Hall, of goodly exterior, and, like a York pie, at this season filled with agreeable and interesting contents . . . I cannot trust myself with a message to Mrs Hopwood, but shall be very much obliged to your Lordship to frame one, suitable to my profession, worthy of its object, and not forgetful of my feelings; let it be clerical, elevated, and tender.

P——'s [probably, Sir George Philips'] single turnips turned out extremely well; he is about to publish a tract 'On the Effect of Solitude on Vegetables'.

I remain, dear Lord Crewe, very truly yours,
Sydney Smith

This letter shows why it was so hard to dislike Sydney, but it is also rather sad. Sydney felt constrained by his orders, and it is this constraint to which he alludes when he tells Lord Crewe that he could not 'trust' himself with a message to Mrs Hopwood. A man of God, thought Sydney, suffered from the handicap that he could not fully express his sexuality. 'As the French say', runs one of Sydney's *bons mots*, 'there are three sexes – men, women, and clergymen.'[7] This chafing at professional constraint helps to explain why Sydney found writing for the *Edinburgh Review* attractive. Under a cloak of anonymity he could say things which he would never have been able to get away with when writing in his own name.

One new friendship which Sydney made during these Yorkshire years is especially important. Towards the end of October 1809, when he had been at Heslington four months, he travelled north to the seaside village of Howick in Northumberland, the home of Earl Grey, Fox's successor as leader of the Whigs. It was Sydney's second visit – he had also gone in the autumn of the previous year. The introduction, made by Lord and Lady Holland, was a success on both sides. 'Sydney Smith passed ten days here, and enlivened us extremely', Grey wrote to Brougham after this second visit. Sydney, for his part, invited Grey to stay at his Yorkshire 'cottage' on his way to town.[8]

For as long as he was rusticated in Yorkshire, Sydney nearly always paid an autumn visit to Howick. He looked forward to the journey north, and thoroughly enjoyed himself once he arrived. Sydney approved of the freedom Lord and Lady Grey gave their children; they were permitted to roam the countryside, to wander on their own over the cliffs near the house, and to call their father by his pet name of 'Car'. It was a large and happy household; the Greys had fifteen children, all except one of whom grew to maturity. Sydney, who loved to be in a lively atmosphere, was envious of Lord and Lady Grey. Soon after he returned from this second visit, he told Lady Holland that 'there is more happiness in a multitude of children than safety in a multitude of counsellors; and if I was a rich man, I should like to have, and would have 20 children.' Sydney was, to the tips of his fingers, a family man.

Letters soon began to pass to and fro between Heslington and Howick. Sydney, with his keen eye for strange inventions, was always thinking of ways to improve the Greys' domestic comfort: a patent iron-back for coping with smoking chimneys, ordered at York and sent up by wagon, a special rake, also sent by wagon, a recipe for lemon juice using citric acid. There is something touching about this, the brilliant Yorkshire parson on terms of easy familiarity with the aristocratic leader of the Whigs, the quick bridging of the social gulf that would otherwise have separated them.

A price, however, had to be paid. There is an air of unreality about this relationship between Sydney and Lord Grey. The picture of Grey's personality that emerges from Sydney's letters is idealized. The earl, he told Lady Holland, had 'a fine nature, a just and vigorous understanding, a sensitive disposition . . . His excellences are courage, discretion, and practical sense; his deficiency, a want of executive coarseness.' Sydney conjures up an image of a man who regarded politics as a hobby and therefore had little chance of success, but Grey was nothing of the kind. Both in public and in private life the leading trait of his personality was the will to dominate. His high forehead and small, cold eyes gave him a disdainful air, and accurately reflected his imperious temper. He took adverse criticism badly and was uneasy in the company of intellectuals, whom he found threatening.

Sydney also took a roseate view of Grey's marriage. He portrays the earl as a devoted husband and father, an assessment which was wide of the mark. Grey was a fond family man – while he was at Howick. His life in London was altogether more risqué. In his youth he had been a drinking companion of Charles James Fox, and his appreciation of the value of chastity had not been well developed; Grey was the father of the illegitimate child born to Georgiana, duchess of Devonshire, in France in 1792. Old habits die hard or rather, in Charles Grey's case, they never die at all. His affairs with, for instance, Sheridan's second wife and also with Princess Lieven, the wife of the Russian ambassador to London, were a frequent topic of conversation in polite society.[9] Sydney must have known about them but kept a diplomatic silence on the subject.

Being rector of Foston was not always a dull life. There were long annual visits to London and Howick. Friends stayed at Heslington from time to time. Sydney's daily routine – writing articles and letters to friends, reading, conversing with his family, walking around the twelve-acre farm with his children – was quite varied. There was, however, still no disguising the fact that his present life, when contrasted with his London literary life, was extremely unexciting. Sydney, a very resilient man, nevertheless managed to prevent himself from becoming too downcast. He explained how he set about doing this in a forthright letter to Lady Holland:

I hear you laugh at me for being happy in the country, and upon this I have a few words to say. In the first place whether one lives or dies I hold and always have held to be of infinitely less moment than is generally supposed; but if life is the choice then it is common sense to amuse yourself with the best you can find where you happen to be placed. I am not leading precisely the life I should choose, but that which (all things considered, as well as I could consider them) appeared to be the most eligible. I am resolved therefore to like it and to reconcile myself to it; which is more manly than to feign myself above it, and to send up complaints by the post, of being thrown away, and being desolate and such like trash. I am prepared therefore either way. If the chances of life ever enable me to emerge, I will shew you that I have not been wholly occupied by small and sordid pursuits. If (as the greater probability is) I am come to the end of my career, I give myself quietly up to horticulture, and the annual augmentation of my family. In short, if my lot be to crawl, I will crawl contentedly; if to fly, I will fly with alacrity; but as long as I can possibly avoid it I will never be unhappy.

This letter, written when Sydney had been living in Yorkshire three months, breathes the spirit of a world we have lost: an eighteenth-century world in which death is accepted as matter of fact, and in which success or failure in life depends upon patronage, and thus upon chance. Sydney knew that his future prospects were governed by the arbitrary fickleness of political opportunity. His stoicism in the face of this unpleasant reality did not come easily to him; indeed he admits as much in this letter.

There is, indisputably, much nobility in Sydney. Here is a man of thirty-eight, in the prime of his literary powers, struggling to adapt to a new existence 200 miles from the 'sacred parallelogram'. It was not an inviting prospect, after the great promise of the London years. Sydney had no means of telling how long his incarceration in Yorkshire would last. Had he known the bitter truth – that he would be rector of Foston for a further two decades – this letter of September 1809 might have been a lot less sanguine. What Sydney had to adjust to, and what we have to adjust to as well, is a changed rhythm in his life. Things move more slowly and his social experience is less rich. But, despite trials and tribulations, the centre of Sydney holds. His was a determined soul. He did not always achieve his goals but he never ceased to strive.

That striving preserved the strength of Sydney's inner radiance and fire.

Once he had settled in at Heslington, he formed the habit of rising early, being at work by six-thirty, a regime which he had not adhered to since his days at Winchester. A letter to Brougham, who was staying at the time at the house of Lord Roberts, shows Sydney in fine form; so fine indeed that, in his ebullience of spirits, he runs away with himself. As he sat beside his candle in the morning darkness at Heslington, he thought about the household at the home of Lord Roberts, especially about the 'young nobles' staying there, who 'having perpetrated their separate acts of Adultery, are gliding in short Shirts and Night caps thro' the passages to regain their apartments'. Not, of course, that Henry Brougham would participate in such sexual fun and games:

> Your conduct while at Lord Roberts is perfectly gentlemanlike, and you enjoy the customary privileges of every Well bred man. But were you to claim any right of insinuating your hand under the Petticoats of every female in that temple of Chastity, its humorous and droll proprietor would probably propose a few regulations upon that point; and if your hands were pinion'd to your pockets, it would only be a just consequence of their Lascivious and extravagant excursions.

He went on to praise Brougham for an article he had written in the latest issue of the *Edinburgh Review*: 'Your review as I told Jeffrey is long and Vigorous like the Penis of a Jackass.' Brougham did not take this as a compliment. Sydney was puzzled by his displeasure, writing to John Allen that he found such 'prudery . . . very odd'.

Although Sydney greatly enjoyed his annual visits to London and Howick, he was very reluctant to leave his wife and growing family – because of financial pressure he always, in these Heslington years, went alone. His unease when away from home comes out with painful clarity in a letter written by Catharine to a family friend:

> There are few people perhaps more nervous than he is & more alive to all the indescribable agitations that a very anxious & a very eager mind gives birth to. . . . When in London he sometimes keeps a letter from home half the day in his pocket unopen'd, fearing lest it should contain ill news, yet too nervous to venture

on the certainty that would follow the reading (of) it . . . This is a piece of secret history that he perhaps would not care to own.

Sydney usually went to London in April but in 1810 he started out much earlier, in February. He decided to brave the treacherous winter roads in order to see his brother Cecil, back in England because he was in yet another scrape. Restoration of his post as Accountant General, following the protracted investigation of his irregular currency dealings, had not lasted long. In December 1807 a new governor, Sir George Barlow, arrived in Madras. Sir George caused chaos in the presidency: English officers mutinied and many civilians were turned out of their jobs. Cecil was sacked as Accountant General but was offered a circuit judgeship by Barlow instead. Cecil only had two objections to Barlow's placatory proposal: he was not a lawyer and he could not speak Hindi. Rebuffing Barlow, he journeyed to London in hopes of getting his old post back. Sydney helped his brother draw up his defence, and Bobus also did what he could, reading all the papers relating to the case and writing to Lord Holland on Cecil's behalf. The Smith family was only ever cohesive in a crisis. Cecil was reinstated.[10]

During this first London visit Sydney also preached at Kensington Palace at the request of the Princess of Wales. He took as his text a verse from the Sermon on the Mount: 'He maketh the sun to shine on the righteous and the unrighteous'. Since Sydney preached on his favourite theme of religious toleration, the way in which he applied his text is fairly clear. After the service the Princess sent for him and was very complimentary, a welcome sign of royal favour. Not everyone in the congregation was pleased by Sydney's cordial reception. Lord Glenbervie, an Irish peer and minor Tory office holder, thought that Sydney 'swallowed' the Princess's remarks 'with the smirking complacency of a man who manifestly thought he deserved them all'. The sermon, continued Glenbervie, was political, not scriptural, and the appearance of the preacher had been unedifying: 'Sydney Smith has the neck of a little bull and two hands like thick raw beef steaks. He uses much action for an English clergyman and particularly has an awkward habit of clenching his right fist.'

Glenbervie was not the only person who was angered. Sydney suffered the indignity of being denied use of the pulpit at the Berkeley Chapel in John Street, Mayfair, the place where he had established a reputation as a leading London preacher a few years previously. The proprietor's petulant rudeness was enormously irritating. Sydney, after all, had transformed the chapel's reputation. You will remember Catharine's eulogy: 'The chapel, in spite of its advantageous position, was nearly deserted . . . In a few months, not a seat to be had! Ladies & Gentlemen often standing in the aisles during the whole Service.' Religious toleration was, in 1810, a red-hot political issue.

Back at home the summer was enlivened by a visit from Lord and Lady Holland. Putting her ladyship up required a modest expansion of the facilities at Heslington. 'We have now another bed in which a maid or a philosopher, or a maid with a philosopher might be put. God grant in this latter event that they might both merit their respective appellations the ensuing morning.' In the autumn there was a steady stream of visits from people in Edinburgh: Jeffrey, Murray and Jane Apreece. Some came from the north, some from the south. Sydney was, as always, delighted to see Francis Horner; and Cecil also made his way to Yorkshire, prior to his return to India.

The winter of 1810 was given over to domestic life. Sydney also wrote an article for the *Edinburgh Review* on the ill-fated Walcheren expedition, launched amid great expectations in the summer of the previous year. War was a subject Sydney was passionate about. There were few things he hated more; he could not bear its futility, its waste, its hideous expense. 'There is', he once wrote, 'more of misery inflicted upon mankind by one year of war than by all the civil peculations and oppressions of a century.' The aim of the Walcheren expedition had been to seize the Dutch fleet as well as take the town of Flushing, but the attack was a fiasco from start to finish. Sydney unfolds the drama in a deliberately low key, allowing the facts to speak for themselves and conveying very powerfully an impression of cumulative idiocy. He is especially good on the lack of medical preparations. The force left England in mid-August, the time of year when the annual marsh fever, sweeping across the islands at the mouth of the Scheldt, was at its height. As a good journalist, he uses official documents to show that the government never took medical advice before deciding the timing of the attack. But he also does more, researching the matter thoroughly and quoting, with devastating effect, from a book on an earlier Netherlands campaign in 1747. As in 1809 the English army had been defeated by disease, the book stating that the Walcheren epidemics always began at the end of July.

Only once, when discussing the role played by the Secretary for War, Lord Castlereagh, did Sydney permit himself to be mischievous.

Before the force set out members of Cabinet had expressed lack of confidence in Castlereagh, but only after its ignominious return was a serious effort made to turn him out. 'The Secretary for War and Colonies then resigned, and shot the Secretary for Foreign Affairs through the thigh on Wimbledon Common', a reference to the famous duel between Castlereagh and Bobus's great friend George Canning.[11]

Sydney made two visits to London in 1811; there was a stay of two months from mid-April until mid-June and then, unusually, he was a guest at Holland House for three weeks in September. The second foray south was in order to see Bobus, home at last and rich after eight years in Bengal. Before leaving India, Bobus had made Sydney an offer he knew would be refused. He would stay on an extra year in Bengal, setting aside his earnings – an income of £5000 a year as Advocate General, with the potential for at least as much again from private practice – for his younger brother's use. Sydney's reaction to Bobus's pseudo-munificence is paraphrased by Catharine:

How strangely must Bobus in these few years have forgotten the devotion and love I have ever borne him! That from any selfish motive I should risk an additional day of that trying climate to his health, already impair'd by a severe attack of illness! A Man in whose worldly success the pride and happiness of my *own* life was centred; who (with his wife) I knew to be *yearning* after their absent children, and counting the hours till they embraced them again; if he would have given me the whole of his fortune could it have given *me* peace of mind, had his life been sacrificed by the additional year spent there for my advantage?[12]

An offer of sums already earned would, added Catharine archly, have been gratefully received.

By the end of the summer of 1812, it was apparent to Sydney that a crisis was in the offing. His position had always been insecure: there was not a suitable parsonage at Foston and he felt that he ought not to go on endlessly renting houses. When he had first moved north he had promised Vernon-Harcourt that he would search for another living nearer London and that, if he failed to find one, he would start building by the autumn of 1812 in order to be ready to move in by March 1814. This was a brave decision on Sydney's part: every penny that went towards building a parsonage had to come out of the incumbent's own pocket, and he got nothing towards the cost from his successor once he vacated the benefice. All the church did was to help with loans.

Building a parsonage at Foston would stretch Sydney's financial resources. He had some savings. There was the sum of £1000 which Mrs Pybus had wisely insisted should be set aside for Catharine and Sydney jointly as part of the marriage settlement. Sydney had also invested the profit of £730 which he had made from teaching the elder of the two Hicks Beach boys. Assuming both these sums had earned compound interest at 3%, there would have been around £2500 in the bank. Building at Foston would cost more. Sydney wanted a house which reached the standards of spaciousness expected by the Georgian clergy. He also had to resolve the problem of what was to be done with the 110 acres of uncultivated land which were not let out to Farmer Horner. Sydney decided to spend heavily on outbuildings, farming equipment and fencing so that the land could be farmed.

All the difficulties would have been overcome had he been able to save out of current income, but he had failed to do so. Lack of sufficient means did not stand in his way. On entering the living in 1806 he had doubled Farmer Horner's annual rent to £500. The great agricultural boom, which had been the backdrop to the terrible row with his father over purchase of a farm, intensified during Sydney's early years as rector of Foston. By 1812 the living was probably worth at least £1000 a year. On top of this there was also Catharine's private income of at least £250 a year. Very few people earned £1250 a year in the first decade of the nineteenth century. An agricultural labourer could count himself lucky if he was paid ten shillings (50p) a week. An annual income of £500 placed a man on the fringes of the landed gentry. Sydney's financial problems did not arise because he was careless about money; on the contrary he watched his expenditure carefully. He spent a lot because of the company he kept. It was hard for a man to mix in aristocratic society, visiting London and Howick every year, and having Lord and Lady Holland to stay at his house, without running through a good deal of cash. Sydney had high social expectations, and these had to be paid for.

His best hope lay with King George III, who could assist him in either of two ways: he could die or he could become permanently incapable of ruling. Regency or succession: Sydney took the optimistic view that, once the Prince Regent was in power, the Whigs would return to office and Lord Holland would fulfil his promise of promotion, made after publication of *Peter Plymley*. The king became very ill in the autumn of 1810, but by the following January his doctors thought they could discern signs of recovery. 'This revival of his Majesty has revived my slumbering architecture', Sydney told Jeffrey. It was a resolution of his difficulties that Sydney strove hard to avoid. He entered into negotiations for an exchange of livings with 'various clergy', but only one scheme offered much hope. This involved Sydney moving to a living in Hertfordshire. Unfortunately the college which owned it would not give its consent. There remained only one possibility: a vacancy for the readership of Gray's Inn. Sydney handed in his application in October 1811 but without conviction, telling Lady Holland in advance that he would not succeed. He was in a despondent mood.

As expected, the readership passed Sydney by. Nothing else came up in the spring and summer of 1812, so Sydney decided to build. Plans for a new parsonage and outbuildings were drawn up by Peter Atkinson the younger, architect of the Ouse Bridge at York, and submitted to Sydney on 21 September. He turned them down: 'You build for glory, sir; I, for use.' Sydney also felt that if he was in charge he could save on materials. So he took out his ruler and compasses, sat down with his wife, and made his own architectural plans.[13]

Within a few weeks Sydney was at work on his new house, writing to Lord Holland in mid-October: 'I am very busy in building my Cemetery at Foston, but I will be a merry corpse and kick against worms, and corruption as long as I can.' A load of timber was transported from Hull (Sydney purchased it himself, bargaining hard to get the price down) and a carpenter and mason were employed. Every effort was made to save money. Sydney even invited over a skilled brickmaker from Leeds, with a remit to inspect the local clay. His verdict being favourable, large heaps were dug up to be tempered by the winter's frost.

At this point Vernon-Harcourt unexpectedly intervened, making it plain to Lord and Lady Holland that he did not want them to think that he was forcing Sydney to build. In December 1812 messages were passed between Sydney and the archbishop, John Allen acting as intermediary. In mid-January William, one of the archbishop's clerical sons, wrote to Sydney giving him express permission not to carry on. Vernon-Harcourt's vacillation, reminiscent of his previous dealings with Sydney, does him no credit. Although Sydney was polite, he was very angry indeed. In a letter to Lady Holland he compared himself to an Indian woman condemned to die by suttee. 'It would be a bad comfort to an Indian widow, who was half-burnt, if the head Brahmin were to call out to her, "Remember, *it is your own act and deed*; I never ordered you to burn yourself, and I must take the liberty of telling you that you are a fool for your pains".'[14]

Fool or not, Sydney was determined to press ahead. 'I live trowel in hand', he told Jeffrey in April 1813. A few weeks earlier Sydney had arranged a loan of £1600 with Queen Anne's Bounty, then the church's board of central finance. As he had expected, his savings were not sufficient to cover the expense of building. There was, into the bargain, an unwanted emergency. Sydney's cost-saving scheme for bricks had not worked out. He moulded them, he hardened them, he paid taxes on them, and he sent 150,000 of them for firing, but they were then found to be useless. Bricks now had to be brought from a distance. Sydney was advised to use oxen to fetch and carry. He bought four – Lug and Tug, Haul and Crawl. It was not a wise purchase. They were expensive to feed and hopeless at brick-carrying. The last leg of the journey to Foston went through sandy soil, terrain which defeated the oxen's combined effort; Lug and Tug, Haul and Crawl would lie down exhausted and roar. James Horner bought the oxen for fattening and Sydney purchased a team of horses, which served him well. The old parsonage at Foston was turned into foundations for the new, and the first stone was laid in June 1813.

While the trowel was in his hand, Sydney spent a good deal of time worrying about his elder brother. Bobus rarely wrote. He had been ill at least twice, once very severely, while he was in India, and his career in England was not going well. He had purchased a parliamentary seat (Grantham in Lincolnshire) which enabled him to enter Parliament at the general election held towards the close of 1812, but his maiden speech the following February had been a failure.[15] He had not come up to Yorkshire since his return from the sub-continent, and the last time the brothers had met had been in the autumn of 1811, when Sydney had made a special visit to London in order to be part of the welcoming party. However, neglect did not dim feeling and in May 1813, Sydney wrote very affectionately, opening his heart:

Pray take care of yourself. Let us contrive to last out for the same or nearly the same time: weary will be the latter half of my pilgrimage, if you leave me in the lurch! By the bye, I wish Mrs Smith and you would promise to inform me if you are ever seriously ill. I should come up to you at a moment's warning, and should be very unhappy if the opportunity were not given me of doing so.

In view of subsequent events, this reads like a premonition.

Bobus did eventually visit his brother, coming up to Heslington in August. He then went with his family to Hinckley in Leicestershire, in search of medical care for his elder daughter Caroline, who had a slight curvature of the spine. At Hinckley, Sydney's worst fears were realized. Caroline, as well as Bobus's fourth child Henrietta, who had been born in India, went down with typhus. Henrietta, along with two nurses, died. The two spinsters in the family circle, Caroline Fox, Lord Holland's sister, and Mrs Smith's sister, 'Aunt Ebey', travelled to Hinckley to nurse Caroline, while Mrs Smith journeyed on with Bobus, who was in a very distressed state. They got no further than Northampton. Bobus also had typhus and was on the verge of death.

Bobus's wife now wrote a pleading letter to Sydney, asking him to come to his brother's aid. Catharine was mortified. 'Never *can* I forget the distress this occasion'd *me*! I had then 3 Children, and in a short time was to be confined. [A son, Windham, was born in September.] To risk the *life* of my Husband by his thus encountering a disorder so malignant as this fever had shewn itself to be, and where no *real* good could follow from it, did appear to me like *Madness*!'[16] Sydney was not swayed. Amid a welter of considerations one thought dominated his mind: 'If any evil were to happen to Bobus, I should reproach myself all my life.' He wrote to John Allen, asking for medical advice. Allen wrote back, telling him to take a number of obvious precautions and adding, '*above all, don't be afraid*'.[17] It was an injunction with which Sydney was unable to comply. He was very much afraid and set off for Northampton without any lively hope of ever coming back. He left a simple message for his wife: 'Kate, if I do die, you must always keep the day of my death.'

Bobus pulled through and Sydney, much to his own surprise, survived unscathed. Sadly, nearness to death did not bring the brothers closer together. Bobus quickly went back to his old lethargic ways. Early in January 1814, four months after the agonizing trek to Northampton, Sydney mentions his brother in a letter to Lady Holland: 'Bobus I presume is recovered as I have heard nothing of him for some time. I am forced to remind him once or twice a year that there is such a person as myself on the face of the earth, but whether I excite a full belief of that important truth may be doubt-ful.'

This was, in the circumstances, one of the saddest letters Sydney ever wrote. His was a common predicament. Relationships tend to develop a distinctive pattern. Dire events can disrupt this for a time but the underlying configuration usually reasserts itself. With Bobus and Sydney all the effort came from Sydney. Not that Bobus was insensitive or unfeeling; the problem, rather, was that he was the reverse. Bobus was slow to come to terms with Henrietta's death. His bereavement was so severe that it put an end to his political career. He was a follower of Canning, and Canning in July 1814 achieved a rapprochement with Lord Liverpool, also at school with Bobus and now prime minister. Canning proposed Bobus for an unsalaried post at the India Board, a suggestion that won prime ministerial approval: 'I shall be delighted to see Bobus at the India Board.' Bobus, however, turned the offer down. His health, he said, would probably not stand up under the pressure of the likely demands.[18] No further offers of office came his way. Sydney's fervent desire, that the two brothers would both have successful careers in England, could never now come to fruition.

During the winter and early spring of 1814, Sydney's eye was constantly on the calendar. His house at Heslington was let to another tenant from Lady Day, 25 March. Despite the loss of eight weeks of work on the new parsonage due to bad weather, he just managed to beat the deadline by five days. Transporting the family was a troublesome task. A closed-in carriage was hired to convey Catharine with Windham, now six months old but never previously out of the house. Wagons took most of the furniture the previous day; the family spent their last night at Heslington on bedding placed on the floor. All went well on the journey until they were a short distance from Foston rectory. Windham started to cry, Catharine failed to pacify him with her breast and the hired coach got stuck in the sand; so Catharine stepped out with her baby in her arms and, although she lost a shoe in the morass, struggled on into her new abode.

The three older children, of course, enjoyed the Heath Robinson situation enormously. Their first tea at Foston rectory was taken on piled-up boxes. Some of the rooms were plasterless and had no doors; there were no carpets and few chairs. Years later Saba could still recall the sound of her father's mellow yet stentorian voice as he gave instructions, until midnight, to the men bringing the last of the family's belongings by wagon. Sydney was worried about damp. As a precaution he had kept fires burning day and night in every room for eight weeks prior to the move. Once the family settled in, the housemaid was given the task of wiping condensation off the windows three or four times a day. Anxious to prevent fires from going out at night, Catharine would go from room to room 'like an unquiet Ghost', making sure that coal-buckets were full.[19] She was uneasy yet contented: she had a permanent home at last.

10

A CLOSE PRISONER

'I like my new house very much . . . but the expense of it will
keep me a very poor man, a close prisoner here for life.'
SYDNEY SMITH TO FRANCIS JEFFREY, December 1814

The family had only been at Foston rectory a few days when Sydney
heard of the death of his brother Cecil. It is hard not to feel compassion
for Cecil. He had intelligence and charm, he had great gaiety of spirit,
and he had many friends; but he was also easily led and circumstances
conspired against him. If he had married, say, Caroline Vernon in
preference to Eliza, all might have been well. As it was, he dissipated
his Indian wealth, a feat in itself, then he lost his wife, his natural
ebullience followed close behind, and the cycle of misfortune was
completed when his health gave way. Despairing of recovery in the
treacherous climate of India, he had set out for home but had got no
further than Cape Town. So ill was he that he had to be carried from
the ship in a sedan chair. He died on 8 December 1813, at the age of
forty-one. Cecil was no more but his debts lived on; they were still
being sorted out more than a decade later.

Sydney was happy in his 'snug' new parsonage. This is the evocative
word he uses to describe it in a letter to John Allen, and he uses the
same word a little later in a letter to Lady Holland. Warmth, comfort
and domesticity are what Sydney aimed for. He felt that, with the
building of his house, he was engaged in an important enterprise:
helping to secure the happiness of his family and of himself. He
articulated his thoughts in a letter to Jeffrey: 'The haunts of Happiness
are varied, and rather unaccountable; but I have more often seen her
among little children, and home firesides, and in country houses, than
anywhere else – at least, I think so.'

Foston rectory, which still stands today, has many fireplaces: 'What
makes a fire so pleasant is, I think, that it is a live thing in a dead room.'

That in the drawing-room is especially lively, benefiting as it does from one of Sydney's most successful inventions – an air vent, which can be opened and closed, runs under the floorboards from the outside wall to the middle of the fire. Sydney also thought that light was very important. The windows in the drawing-room reach nearly to the floor; lift up the middle one, walk down three stone steps and you are in the garden. A further ingredient in Sydney's recipe for domestic happiness was gay informality. Bright colours were everywhere; the wallpaper in the drawing-room, for example, was a strong chrome yellow with a floral pattern. Empty spaces were broken up with books, chairs, tables and wardrobes. Nooks and crannies were covered with large Piranesi prints, mounted but unframed. Nothing was left bare.[1]

How much of Sydney's life and personality went into the making of this house. We see – as a shadow, as it were, upon the wall – a small boy forced to sit for hours in the gloaming light, waiting for a signal from his father allowing him to leave the table. We see a man who felt stalked by feelings of melancholy and was anxious to make surroundings for himself that would combat them. We see a proud husband and father who was determined to make his family happy. And we see, too, a man who was in the wrong profession, who knew he was in the wrong profession, but who felt strongly the call of duty, was caring and conscientious, and whose will to do what he knew to be right was not undermined by his indecisive bishop.

Sydney opted for a simple Georgian design, without flamboyance or unnecessary finery. The roof is pantiled and low-pitched, and the upstairs bedrooms are built into the roof space, a clever and economical idea. The ceilings are on the low side and there are no cornices. The rose-coloured brick gives a soft glow. If you want to draw close to Sydney you should visit Foston rectory: it is, as one of his friends put it, a 'fascimile of its master's mind'. The house has been owned by the Wormald family since 1939. A severe fire in 1962 destroyed the roof and part of the upper storey, but it has been lovingly restored.

When Sydney moved into Foston rectory he was not far short of his forty-third birthday. There were some things about himself which he did not much like, particularly the fact that, like the duke of Bedford's pigs at Woburn, he was beginning to exhibit a wonderful capacity for 'success and farina'. 'I am', he told John Murray a little later on, 'very well, doubling in size every year, and becoming more and more fit for the butcher.' Sydney regretted the middle-aged spread but did precious little to combat it. There were also other physical changes. His hair, which was profuse and exceptionally fine to the touch, was starting to lighten; later in life it would turn silvery before ending up snow-white. Alongside changes were continuities: he was still swarthy, his complexion had not changed from reddish brown, and his features, dominated by his dark eyes and Roman nose, still had great power, albeit not enhanced by the steady growth of two double chins. Increasing corpulence helped Sydney in one way: it meant that he radiated even more good nature and benevolence. 'His faunlike face', commented Crabb Robinson, 'is a sort of promise of a good thing when he does but open his lips'. Sydney's remarkably sanguine temperament never let him down. As he put it in one of his letters, 'My constitutional gaiety of spirit comes to my aid in all the difficulties of life.'

It had not been possible at Heslington to plan for permanence, but Sydney's household did now take a settled shape. His most faithful servant was Annie Kaye, who came to work for him when she was nineteen and nursed him at his death. Over the years Annie imperceptibly graduated from servant into friend. Her advice was sought on thorny issues and she later accompanied Sydney on a continental holiday. The garden was ruled by Molly Mills. With her 'short red petticoat, legs like millposts, high cheek-bones red and shrivelled like winter apples', Molly was every inch the image of a well-built countrywoman and was also the wit of the village, giving Sydney as good as she got. The handyman was Jack Robinson, who had been on parish relief when Sydney took him up and turned him into a carpenter. Jack, who had a face like a 'full moon', made most of the rectory furniture. Sydney felt that he could not afford a man-servant so he had a maid instead. Rachel Masterman, nicknamed Bunch, became almost as devoted as Annie Kaye, eventually following Sydney out of Yorkshire. In the mornings at Foston she helped Sydney to shave, preparing a thick lather in a huge wooden bowl, using a large paint brush. (This was another of Sydney's rituals.) She was the workaday family butler, Jack Robinson helping out on important occasions. Sydney taught Bunch how to wait at table, making her repeat to guests the litany of her crimes: 'plate-snatching, gravy-spilling, door-slamming, blue-bottle fly-catching' (standing with her mouth open) and so on.

Bunch did not mind being teased by Sydney, who was able to talk to his servants on level terms. He did not save up his witticisms for his friends; Annie Kaye and Molly Mills were told at least as many jokes as Lord and Lady Holland. There was in Sydney a fine sense of the human. He set out for himself, in a private memorandum, some 'Maxims and Rules of Life'. The first runs: 'Remember that every person, however low, has rights and feelings. In all contentions, let peace be rather your object, than triumph: value triumph only as the means of peace.' This maxim was vitally important to Sydney; it summed up what was, for him, the essence of Christianity.[2]

Bitty, the pet donkey, came with them from Heslington. The children also had a tame fawn, which lasted until it took to eating Bunch's clothes. Then there was a lame goose, eventually roasted as a punishment for eating all the fruit in the garden. The little phaeton which had brought Sydney from London was too small for a growing family, so he replaced it with an ancient green chariot he found in a back street at York. The village tailor lined it and the village blacksmith repaired it; the pole was removed and a pair of shafts substituted, enabling Sydney to use one of the cart horses he had bought to convey his bricks for the house to pull it along. Sydney christened this dilapidated conveyance the 'Immortal'. The family drove about the countryside in it and used it to take them to church on Sundays. The old rectory had abutted the churchyard but the new one was a mile away. At the bottom of the rectory drive was a 'screeching gate'. Here the Immortal was brought to a stop, and Sydney gently asked the ladies in the party to recollect the things they had left behind.

The parish, neglected for at least a century, gained much from having a resident rector. It was a small, close community – only twelve families at Foston and thirty-three at Thornton – the kind of place where a clergyman could do a great deal of good. Sydney looked after the poor, distributing milk to them in cans marked with his own initials. He gave them advice on diet and helped them in times of distress. As soon as he took over the parish he planted a number of small gardens with fruit trees, allowing the villagers to gather the produce. These plots, affectionately known as 'Sydney's orchards', were a long-term success: as late as the 1890s the gnarled old trees were still laden every year with pink and white blossom. Now that Sydney was living in the parish he extended his horticultural activities, setting aside part of his glebe as allotments at nominal rents. Any family that asked was given a plot on which to grow potatoes and, sometimes, keep a pig. This was an imaginative initiative. The poor in Georgian England were never far from the borderlands of starvation. A small area that they could cultivate and could think of as their own made a huge difference to them. Sydney was ahead of his time; it was not until later in the nineteenth century that provision of allotments became a method of combating poverty that was frequently advocated and practised by clergy.[3]

It was as a makeshift doctor that Sydney really excelled. He had studied anatomy at Oxford, and at Edinburgh he had gone to clinical lectures given in local hospitals. He read medical books all his life, gave advice to friends, and cared for his own children, attending two of them through a 'good stout fever of the typhus kind' and getting out the leech bottle when Douglas had croup. Being Sydney, he thought up some inventions. In his study at the new rectory was a large bag containing his 'rheumatic armour': a helmet, a collar, shoulder pads and boots, all hollow, all made of tin and all filled with hot water when required. Annie Kaye became Sydney's 'apothecary's boy', dispensing medicines to his instructions. The bottles were given jovial names: Rub-a-dub, Dead-stop, Up-with-it-then. Copious notes were kept on every parishioner and drugs were ordered from London. Sydney's greatest test came in the autumn and early winter of 1816, when there was a serious infectious fever in the village. Mary Hopper, Hannah Snowdon and William Gallery died, and many others were very ill. Sydney visited the sick daily, bringing them medicine and food.[4]

It is not only what Sydney did that is important, it is also what he was. The friend of Grey and Holland, the founder of the *Edinburgh Review*, the author of one of the finest pieces of satirical writing since Swift, could forget his achievements, could lay aside his dignity and deal with people man to man. Sydney once asked Thomas Johnson, the local tailor, to make some alterations to the Immortal. When he called at Johnson's shop to check that the work had been carried out, he told the tailor he had not done it correctly, a claim which Johnson vehemently denied. Looking straight into Sydney's eyes, Johnson told him that if he repeated what he had just said, he would throw his scissors at Sydney's head. Sydney repeated the accusation, so the tailor threw the scissors. Sydney ducked, turned on his heel and stormed out. But within a few minutes he had come back to apologize. Catharine had misunderstood the instructions he had given her, and Johnson had followed what she had told him to the letter.

Sydney was not always as emotionally democratic. He treated Thomas Johnson in the way that he did because he liked him: they were firm friends. Where the emotional link was lacking, Sydney could on occasion be stiff with his parishioners. When a young girl stole some fruit from his garden, he made her stand all day on the rectory lawn, a sign with 'THIEF' written on it around her neck.

This is a scene from another rural England, an England of public penance, stocks and ducking stools, of humiliation and social control. Sydney's method of punishing the young thief is the sort of authoritarian action one would expect from a Georgian rural magistrate, which, indeed, is what he was. He joined the Bench in January 1814, three months before moving in to his new rectory. Being a JP gave partial fulfilment to his lifelong wish to become a lawyer. It also transformed his relationship with his parishioners; no longer only a parish priest, Sydney was now also a leader in local society. Descended, as he put it, from a 'long line of Tinkers and Taylors', Sydney was a tinker no more.

To be a magistrate was to wield much power. The Bench governed the localities: there were no local councils and there was no police. The relationship between central and local government was dramatically different in the early nineteenth century from what it is today. Since there were no telephones and no trains, no civil service and poor roads, self-reliance was forced upon the Bench. Magistrates in many instances had to make their own decisions, often with little to guide them – there was a paucity of legislation, with the result that, when it came to such matters as what was to be done to relieve the sufferings of the aged, the sick and the unemployed, JPs had to meet and thrash out their own policy.

A JP's first duty was to keep order. He could always call upon the yeomanry in an emergency, but otherwise he managed as best he could; if necessary, special constables were sworn in. Three years before Sydney joined the Bench the torch of Luddism, with rick-burning, occasional violence and breaking up of machinery, had begun to flare in northern England. Disturbance, fortunately, never reached Foston.

Most of Sydney's time as a JP was taken up with caring for the disadvantaged and the poor. Much of this work was done at home. His study, to the right of the entrance door at Foston rectory, doubled as a justice room. It was to this room, overlooking the garden, that local men and women came for help, and also with their grievances and disputes. Every fortnight Sydney also administered justice at a local public house, the Lobster Inn. He had a special little wooden hammer which he used to keep order (another of his rituals). He disliked inflicting heavy punishments, preferring to assert his authority through dramatic gestures and rhetorical flourishes. When faced with a hardened case of young criminality, he would turn to his clerk and say: 'John, bring me my private gallows.'[5] Sydney always was a touch theatrical. As a JP he allowed this side of his personality full rein.

Those who appeared before Sydney could be sure that they would receive justice, not the sentence of the law. The independence of the magistracy was not a fiction with Sydney; he 'cherry picked' laws passed by the Tory government in London, refusing to apply those he considered unjust. He was especially soft on poachers, because he believed that the contemporary Game Laws were unfair in their treatment of the working man, who needed the occasional rabbit or hare to eke out his slender income.

The key to Sydney's popularity as a JP – and he was immensely popular – was his ability to sympathize with the poor. The fineness of his judgement, the way in which his opinions are never cluttered by cant, is displayed in a highly entertaining article in the *Edinburgh Review* on a subject close to the poor man's heart: alcohol. Sydney confronted the divisions in his own society head on. The rich frequented inns, the poor went to alehouses. Licensing, meanwhile, was in the hands of local JPs without appeal or redress, not an arrangement which commended itself to Sydney. He poured scorn on the annual 'brewster sessions', where the Bench decided the fate of the local pubs for the ensuing year:

> What the poor shall drink – how they shall drink it – in pint cups or quart mugs – hot or cold – in the morning or the evening – whether the Three Pigeons shall be shut up, and the Shoulder of Mutton be opened – whether the Black Horse shall continue to swing in the air – or the White Horse, with animated crest and tail, no longer portend spirits within: all these great questions depend upon little clumps of squires and parsons gathered together in alehouses in the month of September – so portentous to publicans and partridges, to sots and sportsmen, to guzzling and game.

By restricting the number of alehouses, Sydney claimed that JPs were blighting the lives of the poor. They had fewer pubs to choose from when they wanted a drink in the evenings, and when they travelled there were fewer places where they could stay. 'Pull off your superfine, Mr Justice – put on a fustian jacket and corduroy – come in covered with mud, and ask for a night's lodging – and then see what inconveniences you are entailing upon the lower orders, by refusing to extend the number of public houses!' This sort of argument made Sydney as popular with those who gathered in the evening at the Lobster as it made him unpopular with other members of the local Bench.

Not only was Sydney an extremely popular JP, he was also a very unconventional one. Some of the farmers around Foston kept huge mastiffs which they made no effort to restrain. When Sydney was out on his visits he was often met by one of these brutes. He tried scolding, he tried warning, he tried preaching: all to no avail. Then he had a flash of inspiration. A mysterious item appeared in the local press; a farmer had been tried at Northampton Sessions for keeping unconfined dogs. Not only was he reprimanded by the Bench and fined five pounds, he was also sentenced to three months in jail. Humour and imagination succeeded where cajoling and preaching had failed.

Sydney sometimes discussed interesting or difficult cases with other magistrates. On one occasion he wrote to his friend Francis Cholmeley about a local mole-catcher, who was trying to fight off a bastardy order. The letter illustrates Sydney's distinctive style of lateral thinking. Not content with discussing the case, he also made a reference to the French naturalist Buffon, besides revealing one of the runnels along which his own imagination habitually flowed:

> It is right enough that a mole catcher should have his relaxations, and there is more excuse for persons of that business than any other, from the effects of association. You are not perhaps aware that the mole of all four footed animals has the largest member of generation, and is supposed by Buffon to enjoy the greatest pleasure; his venereal endowments have drawn from the pen of that naturalist a most splendid and eloquent eulogium, to which I refer you. I have just heard the cause and am sorry to be compelled to give it against the fair one – I will explain on what grounds when I see you.[6]

It seems strange that Sydney ever became a JP at all. The work was unpaid but was, in most other respects, unsuitable for a man in orders.

The clerical JP was both judge and pastor, contradictory roles. Nowadays clergy are not even allowed to sit on juries. Sydney recognized that there could be a conflict of interest between his priestly and magisterial roles; he was careful, for instance, not to sit in judgement over a parishioner accused of a serious offence. But he would have strenuously denied that a man of God should not also be a man of law. As Sydney saw it, it was his duty to care for the whole man, body and soul. By joining the Bench, he believed he was fulfilling his priestly ministry, not trying to escape from it.

Nor, as it happens, was Sydney doing anything out of the ordinary. The countryside of early nineteenth-century England was a world in which the clergyman, the 'resident Moses' as he was sometimes called, played a major role. He was the learned man, the man who, like as not, knew about law. Often he was the only man in his community with a university education; two-thirds of those who graduated from Oxford and Cambridge (the only English universities) went on to take orders. One in six rectors and vicars was a JP; and one in four JPs was a rector or vicar. Sydney followed convention in joining the Bench, even if he flouted it by his liberal exercise of magisterial power.

In addition to his duties as a JP, Sydney also became a turnpike trustee. In an area such as his part of Yorkshire, where there was a large programme of road building, this was more time-consuming and burdensome than it might appear. Turnpike trustees had to supervise the building of new roads; they also had to get the agreement of the parishes through which the roads would pass. Turnpike business cost Sydney dear; a dispute at a magistrates' meeting at Malton was to turn into a vendetta against him that was very nasty indeed, threatening things more precious to Sydney than the continuance of his magisterial career.

Once he was a magistrate Sydney felt he had the authority to write on social issues, an area which he had previously avoided. In an article in the *Edinburgh Review* for April 1814, only three months after he joined the Bench, Sydney nailed his liberal colours to the mast. His choice of subject looks bizarre: a local asylum for the mentally ill with only sixty or so inmates, run by Quakers for Quakers and using novel methods of care. In fact the choice was an inspired one.

The Retreat, as it was known, had been founded by William Tuke, a prominent member of the Quaker business community at York, in 1792. Tuke, as Ann Digby shows in her excellent book on the Retreat, was not trying out a pet theory or deliberately striving to be inventive.

The Retreat was the child of pure impulse, of Tuke's righteous anger. Incensed by the brutal treatment meted out to a fellow Quaker at the York Asylum, one of only four provincial mental hospitals then in England, Tuke decided that he could do better himself. So, despite the fact that he was devoid of all medical qualifications, he set up the Retreat, initially taking sole charge of everything, even the prescribing of medicines. It did not take Tuke long to find out that the medical remedies then in use did nothing to relieve symptoms of mental derangement, so he used them only to counter physical disease. He also profoundly disapproved of the prison-like appearance, and regime, of the rival York asylum. Everything was done to make the patients at the Retreat feel at home. Each ward was, in Tuke's words, a 'little family' of at most ten. The very walls spoke to the inmates, telling them they were not a sub-species, devoid of all rhyme and reason – the conventional view of their condition – but men and women in desperate need of love. Tuke went to inordinate lengths to reduce the patients' sense of incarceration; the windows had no bars to them and their iron frames were encased with wood and then painted. The grounds, stretching over eleven acres, were filled with rabbits, chickens and a variety of birds. This was a wise move; it was found that caring for animals had therapeutic value. *Mens sana in corpore sano* was Tuke's motto. So he set the patients simple physical tasks: women churned butter, knitted and mangled clothes, while men pumped water, chopped wood and cleaned shoes. Tuke had unwittingly invented occupational therapy. Relations between patients and staff were close and direct; there was a lot of informal discussion, and some convalescents were allowed to join a party which went each week to Quaker meeting in York. Visits to see family and friends were encouraged for those who were on the mend. It reads like a description of the regimen in an advanced mental hospital in the 1950s.

Tuke, needless to say, clashed with the medical establishment of the day. The Quaker tea and coffee merchant was proposing a revolution in patient care. Tension was not helped by his evident skill: discharge rates from the Retreat were high. No profession takes kindly to the incursions of rank amateurs, especially if they successfully challenge its authority. The leading medical men of the time, in their stand against the methods advocated by Tuke, were sure that they were on firm ground. It was self-evident, so their thinking ran, that the mad had lost all semblance of reason. The only way to bring them back to their senses was to frighten them. There was no shortage of ideas:

elaborate systems of plumbing to deliver forcible streams of water on to the head; hidden trap-doors in corridors, so that the unsuspecting lunatic could be plunged into a 'bath of surprise'; even coffins with holes drilled in the lid, into which patients were fastened before being lowered under water. One of the few things that can be said in favour of the 'mad doctors', as they were known, is that they treated rich and poor alike. When George III exhibited signs of apparent mental illness, he was chained to a stake, he was beaten and starved, and was also 'kept in subjection by menacing and violent language'. Inmates of Bethlem ('Bedlam'), England's premier mental hospital, were put in straitjackets, handcuffs and leg-locks, and the most violent were chained to the wall. William Tuke did away with chains and used straitjackets very sparingly.[7]

Where did Tuke get the inspiration for his radical and exciting venture from? The explanation is breathtakingly simple. Tuke was a man who had nothing: no medical qualifications, no experience of dealing with mentally ill people, no special insights into the causes, or possible cures, of mental illness; nothing, that is, except the enormous power of his deeply held religious faith. Central in Quaker theology is insistence that every man has within him an unquenchable inner light that nothing, not even madness, can ever put out. It is the tenacity with which Tuke clung to this conviction which explains his humane treatment of the mad. He tried to create, at the Retreat, a healing religious community: the friendly surroundings, small wards and informal discussion groups were modelled on the Quaker meeting.

Sydney played an important role in gaining for the Retreat well-deserved fame and recognition. In 1813, Tuke's grandson Samuel published *A Description of the Retreat*, the first book in England to deal with the therapeutic practice of a particular mental institution. This volume created a huge stir locally but did not immediately make much impression further abroad. Sydney's article in the *Edinburgh Review* a year later gave Samuel Tuke's book the prominence that was required in order to set in motion a national movement for reform. Sydney was nothing if not bold, stating that the Retreat was 'the best managed asylum for the insane that has ever yet been established', and that its influence would gradually 'bring into repute a milder and better method' of treating the mentally ill.

This judgement shows Sydney at his courageous and broadminded best. His mischievous side doubtless delighted in giving categorical support to an experimental asylum, where the attitude towards patient care was regarded as outrageous by the medical establishment. But beneath Sydney's mischief lay a deep seriousness. He sided with William and Samuel Tuke because he believed in them as men. Quakers, Sydney thought, had qualities other people lacked. There was a group of them at Thornton, the hamlet in his parish, and he was very impressed by the simplicity and sincerity of their lives. During the epidemic fever of the autumn and early winter of 1816 which killed Mary Hopper, Hannah Snowdon and William Gallery, these Quakers went even higher in Sydney's estimation: their courage knew no bounds. The same moral qualities were evident at the Retreat; the health of the patient, Sydney pointed out to good effect, was put before the safety of the staff. Sydney thought that any regime in a mental hospital that relied upon notions of custodial care, an attitude which was prevalent until the middle of the twentieth century, was wrong. The patient must come first. Sydney was also inspired by the Tukes' optimistic belief in the underlying rationality of the insane, and by their insistence that the feelings of patients should be respected and that they must be treated as adults. These notions dovetailed with Sydney's understanding of the essentials of the Christian faith. The poorest outcast, he had told his prosperous London congregation, has some pride in reserve. He wholeheartedly agreed with the Tukes' spiritual values.

Sydney ended his first article on social policy on a Delphic note: 'we have no doubt of the existence of great abuses in the interior of many madhouses'.[8] This was an oblique reference to a tremendous local row which had broken out the previous year as the result of publication of Samuel Tuke's book. Dr Best, the physician at the rival York Asylum, did not like some disparaging remarks Tuke made about traditional methods of treatment. Under a flimsy cover of anonymity, he attacked the Retreat in letters to the *York Chronicle* in September 1813. The Tukes counterattacked, encouraging supporters to pay £20 in order to qualify as governors of the York Asylum. Having packed the governing body, they then demanded an inquiry. A month before Sydney's article was published, four secret cells were found; only eight and a half feet square, they were used as sleeping quarters by thirteen women. Excrement covered the walls, and once the door was closed for the night the women were left in total darkness. Later in 1814 there were revelations of embezzlement, rape and even murder. To cap it all, the records of the asylum had been tampered with in order to conceal the number of deaths. Dr Best was forced to resign and nearly all the staff were sacked.

The bandwagon of publicity now began to gather pace. Tuke's *Description* was read by a London Quaker, Edward Wakefield. So impressed was he that he decided to set up a metropolitan asylum, to be run on the lines of the Retreat. As part of his preparations for this new venture, Wakefield visited Bethlem. He was so appalled by the conditions he found there that he returned, bringing with him a number of sympathetic M Ps. This vocal group successfully pressed for a parliamentary inquiry. The first meeting of the House of Commons select committee on the state of madhouses was held in May 1815, and the first witnesses brought before it gave evidence about conditions at the York Asylum. Later, William Tuke was given a chance to explain what happened at the Retreat. The committee came down firmly in favour of Tuke's methods. 'Moral treatment', as it was known, soon became *de rigueur*. In the early 1820s as many people visited the Retreat as went to see York Minster. Elizabeth Fry, the famous Quaker prison reformer, came; so did the duke of Wellington and the Grand Duke Nicholas of Russia. Asylums in America were modelled upon the Retreat, as were a number of private establishments which were set up at home.

Sydney deserves a place, alongside the Tukes and Edward Wakefield, among the earliest pioneers of humane treatment of the mentally ill. The principles for which Sydney fought – the primacy of patient care over notions of custodial incarceration, the importance of fostering a sense of self-respect among the insane, the desirability of small, homely asylums – could have changed for the better the whole history of English psychiatric medicine. It was not to be. Andrew Scull has skilfully charted the way in which William Tuke's vision was allowed to fade. Local magistrates, counting the pennies, built from the mid-1840s onwards prison-like county asylums, each crammed with 1000 patients or more. Wards in these institutions were massive, there was no occupational therapy and, after mid-century, discharge rates fell sharply. By the late Victorian era, asylums had become social dustbins, full of incurables. Even the Retreat became less effective as a healing comunity.[9] It was not until the middle of the twentieth century that the therapeutic value of the moral treatment which Sydney had advocated came once again to be fully appreciated.

The early months of 1814 were relatively eventful for Sydney; there was his appointment to the magistracy in January, the occupation of Foston rectory in March, and the article on 'Mad Quakers' came out in April. The summer, although quieter, was enlivened by an important incident. One day in August a loud cry went up from the servants: a coach and four, with outriders, was stuck fast in a nearby ploughed field. The visitors were guided, not without difficulty, up to the house. Out stepped Lord and Lady Carlisle.

Frederick Howard, fifth earl of Carlisle, now aged sixty-six, was one of the greatest noblemen in England. A boon companion in his youth of Charles James Fox, his major political appointment had been a brief spell as Lord Lieutenant of Ireland. Sydney was privileged to receive a visit. The earl was a taciturn man and his later years were marred by physical illness and a nervous disorder. He made little effort to cultivate friendships with his neighbours. Apart from seeing Sydney, there are only two recorded instances of his making social contacts in Yorkshire.

The earl did not care for Foston rectory ('it is a red business in the middle of a red fallow field'[10]) but he was pleased with Sydney. The rector of Foston was soon making frequent visits to Castle Howard, the great Baroque mansion belonging to the Howard family, situated five miles away to the north. It was not long before he had the run of the library whenever the earl was in town.

Sydney was impressed by the old earl's sprightliness. He stayed at Castle Howard with Catharine for two or three days in January 1815, reporting to Lady Holland that the master of the house 'has ten years of life in his pocket which surprised me for I thought the parish sexton borrowed money upon him', a calculation of Carlisle's likely life-expectancy which proved remarkably accurate. Sydney, drawing upon his vast reserves of charm, quite soon broke through the earl's considerable reserve. When Lord Carlisle sent over a deer, Sydney was not content with a note of thanks. He also let his lordship in on one of his secret inventions: a novel larder for meat. 'We let the Venison down into the Well where it remained in a temperature of 40, while yours was in one of 80, and it literally would have kept 4 or 5 days longer. Why not make a Venison Larder 10 yards under ground?'

Sydney had known the earl's son, George Howard, Viscount Morpeth, for at least six years. Morpeth, thought Sydney, was 'a man of excellent understanding, very polished manners, and a good heart; but I should suspect very irritable and very sensitive; the last to a fault'. Irritable or not, he was one of the closest friends of Lord Holland and Bobus: the three of them had been together at Eton. Sydney recognized that it was important to get on well with Morpeth, and gradually became happier in his company.

Sydney was never as close to Morpeth as he was to his wife Georgiana, the eldest daughter of the fifth duke of Devonshire and his famous duchess. Georgiana's portrait is at Castle Howard; although lacking the beauty of her mother, she has a pleasant, rounded face and looks very amiable. Appearances belie reality: Georgiana's was a tormented and tortured soul. Her private diary is littered with references to difficulties, inward turmoils and religious resolutions, made and broken. Although she had an especial horror of childbirth, she had many children; six sons and six daughters grew to maturity. Indicative of her state of mind is an entry in her diary for 24 April 1814: 'Pain, suffering, religion, patience, fortitude, virtue. Oh my God give to thy unworthy servant thy Grace. Let me be enabled to bear to go through my approaching trials.'

Her eleventh child was born in May 1818 and afterwards she seems to have suffered a prolonged clinical depression, with a hint of demonic possession. The details of her condition are cloudy but she was acknowledged to be ill. The brevity and poignancy of her diary entries suggest that she felt utterly helpless: 20 January 1819, 'I felt very low'; 26 January, 'struggle with the fiend'. She then became pregnant again and her psychological state worsened: 5 September 1819, 'Great Depression'; 29 October, 'great depression and misery but a determination to persevere in well doing & to leave the rest to Heaven'.

In February 1820, a short while before her twelfth confinement, Sydney wrote her a deservedly famous letter of consolation. He begins by saying that he hopes the 'blue Daemons' are 'got under', and then continues:

Nobody has suffered more from low spirits than I have done, so I feel for you. 1. Live as well and drink as much wine as you dare. 2. Go into the shower-bath with a small quantity of water at a temperature low enough to give you a *slight sensation of cold* – 75 or 80°. 3. Amusing books. 4. Short views of human life not farther than dinner or tea. 5. Be as busy as you can. 6. See as much as you can of those friends who respect and like you; 7. and of those acquaintance who amuse you. 8. Make no secret of low spirits to your friends but talk of them fully: they are always the worse for dignified concealment. 9. Attend to the effects tea and coffee produce upon you. 10. Compare your lot with that of other people. 11. Don't expect too much of human life, a sorry business at the best. 12. Avoid poetry, dramatic representations (except comedy), music, serious novels, melancholy sentimental people, and everything likely to excite feeling or emotion not ending in active benevolence. 13. *Do good* and endeavour to please everybody of every degree. 14. Be as much as you can in the open air without fatigue. 15. Make the room where you commonly sit gay and pleasant. 16. Struggle by little and little against idleness. 17. Don't be too severe upon yourself, or underrate yourself, but do yourself justice. 18. Keep good blazing fires. 19. Be firm and constant in the exercise of rational religion. 20. Believe me dear Lady Georgiana very truly yours, Sydney Smith.[11]

This letter, like the rest of Sydney's correspondence, is an intensely private document. For a third party to see a letter between friends, let alone for the letter to be published, sounded, thought Sydney, the death-knell of the intimacy that was the essential concomitant of all pleasurable letter-writing. Sydney lived out his convictions, systematically burning all personal letters he received and only keeping business correspondence. We, as readers, have the joy of discovering something that was intended to remain hidden. Sydney, for his part, never felt the need to justify himself to posterity. His correspondence has, in consequence, a directness and a naturalness which have rarely, if ever, been equalled.

Although this letter to Lady Georgiana is a wonderfully fresh piece of writing, it is not entirely satisfactory. Sydney was trying to be helpful but he did not always succeed. Lady Georgiana must have smiled at Sydney's third injunction: 'Amusing books'. It is not hard to paraphrase her thoughts. 'Dear Sydney, he tries so hard and means so well but, like everyone else, even my own dear husband, he just does not understand. He wants me to read amusing books when it takes all the effort that I can muster to write a one-line entry in my diary.' Some of Sydney's recommendations, especially his suggestion that it is important to take 'short views of human life not farther than dinner or tea', are addressed to the chronically depressed, but most of the letter is written for those who often feel out of sorts without ever being psychologically ill. Sydney advocated for Lady Georgiana what he advocated for himself: a balanced and active life, striving to keep the mind occupied with present concerns, steering it away from melancholy thoughts. It is in some ways an attractive strategy, but its main drawback is that it discourages the low-spirited person from confronting feelings of hopelessness, learning not to fear them and, gaining strength through the experience, enriching and improving his or her life. Emotion, for Sydney, is a deep and dark pool which is best left undisturbed. 'Avoid poetry, dramatic representations (except comedy), music, serious novels, melancholy sentimental people, and everything likely to excite feeling or emotion not ending in active benevolence.'

These defensive remarks are combined with great psychological insight. Sydney traced depression to its root: a distorted view of the self. 'Don't be too severe upon yourself, or underrate yourself, but do yourself justice.' Sydney realized that the depressed person is cut off from his or her own depths; there is a loss of the sense of self-value, a fatal tendency to indulge in belittlement. Sydney also stressed the importance of a psycho-therapeutic approach to alleviation of suffering. It was essential, when feeling depressed, to try to break out of the prison that is the self. 'Make no secret of low spirits to your friends but talk of them fully: they are always the worse for dignified concealment.' It could well be that this advice stemmed from Sydney's admiration of the methods of mental healing used at the Retreat.

When Sydney mentioned his own low spirits to Lady Georgiana, he was thinking primarily of the burden of financial worry he faced for several years after building at Foston. Catharine speaks of Sydney's sleeplessness, of his agitation and alarm, the fears of a man 'naturally timid and distrustful of the future'. There were 'moments of *dreadful despondence*' which 'sunk his commonly buoyant spirits to a *most afflicting degree*'. Saba is more haunted, more precise, more specific; now in her teens she could still recall, many years later, the picture of Sydney as he sat at his desk in the evenings, slowly and painfully working his way through the mounting bills. His face would drop into his hands and he would exclaim: 'Ah! I see, I shall end my old-age in a gaol!'[12]

Sydney spent around £4000 on the rectory and farm at Foston, so his savings of £2500 or so, supplemented by the loan of £1600 from Queen Anne's Bounty, just about covered the cost. The principal reason for his feelings of despondency over the project was that it had been badly timed. The great agrarian boom, which had benefited him so enormously during his early years in Yorkshire, reached its zenith in

1813. Great booms, of course, are followed by great depressions. Deflation started in 1814, the year in which Sydney moved into his new home, and was very fierce. The values of benefices went down everywhere and the fall at Foston was worse than most. In February 1816, Sydney told Lady Holland that the living was bringing him in 'barely £900 pr.ann.', implying that he had previously been making quite a lot more; and by the summer of 1820 his income was down by a further third, to £600. After repaying £130 to Queen Anne's Bounty, he was left with £470 a year. Compared with the vast majority of his clerical contemporaries, Sydney had little to complain about. Most clergy could consider themselves lucky if they had an income of £250 a year in 1820. His relative wealth did not, of course, come into Sydney's calculations. What he was concerned about was the indecent speed with which the value of his living had gone down.

He also faced a further financial problem. As soon as he had moved into Foston rectory, he had begun to farm the 110 acres of glebe which were not let out to Farmer Horner. His aim was to get a decent return on the capital invested in outbuildings, farming equipment and fencing. In the midst of an agrarian depression this was not possible. It did not help that Sydney, although an enthusiastic farmer, was totally inexperienced. He tried to ensure that his workmen did not take advantage of his agricultural virginity. In order to keep them under firm control he rigged up an enormous speaking trumpet which was always ready to hand, and which he used while standing on the stone steps outside the drawing-room. He also had a telescope, supported in a leather sling. Sydney's instinctive feel for animals was an important bonus. Their comfort was never neglected. In every field Sydney rigged up a 'universal scratcher', a series of sharp-edged poles set at different heights to enable all the animals to relieve their frustrations to their heart's content.[13]

Sydney's playful and restless mind was incapable of resisting the itch to experiment. This was, in one sense, a strength. Sydney constantly questioned traditional farming methods. He wrote a detailed letter to his friend Francis Cholmeley on growing beans – distances between rows, number of ploughings and hoeings, methods of sowing, and so on – and told the archbishop's son William that he always left a portion of ploughed land unlimed in order to work out whether the extra cost of liming paid dividends. But zeal for innovation is always hazardous for beginners, as Sydney found to his cost. An entertaining letter to the *Farmer's Magazine* describes his two most serious blunders: keeping Scottish sheep and using oxen for ploughing. Ten or twelve per cent of the sheep always died of rot, they consumed prodigious quantities of turnips and clover, and stubbornly refused to fatten. They also had an alarming homing instinct. 'They crawled through hedges where I should have thought a rabbit could hardly have found admission; and, where crawling would not do, they had recourse to leaping. Five or six times they all assembled, and set out on their return to the North.' The oxen ate twice as much as Sydney's horses and did half as much work. They were also almost as vexatious as the sheep. 'They ran against my gate-posts, lay down in the cart whenever they were tired, and ran away at the sight of a stranger.'

There is probably a lot of hyperbole in all this. Sydney was for ever making jokes at the expense of anything that was Scottish, so his comments about his sheep should not be taken at face value. It also seems curious that he should use oxen for ploughing, since he had already had plenty of experience of their inefficiency when trying to get them to convey his bricks. The letter might, indeed, be a hoax; there is no way of telling. For what it is worth he told the *Farmer's Magazine* that his dalliance with Scottish sheep and with oxen for ploughing had cost him between £300 and £400.[14]

The main difficulty was the weather. 'Hideous ruin and Combustion among the farmers in this part of the World', Sydney told Lord Holland's sister Caroline in October 1815. 'Blustring Squires are collapsing very fast under the punctures of Adversity. No rents paid.' This sounds bad enough but there was worse to come. The harvest of 1816 was a complete disaster. 'The Crops are all double in this neighbourhood,' Sydney wrote to Lord Grey, 'that is upon the old Crop a new one has made its appearance and is in a very high state of vegetation.' Good flour was too expensive to be had. For a year the household at the rectory went without bread; the sprouted wheat produced 'thin, unleavened, sweet-tasting cakes, like frost-bitten potatoes', and Sydney and his family had to be content with those. It was the dire unproductivity of the land around Foston that probably caused the savage infectious fever that broke out at Thornton in the autumn and early winter of 1816.

Sprouting wheat was not the only thing on Sydney's mind during these months; he was also worried about one of his great friends. Francis Horner's health had been bad for some time but had worsened in the summer of 1816, when he developed congestion of the lungs. With her customary generosity to her friends, Lady Holland put some rooms at Holland House at his disposal for the winter, offering to nurse him herself. On medical advice Horner decided to go to Italy instead. He wrote a fairly buoyant and gossipy letter to Sydney and Catharine from Turin on 16 November, and Sydney wrote back by return. 'It gives us the greatest pleasure to find you have got so far so well. Our kindest affections and warmest good wishes move on with you, and hang like a dew on the glasses of your carriage. God bless you, my dear Horner!'[15] There is a quite extraordinary distilled passion in Sydney's adieu: what a sense of lingering there is, what a desire always to be there.

Sydney's next communication from Horner was a sad, half-finished letter, written from Pisa in mid-January and not received until March. Already, Horner was dead. Sydney was grievously afflicted. 'Looking back on my own mind', he told John Whishaw, 'I never remember to have felt any event more deeply.' It had been a special relationship; Horner, uniquely, had offered Sydney something that came close to moral guidance. 'It will be useful to us in all the great occasions of life', Sydney wrote to Lord Holland, 'to reflect how Horner would act and think in them if God had suffered him to live.' Horner's great gift had been to combine goodness and intellectual power. He was venerated by Sydney, Bobus, Jeffrey and Lord and Lady Holland, and was respected by most of the members of the House of Commons. He had died, before reaching high office, at the age of thirty-eight. It is testimony to the esteem in which he was held that, although he did not come from a wealthy or influential family, although he had never written a famous work, and although he was never in the Cabinet, there is nevertheless a monument to him in Westminster Abbey.

Horner's death, and the atrocious harvest of 1816, mark a nadir in Sydney's fortunes. He did not complain about his crops in 1817, from which it is reasonable to infer that they were a good deal better than they had been the previous year. Conditions in 1818 were tough but Sydney acquitted himself well. There was severe wet in the spring ('the earth that ought to be as hard as a biscuit is as soft as dough') and then a summer drought ('the cattle are drinking ale and porter'). Local farmers found the going hard: the potato crop failed and there was no hay. Sydney for once had something to boast about: '*I* have a fine crop of Talavera wheat', he told Lord Grey.[16]

This was the turning-point. Sydney's harvest in 1819 was 'abundant'. There was another drought the next year ('about three or four ounces of rain here, that is all'), but his crop was still 'good'.

Sydney's method of getting in the harvest for 1821 was novel. 'I have saved all my Corn', he informed Lady Grey, 'by injecting great quantities of fermented Liquors into the workmen, and making them work all night.' All in all, considering his lack of experience, Sydney had come through the post-war agrarian crisis well. General economic conditions had dragged down the value of his living, but he had made considerable progress with the 110 acres he looked after himself.[17] Perseverance pulled him through.

11

A STRANGE REFORMER

'An excellent and well-arranged dinner is a most pleasing occurrence . . . who knows that the kitchen chimney caught fire half an hour before . . . and that a poor little wretch, of six or seven years old, was sent up in the midst of the flames to put it out?'

SYDNEY SMITH, *Edinburgh Review*, October 1819

Sydney's success with his crop of Talavera wheat in 1818 lifted his spirits. In December he took the family up to London, staying until late February. Back in 1816 he had told Lady Holland that such an expedition, much as he wished it, was out of the question because of expense: taking Catharine and the children to Town for three months would cost £100. Now, despite the continuing reduction in the value of Foston, financial considerations were less pressing, principally because Sydney was feeling more confident about his farming ability. The journey from Foston was a joyous struggle. 'You cannot conceive the blunders and agony, the dust and distraction, the roaring and raving with which a family like mine is conveyed through three degrees of latitude to its place of destination.' Once the Smiths finally arrived in London, they stayed at Bobus's house in Savile Row, from where they launched expeditions to see the sights: the British Museum, St Paul's Cathedral, the Royal Mint, the Custom House, the terrace running from Vauxhall to Westminster Bridge. Sydney's children loved the excitement and the crowds. 'It is the first time they have ever seen four people together, except on remarkably fine days at the parish church.' Sydney was apprehensive how Saba, now seventeen, would fare in society. His worries were soon dispelled. 'Saba made a better figure than I imagined she would – was not bad looking . . . nor rurally timid, nor deficient in conversation', is the substance of Sydney's report to Jeffrey. He ends on a proud note: 'Mrs Sydney was very popular.'

Sydney only took three children with him to London; Douglas had started at Westminster School in September. Sending him there was an extraordinary decision. Sydney had hated his own time at Winchester, and had nothing except contempt for those who sent their children to public schools. You will remember the first of the popular fallacies which he recorded in one of his commonplace books: 'Because I have gone through it, my son shall go through it also.' At first he was opposed to a public-school education for his elder son. He had raised the issue of the boy's future with his godfather, Francis Horner. The public school option was ruled out as expensive and useless; it would be better if Douglas was sent to a small private establishment, the course of action advocated by Sydney in the *Edinburgh Review* article, written in 1810, in which he had drawn up the list of Englishmen who had achieved fame despite not going to Eton or Westminster.

Bobus, always a powerful influence, seems to have been partly responsible for Sydney's change of mind. He took a house at Scarborough during the summer of 1817, Sydney and the family came and visited him there, and Douglas's education was discussed by the two brothers. Bobus was in favour of Westminster and offered to pay half the fees, calculated by Sydney at somewhere between £150 and £200 a year. Fatherly pride was a further factor. Sydney had high hopes of his elder son. 'I begin to suspect that my little boy will turn out extremely clever', he had told Lady Holland in February 1811; Douglas, at the time, was on the eve of his sixth birthday.[1] Sydney's own circumstances decided the matter. He felt that he would never get a bishopric because the Whigs had no chance of regaining power. Even if the value of Foston recovered, the living would never provide the substantial sums he was looking for in order to launch his sons on successful careers. Pressured by what he saw as his own dull prospects, Sydney decided that the least he could do was to give Douglas a good start by sending him to Westminster. He also made future plans for the boy, asking Lord Holland to use his influence to secure a position for Douglas in India:

It is better to lose sight of a Child than to retain him near you in poverty, obscurity and dependance.
  Fortune I believe has done for me all she ever means to do, and I have no better prospect for Douglas than that concerning which I am writing to you.

This letter shows the full extent of Sydney's underlying lack of self-confidence. He was distrustful of the future and, when events conspired against him, he fell back upon the same career path for Douglas as Robert Smith had adopted for Cecil and Courtney: use of friendly contacts in order to open up opportunities in the formidably lucrative Indian Civil Service. Sydney had not shaken himself free of *nouveau-riche* attitudes, but the India scheme came to nothing.

Sending Douglas to Westminster was idiotic: it was the most brutal school in England. The boys fought each other at Milling Green, a small patch of grass located, of all places, in the cloisters of Westminster Abbey. Fights were scheduled for 7 AM and were conducted according to the rules of the prize ring. Combatants quite often suffered severe injuries, fighting until they were virtually unconscious. Violence was not confined to Milling Green. The boys defended Dean's Yard as though it were their own property; even adults, ignorant or brave enough to attempt to walk across, were set upon. There were also frequent fights with the boys who lived in the dilapidated tenements to the south of the school, towards the river. Westminster boys called their opponents 'Skies', supposedly a shortened form of Volsci, and considered that it was incumbent upon themselves to show Roman valour in repulsing the barbarians.

Douglas was quickly blooded at Westminster. He had not been there more than a few weeks when his father reported to Lady Holland that he had fought his first fight, coming off victorious; Douglas was, Sydney adds, now 'completely established'. It speaks volumes for Sydney's naïvety that he should think a single success at fisticuffs sufficient to 'completely establish' a boy under the barbaric regime in force at Westminster. Douglas was soon to show that he was not established at all. Within a week of winning his first fight he caught typhus, and Catharine had to hurry up to London to nurse him.

Sydney's rough treatment of his elder son becomes even more culpable when Douglas's character is considered. He was a nervous boy who suffered from a stammer; just the kind of person who was likely, as Sydney had recorded in his commonplace book, to have 'his eye nearly knocked out' at an English public school of the period. Also, like his godfather, Douglas was deferential to his parents and extremely anxious to please. He showed this side of his personality during the bout of typhus. Confined to bed for six weeks, Douglas was not idle. He had been sent to Westminster because Sydney and Catharine hoped he would get a king's scholarship. The examination was to be held the following March and Douglas was so determined to do well that he studied hard at his Latin grammar even while he was ill. Eight king's scholars were elected, Douglas being placed sixth. Catharine was happy, for the boy's sake: 'I verily believe it would have broken his heart had he fail'd so very desirous was he on the first occasion that had occurr'd in his young life to repay us by his success for all the anxious and agitating fears his dear Father had felt about him for the future.'

Douglas's trials were far from over. As a junior scholar he was outrageously bullied by an older boy, the eldest son of a clergyman, later bishop of Bristol. Douglas lost the key to this boy's desk. He responded by beating Douglas across the hand every day for a month with a walking stick; Douglas worried for a while that his thumb was broken and could not hold his pen in school. The critical moment came when Douglas was attacked once again by the same boy. So badly was he hurt that he wrote to Sydney saying that some reason for going home must be invented, or he would be compelled to run away. Emily happened to be ill and Sydney wrote to the headmaster of Westminster, stating that she was most anxious to see her brother. So Douglas went back to Foston. And his problem? By a supreme irony, his eye had nearly been knocked out. Catharine was distraught. The whole of one of Douglas's eyeballs was 'the deep colour of blood; he could scarcely bear to open it, and the weakness of sight . . . from the great state of inflammation of all the surrounding parts such as to make him firmly believe he should lose it altogether.' (None of the masters had noticed Douglas's plight; it was perfectly normal for boys to come to lessons immediately after doing battle at Milling Green.) Douglas was stoic about his injuries. 'Shelter me for a little while from this Monster who leaves College at the coming holidays, and I will cheerfully return again.'

Douglas went back, did well, and ended up as captain of school. He never, however, managed to overcome the physical weakness brought on by the attack of typhus which had struck him down soon after he entered the school. Sydney admits as much in a letter written to Lady Mary Bennet in November 1822, by which time his elder son had been at Westminster four years. 'You will be sorry to hear that Douglas has had bad health ever since he went to Westminster, and has been taken thence to be nursed in a typhus fever, from which he is slowly recovering. Mrs Sydney set off for London last week and is likely to remain there some time.' Keeping Douglas at Westminster was a hideously dangerous experiment which a less ambitious, and more socially secure, father would have been sensible enough to avoid.

Culminating in the family visit to London, 1818 was an important transitional year for Sydney. Despite the worry caused by Douglas's attack of typhus, he was beginning to throw off the lethargy which had intermittently weighed him down ever since he had moved into Foston rectory. It is a sign of his improved spirits that he started to think about doing some writing again. The article on the Tukes, which had appeared in the issue of the *Edinburgh Review* for April 1814, was his last literary effort; magisterial, clerical and agricultural duties had, in the interim, taken up all his time. Now there was space, once more, for intellectual work. Provided, that is, that he was well paid for what he did. On 9 July he told Jeffrey that 'if you can afford me £40 each for 5 sheets the quantity I could do with ease to myself in the course of a year, it would attach me to the review, and make me think it worth my while.' Not even Douglas's illness slowed Sydney down. He wrote one article for the September 1818 issue and two for December's. Once he was in full flow, there was no holding him back. Between September 1818 and October 1824 he wrote a total of twenty-eight pieces, with a further six over the next two years. Seven were on travel narratives and five on literary subjects. The remaining twenty-two range across political, social and economic affairs, an impressive body of work that firmly established Sydney's reputation as one of the leading social commentators of the age.

Sometimes Sydney did the necessary background research himself; on other occasions he relied upon facts which were already in the public domain, presenting them in a way that made his case forceful and effective. He used the latter technique in an article on boy chimney sweeps in the issue of the *Edinburgh Review* for October 1819. The evidence was drawn from the report of a parliamentary Select Committee, published in June 1817: Sydney added the wit. He went on the attack in his first paragraph:

> An excellent and well-arranged dinner is a most pleasing occurrence, and a great triumph of civilised life . . . In the midst of all this, who knows that the kitchen chimney caught fire half an hour before dinner – and that a poor little wretch, of six or seven years old, was sent up in the midst of the flames to put it out?

'What', asked Sydney rhetorically, 'is a toasted child, compared to the agonies of the mistress of the house with a deranged dinner?'

As in his earlier article on the Walcheren expedition, Sydney let the facts speak for themselves. Sweeps left cards at doors: '*Little boys for small flues*'.[2] To clean cramped chimneys, where the flue could measure as little as eight inches by nine, it was not unknown to employ boys as young as five or six. Often, of course, the boys got stuck. Imaginative employers used home-grown methods to remove them. One Edinburgh chimney sweep fastened a rope around a boy's foot, pulling for about a quarter of an hour; when this tactic failed he attached the rope to a crow-bar, called in the help of his assistant, and they both pulled for about a quarter of an hour more. The rope did not manage to survive this gruelling experience; nor, for that matter, did the boy.

Boys, complained Sydney, were quite often sent up chimneys that were on fire. When they yelled out in pain, their burns were assuaged with a bucket of water deftly poured down upon them from above. Hours were hard and long; many children had to start work at two or three in the morning, because people wanted their chimneys cleaned before the household was awake. The workload in Christmas week was especially severe. Despite the filthy working conditions, long hours and frequent danger, some of the more enterprising youngsters tacked on other work. Recovering watches from privies was one of the most popular sidelines.

Sydney's article was brilliant but flawed. He was excellent at diagnosis but bad at prescribing a cure. The owners of houses, Sydney argued, should be 'encouraged' to use machinery to sweep their chimneys, stopping short of the more radical proposal that use of machinery be made compulsory except in cases where it could be shown that the shape of the chimney made this impossible. To understand why Sydney was poor at devising means of social reform, it is necessary to recognize the unusual position he occupied within the Whig party. Contemporary Whiggism was an uneasy alliance between aristocratic landowners and professional men, many of them educated at one or other of the Scottish universities. Sydney was on terms of the greatest intimacy with the leaders of both groups within the party. He had started the *Edinburgh Review* with Jeffrey and Horner, he was a close friend of Romilly and Mackintosh, he went every year to Howick, and was virtually part of the family circle at Holland House. Given his social background, his taste for law, his innate ability and, most of all, his role as the founder of the *Edinburgh Review*, Sydney's natural place was among the professional men in the party. This place was not taken up. When it came to social policy, he sided with the aristocrats. Lord Grey and Lord Holland believed that the role of government was to administer, not to reform; measures of social improvement should be left to the magistracy. This non-interventionist stance promoted the interests of the Whig grandees to perfection; for it was they, of course, who wielded the power in their localities. The professional men, who were landless, wanted to use Parliament as the instrument of social change; for, with their energy, ideas and debating skills, it was in the House that they shone. Sydney took a different line. When Lord Shaftesbury introduced his Ten Hour Bill in 1844, Sydney was outraged. 'It does seem to me very absurd to hinder a Woman of 30 from working as long as she pleases but mankind are getting mad with humanity, and Samaritanism.'[3] It was belief in *laissez-faire* which also lay behind Sydney's rejection of legislation as a suitable method for curbing the use of boy chimney sweeps.

Why did Sydney desert his natural allies? One could cynically argue that he was looking to the main chance. Lawyers in the mould of Romilly and Brougham, an editor of the stature of Jeffrey, could afford to take independent views. Sydney, who was reliant on patronage in order to gain ecclesiastical promotion, could not. Bobus, conservative in his social attitudes, was also an influence. Nor should we forget the idiosyncratic orientation of Sydney's mind, his sheer sense of fun. When he sat down to write about climbing boys, his main aim was to amuse. Remedies were consigned to a weak and rambling final paragraph. Great wits do not make good social reformers.

In October 1821 the household at Foston rectory became quite excited. Their animation had a surprising source: news concerning Sydney's spinster aunt Mary, who lived with his wealthy uncle John. For many years Mary had had nothing to do with her famous nephew. Suddenly, and quite out of the blue, she had written to Sydney proposing a visit, which had duly taken place in the spring of the previous year. In April 1821, when on the point of death, she made her will. It was proved on 24 October and the contents were known in Yorkshire within a matter of days. Most relatives received something, but those who lived at Foston rectory did best of all. 'I bequeathe to Mrs Caroline Smith, the wife of my nephew the Reverend Sidney Smith' – despite the visit in the spring of 1820, Mary still found it impossible to distinguish between Sydney's wife and Bobus's – 'the sum of £500'; Saba and Emily both benefited by £100; while, for Sydney, there were three London properties: the Guildhall Coffee House and Tavern, situated in Cheapside, and a pair of nearby dwellings. Valued at £8000, this bequest produced rents of £400 a year, two-thirds as much as Sydney's income from Foston. Sydney was delighted; he had seen so little of Aunt Mary since he reached adulthood that his financial expectations were not pitched high. 'I thought she would have left me about a thousand pounds . . . However she behaved very well and is now in heaven.'[4]

There was also bad news. These tidings, which were a matter of intimate concern to Catharine, are conveyed in a typically hurried and breathless note which he wrote to Lady Morpeth.

If Saba had not been present at our tete a tete yesterday I could more naturally have accounted for my illness. I have for some time been getting provokingly fat, & as neither medicines nor exercise nor abstinence were of any avail, I resigned myself to the evil with great composure, feeling that at my age it matter'd very little whether I looked more or less clumsy. About a fortnight ago however I was *astonished*, & the whole business was put beyond a doubt. A few days since I told Sydney the melancholy truth, luckily as it happened before I was attacked by that succession of fainting & shivering fits the other night that frightened my poor girls out of their senses; but which I concluded would prove the end of the affair. This however is not to be, it seems; for I am getting quite well again tho' still *horribly* nervous. I have as yet named it to no one but Sydney, & really feel almost unwilling that it should be known, as if I were unmarried. It seems so ridiculous after 8 years cessation.[5]

Saba, still innocent, was nineteen at the time. Catharine, who at forty-seven ought to have been comfortably past child-bearing age, miscarried a short while afterwards.

Nearly eighteen months later, in March 1823, Sydney had a further piece of financial good fortune. Without prior consultation, Lord Carlisle, Lord Morpeth and Lady Georgiana all wrote to Georgiana's father, the fifth duke of Devonshire, asking him to appoint the rector of Foston to the vacant living of Londesborough. Londesborough was within driving distance of Foston; more to the point, it was worth £800 a year. Since the value of Foston had by now recovered to the same figure, the two livings would make Sydney one of the highest paid clergymen in England.

The duke consented. Catharine was extraordinarily relieved; she knew how much the years of anxiety had cost Sydney. She paints an attractively homely picture of life at the rectory when the startling news was received. 'Before the answer arrived, old Lord Carlisle told Sydney of the application. He was permitted to tell me, but no one else. Saba and Emily saw there was a something – a mystery! – evidently a very pleasant one! Every possible and impossible thing was guessed. Still at fault! At last the letter came! The joy, the happiness felt by every inhabitant of the Parsonage were unbounded, as was their gratitude!'[6]

The way in which Sydney obtained his new living was far from straightforward; indeed negotiations were unappealingly similar to the earlier unsuccessful effort, in 1808, to share Harefield with William Otter. The arrangement was that Sydney would hold Londesborough until the duke's nephew, W. G. Howard, reached the canonical age to become the incumbent, a situation which would not arise for a further nine years. To seal the pact between the two sides, Sydney signed a resignation bond. The function of this device was to secure legally binding agreement to quit a living in favour of the person mentioned in the bond at a specified future date. Resignation bonds were used quite rarely and were not popular with bishops. Five years after Sydney got hold of Londesborough, they were made illegal, except in cases where both the appointee and the prospective parson were related, either by blood or marriage, to the patron. Fortunately for Sydney the Act was not made retroactive.[7] Still there is no avoiding the fact that he had taken part in a scheme which, although not as yet illegal, was covert and reprehensible.

Sydney did not allow his unexpected success to compromise his libertarian principles. Two weeks after he had written to the duke of Devonshire to thank him for the presentation to Londesborough, a meeting of the North Riding clergy was held at the Three Tuns, Thirsk, in order to petition Parliament against any further concessions to Catholics. Sydney drew up a counter-petition, also signed by Wrangham as well by Vernon-Harcourt's clerical son William, and went along to speak. It was his first political meeting and his first speech.

Sydney's tone was the same as in his Malton sermon of 1809: aggressive condescension. The meeting was futile, a complete waste of energy and time. 'I am sick of these little trumpery Clerico-political meetings . . . Here we are, a set of obscure country clergymen, at the Three Tuns, Thirsk, like flies on the chariot wheel; perched upon a question of which we can neither see the diameter, nor control the motion, nor influence the moving force.' Plundering his stock of medical imagery, he described anti-reformers as a set of 'holy hypochondriacs' who suffered from 'protestant epilepsy'.

The best part of Sydney's speech was when he turned his opponents' main argument against themselves. The spirit of Catholicism was held to be unchangeable and unchanged, always obdurate and intolerant. Not so, claimed Sydney. The history of the cantons of Switzerland showed that, with mutual goodwill, Catholics and Protestants could live together amicably. It was the militant pro-Establishment men who stood in the way of progress. 'If I could say that any human spirit was unchanged and unchangeable, I should say so of that miserable spirit of religious persecution, of that monastic meanness, of that monopoly of heaven, which says to other human beings, "if you will not hold up your hands in prayer as I hold mine – if you will not worship your God as I worship mine, I will blast you with civil incapacities, and keep you for ever in the dust".'

Considering the pro-Tory sympathies of the local clergy, the voting went well: ten men for further concessions, and twenty against. Reformers lost the vote, but they won the propaganda war. The *York Herald*, a Whig paper, devoted three columns to the speeches of Wrangham, Vernon-Harcourt and Sydney, an expansive coverage which, conveniently, left no room for the efforts of their opponents. Its Tory rival, the *Yorkshire Gazette*, was caught napping and did not file a report. But it did run, two weeks later, a long letter from an anonymous clerical correspondent roundly abusing Sydney.

The clerical debate at the Three Tuns, Thirsk, was not the only controversy in which Sydney was involved in 1823. In September a new Prison Act came into force. Among other things this outlawed an outrageous practice followed by the local North Riding Bench. Prisoners awaiting trial were divided into two classes: those who could afford their own food in jail and those who could not. North Riding justices required poor untried prisoners to pay for their keep by working at the treadmill. On 13 October 1823, under the shadow, as it were, of the new Prison Act, the North Riding Bench passed a resolution stating that poor untried prisoners who were unwilling to work at the treadmill were to be put on a diet of bread and water.

Sydney lambasted his brother justices in a powerful article in the

Edinburgh Review. Since there were only two Assizes a year (a third was not introduced until 1843) some untried prisoners were kept in jail from August until March. In these circumstances, being put to the treadmill was no light matter. This is a strong argument but Sydney had even stronger ones to make. The North Riding Bench was flouting justice. Punishment was being inflicted upon innocent men; about half of all committed prisoners were acquitted, Sydney pointed out. The judicial system was being undermined. For, if men were put to the treadmill prior to trial, it was of no consequence whether they were acquitted or not – either way they were being humiliated and, effectively, sentenced: 'The verdict of the jury has pronounced him steady in his morals; the conduct of the justices has made him stiff in his joints.' The notion that working the treadmill was a suitable way for an untried prisoner to earn his keep was laughable. 'The gayest and most joyous of human beings is a treader, untried by a jury of his countrymen, in the fifth month of lifting up the leg, and striving against the law of gravity, supported by the glorious information which he receives from the turnkey, that he has all the time been grinding flour on the other side of the wall!'[8] Sydney vanquished his opponents in a righteous cause but made himself locally still more unpopular.

One of Sydney's abiding interests was legal reform. A select committee on criminal law was appointed in March 1819 on the motion of his friend Sir James Mackintosh. Another of Sydney's friends, Lord Lansdowne (as Lord Henry Petty he had been a pupil of Dugald Stewart's in Edinburgh in the 1790s), was a member, and Sydney wrote to him at length expounding his views. In the mid-1820s Sydney corresponded several times on penal issues with the Home Secretary, Sir Robert Peel. Sydney also went public as well as private, writing four articles for the *Edinburgh Review* on prisons and criminal law.

Sydney stood four-square behind the contemporary 'march of mind'. Facts. Figures. Investigation. Reform. 'The great panacea is publicity.' Here speaks the victor in the struggle to clean up the York Asylum. He also campaigned vigorously for natural justice. The poor were not getting a fair deal. They had no money to pay for witnesses to attend trial and could not, for the same reason, issue subpoenas. Their defence should be paid for out of the public purse. 'Would it not be a wise application of compassionate funds, to give them this fair chance of establishing their innocence?' Sydney would have been strongly in favour of legal aid.

Thus far a progressive reformer but no further. Sydney was convinced that the contemporary prison system, far from stemming the swelling tide of crime, merely added to its speed and vigour:

> There are, in every county in England, large public schools, maintained at the expense of the county, for the encouragement of profligacy and vice, and for providing a proper succession of housebreakers, profligates, and thieves . . . There is not, to be sure, a formal arrangement of lectures, after the manner of our Universities; but the petty larcenous stripling, being left destitute of every species of employment, and locked up with accomplished villains as idle as himself, listens to their pleasant narrative of successful crimes, and pants for the hour of freedom, that he may begin the same bold and interesting career.

Sydney believed that the regime in prison should be based solely upon deterrence: 'Coarse men should be made sorrowful and penitent by plain food.' There should be as much solitary confinement as possible, subject to the proviso that the balance of the mind must not be put in jeopardy, and no paid work: 'We would banish all the looms of Preston jail, and substitute nothing but the tread-wheel, or the capstan, or some species of labour where the labourer could not see the results of his toil.' Prison sentences should, at the same time, be shortened. Sydney was an advocate of the short, sharp shock.

There is little about Sydney's social thinking that is coherent. The man who had stood up to his fellow magistrates on the North Riding Bench was able to speak of prisoners as though they were a sub-species, devoid of thought or feeling. Consider, for example, these remarks made in a letter to Peel:

> A sentence of transportation to Botany Bay translated into common sense is this: 'Because you have committed this offence, the Sentence of the Court is that you shall no longer be burthened with the support of your wife and family. You shall be immediately removed from a very bad climate, and a country overburthened with people, to one of the finest Regions of the Earth where the demand for human labour is every hour increasing, and where it is highly probable you may ultimately regain your character and improve your fortune. The Court has been induced to pass this sentence upon you in consequence of the

many aggravating circumstances of your case, and they hope your fate will be a warning to others.'[9]

He would have found it hard to persuade the Tolpuddle martyrs that transportation was a boon, a hallowed blessing in strange disguise.

Sydney's four articles on the Game Laws are much more liberal. Here was a subject tailor-made for his formidable skills: his mischievous sense of fun, his strong instinct for natural justice, his nose for absurd bombast and thinly veiled hypocrisy. The Game Laws, as they stood around 1820, were barbarous and extraordinary. No man could legally shoot game who did not pay at least £100 a year in rent. This prohibition was absolute: the bailiff of an estate, even if he had the owner's permission, did not have the right to shoot. A second extraordinary enactment was that those who were allowed to massacre pheasants and partridges could do so everywhere; their rights were in no way restricted to their own land. Thirdly there was no market for game; it was an offence both to purchase and to sell. Finally the penalties for poaching were draconian; poachers caught at night bearing arms faced transportation.

Sydney was his facetious best. He could not understand why the qualification to shoot game was based solely upon the ownership of land. If landowners had privileges, why should not holders of other types of wealth have them too? 'What amusement can there be morally lawful to a holder of turnip land, and criminal in a possessor of Exchequer bills? What delights ought to be tolerated to Long Annuities, from which wheat and beans should be excluded?' It was unfair to restrict consumption of game to the landed gentry. It would be just as reasonable that 'maritime Englishmen should alone eat oysters and lobsters'. The arguments used to defend the Game Laws were specious. It was said that, if current regulations were done away with, the poor would become idle and dissipated, implying that they had been enacted for the poor's benefit. If true, this defence was capable of considerable extension. Why not have a similar property qualification for all those who played bowls or skittles, and 'prevent small landowners from going to races, or following a pack of hounds?' The argument was, of course, mere pretence: 'it is monopoly calling in the aid of hypocrisy, and tyranny veiling itself in the garb of philosophical humanity.'

Sydney's proposals for legislative change breathe a spirit of modernity. Every man, whether tenant or owner, should have the right to shoot game on his own land, and also on land belonging to others with their permission. The market in pheasants and partridges should be restored, an enactment which would greatly reduce poaching. Sydney, who had been impressed by Dugald Stewart's exposition of Adam Smith's free market economics, believed that the most certain method of checking the poacher was by underselling him. Harsh penalties for illegal shooting of game should be abolished because they encouraged poachers to go out in groups for their mutual protection.[10]

One aspect of the situation in the English countryside attracted Sydney's especial displeasure. Some landowners had recently resorted to the hideous practice of protecting their property with spring guns. Sydney thought it would be more humane if gentry were given summary power of life and death. They would then kill only poachers and 'perhaps might spare a friend or an acquaintance – or a father of a family with ten children – or a small freeholder who voted for Administration'. Sydney argued that legalizing spring guns would lead to trespassers being given a lower legal status than hunting dogs: it had long been illegal, Sydney reminded his readers, to kill a pointer in pursuit of game. 'The least worthy of God's creatures must fall – the rustic without a soul – not the Christian partridge – not the immortal pheasant – not the rational woodcock, or the accountable hare.'

From his reading of English common law Sydney was convinced that killing a trespasser with a spring gun was murder and setting one up an indictable offence. It was incumbent upon landlords to use minimum force. Why not let intruders down into five feet of liquid mud or contain them in a box? He concludes his argument with conviction and passion. To plant a spring gun is to 'want that sacred regard to human life which is one of the corner stones of civil society'. It is impossible to dissent.

What are we to make of Sydney's social thought, against the backcloth of history and within the context of his own times? On mental health he stood side by side with Quaker reformers, establishing a rapprochement between Anglican rationalism and religious Dissent. It is a tragedy that Sydney did not take this fruitful union further. He had considerable personal regard for Elizabeth Fry but disapproved of her ideas.[11] Humane treatment for the mentally ill, animal treatment – weeks, indeed months, spent at the treadmill – for convicted prisoners: Sydney's social philosophy does not add up. His stance on many issues was that of an old-fashioned, aristocratic Whig:

anti-Shaftesbury, pro-*laissez-faire*. The final impression is one of incoherence, of sadness at the contrast between what was and what might have been. Sydney was a man of enormous sensitivity, of flashing intuitive insight, and of the broadest human sympathies; but he never managed to meld thought and feeling in order to fashion a unified response to the world.

12

AT THE RISK OF MY LIFE

'I pass over the expressions of violent and unmannerly abuse
in Mr Read's [letter] . . . As I cannot risk my life for this sort
of language, I never use it'

SYDNEY SMITH TO THE EARL OF CARLISLE,
September 1824

One day in September 1824 a meeting of magistrates was convened at
Malton. In the chair was Sir George Cayley, a local squire two years
younger than Sydney; he was a prolific inventor and is now generally
regarded as the father of aviation. The meeting was quite crowded:
twenty-eight clergy and gentry were gathered around the table, with
Sydney towards the middle. The meeting was also quite tense: the
main subject on the agenda was a proposed new road at Malton, the
sort of subject that was likely to stir up passions. Sydney was speaking
in favour. Suddenly the Revd T. C. R. Read, incumbent of the nearby
living of Sand Hutton, stood up and tried to interrupt. The two men
were almost opposite each other, only a few feet away. Sydney carried
on with his speech, taking no notice of Read. The incumbent of Sand
Hutton, angered by the slight, became more irritable by the moment.
Suddenly, he could contain himself no longer. 'We have been
described', he spluttered, 'as the nine enemies of McAdam, which I
deny.'

Everyone around the table knew to what Read was referring.
Sydney had recently written an article on the Malton road in the local
press, and the article had appeared under the heading 'The Nine
Enemies of McAdam'. (Read had been shown the article prior to
publication and had raised no objection, but was understandably
incensed by the title.) What happened next was soon to become fuel
for controversy. No one doubted that Sydney silenced Read; what was
open to debate was the words that he used. Read's version was fiery:

'Sir, if you raise your voice and do not hold your noise, I shall say something to you which you will not easily forget.'[1]

Read visited Lord Carlisle at Castle Howard and asked him to arbitrate. It was not an easy task. 'A sad mistake prevails somewhere,' Lord Carlisle told Read. 'Until the saddle is put upon the right horse, I own I do not see my way towards successful mediation. But I do not despair.' Sydney behaved exactly as his father would have done in similar circumstances, standing his ground, denying he had done anything wrong, and attacking the probity of his opponent. Read, he told Lord Carlisle, was not to be trusted: 'of all the men I ever saw in my life at a public meeting he is the most touchy and quarrelsome.' Sydney categorically denied that he had used the words that were alleged. To prove his innocence he wrote letters to every magistrate who had been present at the meeting. Only two were willing to state that Sydney had used offensive language, and neither was prepared to support the veracity of the *ipsissima verba* as reported by Read. Read countered by saying that precise reportage was irrelevant; what mattered was whether he had been 'insulted' or not.[2]

Indeed it did. This dispute with Read looks minor but, in fact, was not. Sydney alluded to the possibly desperate implications in a letter to Lord Carlisle. 'I pass over the expressions of violent and unmannerly abuse in Mr Read's [letter], so common among quarrelling clergymen. As I cannot risk my life for this sort of language, I never use it.' Sydney was well aware that Read might, at any time, challenge him to a duel. Hence the pains he took to establish his innocence. If challenged he would, under the aristocratic code of honour, have been obliged to accept. Taking up a challenge was required of everyone, royalty and leading politicians included. The duke of York fought a duel in 1789, William Pitt the Younger in 1798, Canning against Castlereagh in 1809, Wellington in 1829. The chances of death, about one in six, were comparable to those in Russian roulette.

The knock, so to speak, never came at Sydney's door. The dispute with Read died away, Sydney protesting his innocence and Read refusing to be reconciled. This is not to say that Sydney escaped from the episode unscathed. Read's anger brought to the surface a great deal of simmering discontent. Sydney was already unpopular; his enemies now felt that they had an excellent opportunity to take him down a peg. The sense of the inappropriateness of Sydney's behaviour was well expressed by Colonel Cholmley, a local landowner and a friend of Read's. 'Really I think a clergyman residing in the county, without an acre of land in the county belonging to him, ought to know better than to attempt to be a leading character in county business'. Sydney, Cholmley was saying, was a landless parvenu, a tinker in court dress.

Those who disliked Sydney were soon to discover that they had a new ally: the fifth earl of Carlisle. Carlisle was initially firm but friendly. He confided his thoughts on the dispute between Read and Sydney to some private jottings; the letter, interestingly, was never sent to Sydney. His lordship was sure (and here his instincts were undoubtedly correct) that if Read appealed to the public, he would have little difficulty in establishing Sydney as the aggressor.[3] It is easy enough to understand what Carlisle meant. Sydney's tone towards his neighbours was condescending and he had attacked too many things which the gentry and clergy around Foston held dear. Carlisle felt that Sydney should apologize to Read and also make more effort to make himself locally popular. No apology came.

In October, Lord Carlisle wrote Sydney a letter in which he was careful not to mention the altercation at the magistrates' meeting, concentrating instead upon the content of Sydney's recent writings. The ostensible cause of Carlisle's concern was an article which had appeared in the *Edinburgh Review* a few months earlier, in July. It was, thought Carlisle, an 'excessive eulogy' of America and all things American. This criticism was one-sided and unfair. Sydney had certainly praised American economy in government and lack of economy in religious toleration, favourite themes, but he had also had some harsh things to say. A number of Americans, he complained, were uncouth. 'We are terribly afraid that some Americans spit upon the floor, even when that floor is covered by good carpets. Now, all claims to civilization are suspended till this secretion is otherwise disposed of. No English gentleman has spit upon the floor since the Heptarchy.' Sydney's was a typical English reaction. When Charles Dickens visited America in 1842 he was also appalled: 'in every bar-room and hotel passage the stone floor looks as if it were paved with open oysters.' Uncouthness was a light matter in comparison with America's main spot and stain, her 'great disgrace and danger': slavery. Sydney forecast the American Civil War. 'The existence of slavery . . . will one day entail (and ought to entail) a bloody servile war upon the Americans – which will separate America into slave states and states disclaiming slavery.' No 'excessive eulogy' here!

After referring briefly to Sydney's article on America, Lord Carlisle launched himself into a passionate admonition. He was concerned that Sydney was piling up for himself treasure in Hell and would reap, at some indeterminate time in the future, a bitter reward. 'Elevated spirits can only support themselves to a certain period of life; when these begin to fail, then comes the hour of vengeance for slaps and bruises which timid & patient sufferers have bonded, like corn, and let out of the storehouse upon the sick Lion, who may not then be a match for a Jackass.' Well and finely said. Sydney was making himself dangerously exposed. 'When you are so capable of giving us both instruction & pleasure, why run amuck at every component part of society: Order, Class, Profession, the Bar, the Bench, rural residents, West Indian proprietors, youthful sportsmen, brother Magistrates?' Sydney ought to become more agile, more feline. 'You may stroke, but do not strike the world. All this, I know, will appear assuming & unpalatable, but if you take it as it is meant, you may turn it to use, and I risk it.'[4] It is an eloquent letter, a sympathetic letter, a loving letter, a wise letter. Above all it is a letter that comes straight from Lord Carlisle's heart.

Sydney's reply on 30 October was tactful and cautious. Falling out with the incumbent of Sand Hutton was one thing; getting on the wrong side of one of the greatest noblemen in England was a different matter altogether. His was a contrite heart. 'There is moderation to be used in the frequency of attacks, & in the bitterness of attacks, & in both these points I believe I have sinned.' He regretted the past and would amend in the future. 'I will attack less frequently, & joke less severely.' This is a very important statement. Faced by opposition from Lord Carlisle, Sydney had agreed to back off in his literary career.

He added a note to this letter: 'I had sent a severe article upon the Catholic Question before your letter came; but after that, I will seriously remember your useful & valuable advice.'[5] The article to which Sydney alluded was a review of *Memoirs of Captain Rock*, a burlesque on Irish history which, although published anonymously, was well-known to be by one of Sydney's friends, the diminutive Irish poet Tom Moore. Not only had Sydney sent off this piece, but it had already been published in the October issue of the *Review*. Had it not been for the inefficiency of late Georgian communications, this 'severe article' would already have found its way to Castle Howard.

Once he saw it Lord Carlisle became extremely nasty; he refused to see Sydney and, more damagingly, he interfered with his career. Unfortunately for Sydney, Archbishop Vernon-Harcourt was one of the earl's good friends – the two men had known each other for at least twenty years. Behind Sydney's back, Lord Carlisle went to see the archbishop. The first intimation Sydney had of the meeting was when he received a letter from Vernon-Harcourt, calling him for an interview. Sydney duly went to Harcourt's palace at Bishopthorpe and found the experience acutely embarrassing. When he got home he sat down at his desk and, on 10 January 1825, wrote Lord Carlisle the longest letter of his entire life.

Discretion called for an abject apology, even though Carlisle was in the wrong, but Sydney threw discretion to the winds. Ambition did not match what was for him the overwhelming moral imperative of preserving his reputation as an independent man, as someone who was fearless in the pursuit of truth. Sydney refused, now, to be pushed around. 'My opinions & the free Expression of them I will surrender to no man alive, and nor will I hold myself accountable to any man for the Exercise of this right.' He had told Carlisle the article had already been sent off to the *Edinburgh Review*. In approaching his diocesan before he had had a chance to change his style of writing, Carlisle was behaving badly. 'Your resentment is premature, unjust and repugnant to the Spirit and good feeling of the amicable treaty which subsisted between us.' Strong words. Sydney was so angry that he talked down to Lord Carlisle, treating him like a child suffering from a temper tantrum. 'You talk me over with the greatest Severity, dispose the Archbishop against me, suspend all intercourse, and feel in a high degree incens'd because I have not followed advice before I received it and listen'd to warnings made after the Event.'[6]

In this letter Sydney also raised the stakes, claiming that the earl had told the archbishop that Sydney's opinions were unlawful. According to Sydney's account, Carlisle had said that the review of *Captain Rock* was 'seditious' and therefore liable to prosecution by the Attorney General. What had enraged Carlisle was a passage in which Sydney had predicted that the civil disabilities of Irish Catholics would never be removed 'till they are removed by fear'. Carlisle, a former Lord Lieutenant of Ireland, had interpreted this as a statement designed to 'rouse the persecuted', not to 'warn the persecutors'. 'I respectfully but firmly deny the Justice of the conjecture,' was Sydney's reasonable rejoinder.

Over the next week or so, two more letters were sent from Castle Howard with two from Foston rectory in reply. They did not do any good. Carlisle flatly denied that he had accused Sydney of sedition to the archbishop, saying that his only complaint was the embarrassment caused by some acerbic remarks which Sydney had made at the expense of the duke of York, a royal personage with whom Lord Carlisle was acquainted; and Sydney, for his part, stuck to his guns. Neither man would back down.

They never met again. The master of Castle Howard died in September 1825, fulfilling Sydney's prediction, made in February 1815, that he still had 'ten years of life in his pocket'. Sydney was furious at the treatment he had received, but did not let it be known . Writing to Lady Grey in October 1825 he gives a graphic account of Carlisle's final hours. 'The old Lord slipped through the fingers of the Physicians in a moment. He was always very kind to me.' Appearances must always be kept up. It would not do to let Lady Grey know that there had been a breach with a Whig aristocrat as influential as Lord Carlisle. Maintaining the pretence of continuing cordiality was made much easier by the fact that the row with the old earl mercifully did not sully Sydney's relations with Morpeth and Lady Georgiana.

Although it had led to the breach with Lord Carlisle, Sydney refused to end his campaign on behalf of those who were disadvantaged on account of their religious faith. On the contrary he redoubled his efforts. His honour and integrity were at stake, he felt. In March 1825 the clergy of the East Riding proposed to their archdeacon – who, as in the North Riding two years earlier, happened to be Wrangham – that they should meet to petition Parliament against the Catholic claims. Sydney thought that the idea was 'mischievous' and tried to persuade Wrangham not to give way. Sydney had to be content with a pyrrhic victory: Wrangham gave his consent to the meeting but was ill (probably a diplomatic disorder) on the fateful day.

The debate at the Tiger Inn, Beverley, held on 11 April, did not go anything like as well for reformers as the earlier confrontation at the Three Tuns, Thirsk. Sydney, present in his capacity as rector of Londesborough, found that even his curate, Mr Milestones, voted on the other side. To Sydney's credit he encouraged Milestones to make a public stand on behalf of conscience, and made amusing reference to the difference of opinion between rector and curate in the speech in which he introduced his own counter-petition. This was the best moment in a bad day. No Wrangham; no William Vernon-Harcourt; and, as the Tory *Yorkshire Gazette* gleefully reported, unanimous opposition to further concessions, 'one individual alone excepted, the Rector of Londesborough'. Instead of advertising the weakness of the reformist cause, it would have been better if Sydney had followed Wrangham's lead and stayed at home. But it was not in his nature. Not turning up would have looked too much like cowardice.

Sydney's speech was disappointing; he mostly served up old wine in old bottles, and his prose was not enlivened with memorable images. He also made yet another *faux pas*, tactlessly reminding his clerical brethren of their provincialism, in which he, by clear implications, did not share. 'If you go into a parsonage-house in the country . . . you see sometimes a style and fashion of furniture which does very well for us, but which has had its day in London . . . from the gentleman's houses of the provinces these pieces of furniture, as soon as they are discovered to be unfashionable, descend to the farm-house, then to the cottages, then to the faggot-heap, then to the dunghill. As it is with furniture so it is with arguments.' In the rest of his speech Sydney rehearsed old debating points, emphasizing the more liberal spirit of contemporary Catholicism and the danger that a disaffected Ireland would pose in time of war.[7]

Early in February 1826, Sydney returned to the attack, publishing *A Letter to the Electors upon the Catholic Question*. Morpeth, now Lord Carlisle, was sent a copy, as was George Canning, the butt of Sydney's humour in *Peter Plymley*. Sydney's pamphlet did well, selling a thousand copies by the end of March, at which point a print-run of another thousand was arranged. It is a much more powerful production than his speech at Beverley ten months earlier: there are ingenious arguments, memorable images, effective debating techniques. Sydney opened in front of his readers a vista of liberty. 'No chains, no prisons, no bonfires for man's faith . . . *no oppression, no tyranny in belief: a free altar, an open road to heaven; no human insolence, no human narrowness, hallowed by the name of God.*'[8] 'An open road to heaven': an evocative and fine phrase, a potent clarion call.

Sydney's confidence, which had sagged under the weight of the controversy with old Lord Carlisle, had now returned. He even repeated, albeit in less provocative terms, the argument from fear: every year increased the size and wealth of the Catholic population in Ireland, and thus the strength of its rightful demand for emancipation. The cleverest section of the pamphlet is that in which Sydney took the catchwords of his opponents and turned them to his own advantage:

My cry then is, *No Popery*; therefore emancipate the Catholics, that they may not join with foreign Papists in time of war. *Church for ever*; therefore emancipate the Catholics, that they may not help to pull it down. *King for ever*; therefore emancipate the Catholics, that they may become his loyal subjects. *Great Britain for ever*; therefore emancipate the Catholics, that they may not put an end to its perpetuity.[9]

This is a new Sydney, a Sydney capable of eloquent demagoguery, the words of a man able to sway political debate. He was destined to make even greater impact in later years.

'I must not die without seeing Paris', Sydney wrote in 1820. 'Figure to yourself what a horrid death – to die without seeing Paris!' He had visited France after leaving Winchester, but had got no further than Normandy; his first chance to sample the delights of Parisian life came in the spring of 1826. The longed-for opportunity came through the kindness of Lord and Lady Holland, who had been staying there since the previous September and sent Sydney an invitation. The jaunt was a pleasing by-product of his greatly increased affluence; it was Aunt Mary ('now in heaven') and the proceeds from his new living of Londesborough that made the trip possible. Sydney did not feel rich enough to take Catharine, although he did write to her every day he was away from home. His wife treasured his letters, underlining those sentences and clauses referring to a planned future holiday for the family: '*You shall all see France; I am resolved upon that*'; '*it will be, I think, here we shall lodge*'.[10]

Sydney arrived at Dover on 14 April, where he stayed at the Ship Inn. Before embarking on a Post Office packet boat for France, he climbed the cliffs of Dover by a staircase cut into the rock. He found it a strain: 'The top of the cliff is reached with great ease, or at least what I call great ease, which means the loss of above a pound of liquid flesh and as much puffing and blowing as would grind a bushel of wheat.' This is the first reference in Sydney's letters to the ill-effects of overweight. He made periodic forays against his increasing corpulence, giving up alcohol and cutting down on 'boiled and roast', but they never lasted long. He was a man who accepted what he was: 'I am, you know, of the family of Falstaff.' Now on the eve of his fifty-fifth birthday, he was to find his obesity an increasing problem.

Sea-journeys terrified Sydney; on this occasion he was one of the few passengers who was not sick, a slice of luck he put down to his prudence in drinking a large glass of brandy as soon as he went on board. Once ashore, the exiled Huguenot was in his element. His reactions to the people he met and the places he visited are so fresh that it is as if the initial tour, thirty-eight years earlier, had never happened. At Calais he stayed at Dessin's: 'I never ate so good a dinner, nor was in so good an hotel.' Everywhere he was struck by the politeness of the people: 'I have not seen a cobbler who is not better bred than an English gentleman.'

From Calais he travelled via Boulogne, Abbeville, Amiens and Beauvais to Paris. He stayed overnight at the Hôtel d'Orvilliers, but moved next day to the Hôtel Virginie in the Rue St Honoré, where he had a spacious apartment comprising sitting-room, bedroom and balcony. On his first night Sydney went to a café where he had a poor dinner. 'Not understanding their language of the kitchen' (strange in such a gourmet and in such an able linguist) 'I chose the first thing upon the list, and chose badly.' He was, however, impressed by the price. The meal, including half a bottle of brandy and liqueurs, came to the equivalent of only 4s 10d. A similar dinner in London, Sydney thought, would have cost 30s. The disparity in restaurant prices between London and Paris lasted long after 1826.

Sydney stayed in Paris for three weeks. He was an impatient sightseer, a man with a surprisingly casual attitude towards the artistic world. What struck him most about the Louvre was the gallery itself, which he reckoned could not be less than a quarter of a mile long. The pictures and sculptures claimed less of his attention: 'I saw all the statues and pictures thoroughly so as to judge of and compare them amounting to many thousands in 32 minutes.' This lack of interest in art is strange in a man with such a powerful visual imagination.

Some of Sydney's choices of entertainment were a touch bizarre. He went to an abattoir in Montmartre where 'they kill every week 600 oxen, 4000 sheep and 2000 calves'. He found this a 'very useful institution' – animals had previously been slaughtered in the streets – 'but a sight not worth seeing'. He liked rather more the cemetery of Père Lachaise, which dated from the late eighteenth century and covered some 200 acres. 'The tombs are placed in little gardens by the relations and covered with flowers and you see people mourning and weeping over the graves of their friends. I was much pleased and affected by it.'

Sydney spent a lot of his time in Paris among English friends. Even without taking Lord and Lady Holland and their family into account, there was a large English contingent either resident or on holiday: the duke of Bedford, Lord Granville, who was British ambassador, the marquess of Bath, Sir Thomas Hardy, Nelson's captain, Lady Grantham, who 'spoke with great praise of you and your daughters', Sydney told Catharine, and several others. The duke of Bedford mistook Sydney for Sir Sidney Smith and refused him entry to his apartment, not the first time the confusion of identities had occurred. The duke met Sydney soon afterwards in the street and realized his error. To put matters right he wrote Sydney an apologetic letter which, compounding the duke's embarrassment, was sent to Sir Sidney. So vain was he that he failed to work out that, had he called upon the duke, he would have been slighted. Sir Sidney continued the merry-go-round by sending the duke's letter back to Sydney, apologizing for his ill-manners in opening it and offering to take his namesake to some shows. This series of events greatly amused Sydney.

The duke of Bedford also took Sydney to meet the most remarkable of all the men then living in Paris, Charles-Maurice de Talleyrand-Périgord. Talleyrand was among the list of those who frequented Holland House. Now seventy-two, he had been born into one of the oldest aristocratic families in France. The Great Survivor had been present at the coronation of Louis XVI, had taken part in the Revolution of 1789, and had been Minister for Foreign Affairs under both Bonaparte and the restored Bourbons. No one could fathom Talleyrand. Although he was ugly and a cripple (a nurse had let him drop from a cabinet when a young child, crushing a bone in his foot which would never mend), many women fell for his indefinable charm. Talleyrand's outward behaviour did not express the inner man. His manners were exquisite but his tongue was malicious; and although his demeanour was always one of impenetrable calm, this concealed a ruthless capacity to exploit the main chance. He was a deadly vulture with the immaculate plumage of a bird of paradise. Napoleon, with predictable earthiness, summed up Talleyrand's character better than anyone, describing him as 'a pile of shit in a silk stocking'.

The unscrupulous acquisition of great power had gone hand in hand in Talleyrand's career with the unscrupulous acquisition of great wealth. Prince of a small principality in Italy, he had accumulated vast estates and now lived in Paris, in the Rue St Florentin, surrounded by a 'court' which would not have disgraced a medieval monarch. Or a medieval bishop for that matter. Talleyrand united in himself the kingdom of Mammon and the kingdom of God: he was a disciple of Voltaire dressed in the incongruous habiliment of an episcopal cope and mitre – one of his uncles was a cardinal and he had himself been briefly bishop of Autun. Currently, however, he was excommunicated, a fact not unconnected with his marriage to a notorious courtesan. When Sydney visited the Rue St Florentin the couple had long since separated. Talleyrand's strong desire for the company of women was now met, at least in part, by his beautiful niece Dorothea, duchess of Dino. Although thirty-nine years younger than her uncle, the duchess dedicated herself to Talleyrand to the end of his long and turbulent life.

Sydney enjoyed being with the Prince and Dorothea. They were, he informed Catharine, 'very civil'. Civil, in Sydney's vocabulary, was a condensed way of saying cultured, interesting and amusing. Sydney was also pleased by the magnificent cuisine, noting that Talleyrand's cook Carême 'is said to be the best in Paris'.

The food was excellent, the company congenial. Sydney sat near the comte de Montrond, one of Talleyrand's oldest friends. Montrond was a gambler, a womanizer and a wit; he still used, in conversation, the coarse style which had been fashionable around the turn of the century but which was now fast becoming outmoded. Sydney found Montrond entertaining; he was, he told Catharine, 'the Luttrell of Paris – a very witty, agreeable man with whom I made great friends'. Sydney, Bohemian himself, was always attracted by those, whether men or women, who had a little devil in them.

Sydney also had breakfast with the duc de Broglie, one of the foremost public figures of the day. The duke, like Montrond a regular member of Talleyrand's circle, was married to a daughter of Madame de Staël, giving him admirable avant-garde credentials which he failed to live up to. His politics were those of an English Whig, his way of life respectably boring. Sydney's comment is crushing. The duke and his wife, he wrote to Catharine, were 'virtuous sensible disagreeable people, and gave bad breakfasts without a table-cloth'.

When he was not making forays into French aristocratic society, Sydney was witnessing some of the public life of the capital. There was a visit to the Assembly of Deputies; he could not easily hear what was said because his seat was badly placed, but he thought the deputies read their speeches 'like very bad parsons'. There was also a glimpse of royalty when he watched a procession in the company of Lady Holland. Catholic ritual had not ceased to offend Sydney's Protestant sensibilities. 'There were about 1200 priests, 4 cardinals, a piece of the Real Cross, and one of the Nails, carried under a canopy upon a velvet cushion . . . a more absurd disgraceful and ridiculous or a finer sight I never saw.' Despite his prejudices Sydney was able to grasp political realities. 'The Bourbons are too foolish and too absurd. Nothing can keep them on the throne.' The restored monarchy of 1815 had, in fact, four more years to run.

Sydney left Paris on Tuesday 9 May. He stayed in London with Bobus on his way back, and then returned to Foston. The holiday had been an almost unqualified success. Apart from minor irritations like the semi-public nature of lavatories in the streets (an annoyance to visitors for many more years to come) or the sharpness of the cobblestones, he had nothing but praise. 'Paris', thought Sydney, was merely an abbreviation for 'Paradise'. He especially liked French food, bringing back with him *Le Cuisinier Bourgeois* with the intention of trying out some of the recipes. Laden with presents for the family, he bought for himself, at a cost of six shillings, only the seal bearing a French aristocratic coat of arms which, when he used it on his own letters, so puzzled and surprised his English correspondents.[11]

He was only at home a few weeks. Towards the end of June he had to make another journey: his father, whose mind had gone the previous year, was near death. Robert Smith, now eighty-six, was very ill but he was also very well off. His insatiable desire for a 'small farm' – the desire which had provoked, in 1800 and again in 1802, terrible rows with Sydney – had been satisfied when, around 1810, he had become the owner of Bishop's Lydeard House in Somerset, a fine mid-eighteenth-century mansion set in 100 acres. He lived with his grandson Cecil, now married and in orders but not pursuing an active clerical career. Once he reached his dotage, Robert Smith was fairly easy to handle. Sydney had gone to see him five years earlier and was surprised by the extent of the personality change. 'My father is one of the very few people I have ever seen improved by age. He is become careless, indulgent, and anacreontic.' Softened by the age of eighty-one, Robert Smith was softened still further five years later. Once, as Sydney sat at the dying man's bedside, he turned to his son and said in a tone of quiet affection: 'I say little but I feel a good deal, & am very much obliged to you for coming to see me.' These words made a powerful appeal to the young, insecure boy within Sydney, the boy desperately in search of his father's love. That love, alas, had come too late. Only at the gates of death did Robert Smith let his defences down.

The visit, unhappily, was not without pain. Sydney put his head for business to good use, sorting out his father's testamentary papers. For a man who had always pleaded poverty, who had been so hard up that he had tried to get his hands on Catharine's marriage settlement, Robert Smith was remarkably wealthy. Sydney reckoned that the estate was worth between £40,000 and £50,000, a masterly display of Robert Smith's miserly credentials. Bobus had known for 'some years' that his annual present of £500 went to augment capital, not income, but had carried on with the payments because of the pleasure they gave his father. Courtney had also kept up his contribution of £250 a year, but his enthusiasm had been less marked. (Between 1811 and 1816 he had given nothing at all and had had to catch up with a lump sum payment of £1500.) Bobus over the years had made over more than £10,000, Courtney just over £5000.

These are substantial gifts, but they in no way justify what Robert Smith had done. In his will, drawn up in October 1822, Sydney was left £6000. The stinginess of the sum, less than 15 per cent of Robert Smith's assets, now stood revealed. Sydney was both hurt and angry, telling Bobus that the size of the bequest was a 'gross act of injustice: I must say I have serious complaint against my Father, but I cannot help myself.' Bobus took the extremely heavy hint. A codicil was added to the will, increasing Sydney's share from £6000 to £10,000. Robert Smith, with typical and unnecessary spitefulness, stated in the codicil that the change was 'recommended by my oldest son'.[12]

Sydney returned to Foston early in August. Travelling down to Bishop's Lydeard had exhausted him and the journey back was no better. 'I am still very weak, and have no expectation of recovering till the Hot Weather is over,' he told Cecil after he had been home a few days. This was to be a frequent refrain in future years: heat exacerbating problems brought on by excess weight. In the same letter Sydney made a request. He had brought back to Foston either originals or copies of all his father's testamentary papers; all, that is, except one. 'The paper I allude to is that containing directions respecting the future management of Young Pyke, and a statement of his own feelings. It is without date, I believe.' Cecil was reluctant to comply. In a further letter, written two weeks later, Sydney felt obliged to give his nephew a gentle, but firm, reprimand. 'The paper in question is certainly a testamentary paper as much as any other of which I have copies ... You should remember there is no fact mentioned in it with which I have not been long acquainted, that I have read the paper, and that therefore all idea of Secrecy is out of the question as far as I am concern'd.'[13]

Charles Pyke had been born in April 1814. His mother, Jemima, had lived for some years with Robert Smith as his 'housemaid'. Robert paid for the boy's education and left him £500 in his will; he also gave Jemima a modest allowance, continued after his death. The birth of this bastard son was one of the secrets, like Cecil's debts and Eliza's infidelities, which the Smith family clasped tightly to its bosom. There is no record of Sydney having expressed an opinion on his father's behaviour, but it is likely that he was both sickened and embarrassed by it. How, after all, was it that Sydney described Robert Smith? 'A good kind of man, who disappeared about the time of the assizes . . .' Would that he had!

The birth of Charles Pyke throws an interesting sidelight on Sydney's upbringing. It is hard to believe that Robert Smith was faithful to his wife. All that is known about him – his relentlessly high self-opinion, his restlessness, his constant travels abroad, his irresponsibility – suggests that he was a philanderer. There is a delicate hint to this effect in Catharine's 'Narrative'. Her father-in-law, she wrote, 'delighted in making conquests – his gratification was ample, and no woman was ever more vain of them'. If, indeed, Robert Smith did have a number of affairs, it would help to explain the strain of puritanism – one of his most surprising qualities – to be found in Sydney.

Sydney, worried that Saba and Emily might become too countrified, wanted to introduce them to social circles beyond the narrow confines of Foston but heeded the expense. Apart from the long visit to London in the winter of 1818–19, the girls had no experience of life in a broader, urban and literary society. By 1826, Saba had reached twenty-four, Emily was nineteen. In January 1827, Sydney decided to set out on a trip to Edinburgh, where he would stay with Francis Jeffrey. The idea was that Sydney would go on ahead by stage coach, with Catharine and the two girls following on behind in Sydney's carriage. Unfortunately there was a delay. Catharine sprained her ankle, the twelve leeches put on the injury did little good, and she was unable for some time to put her foot to the ground. The delay meant that the itinerary had to be simplified: a visit to Lord and Lady Grey at Howick, and also to friends at Durham, had to be cancelled. After many hurried exchanges of letters and several changes of plan, the party left Foston on 6 February.

The month spent at Edinburgh did not go as well as Sydney hoped: Catharine's injured ankle refused to heal, so she was confined to her sofa, unable to walk. In addition a throat infection, which had troubled her on and off for a year, returned. An invitation to stay for a few days with Sir Walter Scott had to be turned down. Sydney tried to be as philosophical as he could: 'We must therefore make the best of our Way back, put the old Lady into Dock and make her ready for Sea again.'[14]

The party returned to Foston in mid-March. The same month the *Edinburgh Review* carried yet another broadside by Sydney on Catholic emancipation and the Irish question, his fifth article on the subject. As with *Peter Plymley*, Sydney's timing was politically adept. The parliamentary election of 1826 had returned an increased number of Irish MPs committed to emancipation; and on 5 March 1827, a resolution in the House of Commons on the Catholic claims had been lost by only four votes. Sydney caught the tide's turn. Three developments, he argues, had made emancipation inevitable. There was the high level of the national debt – £840 million – brought about by war and colonial expansion: 'every rock in the ocean where a cormorant can perch is occupied by our troops'. An expensive war in Ireland, in these circumstances, would be a financial catastrophe which any English government would use every means in its power to avert. Financial constraints were being reinforced by political change: Ireland was becoming increasingly restive, with discontent being stirred up by O'Connell's Catholic Association. A new dimension to the Irish question had also been created by the rise of the 'democratic party' in England. The government now worried that a Catholic rising might trigger riots in the industrial heartlands of England. In the context of politics in the late 1820s, Sydney was articulating a genuine fear.

In this article Sydney adopts a challenging tone. The arguments which had so angered the fifth earl of Carlisle in the earlier review of Tom Moore's *Memoirs of Captain Rock* were not only represented, they were given a fresher, sharper focus. It was the 'violence' of O'Connell's Catholic Association which was forcing the English government to contemplate giving up its policy of exploitation and tyranny. 'The mild and the long-suffering may suffer for ever in this world.' (A provocation to insurrection, old Lord Carlisle would have said, putting the author at risk of prosecution by the Attorney General.) Sydney also had some harsh words to say on the subject of royalty and royal dukes:

Of all human nonsense, it is surely the greatest to talk of respect to the late king – respect to the memory of the Duke of York – by not voting for the Catholic question. Bad enough to burn widows when the husband dies – bad enough to burn horses, dogs, butlers, footmen, and coachmen, on the funeral pile of a Scythian warrior – but to offer up the happiness of seven millions of people to the memory of the dead, is certainly the most insane sepulchral oblation of which history makes mention.

It would be easy to get the impression from this article that Sydney had resolved not only to continue with his career as an Edinburgh reviewer but to be as forthright as he had ever been. The truth is more complex. He desperately wanted to assert his literary independence and yet, at the same time, the row of 1824 had shown him that he would have to give up his connection with the *Edinburgh Review* if he was ever to become a bishop. Even as he wrote this no-holds-barred article on Ireland, he was probably beginning to think of withdrawing. Certainly the idea was uppermost in his mind seven or eight months later. 'I am', he told the duke of Devonshire in November 1827, 'fast backing out.'[15]

13

THE OAK WILL SPRING UP

'Show me a deep and tenacious earth – and I am sure the oak will spring up in it.'

SYDNEY SMITH, 1831

On 17 February 1827, Lord Liverpool, prime minister since 1812, had a paralytic stroke, his illness bringing to an end half a century of virtually continuous Tory rule. On 9 April George IV sent for George Canning, and the 'Junction Ministry' was formed. Canning's elevation to the premiership got a mixed reception at Holland House. Lady Holland's loathing for him had not lessened with the years, but her husband, more emotionally balanced, took a pragmatic attitude, giving the new prime minister his qualified support. Sydney was more interested in the fact that Lord Holland gave in his name to Canning for a bishopric. (The baron was obviously hopeful that the new prime minister had forgiven the mauling he had received at Sydney's hands in *Peter Plymley*.) Things seemed to be looking up. The new foreign secretary was Sydney's friend John Ward, created earl of Dudley. Another old Edinburgh chum, Henry Petty, third marquess of Lansdowne, was also in the Cabinet. A further crucial appointment, from Sydney's point of view, was Lord Lyndhurst as Lord Chancellor: chancellors had a lot of ecclesiastical largesse to give away. Lyndhurst was brilliant and charming; he knew Sydney quite well and, though a Tory, wanted to be of help.

Sydney had an even stauncher ally in Lady Lyndhurst; she was, he told Wrangham, 'a very handsome, good natur'd person, who is always very civil and obliging to me'. Sydney was less highly favoured than a lot of other men. With them Lady Lyndhurst dispensed with civility and concentrated upon the greater simplicity of being obliging. The Lyndhursts had a 'free' marriage; Charles Grey may well have been one of Lady Lyndhurst's numerous lovers.[1] She was just the kind of woman that Sydney liked: sexually attractive, witty and relaxed in the company of men. Being on easy terms with beautiful women was good for Sydney's morale He was a risk-taker, a man who liked to push himself close to the edge, to enjoy the frisson of excitement without ever crossing the border of sexual propriety, always careful never to compromise himself. It was a path he was to follow successfully to the end of his life.

In August, Sydney took the family on holiday to Scarborough. While he was there he heard the news of his father's death at the age of eighty-seven. Thanks to Bobus's timely intervention the previous year, Sydney now had an extra £10,000 of capital, a very tidy sum. He did not travel down to Somerset for the funeral, leaving the arrangements to his clerical nephew Cecil. Sydney was offered a memento which he politely refused. 'I lov'd my father in spite of his numerous faults & imperfections, and any memorial of him would fill me with Melancholy. My plan is to have no memorial of the friends I lov'd; they make me wretched. Therefore, I will accept nothing of any sort or kind however trifling.' This is the only time that Sydney stated that he loved his father. He was, I think, whistling in the wind: his actions are more eloquent than his words. After the 'reconciliation' in 1805, brought about by the need to co-operate over carrying forward Cecil's plans for a divorce, father and son hardly ever wrote to each other and only met infrequently. This speaks of acquiescence in a deliberate emotional distancing, not of love. Robert Smith never ceased to be highly critical of Sydney. In April 1826, just two months before Sydney's final visit to Bishop's Lydeard (the visit during which Robert said he was 'very much obliged' to him for coming), Sydney's father wrote a friend a note of blistering complaint against his second son: '*Sydney never writes me, whether he is affronted* [by] *the truth* I told him that his wife wanted good temper *I know not.*'[2] Behind the broad grin of Robert Smith's senility there could still be bared teeth.

Sydney is not to be blamed for the failure of the relationship. Loving Robert Smith was a superhuman task. He was an enormously strong character who made excessive emotional demands upon other people while requiring absolute respect and obedience in return – a recipe for conflict with all four of his sons. Sydney never learnt how to love his father, he learnt how to escape from him. A memento would have brought to mind far more pain than it would have recalled pleasure.

Another death took place while Sydney was at Scarborough: that of Canning on 8 August. Fortunately for Sydney, Lord Holland was on good terms with the new prime minister, Lord Goderich; it was also helpful that Dudley, Lansdowne and Lyndhurst were still in office. Hope, though, vied with despondency. Sydney thought that the new ministry was insecure, and indeed it was one of the weakest in history; Goderich himself was called by Disraeli, in a brilliant phrase, a 'transient and embarrassed phantom'. Sydney reveals his downcast state of mind in a letter written towards the end of August. 'If the [Goderich] administration remain in three years, which is not probable, and I am alive & not forgotten, and no great Lord comes across me for his Son's Tutor, or the Brother of his Harlot, I may possibly get a Stall in some Cathedral.'

In October, Sydney went up to town, dining with several ministers. The time seemed ripe but the fruit obstinately refused to fall from the tree. Lord Lyndhurst told Sydney that he had found a rich living for him in Kent, only to discover that he had already promised it to someone else. In December, Lord Fitzwilliam wrote, saying that he had read in 'London papers' that Sydney was to be rector of St George's, Bloomsbury, the church where his parents had married. St George's was of more than sentimental interest to Sydney. It was within easy walking distance of 'the sacred parallelogram'; equally to the point, it brought in a good income. The news in 'London papers' was, however, wrong. Dudley, who was privy to the negotiations over the choice of the new rector, put his finger on the reason for Sydney's failure. 'So conspicuous a piece of preferment could not be given to so strange a monster as an Oxford Whig without a clamour against him among his own parsons as he could not bear up against.'[3] The failure to obtain St George's, Bloomsbury, was a warning to Sydney, a warning that he did not heed. If government got cold feet over making him a London incumbent, his chances of a bishopric were slim indeed.

The visit to London in October 1827 was not entirely self-serving; Sydney was also there to make arrangements for the marriage of Emily, affectionately known as 'Duck'. The ceremony, which took place at Foston on New Year's Day 1828, was conducted by the archbishop of York, still a firm friend despite the uncongenial role he had been forced to play in Sydney's row with the fifth earl of Carlisle. Emily made a good match although not a great one. Her bridegroom, Nathaniel Hibbert, was a barrister on the northern circuit. His father, George, had been briefly a Whig MP and was a rich man, one of the founders of the West India Docks. Nathaniel's mother, Elizabeth, was of Huguenot descent, a fact of obvious appeal to Sydney. He was happy for his daughter but desperately sad to see her go. 'I feel as if I had lost a Limb and was walking about with one Leg', he wrote to Lady Grey while the newly-weds were on their honeymoon. 'Nobody', he continues, 'pities this descripton of Invalids.'

The Goderich ministry fell within a week of Emily's marriage: Wellington, victor over Bobus in a fight at Eton, took over as prime minister. Although the 'Iron Duke' was an implacable Tory, there was still hope for Sydney; Dudley continued as foreign secretary and Lyndhurst remained lord chancellor. Victory, in fact, was snatched out of the jaws of defeat. The hoped-for, but never expected, letter came from Lady Lyndhurst after Wellington had been in office scarcely two weeks: 'My husband . . . was willing that I should have the pleasure of first communicating to you this good news.' Always it was the women – Lady Lyndhurst, Lady Grey, Georgiana, Lady Carlisle, Lady Holland – who pushed hardest for Sydney.

In the current negotiations Lady Lyndhurst had enlisted the support of the foreign secretary. Dudley wrote to that most easy-going of monarchs, George IV, pressing Sydney's claims, and received a typically laconic reply. 'Tell Dudley I suppose he has seen SS where I once dined with him [at Holland House], and a more profligate parson I never met.' Having enjoyed himself a second time at Sydney's expense – he had clearly not forgotten the sweetness of his verbal victory over Sydney at the dinner hosted by Lord and Lady Holland in July 1807 – the king acceded to the foreign secretary's request.

Sydney was now a prebendary in the cathedral church at Bristol. He would have to live in the ancient sea port for four months each year, taking church services, light duties for which he was rewarded with an extra £400 a year.[4] He kept his livings at Foston and Londesborough; and to these, later in 1828, was added the vicarage of Halberton in Devon, obtained as a direct result of holding the prebend at Bristol. More money was not what Sydney was primarily after; what he sought was recognition. Always it had been a tough grain of insecurity within him which had nourished his ambition, driving him on.

Preferment, Sydney knew, was coming to him late. Now close on fifty-seven, he would be lucky if his future years of active life extended beyond single figures: only one in ten of his clerical contemporaries lived beyond seventy. Tardy success in his clerical career turned one of the more bitter remarks in Sydney's *Sermons* into an unhappy prognostication. 'The aged . . . enjoy some of the privileges of the dead; they experience that justice, which those who are actively engaged on the theatre of the world so seldom receive.'[5]

Appointment as a cathedral dignitary was a beginning, a much-desired further step up the ecclesiastical ladder, and it was also an ending. Sydney, in November 1827, had been 'fast backing out' of the *Edinburgh Review*; now, following receipt of Lady Lyndhurst's letter, he withdrew altogether. Sydney realized that it would not be feasible to be both a man aspiring to a bishopric and a literary firebrand. Desiring fame and power, he sacrificed his satirical career.

Sydney did not enjoy the biannual visit to Bristol; the two round trips, via the metropolis, added up to 1,300 miles, 'the distance from London to Naples'. While in residence, Sydney occupied a large prebendal house in Lower College Green. He was restless and uncomfortable in his new surroundings ; he missed Catharine, was deprived of domestic bustle, had little to do and made no new friends. For the first time in his adult life he felt lonely. He explains his predicament in a letter to his great friend, Georgiana, Lady Carlisle. 'I am living quite alone in a large Gothic room with painted glass, and waited upon by an old woman with only one Gothic tooth. About 6 o'clock when it is dark the various ghosts by which the house is haunted come into the room, and converse with me: Deans the colour of Rogers, Ancient Sextons of the Cathedral, Prebendaries now no more, elderly ladies who liv'd near, and came regularly during their lives to Morning Service.'[6] The Gothic and the grotesque: a pair of absorbing preoccupations for Sydney.

The only time he had any fun was when he was asked to deliver the annual commemorative sermon on 5 November 1828, Guy Fawkes Day. Bristol was one of the most staunchly Protestant cities in England. Failure of the Catholic plot to blow up Parliament was remembered amid general rejoicing. The mayor and corporation went in procession to the cathedral and, after the service, there was a sumptuous dinner. Sydney put a large fly in the ointment of festivity. With predictable lack of tact, he preached on religious toleration. The mayor and corporation were outraged, as of course Sydney knew they would be. He had, he felt, good reason to feel proud of himself. 'I told you I would make a splash at Bristol on 5th November, & accordingly I let off in the Minster no ordinary collection of Squibs, Crackers, and *Roman* Candles', he told one of his friends.[7]

Why did Sydney put on this verbal firework display? His was the joy of a man who has been fighting for a cause in which he passionately believes for over a quarter of a century, who has faced for most of that time what seems like a hopeless uphill task, and who suddenly finds, much to his surprise, that there is a real chance of success. Catholic emancipation was finally at the top of the political agenda; indeed, within a matter of months, it was to find its way on to the statute book. There was thus more than a whiff of triumphalism about Sydney's Guy Fawkes sermon. He amused himself but wisely decided not to take matters further, resisting pressure from pro-Catholic local papers to have the sermon published.

The year 1829 began badly. Douglas, not for the first time, was ill. He had a fall, spraining both his feet; much more seriously he became blind in both eyes. Sydney's elder son had lived a lot of his life in the shadow of the sick-room. When new-born he had been hurriedly baptized for fear he would not live. His health had been poor throughout his years at Westminster and he had a further 'long illness' when he was twenty. At Christ Church, Oxford, he did not take Honours because he lacked confidence in his ability to compete successfully in such an intense examination. The plan now was for him to sit Bar exams but ill-health was again holding him back. Towards the close of 1827, just over a year before his current blindness set in, Sydney had feared for Douglas's life; pleurisy was the culprit this time.[8]

Death came to Douglas unbidden and unexpected. The blindness of early 1829 seems quickly to have eased. We hear no more about his condition until the start of the second week in April, when Sydney was in London looking after him. On 9 April he was bled, showing a 'very marked and immediate improvement'. 'I shall stay a day or two longer in Town to see what progress he makes, and will tell you when I think him safe', Sydney wrote to Lady Grey. Sydney was building castles in the air. Within less than a week Douglas was dead.

Waves of suffering flowed through Sydney's heart. It was by far the worst emotional shock he had ever received, much more agonizing than the pangs of hurt that followed Horner's death. Part of the force of the tragedy came from the fact that it caught Sydney unprepared. Three months after Douglas's sudden demise, he realized the full force of his feelings. 'I did not know I had cared so much for anybody,' he wrote. 'The habit of providing for human beings, and watching over them for so many years generates a fund of affection of the magnitude of which I was not aware.'

This expresses exactly the experience of deep bereavement: the discovery within the self of a hitherto unsuspected fire, that licks us, and then licks us again, with its flames. Nearly a month later, in early August, Sydney was still absorbed in the mystery of his own suffering, and of human relations. 'I have from time to time bitter visitations of sorrow. I never suspected how children weave themselves about the heart. My son had that quality which is longest remembered by those who remain behind – a deep and earnest affection and respect for his parents.' Sydney had lost more than a son; he had lost a young man for whom he felt a degree of fatherly pride that bordered upon mild idolatry. The full weight of parental expectation had been placed upon Douglas's frail shoulders, he had striven to sustain the burden and the effort had destroyed, one by one, the fibres of his strength. To describe him as a tragic figure is not to overstate.

Douglas's death came at a difficult time for Sydney. His life was in a state of flux. He had been quick to realize that dividing his time between Yorkshire and the West Country was not practicable in the long run. The obvious solution was to exchange Foston for a living near Bristol. Cecil, conveniently situated at Bishop's Lydeard, was asked to keep an eye out for a suitable vacancy.[9] After one or two false starts Cecil found the rectory of Combe Florey, two miles from his own home and seven miles north of Taunton. Sydney, as was his custom, proceeded with caution. The living was held by the son of Mr Escott, a 'gentleman of large fortune'. Foston was worth a good deal more than Combe Florey and Sydney did not trust Escott. He had voiced his concern in a letter to Cecil at the end of October 1828. 'I must have another good look at the premises before I would allow the negotiation to be set on foot, and I should wish also thoroughly to investigate the value, taking it for certain that he would defraud me if he could.'[10] In financial matters Sydney was always influenced by the memory of his father's reckless deal-making.

Sydney's forebodings proved to be ill-founded. Negotiations for the exchange went smoothly and Sydney became rector of Combe Florey in March 1829. A further link with Yorkshire was severed three days after Douglas's death, Sydney giving up Londesborough three years before his agreement with the duke of Devonshire ran out. He left Foston on 30 May 1829; he was four days away from his fifty-eighth birthday and his wife was fifty-five. Although he kept up his correspondence with Yorkshire friends, and regularly took in a York newspaper, he never set foot in the county again.[11]

The new life at Combe Florey was some small consolation for the loss of Douglas. The place was, to Sydney, 'our little Paradise'. Built in the reign of Queen Anne, the rectory is in the lower part of the combe. Above it is a wood and, further up, a fine table-land with the Quantock Hills on one side and the Vale of Taunton on the other. The combe supports scores of plants, a botanical profusion which made a great impact upon Sydney; in his letters he calls Combe Florey the 'valley of flowers'. Sydney was also very fond of his new garden. It had an avenue lined with elms, there were many circular flower-beds, and groups of conifers and cedars were dotted about the undulating lawns. The beauty was enhanced by the mild climate. Hydrangeas and magnolias flowered throughout the year and, on at least one occasion, Sydney was able in November to eat grapes grown out of doors.

The rectory at Combe Florey is quite near the church; it is a short stroll from one to the other, round a gentle bend. The church itself is brownish pink, the colour of the local earth; parts of it can be traced back to the thirteenth century but it was extensively rebuilt around 1480. On the south side an ancient yew spreads out a long, gnarled arm which touches the church roof. Behind the church to the north, but hidden from view, is Combe Florey House, later to become the residence of the Waugh family. Evelyn Waugh, a Catholic, is buried in a simple grave just inside the grounds of the house and hard up against the church wall.

One of Sydney's first visitors, late in August 1829, was Francis Jeffrey. The two men, bound together by mutual affection and respect, had seen little of each other over the years. Sadly the famous literary critic, who was to become Lord Advocate the next year, never visited Combe Florey again. During his visit Sydney and Jeffrey sat for hours, talking together in high summer, on the lawn. Surrounding them was the greater part of the roof of Combe Florey rectory. Sydney loved altering houses. His main requirement was always the same: there must be light and then more light. Most important of all was a large room to work in; this should look out into the garden and should have a three-sided bay window. At Combe Florey this essential ingredient of Sydney's comfort was obtained by throwing together a passage, a pantry and a shoe-hole. As an added decorative touch, Sydney provided the bay window with a balcony. There was a large library, lined with books. 'No furniture', Sydney once wrote, 'is so charming as books': the volumes, as was characteristic of their owner, were chosen as much for their bright bindings as for their content. The changes made at Combe Florey rectory all served the purpose of keeping at bay Sydney's ancient enemy, the 'Black Dog' of depression. Full use was made of the garden in summertime. Fresh roses were put on people's plates at breakfast; and a favourite command to one of the servants (Annie Kaye had followed Sydney into Somerset, along with Bunch) was to 'glorify the room'. The three Venetian blinds of the bay were then flung open, revealing the garden in every direction and letting in a blaze of sunshine.[12]

Sydney was less active than he had been at Foston. He no longer took a leading role in county business, did not attend Quarter Sessions and was not a turnpike trustee. There were no schemes of allotments or orchards for the poor, and no grand plans to revivify the parish. Sydney wrote a brief, tell-tale, note to John Murray after he had been at Combe Florey for some eight months. 'I love liberty, but hope it can be so managed that I shall have soft beds, good dinners, fine linen, etc., for the rest of my life. I am too old to fight or to suffer.'

Lazy most of the time, Sydney was still capable of great energy in an emergency. He went to court to plead on behalf of a young parishioner, the son of a partially deranged woman, wrongly accused of theft; one winter's night, lantern in hand, he visited a poor cottager seized with epileptic fits (what painful memories of his mother this experience must have stirred!); and, when his footman ate a huge quantity of rat poison accidentally left in the kitchen by the gardener, Sydney watched over him day and night for ten days.

Nor did Sydney's wit desert him. In the winter of 1831–2 he explained to Lady Grey how pleasant it was at Combe Florey. 'We have had', he told her, 'the Mildest Weather possible; a great part of the Vegetable World is deceived and beginning to blossom, not merely foolish young plants without Experience, but old plants that have been deceived before by premature Springs, and for such one has no pity. It is as if Lady Glengall' (a notorious scandalmonger) 'were to complain of being seduced, and betrayed.'

Sydney also amused his parishioners. One of his jokes was to fix antlers on to leather caps, then buckle these to the heads of two donkeys named Jack and Jill. When they were not making people laugh, the two 'deer' were pulling Sydney around the garden in a low chair.[13] This jest was, in fact, less innocent than it seemed; the occupants of Combe Florey House had a deer park, and Sydney, by dressing up his two donkeys, was parodying their social pretension, the sort of cruel trick which had got him into trouble with his Yorkshire neighbours.

After Sydney had been at Combe Florey for a little over a year, politics impinged upon his life once more. George IV died on 26 June 1830. With William IV on the throne, Lord Grey stated in the House of Lords that Wellington's Tory administration would not last five months. It proved a remarkably prescient prognostication. On 2 November the 'Iron Duke' made a famous blunder, declaring that he would under no circumstances introduce any measure of parliamentary reform. Two weeks later Grey was asked to form a government; the Whigs were back in Downing Street.

Sydney was overjoyed. 'That a man should be placed where providence intended him to be, that honesty and Virtue should at last meet with its reward is a pleasure which rarely occurs in human life', he told Lady Grey. Sydney was pleased for 'Charles the Tall' and he was also pleased for himself. Never, probably, in the history of England has a cleric, not yet a bishop, found himself so well connected politically. Of the thirteen men in Grey's Cabinet, Sydney had spent quite a lot of his life with four and knew well another three. Grey was prime minister, and Brougham, Lord Holland and Morpeth, now Lord Carlisle, were also in the Cabinet. The new Home Secretary, Melbourne, had known Sydney for nearly thirty years (he had been one of the guests at the Holland House dinner, given for the Prince Regent in July 1807, at which Sydney had made his celebrated *faux pas*) and Lord Lansdowne, in power under Canning and Goderich, was back again as Lord President of the Council. The Lord Privy Seal was Grey's son-in-law Lord Durham, whom Sydney had visited at his country seat of Lambton Hall as long ago as 1820.

Sydney also felt, for the first time in his life, part of the stream of political events. The experience was exhilarating and he wanted to savour it. In his letters to the master and mistress of Howick he had always commented freely on issues of policy, both domestic and foreign; for so long as Grey was to be prime minister he was to write more regularly, offering advice on many matters. Sydney began as he intended to go on. While the administration was being formed he put in front of Grey's nose the credentials of favoured candidates for office: Lord John Russell should be given something (he was made Paymaster-General, later entering the Cabinet in June 1831) and Macaulay, whom Sydney called a 'book in breeches', is 'well worth your attention'.

Sydney soon had an opportunity to defend the administration in public. On 1 March 1831, Lord John Russell introduced to Parliament the first version of the Reform Bill. The proposed measure was radical: 54 constituencies with a minimal number of voters (in contemporary parlance, 'rotten' boroughs) were to be done away with. There was a furore in the Commons; the bill passed its second reading on 22 March by a single vote. The battle for reform was to last a further fifteen months, and England was to be driven closer to revolution than at any period in her modern history. Grey's survival as prime minister, and the slender hold that the Whigs had upon office, depended upon the safe passage of the bill. It was not a time for sitting on the fence.

Sydney joined the fray immediately, speaking at a political meeting held in Taunton on 9 March. It had been suggested that those who controlled pocket boroughs ought to be compensated as a *quid pro quo* for disenfranchisement, a notion which provoked Sydney into making a droll comparison:

When I was a young man, the place in England I remember as most notorious for highwaymen and their exploits was Finchley Common, near the metropolis; but Finchley Common, gentlemen, in the progress of improvement, came to be enclosed, and the highwaymen lost by these means the opportunity of exercising their gallant vocation. I remember a friend of mine proposed to draw up for them a petition to the House of Commons for compensation, which ran in this manner – 'We, your loyal highwaymen of Finchley Common and its neighbourhood, having, at great expense, laid in a stock of blunderbusses, pistols, and other instruments for plundering the public, and finding ourselves impeded in the exercise of our calling by the said enclosure of the said Common of Finchley, humbly petition your Honourable House will be pleased to assign to us such compensation as your Honourable House in its wisdom and justice may think fit', Gentlemen, I must leave the application to you.

Sydney started well and he went on to do even better. On 20 April the Reform Bill was defeated in committee and two days later William IV dissolved Parliament. Political meetings were held throughout the land. On 24 April the freeholders of Devon, who had Sydney among their ranks because he had obtained a living in the county on the back of his prebend at Bristol, met at an inn at the seaside town of Sidmouth. 'Stick to the Bill', Sydney began, 'it is your Magna Charta, and your Runnymede.' This was just what was wanted: a simple and vigorous catch-phrase which would rally support. Sydney poured scorn upon the easy lives of those who were returned to Parliament for rotten boroughs. 'Mr Plumpkin hunts with my Lord – opens him a gate or two, while the hounds are running – dines with my Lord – agrees with my Lord – wishes he could rival the South Down sheep of my Lord – and upon Plumpkin is conferred a portion of the government.' Sydney also made a daring appeal to the deep human desire at times of crisis to close ranks and take sides. Those who opposed reform were political lepers, 'If a man does not vote for the Bill, he is unclean – the plague-spot is upon him . . . purify the air before you approach him – bathe your hands in Chloride of Lime, if you have been contaminated by his touch.'[14] This was shrewd: it is reminiscent of the tactics used by Harold Wilson, a canny politician if ever there was one, to try to destroy the career of Peter Griffiths, Tory MP for Smethwick in Birmingham from 1964 until 1966, for allegedly getting himself elected by marshalling the racist vote.

Sydney's greatest triumph came later in the year. On 8 October the House of Lords threw out the second version of the Reform Bill by forty-one votes. Only two bishops voted for the measure; twenty-one voted against, with a further six episcopal abstentions. 'The Bishops have done it,' exclaimed a well-known political Radical. 'It is the work of the Holy Ghost.' This heavy hint was acted upon: the episcopal palace at Bristol (where the bishop was the father of the boy who had bullied Douglas so mercilessly at Westminster) was burnt down. Being in favour of reform made a clergyman popular but did not endear him to his ecclesiastical superiors.

Three days after the Lords had rejected the Reform Bill there was another political meeting at Taunton. The intention was to use the Guildhall, but the press of people was so great that it was decided to hold proceedings in the massive and battlemented Castle Hall instead. It was in this historic setting, built by a Saxon king and used by Judge Jeffreys for his 'Bloody Assize', that Sydney delivered his most famous speech.

The atmosphere in Castle Hall was highly charged. As Sydney rose to speak a ruffian, perhaps made brave by alcohol, pointed a finger in the direction of St Mary Magdalen, the beautiful parish church, and cried out: 'If we don't have reform directly, we will pull down that church! We will pull it down and repair the roads with its stones.' Sydney rose calmly from his seat, walked slowly and deliberately across the hall, looked the man straight in the face and said to him in a freezing tone of scorn: 'Your language, sir, is highly indecent.' The man sat down, saying not one word.

It was, on Sydney's part, a brilliant actor's entrance: the crowd was hushed, expectant, tense. Sydney's speech was short. He used no rhetoric, drew no resource from a well of fine words. Instead, he fixed in the minds of his audience a curious image: the image of Mrs Partington. This venerable woman, who lived on the beach at Sidmouth (the venue for the meeting of Devon freeholders held the previous April), had no obvious connection with the issue of political reform. Still, Sydney pointed out to his hearers, she was locally famous. During a ferocious storm in 1824, she had done something strange. Here Sydney paused, bent his back double and mimed an old woman trundling a large mop back and forth. Then he paused again. After a few moments, instead of going on with his speech, the mime recommenced, this time more animatedly. Sydney made yet another pause and then delivered a brief peroration. 'The contest was unequal. The Atlantic Ocean beat Mrs Partington.'

Truth had finally sunk in: a great wave of laughter spread across Castle Hall. 'Gentlemen, be at your ease – be quiet and steady. You will beat Mrs Partington.'[15] Sydney had achieved with a single joke what could not have been done in a serious speech: he had made the attempt to halt the Reform Bill look both futile and ridiculous. Within days prints of Dame Partington, trundling her mop and with her face bearing a remarkable resemblance to that of the duke of Wellington, leader of the anti-reform Tories, were in London shops.

Sydney's attitude towards his own preferment was ambivalent. 'The temptation may not come. If it does, I hope I shall not be such a fool as to yield to it' is how he speaks of the possibility of joining the bench of bishops. He had enough self-knowledge to realize that advancement would, in many ways, make him unhappy. The constraints of clerical life, which he fought against, would be greatly multiplied. 'How can a bishop marry? How can he flirt? The most he can say is, "I will see you in the vestry after service".' On the other hand, Sydney was intensely ambitious; and he also believed both that he would make an excellent bishop and that he deserved to be one. The contradictory forces raged within him. He insisted that he despised episcopal pomp and ceremony and yet, at the same time, he went out of his way to be prominent in the Whig cause, a prominence whose clear motive was to place himself at the top of any ministerial list of future episcopal appointments. Hence his defence of the policy of the Talents in *Peter Plymley*, and hence also his three recent speeches on parliamentary reform.

Lord Grey added fuel to the fire of Sydney's ambition. On his first day in Downing Street the new prime minister told one of his sons-in-law: 'Now I shall be able to do something for Sydney Smith.' This remark became known at Combe Florey, where it was interpreted, with every justification, as meaning that the prime minister would make Sydney a bishop at the first opportunity. Favouring family and friends was very much Grey's policy. Lord Durham, married to one of his daughters, was in the Cabinet; one of his sons, Charles, was his private secretary; another son, Henry, was Under-Secretary for the Colonies. It was later alleged that twenty relatives of Grey received during his ministry appointments, sinecures and pensions to a total value of £202,892 6s 2d.

Lord Grey's nepotism was not Sydney's only ground for hope. The Whigs had been out of power for nearly a quarter of a century and the leadership wanted to use its patronage to reward, in the first instance, those who had stood by Whig principles longest. This applied both to the church and to politics. Lord Holland plied Grey with lists of deserving Whig clergy, some of them 'actually starving'.[16]

If Sydney was to reach the episcopal bench he would need assistance from natural causes. There were no ecclesiastical pensions and thus little prospect of any episcopal resignations. The chances of a vacancy were nevertheless high, for a number of bishops had held office a long time and were now very old. When Earl Grey came to power, Bathurst of Norwich was eighty-six, Folliott Cornewall of Worcester seventy-six, Burgess of Salisbury seventy-four, Sparke of Ely seventy-three, Sydney's friend Edward Vernon-Harcourt, archbishop of York, the same age. Unfortunately things did not go Sydney's way. 'The Upper Parsons live vindictively, and evince their aversion to a Whig Ministry by an improved health', he told John Murray in January 1831. The behaviour of Sparke of Ely was especially irritating; he had the 'rancour to recover after three paralytic strokes'.

Through most of 1831, Sydney waited. His chance came on 5 September with the death of Folliott Cornewall of Worcester. The opportunity, however, passed him by. Lord Holland, who took a keen interest in all ecclesiastical negotiations that might be of possible benefit to Sydney, narrates what happened. William IV 'suggested or in a way asked' that the vacant bishopric should go to Carr of Chichester, and Lord Grey put forward the name of Edward Maltby to fill Carr's place. Edward Maltby! That 'excellent man and a great fool'. How galling to be superseded by an old school chum who was, Sydney knew, quite incompetent. But he kept his own counsel and said nothing.

In the spring of 1832 there was another vacancy, this time at Hereford. The deceased bishop was none other than George Hunting-ford, intensely close friend of Henry Addington and an assistant master at Winchester while Sydney was at the school. (Shortly after Sydney left he had returned as Warden, adding the bishopric later.) Once again Sydney was passed over, the plum going instead into the mouth of Edward Grey, youngest brother of the prime minister. This looks like a piece of flagrant nepotism but almost certainly was not. According to Lord Holland the decision, as with Carr's promotion to Worcester, was the king's, testimony supported by Grey's dislike of his brother's pro-Tory attitudes and sympathy towards Evangelicals.[17]

Grey remained prime minister until July 1834. Sparke stayed as bishop of Ely, Bathurst lived on at Norwich, Vernon-Harcourt was hale and hearty at York, Burgess kept going at Salisbury. Sydney felt sure that if a number of 'proper vacancies – that is, ones where candidates were not chosen by the king – had arisen during Grey's premiership, he would have been made a bishop. Saba claimed to have 'papers' showing that it was Grey's intention to put Sydney on the bench. I doubt it. The prime minister was very fond of his old friend and admired his mind, but he was also convinced that promoting Sydney would not be politic. In the heated atmosphere of the times the last thing that Grey wanted was a forest fire of discontent sweeping through the ranks of the mostly Tory bishops and equally Tory parish clergy.

Sydney, for his part, failed to acknowledge that any one of a number of obstacles could trip him up. He dressed extremely casually in what was a very formal age – bishops were still expected to wear wigs. More seriously still, Sydney was sometimes boyish and reckless. A good illustration is an incident that occurred towards the end of his stay in Edinburgh. An apothecary called Gardiner had a shop in George Street. Over the door, high up and well secured, was a bust of the famous Greek doctor, Galen. Four men, including Sydney and Henry Brougham, plotted its removal, at dead of night and in great secrecy.

As the four would-be robbers approached Gardiner's shop, it was noticed that Brougham was missing. Nothing daunted, the other three carried on. One of them mounted the iron railing that was immediately below Galen's bust; and a second, with some help from the third, stood on the first man's shoulders. At this point Henry Brougham, duplicitous Brougham, slippery and unreliable Brougham, played out a brilliant piece of self-parody; for he was detected in the distance, stealing up in the company of the neighbourhood watch. The spirit of such derring-do remained alive within Sydney, as indeed it did within Brougham. The difference is that it was just permissible in a member of the Cabinet but was quite fatal to the chances of an aspiring bishop.

Moreover, Sydney could not hold his tongue. 'Good things', in his own expression, had an awkward habit of slipping out. It was not wise to compare Lord Grenville, a past prime minister, to a reformed prostitute; or say, in the hearing of a future king, that the wickedest man in Europe was a prince. People, unfortunately, remember a joke, particularly a joke directed against themselves, rather better than they remember most other things. Sydney's free use of Scripture – 'Is thy servant a Dog that he should do this thing?' – also counted against him. Even some of Sydney's friends felt that he should show more self-control. For example, at Sydney's death, the portrait painter Benjamin Haydon, an avid listener to his sermons, paid a tribute in which admiration was mixed with sadness. 'He was a Man of great Genius! but he was too careless of his wit, where Religion ought to have restrained him. I have heard him say irresistible things which ought not to have been irresistible on such a subject. Well, he is gone, & he will be missed.'

Sydney was no ivory tower intellectual; on the contrary, he was a muck-raking, highly partisan Whig, the originator of the *Edinburgh Review*, the man who, in *Peter Plymley*, had heaped personal abuse on the heads of two future prime ministers – Canning and Spencer Perceval. It is worth recalling the fifth earl of Carlisle's admonitory words, written in October 1824. 'When you are so capable of giving us both instruction & pleasure, why run amuck at every component part of society: Order, Class, Profession, the Bar, the Bench, rural residents, West Indian proprietors, youthful sportsmen, brother Magistrates?' Sydney's satirical pen had ranged too wide.

Sydney also had theological antagonism to contend with. The Evangelicals, whom he had treated so viciously and so unfairly early in the century, had become numerous and powerful by the 1830s; there were even three Evangelical bishops. Hated at Clapham, Sydney was also hated at Oxford. It was in 1833 that John Keble preached his famous Assize Sermon. Sydney parodied the Catholic spirituality of the newly emerging Oxford Movement, heading his letters 'Washing Day'. Keble and Newman returned the compliment, arguing that the Low Church rationalism that Sydney typified was heresy. In view of the opposition that his appointment to a bishopric would inevitably provoke, it is fair to say that Sydney, despite his closeness to Lord Grey and Lady Holland, was not being wholly realistic in expecting to be promoted.

Lord Grey did not prove an entirely false friend. When, in September 1831, Carr was moved at the king's request from Chichester to Worcester, his canonry at St Paul's became vacant and Grey gave Sydney the post. 'A snug thing' is how Grey puts it (the same adjective as Sydney had used to describe his new rectory at Foston in letters to John Allen and Lady Holland), and 'snug' sums up a canonry at St Paul's very well: duties, as at Bristol, were undemanding and pay exceedingly good. Sydney was now even richer than when he had held both Foston and Londesborough. His post at St Paul's was worth nearly £2300 a year, and then there was more coming in from Combe Florey and Halberton. Adding it all up, Sydney was earning close on £2900 a year. Quite a few bishops made less than this sum; only twenty-five clergy (in a total of around 10,000) were paid more. Sydney's income, adjusted for inflation, is equivalent to after-tax pay of £89,000 in 1990.

Very soon after his appointment to the canonry at St Paul's, Sydney was presented at court. Unfortunately he blotted his copybook, turning up with strings, not buckles, to his shoes. Two or three courtiers looked at him askance, thinking it was a joke. Sydney was very annoyed; his error, he was at pains to point out, was born of ignorance, not impudence.[18] The incident shows, with remarkable clarity, why it would have been unwise to make Sydney a bishop.

From September 1831, Sydney divided his time between Somerset and London. His usual routine was to be at Combe Florey for two months over Christmas and for a further period of two months in the summer, spending the remaining eight months of the year in the metropolis. The official duties of a canon of St Paul's were light; when in residence he could, if he wished, get away with doing virtually nothing except preaching a Sunday sermon. Sydney was not satisfied with a modicum of work, but took his new position very seriously. The dean, Edward Copleston, was also bishop of Llandaff and was therefore away for much of the time. In his absence Sydney took matters into his own hands.

Within a year he had set the affairs of the cathedral upon a new footing. Chaos was turned into order, system took the place of haphazard practice. The main tasks of the dean and chapter – running the cathedral and chapter house, and superintending their repair – were not as easy as they looked. The only way of heating St Paul's, said Sydney, was to heat the county of Middlesex. Controlling the crowds who flocked into the cathedral was very hard. London was less civilized than it is now. Monuments were scribbled upon, dogs and cats, unless checked, roamed at will, and there were even worries that the cathedral might be used, as it had been in the seventeenth century, for purposes of prostitution. In order to maintain decency, it had been the custom for a century to charge two pence for admission outside hours of worship. Arrangements for the financing of upkeep were not sensible. Repairs to the fabric were paid for out of a general fund, but all other expenses came out of the pockets of the dean and the three canons. Non-fabric expenditure was therefore kept to a minimum, and Copleston and the two other canons took no interest in repairs paid for out of the general fund, leaving everything to the cathedral's surveyor, Charles Cockerell, a well-known architect.

Sydney took a different line, giving Cockerell a hard time. There was nothing that was not questioned. Why did not the deputy surveyor keep written records of work done? Why were not estimates obtained? Why did not Cockerell employ cheaper workmen? 'Your idea of respectability seems to be that no tradesman can be respectable who does not charge high prices.'

After the 'initial collision', as Sydney called it, he managed to work with Cockerell reasonably well. The surveyor admired Sydney's zest for business. Nothing was too much trouble. Sydney clambered about on roofs and towers, oblivious to the strain imposed upon his portly frame, arranged for the books in the library to be repaired, introduced mains water in the lower parts of the cathedral, and created an important precedent by being the first person to insist upon insurance of an English ecclesiastical building. It was work of lasting benefit. After Sydney's death, Dean Milman paid him a rare compliment. 'I find traces of him in every particular of Chapter affairs,' he told Catharine; 'and on every occasion, when his hand appears, I find [the] strongest reason for respecting his extraordinarily sound judgment, knowledge of business, and activity of mind.'[19] Sydney, in these early years as a canon of St Paul's, wanted to show that he would make an excellent bishop.

Still, he did not escape controversy. The most protracted dispute started in July 1837 and was, as it happens, with Lord John Russell, the friend whom Sydney had recommended to Grey for promotion in 1830. In 1837, Russell was home secretary and, in his official capacity, wrote to the dean and chapter, saying that because St Paul's was a national building containing valuable works of art the government was anxious that it should be made more accessible, free of charge, to the public. Copleston wrote the initial reply but the rest of the correspondence was handled by Sydney. He felt sufficiently confident of Russell's friendship to have a public row. Lord John implied that the cathedral was rarely, if ever, open without payment. He should, Sydney told him, check his facts; St Paul's was open free of charge, outside times of worship, for about nineteen hours a week. Running the cathedral efficiently was virtually impossible. At times of free opening it was not unknown to see 'beggars, men with burdens, women knitting parties eating luncheon, Dogs, children playing, loud laughing and talking and every kind of scenery incompatible with the solemnity of worship'. Prayer books were torn up. Pews were sometimes turned into 'Cabinets d'aisance'.

The home secretary, making a limp effort to be helpful, suggested that the dean and chapter might wish for extra police support (for several years they had paid for two constables to be on duty inside the cathedral on Sundays). Russell's proposal drew from Sydney a brief reply of piquant irony. 'The Dean and Chapter will I am sure be much obliged to your Lordship for the offered intervention of the London Police.' The correspondence dragged on until November, Sydney thoroughly enjoying himself. The dean and chapter eventually agreed to open the cathedral free of charge for an extra hour each day. Lord John Russell said he was unhappy with the arrangement but would accept it.[20] There matters rested until 1851, when the two pence charge for entry was abolished.

In these years as a London canon, Sydney had a public platform: the pulpit of St Paul's. He had always been a powerful preacher, but now added to this natural gift the force of dignity and the lustre of wisdom that can come with age. The setting certainly helped; during services there were only a few scattered lamps under the dome, producing a sepulchral effect and giving a vague sense of the immensity of the place. All eyes focused upon the pulpit, a situation which Sydney, with his highly honed acting ability, was able to exploit to the full.

Those who had met Sydney at Holland House came to St Paul's a little tremulous, expecting that he would be witty and coarse. Their fears were soon dispelled. Mrs Austin, who later edited some of Sydney's letters, went to hear him preach and was taken aback. 'The moment he appeared in the pulpit, all the weight of his duty, all the authority of his office, were written on his countenance . . . his whole demeanour bespoke the gravity of his purpose . . . As soon as he began to speak, the whole choir, upon which I looked down, exhibited one mass of upraised, attentive, thoughtful faces. It seemed as if his deep, earnest tones were caught with silent eagerness.'

Everyone noticed the voice. It was a human instrument that had a power which was all its own: it was light and mellow but strong. Charles Greville, the diarist, went to hear Sydney preach in December 1834. He was, thought Greville, 'very good; manner impressive, voice sonorous and agreeable, *rather* familiar, but not offensively so, language simple and unadorned, sermon clever and illustrative'. Sydney's preaching was liked even more by George Ticknor, a Harvard professor. Ticknor was something of a connoisseur of sermons, listening to most of the well-known preachers of the day. None of them, he felt, could match Sydney's clarity and force. Here is the entry from Ticknor's diary for Sunday 19 July 1835. 'We went to St Paul's and heard Sydney Smith'; the sermon 'was written with great condensation of thought and purity of style, and sometimes with brilliancy of phrase and expression, and it was delivered with great power and emphasis . . . It was by far the best sermon I ever heard in Great Britain.'[21]

Sydney, standing erect with the light shining upon him in the freezing vastness of St Paul's, is an entirely different figure from the Holland House wit. As a preacher he was a man born to command; there was the heavy frame, the Roman nose, the piercing eye. Those who listened to him were often deeply moved.

Entertainment was an important part of Sydney's new metropolitan life. He held an At Home once a week, from 9 PM until midnight, asked many friends to breakfast (then a substantial meal, usually taken at 10 AM or thereabouts) and, in 1840, was dining out eight or nine times a week. His circle of acquaintance was much larger than when he had last lived in London. There was still the Holland House set – Lord and Lady Holland, Samuel Rogers, Henry Luttrell, John

Whishaw, and so on – but Sydney had made many other friends over the years. He dined quite often with Archbishop Vernon-Harcourt when he was in town, and Sydney got on especially well with the Archbishop's daughter Georgiana; Lady Davy (as Jane Apreece she had first visited Foston in the autumn of 1810) was quite close; there was Mrs Grote ('the Grotesque'), whose husband was a prominent Radical MP; and Sydney was also on good terms with, for instance, Lord and Lady Ashburton and with the fifth earl of Tankerville, whose sister, Lady Mary Bennet, was one of Sydney's regular correspondents. Social life was broad but it was also shallow. Catharine was wearied by the social round and spent an increasing amount of time at Combe Florey, especially in her declining years.

Sydney enjoyed the dinners of the 1830s less than those of the early years of the century. Society was changing. Use of language was becoming more restrained and behaviour more inhibited. It was unlikely, in 1835, that a devout Christian woman would have 'Set your mind on things above' woven into her garter. Sydney, of course, belonged to the moral *ancien régime*, and therefore felt increasingly out of place. There was a second threat to his free and easy ways. It was an age of publicity. 'Literary lions', as the contemporary phrase had it, were followed in the streets; when they went to parties, they found that many of the guests hung upon their every word; they even had to cope with a new breed of admirer – the autograph hunter. The mobbing of literary figures earned the scorn of Harriet Martineau, who entered London society in 1832. 'It is somewhat new to see the place of cards, music masks, my lord's fool, and my lady's monkey, supplied by authors in virtue of their authorship', she noted with disdain. Sydney attracted his full share of popular acclaim. People, said one of his friends, felt 'little inclination to talk in his presence'. This was just the kind of constraint that Sydney found irksome; his dinner-table conversation had developed as spontaneous witty responses to other people's remarks. His unease did not go unnoticed. Charles Greville said that at dinner parties, Sydney often 'came on stage like a great actor, forced to exert himself, but not always in the vein to play his part'.

Sydney did not complain about unwanted hero worship, preferring to use it as raw material for humour. Tom Moore records in his diary an example of Sydney's raillery:

April 3, 1836. Dinner with Miss Rogers. Sydney highly amusing in the evening. His description of the *dining* process, by which people in London extract all they can from new literary lions, was irresistibly comic. 'Here's a new man of genius arrived; put on the stew pan; fry away; we'll soon get it all out of him'. On this and one or two other topics, he set off in a style that kept us all in roars of laughter.

Fame had its compensations. Sydney was elected to The Club, the highly prestigious literary club founded the previous century by Samuel Johnson and David Garrick. Brougham, Lord Holland and Macaulay were among the members. Sydney also had the good fortune to meet Charles Dickens. Sydney was at first put off by his surname, which he thought vulgar (a common reaction at the time), but soon warmed to the young novelist. Dickens first dined at Holland House on 12 August 1837. Sydney was not present at the dinner but he did read *Sketches by Boz*, which had been published in February 1836, a few weeks later. 'I think them written with great power,' he told a correspondent, '& that the Soul of Hogarth has migrated into the Body of Mr Dickens.'

There is, among Dickens's correspondence, a brief undated note to the publisher William Longman: 'I wish you would tell Mr Sydney Smith that of all the men I ever heard of and never saw, I have the greatest curiosity to see and the greatest interest to know him.' Sydney and Dickens saw something of each other over the next few years. In 1839, Sydney invited the novelist to meet Mary Berry and her sister Agnes; it was Mary who had written, many years ago, a poem about buying a new bonnet to wear to one of Sydney's lectures on moral philosophy. The two women, both spinsters, were by now thoroughly old-fashioned, being addicted to use of rouge, pearl-powder and false hair. It was a fruitful suggestion on Sydney's part; Dickens loved to meet colourful characters. One wonders what he made of the sisters' appearance, and how he responded to their conversation, liberally sprinkled as it was with feminine oaths popular half a century earlier. Dickens paid Sydney the compliment of calling his seventh child, somewhat awkwardly, Sydney Smith Haldimand. Sydney became an avid reader of Dickens's books. He found *Nicholas Nickleby* 'very good', and said of the first number of *Martin Chuzzlewit* that he had 'never read a finer piece of writing'.[22] Not since Scott had Sydney found a novelist who was so much to his taste. He was drawn, in both instances, by the power of the pictorial. It is a pity that Sydney did not develop his relationship with Dickens further. They had, both morally and imaginatively, much in common: a love of the ludicrous and the comic, a fine sense of theatre, satirical edge, hatred of everything (and everyone) pretentious or false. Dickens also shared Sydney's deep compassion for the outcast and the poor, a social concern which, as with Sydney, was driven by strongly-held Christian faith.

Sydney liked spotting and encouraging young literary talent. He was fond of telling people that he had 'prophesied' the future greatness of Macaulay from 'the first moment' he had seen him; and John Ruskin said, generously, that he was the first person in the literary circles of London to enthuse about *Modern Painters*; Sydney thought the book would 'work a complete revolution in the world of taste'. He also embraced, with the broad arm of his patronage, Richard Monckton Milnes (later Lord Houghton), although he was irritated by his pushiness. Determined to put Milnes in his place, he minted a number of derogatory nicknames, all of which swiftly gained currency. Sydney's best effort, in this line, was 'In-I-go Jones'. It was not that Milnes in any way resembled the famous architect. Rather was it that he reminded Sydney of a certain William Jones, whose hobby was finding his way around the servants who guarded Buckingham Palace, and then secreting himself in Queen Victoria's private apartments. Unlike a late twentieth century imitator, by name Michael Fagan, Jones surpassed every reasonable expectation by performing the feat more than once. The numerous jests provoked Monckton Milnes into writing Sydney several angry letters, drawing by way of reply a judicious reprimand. 'Never lose your good temper', he told Monckton Milnes; it is 'one of your best qualities, and which has carried you hitherto safely through your *startling eccentricities*. If you turn cross and touchy, you are a lost man.'[23] It is ironic that Sydney, who in his own youth had been nervous and uncertain, should at the age of seventy take it upon himself to give advice to a young man about how he ought to behave in society.

14

PUT ON THE DRAG

'I like, my dear Lord, the road you are travelling, but I don't like the pace you are driving . . . I always feel myself inclined to cry out, Gently, John, gently down hill. Put on the drag.'
SYDNEY SMITH, *A Letter to Lord John Russell*, 1838

On 20 March 1834 another 'limb' was cut off: Saba married Henry – later Sir Henry – Holland, one of the best-known men in London society. As with 'Duck', Archbishop Vernon-Harcourt performed the ceremony. Sydney had known his new son-in-law for a considerable time; the first mention of Holland in Sydney's correspondence occurs in 1822, but the context implies that they were already good friends. The two men shared Edinburgh connections: Holland was one of a small band of able Unitarians who were educated at Scottish universities and then settled in London to make their fortunes.

Henry Holland was, in every way, a more substantial figure than Sydney's other son-in-law, Nathaniel Hibbert.[1] One of the country's leading doctors (he had attended Queen Caroline and later in his career was made physician-in-ordinary to Queen Victoria), he was also a distinguished traveller and a profuse writer on scientific and medical subjects. There is, about Holland, a touch of Renaissance man. He also moved within an exceptionally wide social circle; he met at one time or another in his life six US presidents, and counted among his patients Napoleon III and Talleyrand. His maternal grandmother was a sister of Josiah Wedgwood, and Holland himself had a long and fruitful friendship with Josiah's grandson, Charles Darwin. When he married Saba he was already middle-aged. Fourteen years older than his bride, he had had a London practice since 1816 and had been married before: his first wife, who died in 1830, bore him two sons and two daughters. Holland's children visited Combe Florey in the summer of 1835 and it was not long before they were accepted as part of the family. The marriage with Saba went smoothly and well.

The other surprise in 1834, Lord Grey's retirement in early July, was altogether less pleasant. Sydney did not get on with his successor, Melbourne. Describing Melbourne's social behaviour to Lady Grey, he is positively prudish, complaining that the prime minister 'giggles, and rubs his hands and swears'. Sydney also had no trust in Melbourne's judgement, complaining that he too frequently promoted men lacking credentials for the job in hand. Within a matter of months, Melbourne bore out Sydney's low opinion of his capacity to make sensible appointments. In October 1834 the bishopric of Bristol fell vacant, following the death of Bishop Gray. The appointment went to Joseph Allen, whose sole claim to fame was that he had been tutor to Lord Althorp. 'If', Sydney had written, 'no great Lord comes across me for his son's Tutor, or the Brother of his Harlot, I may possibly . . . '

Worse than Allen's appointment was a conversation Sydney had with Lord Holland. Showing scant respect for Sydney's feelings, Holland said that he was dissatisfied with the choice of Allen: he would far rather have had Samuel Butler, the reforming headmaster of Shrewsbury. This off-the-cuff remark understandably made Sydney exceedingly angry. He let his feelings have full flow:

> You have said to me an hundred times what pleasure it would give you to see me a Bishop, and that you had given in my name to Canning for that purpose: have I done anything to forfeit your good opinion? Is there any one occasion where I have shrunk from expressing and defending Liberal opinions in Church and State? Is there any other clergyman who has done it so long, so much, and I think I may add so successfully? Why then do you pass me over now and not think me worthy even to be thought of, when before coming into office you expressed yourself so desirous of my elevation?
>
> I have no other right to put this question but as a friend of 40 years standing, and I should really be obliged to you to tell me whether I am to consider myself as entirely laid upon the shelf, and passed over by that party for whom I have all my life hazarded so much abuse and misrepresentation. It is not that I care for being a Bishop. If the See of Bristol had been offered to me nothing would have induced me to take it — there is scarcely any

Bishopric I would take; but I think I do not deserve the disgrace from my party of being passed over and the dignity never offered to me.

This letter displays Sydney's usual mixture of honesty and lack of realism. The sense of slight (a family trait) comes across strongly. The *nolo episcopari* – 'It is not that I care for being a Bishop' – does not ring true at all.

Sydney's annoyance was given added vehemence by the fact that his letter to Lord Holland, written in mid-November, was sent a few days after William IV had dismissed Melbourne's ministry: the Tories, under Peel, were back in power. Sydney and Lord Holland held further discussions. Some good news came out of these. Lord Holland clarified what he meant by his casual remark about Samuel Butler. His personal preference, he said reassuringly, had been for Sydney but – then came the bombshell – he had felt unable to support him because three-quarters of Grey's Cabinet had been against making him a bishop. Sydney was shaken by the news. Here were men whom he had known since his youth, and yet they still did not believe in him. There was Brougham, mercurial and devious it is true, but they had managed to get on reasonably well together despite Sydney's insistence that Brougham should be excluded from the editorial committee of the *Edinburgh Review*, and they had been fellow combatants in the Whig cause for over thirty years. With Lansdowne, Sydney also went back a long way. The marquess had been one of Dugald Stewart's pupils in the late 1790s and, like Melbourne, had been a member of the King of Clubs; there was also, adding an extra layer of social cement, Bobus's marriage: the half-sister of Bobus's wife had wedded Lansdowne's father. As for Lord John Russell, had not Sydney helped to lever him into the Cabinet in the first place? Durham was friendly and the sixth earl of Carlisle had been a close friend of Bobus's since the 1780s, while his wife Georgiana trusted Sydney enough to turn to him for spiritual advice.

Worst was the thought that Earl Grey, whose hospitality at Howick Sydney had been receiving since 1808, did not have faith in him either. Had all his relationships been a sham? Was no one loyal to him? No, these thoughts were not to be tolerated. Brougham might well be prepared to stab him in the back, and Melbourne too, but he would go on believing in 'Charles the Tall' to the end. As for the others, he tried to shrug off his disappointment, telling Lady Holland that those who had been against him were worthless men: 'A set of political Cowards not worth serving, who desert a bold and honest man who has always turned out in danger and difficulty'.

Sydney was badly hurt. He was now sixty-three and would be lucky if he had more than a few more years of active life. He had spent twenty years shut away in Yorkshire, the Whigs had unexpectedly been returned to power, he had done all that he could to help their main measure, the Reform Bill, on to the statute book, he had been friends with over half the Cabinet, Earl Grey had been prime minister for more than three and a half years; and yet, despite his sufferings in the Whig cause, and despite the support he had given the party, he had still not gained his much-coveted bishopric. This disloyalty on the part of the Whig leaders was a blow from which Sydney never fully recovered. He was, henceforth, a man who felt he had been unfairly cast aside, a man pained at the thought of having been let down. Peel had less reason to fear his pen than Melbourne.

Although the Whigs were out of Downing Street, Sydney still managed to keep in touch with what was going on. 'I believe', he told Lady Grey on 14 January 1835, 'the new ministry are purporting' – that is, planning – 'some great Coup de Theatre.' It was true. In mid-January, just at the time Sydney wrote this letter to Lady Grey, Peel was recruiting members of an ecclesiastical commission. In a daring move the prime minister had decided to turn the tables on the Whigs: the Tories would take up measures of reform, starting with the church. The official announcement of the formation of the commission came on 4 February. It was a small body, seven politicians and five bishops, and the first meeting was held on 9 February at 10 Downing Street.

Even before the commission convened Sydney had wind of its intentions. 'I have no doubt whatever', he told Lady Grey on 7 February, 'but that Bob or as they call him Bobbin Peel is quite sincere in his Church Reform; Bishops nearly equalized – Pluralities, Canons, and Prebendaries abolished.' Sydney exaggerated but he got the general drift. The commission set itself three tasks: reduction in disparities between episcopal incomes – Durham and Canterbury were worth over £20,000 a year, Llandaff brought in £1043 – curbing of pluralism, the practice whereby many parochial clergy managed to obtain a second living and even, in a few instances, a third and a fourth, and the implementation of such measures as would render cathedrals 'most conducive to the efficiency of the established church'.[2] Sydney, as a canon of St Paul's, was a leading cathedral dignitary; and, as vicar of Halberton and rector of Combe Florey, he was a pluralist. A fight with the Ecclesiastical Commission seemed inevitable. Peel had, unwittingly, mapped out the direction that Sydney's life was to take over the next five years.

The spring and early summer of 1835 passed quietly enough, but Sydney's tranquillity was broken in the second week of July; he had to journey up to Cambridge in order to try to save Windham's university career. Life had never gone smoothly for Sydney's surviving son. Early in 1815 when Windham was less than eighteen months old, Sydney had told the boy's godmother Lady Holland (not an obvious choice as spiritual mentor and guide) that he looked 'more like the result of artificial fatting for a prize than any regular production of nature under an ordinary system of nourishment'. Windham had been eased into Charterhouse, on the nomination of Archbishop Vernon-Harcourt. He went up to Trinity College, Cambridge, in October 1831, soon earning the nickname of 'Assassin' after success-fully killing a bulldog in his rooms. Windham had two great loves: gambling and borrowing large sums. Annoying his father was, I suspect, an important motive in both cases. Sydney and Catharine must shoulder some of the blame for the way in which their son had turned out. From the beginning they had had too high hopes. When the child was two months old, Catharine wrote eulogistically to one of her friends: 'Sydney says he likes him because he looks so wise (indeed he does look very sagacious) & already Saba & I are stored with many a trait of his superior Genius.' Windham, who was no genius, was firmly set on a path which ran in the diametrically opposite direction to that followed by Douglas; whereas Douglas had striven to fulfil his parents' expectations of him, Windham was determined to dash them.

It was not his first scrape since he had been at Trinity. In October 1834, Sydney had paid some 'thumping bills' on his son's behalf. The interview between father and son had embarrassed Sydney more than it had Windham. Nonchalance had been his ploy; the names of most of his creditors had, so he said, slipped his mind. After he left the room Sydney sat disconsolate by the fireside, his face in his hands, slowly saying to himself the Lord's Prayer. When he reached the petition, 'Forgive us our trespasses', he paused and then decided to say the petition twice.

The current débâcle had been triggered by a trifling incident. Windham had laid a bet of £2 or £3 with another undergraduate over a race between two hackney coaches. Windham had won and had written to the loser, asking for the money. The letter, unfortunately, was opened by the loser's father, who sent it on to the Master of Trinity, Christopher Wordsworth (younger brother of the poet). Windham apologized for the breach of college rules in gambling with a fellow undergraduate and the matter was dropped. Windham then made a fatal mistake. Feeling that he was now in the clear he thought that he could safely give vent to his anger, so he wrote once again to the loser's father, expostulating with him for opening his son's mail. This letter was also sent on to Wordsworth. The Master, a strict disciplinarian, took the view that the dispute had now become public – how he reached this conclusion is hard to fathom – and expelled Windham.

By the time Sydney heard about what was going on, the decision had already been taken. Sydney was in an invidious position: trying to persuade a Cambridge college that it has acted wrongly is a task requiring superhuman skill. In his first letter to Wordsworth, Sydney put the case for Windham as well as he could but failed to get the Master to change his mind. He returned to London from where he wrote again, this time with much bitterness. 'You have I believe Children of your own; if you have my earnest prayer is that God may shield them from the Misery and ruin which you have poured with such an unsparing hand upon his unhappy young man.'

Wordsworth ignored Sydney's aggressive remarks and arranged for Windham to be given a place at Caius College. Windham did not take advantage of his good fortune. After leaving university he proved as incapable of holding down a job as he proved fond of continuing to run up huge bills. In 1842, when he was twenty-nine, Sydney paid off creditors owed the massive sum of £4000. On top of this, Windham had failed to meet substantial financial obligations incurred at racecourses. The next year there was a parting of the ways: Windham would in future have his own home at Southampton, and was given an allowance of £500 a year, but would otherwise have to fend for himself.

In October 1835, Sydney fulfilled the promise, made during his visit of 1826, to take Catharine to Paris; Duck and her husband Nathaniel came as well. The party did not get off to a good start. They were delayed in London because Emily was ill, and then a stone got jammed in one of the wheels of the carriage four miles the other side of Canterbury. This made them late in arriving at Dover, they missed all the packet boats and had to kick their heels throughout a rainy day. To cap it all a hurricane blew up in the night. The captain, after much hesitation, decided to set sail at five o'clock the next morning. Sydney, as was his custom, spent the crossing on deck but Catharine, who was very frightened, refused to budge from the carriage. When they disembarked she was brought out 'more dead than alive'.

After the perils and inconveniences of the journey, it was good to be back at Dessin's, the hotel at Calais that was one of Sydney's favourites. It did not let him down: 'such butter was never spread in England, no English hen could lay such Eggs, no English Servant could brew such coffee.' From Calais the party travelled to Montreuil, and then on to Rouen via Abbeville, before making its way at what was virtually a walking pace to Paris.

Sydney's impatience as a tourist had not diminished. He moved restlessly from site to site, often not even being prepared to get out of the carriage. His enthusiasms had waned even before the party reached Paris. At Rouen, for instance, he was resolute in his determination to stay put: 'I refuse to see . . . the square where Joan of Arc was burnt . . . the house where Corneille was born.' This dovetails with what we already know about Sydney. Had he not once said that he lived entirely in the present and the future, and that the past was 'so much dirty linen'? He started by training himself not to dwell upon his own unhappy childhood, and he then broadened this response to the world, striving to cut himself off from the poetic feeling evoked by contact with the past. 'My plan is to have no memorial of the friends I lov'd.'

There was another reason, apart from the perceived need to shore up his psychological defences, for Sydney's anti-Romanticism. The satirist is, by temperament, an iconoclast: he wants to lay bare human pretension, to deflate unworthy reputation, to expose everything that is hypocritical and false. This iconoclastic streak was fully developed in Sydney. He would always, if he could, debunk a grand or solemn occasion. 'It seems necessary', he once wrote, 'that great people should die with some sonorous and quotable saying. Mr Pitt said something not intelligible in his last moments: G. Rose made it out to be, "Save my country, Heaven!" The nurse, on being interrogated, said that he asked for barley-water.' The satirist has his own peculiar quirkiness, is always, to some extent, at odds with his surroundings and with the moral standards of his own world.

Sydney· was in ecstasies over French salads; their vinegar was 'almost Wine, like a Lady who has just lost her Character', a pleasant contrast with the 'Cut Throat Acidity' which he had experienced at home. Sydney was fond of devising recipes for salads and would sometimes, when staying at country houses, reorganize this part of the cuisine. He had harsh things to say about French bread – it was 'too crusty, and wounds the Jaws like a Brick' – but was otherwise very complimentary about both the food and the wine. He had a bon viveur's sense for the special occasion. 'I shall not easily forget a *Matelotte* at the Rochers de Cancailles, an almond tart at Montreuil' (the food is still excellent at the château there) 'or a *Poulet a la Tartare* at Grignon's.'³ A man's memories are one of the keys which we must use if we want to unlock the door that leads in the direction of his heart.

Upon his return Sydney set about finding a permanent London residence for himself: since his appointment at St Paul's in September 1831 he had rented furnished houses. He quite quickly found a place he liked just south of Berkeley Square. Lawyers created problems and Sydney did not move into the 'Hole', as he called it, until February 1836. His purchase of a fourteen-year lease on 33 Charles Street has symbolic importance; reconciled to living permanently in London, he had now decided that he would refuse any offer of a bishopric. After Peel's ministry had fallen in April 1835 and the Whigs under Melbourne had been returned to Downing Street, Sydney had made his new position clear, telling Lord Holland: 'I have entirely lost all wish to be a Bishop . . . in this I am *perfectly honest and sincere* and I make this communication to you to prevent your friendly exertion in my favour.'⁴

Negotiations over the new house were conducted from Combe Florey. The Christmas spent there was not agreeable. Sydney was missing Saba, he was in poor health and he felt depressed and bored. A pessimistic and reflective note starts to creep into his correspondence. 'I am going slowly down the hill of life. One evil in old age is, that as your time is come, you think every little illness is the beginning of the end. When a man expects to be arrested, every knock at the door is an alarm.' Sydney was open about the fact that he lacked 'infinite resources' of his own; he suffered from ennui whenever he was alone, and this produced in him a craving for company. Intensely sensitive to the moods of other people, he was able to respond to the liveliness of those who were around him, using the interaction with them to lift his own spirits.

For someone of Sydney's temperament the countryside is not the place to be. He had found Foston unspeakably dreary. How sad had been the note he had written to John Allen two weeks before moving into Foston rectory in March 1814: 'It is very pleasant in these deserts to see the handwriting of an old friend; it is like the print in the sand seen by Robinson Crusoe.' Now that Sydney was ageing, he felt the limitations of rural life even more acutely. 'One advantage of the country,' he told Saba in June 1835, is that 'a joke once established is good for ever; it is like the stuff which is denominated *everlasting*, and used as pantaloons by careful parents for their children.'[5] Sydney wanted all the time to be drawn out of himself. Piccadilly was the magnet that did the trick.

Events out of Sydney's control now began to dominate his life. On 19 January 1836 the regius professorship of divinity at Oxford fell vacant. Melbourne cast around for a suitable candidate. The prime minister concurred with Sydney's opinion of Evangelicals, regarding them as bigoted and hypocritical; and he found the theological ideas of Newman and his Oxford acolytes incomprehensible. Liberals were the men that Melbourne liked; they wrote plainly — it was one of Melbourne's affectations to consider himself a plain man — and there was the added advantage that they voted Whig. Melbourne's choice fell upon Dr Hampden, on the face of it an adequate if somewhat ineffectual candidate; he was scholarly and he was a Whig, but he was also a dull man without the slightest hint of charisma and his lack of charm was exacerbated by an unduly harsh voice. However, Melbourne made a fatal blunder: he failed to check with sufficient rigour his candidate's theological orthodoxy. Hampden had, in Newman, an enemy who was determined to expose him as a heretic. News of the proposed appointment leaked. Newman sat up all night writing a pamphlet against Hampden, Oxford busied itself raising petitions, and Melbourne had pressure put on him to change his mind by both William IV and William Howley, archbishop of Canterbury. There was much vacillation in Downing Street, but Melbourne eventually decided to stand his ground.

The timing of these asperities could scarcely have been worse from Sydney's point of view. Hampden's appointment was gazetted on 17 February. Four days later William Van Mildert, the bishop of Durham, died from a severe fever. He was followed to the grave by Henry Ryder, the bishop of Lichfield, on 31 March, and by Sparke of Ely on 4 April. Three bishops dead in six weeks! Melbourne, in the spring and summer of 1836, was anxious to make amends to Sydney for his lack of confidence in him the previous year, when he promoted

Joseph Allen to Bristol. Whatever Sydney may have thought of the prime minister, the prime minister thought highly of Sydney; he was impressed by his abilities and was convinced that he had done more than enough to deserve a place on the bench.

Almost certainly it was the row over Hampden that tipped the scales against an offer being made to Sydney. Writing in his diary in August 1836, Lord Holland discusses the episcopal appointments made earlier in the year. 'The Clamour raised about Hampden deterred Melbourne, I think, from taking the marked men on the side of Liberalism'; and he then goes on to make a list, including the names of Thomas Arnold, the famous headmaster of Rugby, and Sydney. The decision was finely judged. Melbourne wanted to brave the inevitable public outcry, but could not bring himself to do it. Guilt at what he saw as his own disloyalty never left him. Richard Monckton Milnes once heard Melbourne praising Sydney, and then adding: 'our not making him a bishop was mere cowardice.' This sentiment was deeply felt; some years after Sydney's death, Melbourne told Samuel Rogers that 'few things filled him with more regret in his past life' than not putting Sydney on the bench.'[6]

Meanwhile, a storm was brewing. Peel's Ecclesiastical Commission had been continued by Melbourne. The commission's aims remained the same: to make the pay of bishops more equal, to cut down pluralism among the parish clergy, and to render cathedrals more 'efficient'. Sydney put the correct gloss on the meaning of efficient. The commission wanted to clip cathedral dignitaries' wings. In particular it wanted to curtail the practice – which seems incredible today but was very much alive in the 1830s – whereby deans and canons were allowed to nominate themselves to livings to which, by virtue of their cathedral offices, they held the patronage.

Sydney took umbrage. He had already benefited from the church's *ancien régime*, having exercised the right, as a prebendary of Bristol, to nominate himself to the Devonshire living of Halberton, and he was anxious to benefit from it further. Sydney's self-serving was open and blatant. 'I think', he told Lord John Russell, the home secretary, on 14 January 1836, 'the only permanent basis of peace will be to leave us our patronage, *as it now is*, for a term of Years equal to the Lives of the present possessors, say 10 or 12 Years.'[7] Nothing could be plainer than that.

The commission had other ideas. In its Second Report, which came out on 4 March, it proposed that deans and canons should continue to have the right to appoint themselves to livings in their own patronage but only 'under certain conditions'. The cathedral dignitaries were up in arms. Meetings were held, sometimes chaired by Sydney. Pressure was brought to bear. It was not without its effect. The Fourth Report, published on 24 June, showed that the commission was in ragged retreat. Chapters were now to have 'as much patronage as may be required' by the members; the rest would go to the bishops. Sydney was still not satisfied; he wanted to keep everything. He failed to persuade the commission in private, so he determined to persuade it in public. The decision to write a pamphlet was taken just before Christmas. So fast did Sydney write its fifty-five pages that it was on the streets by 15 January 1837. 'I wrote it to save my Life – I should have died of bile & rage but for this remedy', he told Lady Ashburton.

Sydney wrote as though he were corresponding with a private individual: his pamphlet was called *A Letter to Archdeacon Singleton*. Singleton was archdeacon of Northumberland; Sydney must have met him at Howick, where he was rector. It is appropriate that Sydney should have addressed his diatribe to a brother clergyman. It is not just that he set out to defend clerical privilege and power. The irony in the title (not, I think, clear to Sydney himself) is that the clergy were, with few exceptions, Tories to a man, and in this short squib Sydney, the great Whig apologist, turns his political coat inside out. *A Letter to Archdeacon Singleton* is, first and foremost, a conservative document. Change, if change there be, must not exceed 'one thing more than was absolutely necessary'.

By 1837, Sydney was becoming disillusioned with the Whigs. He had noted the alteration within himself three years earlier, writing to his friend Richard York in February 1834: 'I am turning more conservative every day, and get severely abus'd by the Democrats.' Sydney was not the only person who was aware of the shift in his political position. In June 1836, R.H. Barham, author of the *Ingoldsby Legends* and, as a minor canon of St Paul's, a man in contact with Sydney from day to day, wrote to a correspondent: 'Mr Smith himself is as lively as ever, though they tell me he is losing caste with his party for turning Tory! Certain it is that the language he now holds is to the full as Conservative as anything that ever dropped from Peel or Lyndhurst.'[8]

Barham, himself a Tory, was guilty of wishful thinking in hinting that Sydney might change sides. He had lived his life as a Whig, and he intended to die a Whig. He made clear his loyalty to the party in a letter to Lady Holland, written in September 1838. 'I am out of temper with Lord Melbourne, and upon the subject of the Church; but in case of an election, I should vote as I always have done, with the Whigs.' A year before Sydney's death a Belgian poet wrote to him, asking for some personal details for inclusion in a review he was writing. Sydney's answer was rather smug. 'I am living amongst the best society in the Metropolis, and at ease in my circumstances; in tolerable health, a mild Whig, a tolerating Churchman, and much given to talking. laughing, and noise.'

'Mild Whiggery' is not an accurate description of Sydney's writings from 1836 onwards; indeed, some of them read as though they had come from the pen of an extreme Tory. There are three reasons why Sydney, although still considering himself a Whig, failed to give the party his public support. He thought that the leadership had acted shabbily in not making him a bishop; like Lord Grey, he was increasingly out of tune with radical elements in the party; thirdly, and most importantly, he interpreted the plans of the Ecclesiastical Commission, begun under Peel and continued under Melbourne, as an unwarranted attack upon the chapter at St Paul's in general, and upon himself in particular.

Reform of the church had never been top of Sydney's agenda. In 1803, at the age of thirty-two, he had written in the *Edinburgh Review* that it would be grossly unfair to stop the clergy from having more than a single living. Why? Because they would all become so poor: 'emoluments which a footman would spurn, can hardly recompense a scholar and a gentleman.' This does not sound like Sydney, it sounds like a reactionary cleric of advanced years living in some rural fastness. Thirty-four years later Sydney used the same argument. Every available means should be employed to maintain the incomes of the clergy: no member of this superior order should, on any account, be reduced to the standard of living enjoyed by 'the upper domestic of a great nobleman'. In the desire to put worldly considerations to the fore, spiritual values are forgotten.

It is not the power of argument that drives Sydney's *Letter*, it is the force of bile. At least Sydney was honest about his motives. 'I have not', he wrote, 'deserved this of my Whig friends.' It was not only that Melbourne's government was firing its arrows of reform directly at him; it was also that the growing influence of the Ecclesiastical Commission — it had been made a permanent body with delegated powers of legislation in August 1836 — greatly strengthened the authority of the episcopal bench. Bishops dominated the commission, which had a quorum of only three; and, under the commission's most recent plans, it would be the bishops who would be given the 'surplus' patronage of deans and canons. Sydney had never found it easy to accept authority. He found it even more difficult now. The leading spirit of the Ecclesiastical Commission was Sydney's own diocesan, Charles James Blomfield, probably the most administratively able of the nineteenth-century bishops. Blomfield's was a personality of great power; if he had chosen politics as a career, he had all the requirements – leadership, energy, ruthlessness, ideas – to make it to Downing Street. Blomfield and Sydney locked horns. '*Charles James, of London*', wrote Sydney, 'will become the *Church of England here upon earth.*'[9]

Sydney scored some good debating points. Why, he asked, were there not any deans or canons on the Ecclesiastical Commission? 'Common sense', if not 'common honesty', suggested that there should be. This was shrewd. Peel had wanted to include three or four cathedral dignitaries when the commission was first set up but Blomfield had squashed the idea. When the commission was reconstituted in 1840, three deans were made members *ex officio*. Sydney also laid bare, with unerring accuracy, episcopal hypocrisy. Central to the Ecclesiastical Commission's plans was a proposal to create a central fund, which would be used to endow desperately needed new urban parishes. Some bishops were congratulating themselves upon their high-mindedness in being willing to make over a little of their income into this new central fund; but these same bishops were also hoping, at the same time, to take over the 'surplus' patronage of the deans and canons. They could not, Sydney pointed out, have it both ways:

> Where then is the sacrifice? They must either give back the patronage or the martyrdom: if they choose to be martyrs – which I hope they will do – let them give us back our patronage: if they prefer the patronage, they must not talk of being martyrs – they cannot effect this double sensuality and combine the sweet flavour of rapine with the aromatic odour of sanctity.

Sydney did not scruple to exploit the antipathy which many of his clerical contemporaries felt towards their diocesans:

> Bishops live in high places with high people, or with little people

who depend upon them . . . They hear only one sort of conversation, and avoid bold reckless men as a lady veils herself from rough breezes . . . What bishops like best in their clergy is a dropping-down-deadness of manner . . . It would be just as rational to give to a frog or rabbit, upon which the Physician is about to experiment, an appeal to the Zoological Society, as to give to a country Curate an appeal to the Archbishop against his purple oppressor.

The best thing in Sydney's pamphlet is an account, from 'an old Dutch Chronicle', of a great meeting of the clergy at Dordrecht; bishops, canons and lower clergy were all there. Suddenly the proceedings were disrupted by an ugly crowd shouting '*Bread! Bread!*' and '*No Bishops!*' The bishops, afraid, threw their dinner out of the window to appease the mob. One of their number, 'Simon of Gloucester', then had a brainwave. Why not order the dinner of the deans and canons, 'which is making ready for them in the chamber below'? This the bishops duly did. Not only were the cathedral dignitaries required to go hungry, they were also pelted by the mob for failing to follow the example of the bishops in sacrificing their food.[10]

This jest at the expense of bishops received a lot of publicity and was widely believed to be true. But even Sydney's most effective arguments were vitiated by his conduct. He complained that the bishops were keen on giving fat livings to their sons and relatives, and then remarked sanctimoniously: 'I have no son nor son-in-law in the Church, for whom I want any patronage.' It was not for lack of trying. In April 1836 Sydney had written to the foreign secretary, Palmerston, saying that he had intended Windham for the church, a fairly incredible idea in itself, and had kept himself at the head of the preferment list at St Paul's in order to provide his son with a good living. But Windham had, as usual, refused to bow to his father's will; Sydney therefore sought for him some public office: 'I care not how small the emolument, I only want the occupation.' So much for not having a son in orders! Still more revealing is a letter from Blomfield to Sydney written on 24 January 1837, little more than a week after Sydney's pamphlet came out. It is clear from this that Sydney had made informal contact with the Ecclesiastical Commission, and had given an assurance that he would cease his attacks provided his own rights of patronage, as a canon of St Paul's, were not interfered with. Private posture undermined public argument. Sydney's tirade against the commission was not only intellectually weak, it was morally weak as well.

The months following publication of *A Letter to Archdeacon Singleton* were uneventful. In May he took Catharine (and, as a special treat, Annie Kaye) on a month's holiday in Belgium and Holland. It was a punishing itinerary: Dunkirk, Ypres, Bruges, Ghent, Antwerp, Rotterdam, The Hague, Amsterdam, Utrecht and Brussels. As though this were not enough, Sydney wanted to do a further stage of 800 miles but this ambitious plan had to be abandoned: Annie Kaye, worn out by the hectic schedule, became lame and was 'turned into a piece of baggage'. Sydney was not impressed by the Low Countries. He found the people poor and ugly – as ugly, indeed, as Macaulay – and the inns were dirty. Worst of all were the roads. They were all paved: 'The shaking is dreadful so that, if you took a bottle of Cream in the Carriage, it would infallibly be Butter before the End of the Stage.' He also complained that the behaviour of the postilions was a danger to life and limb: it was their habit to take a glass of schnapps every three miles.

Sightseeing, as always, did not make for marital harmony. Sydney was happy with the 'aujourdhui of Life': Catharine read masses of tourist books, and wanted to go everywhere and see everything. Sydney's artistic sensibilities were as dull as ever ('I have seen between 7 and 800 large women without Clothes painted by Rubens, till I positively refuse Mrs Smith to see any more'), but he was awestruck by the grandeur and beauty of the Rhine. Sydney was always responsive to the fierceness, the sheer brute strength, of nature. A wide river was unappealing, a narrow ravine exciting. 'The Rhine', he wrote, 'is like an army Tailor, it gains immensely by contracting; the last stage from Coblentz the rocks on each side become precipitous and sublime and I hardly think (which can rarely be said of any kind of excellence) that too much is said about it. Tormorrow we turn our faces towards England.'[11]

Sydney returned to London on 6 June. He found waiting for him a letter from William Cowper, later Baron Mount Temple, nephew to Melbourne and currently his secretary. The letter was about Windham. Ever since the correspondence with Palmerston in April 1836, Sydney had been doing what he could on his son's behalf. Palmerston had not been able to help but the next month Melbourne had seen to it that Windham was given a job, albeit a menial one, in the Audit Office. In April 1837 Sydney had written to Melbourne, asking for something better: '£80 pr Ann and 6 hours Labour is not that upon which a man can rest his Oars.'

Rest his oars or not, a clerkship in the Audit Office was all that Sydney got out of Melbourne for Windham. William Cowper did offer an alternative, but it was exceedingly unattractive: a job as a land-waiter, a degrading post with Customs and Excise. Sydney's rage knew no bounds. He gave his answer to Cowper the day after he was home. 'As to the Land Waiter's place I have too much real confidence in the proper feeling of Lord Melbourne & yourself to suppose for a moment that you are treating me with derision, & have therefore only to say plainly, that my situation in Life places me above the necessity of accepting such an offer, & *ought* perhaps to have guaranteed me from the pain of receiving it.'[12]

Sydney did not see himself as importuning the prime minister. As he told Lord John Russell on 3 April (three months after publication of *A Letter to Archdeacon Singleton*), giving Windham a decent job would be a 'receipt in full for that Mitre to which a long life of depression for liberal principles bravely avowed had doomed me to the age of 63. – Pray shew this letter to Lord Melbourne . . . '

What Melbourne must have thought of this letter is easy to imagine. Windham had been given something the previous year. Sydney, meanwhile, was no longer a loyal Whig; only a few months ago, in his latest pamphlet, he had lambasted the Ecclesiastical Commission and, with it, the government. Yet here he is, asking yet again for a post on behalf of his worthless, gambling son! 'Write to him, Cowper, offer him something really offensive.' Ungenerous perhaps, but under-standable. The fact of the matter – plain for all to see but seemingly hidden from Sydney himself – was that, once *A Letter to Archdeacon Singleton* was published, Sydney was outside the Whig pale. Melbourne made this abundantly clear to Lady Holland. 'Do not dream', he told her, 'of making Sydney Smith anything. It would now offend every party in the country. His pamphlet disgusted the High Church, the religious of the Low Church never liked him, and, as a politician, he never was popular with those who go principally by politics.' This last comment was Melbourne's typically elliptical way of saying that Sydney's attack on the Ecclesiastical Commission had annoyed him very much indeed. He had done nothing about it at the time, but now that Sydney had provoked him he had fought back.

This is one of the most extraordinary episodes in Sydney's career. Here we have a minor church dignitary, who publishes a pamphlet attacking the government of the day and then writes a letter to the prime minister some six months later, asking for a personal favour. Had Sydney temporarily taken leave of his senses? His letter to Lord John Russell on 3 April goes part of the way towards an explanation. 'A receipt in full': that is what Sydney was after. People who are convinced that they have right on their side are apt, at times, to be careless of the means they employ to ensure that right prevails. Nor should we forget the importance of the Holland House connection. Sydney had sat at table with members of the present Cabinet, off and on, for more than thirty years; Melbourne's name appears alongside his in the Dinner Books as early as 1801. Sydney did not write to the prime minister in his capacity as a canon of St Paul's: he wrote to him as a friend of thirty-six years' standing.

Finally, and most importantly, there is Sydney's fierce pride. He was, he believed, the equal of any man. The fact that Melbourne was prime minister did not enter into his calculations. The Whigs had treated him badly, he deserved to be a bishop and, since this was now impossible, he ought to be recompensed in some other manner. This was Sydney's train of thought and he acted on it. His behaviour would have been less preposterous if Windham had been fit for public duties of any kind. Employing Windham was an act of pure charity. It was Lord John Russell who played the Good Samaritan generously giving Windham a post in the Home Office. The outcome was all too predictable: Windham was later dismissed for bad conduct.

Sydney's *Second Letter to Archdeacon Singleton* was published in the spring of 1838. Insult overwhelms argument, evidence that Sydney was still smarting from the humiliations he had suffered during the correspondence with William Cowper the previous June. Blemishes in the prime minister's character had long been evident to Sydney. In this *Second Letter* he concentrates upon the foppish and affected side of Melbourne's personality: 'Every thing about him seems to betoken careless desolation: any one would suppose from his manner that he was playing at chuck-farthing with human happiness; that he was always on the heel of pastime; that he would giggle away the Great Charter.' This was hurtful; every prime minister wants to be taken seriously, wants to make the world feel the full force of his or her *gravitas*. 'Giggle away the Great Charter': a wonderfully evocative image but one that calls to mind Lear's Fool, not the queen's first minister.

The centrepiece of this *Second Letter* is an analysis of the career prospects of the clergy in terms of Adam Smith's free market economics. Sydney compares the clerical profession with a gigantic lottery. All sorts and conditions of men draw ecclesiastical 'tickets' and some surprising people win 'prizes'. 'Butchers, bakers, publicans, schoolmasters, are perpetually seeing their children elevated to the mitre.' Because everyone knew the rules of the game, losers did not have just cause for complaint. Even granted Sydney's highly materialistic assumptions, his argument is still flawed. Men from humble backgrounds did sometimes become bishops (Sydney's schoolmate Edward Maltby, for example), but it did not happen often, certainly not 'perpetually'.

Sydney also made a barefaced defence of nepotism. What was wrong with a canon of St Paul's promoting his own son to a living in his gift? There was a positive need for such 'gentle allurements'. 'You may as well attempt to poultice off the humps of a camel's back, as to cure mankind of these little corruptions.' A vivid way of putting it, but scarcely discreet. Is not a corruption, whether 'little' or large, still a corruption? Sydney, by 1838, had grown intellectually careless, making concessions to his opponents that, in the years of his strength, he would have been astute enough to avoid.

Predictably, he also attacked the bishops. The Ecclesiastical Commission had decided that the best way of making the incomes of bishops more equal – of bringing down the value of Canterbury and raising up that of Llandaff – was to put in place a plan for a modest redistribution of wealth between the sees. The annual 'tax' was light and, when the process was complete, William Howley would still be left with an income of £15,000 a year as archbishop of Canterbury. The leading bishops, who had the wealthiest sees and who dominated the commission, had been soft towards themselves. Sydney exploited their vulnerability. If representation on the commission had been broader, if deans and canons had been chosen, there would have been a different result. 'I could not, as a conscientious man, leave the Archbishop of Canterbury with £15,000 a year . . . This comes of calling a meeting of one species of cattle only. The horned cattle say – "If you want any meat, kill the sheep; don't meddle with us, there is no beef to spare".' The episcopal bench as horned cattle: an example of Sydney's bitterest satirical style. The mighty of the earth had been reduced to the level of the beasts of the field.

Sydney's *Second Letter* strained relations with the master of Castle Howard. The sixth earl objected to Sydney's personal attacks, which he thought unfair and which, of course, did nothing to help the Whig cause. 'You fulminate from your stall your censures upon the Administration, with many of whom you have lived in terms of intimacy'. Lord Carlisle ends his letter with a wise admonition, which echoes in its phrasing some of the remarks his father had made when he wrote his first, cautionary, note to Sydney in October 1824: 'Take care that there is no recoil. A gun that is highly charged often produces that effect.' Carlisle was annoyed but did not take the matter any further. He was altogether more emollient than his father and did not want a battle.

Sydney's answer was written towards the end of May. He portrays himself as the innocent party, provoked into action by the insolent behaviour of Melbourne. So badly had the prime minister treated him that he had even been forced to distance himself from his beloved Holland House. 'A year ago' (that is, at the time of the land-waiter controversy) 'I stated to Lady Holland in the strongest language my opinion of his [Melbourne's] conduct to me, & as a discontented person I have kept away from those head quarters of the Ministry as much as my sincere regard for Lord & Lady Holland would permit, Lady Holland often telling me that I had given her up.'[13] A plea for sympathy, this, but a plea without solid foundation. In the year to May 1837 the Dinner Books show that Sydney went to Holland House on eleven occasions: once in July, four times in September, three times in November, once in December and twice the following April. In the succeeding twelve months the number of visits falls marginally to nine, but they are better spaced out: one in June, one in July, one in August, three in September, two in December and one in January. This is not the behaviour of a 'discontented person'. Sydney had learned, over the years, how to pull on the strings of the human heart.

In the autumn of 1838, Sydney wisely decided to forget about cathedral reform for a while, turning his attention instead to a different topic: the secret ballot. The mechanism of voting had recently become a live issue in contemporary politics. A proposal to introduce secret voting was included in the first draft of the Reform Bill, drawn up in January 1831, but was subsequently dropped. Once parliamentary reform was passed, support for the secret ballot grew; a motion in Parliament in April 1833 attracted 106 votes in favour and 211 against. The pro-ballot campaign was given a fillip by the 1837 election; people were able to see that open voting – landlords making sure that their tenants did as they were told, electors in many boroughs bribed with free ale, food or travel and, in some places, blatant purchasing of votes – was quite as corrupt under a reformed Parliament as it had been under an unreformed one. Sydney knew about the campaign for electoral reform at first hand: the chief spokesman for the ballot in Parliament was George Grote, the diffident and scholarly husband of Sydney's friend Harriet Grote, 'the Grotesque'.

Sydney's pamphlet was published early in the New Year. He was pleased with what he had done, thinking it the best thing he had ever written. Still more satisfying was a glowing tribute from Bobus. 'Since the days of Pascal', said Sydney's elder brother, 'no such piece of Irony, involving so much wisdom, had ever been penned.' It would be hard to be richer in compliment than that. Bobus's praise was overblown – he veered between extremes of adulation and denunciation – but he did rightly divine that Sydney was back on good form. The essential thing was that Sydney had put animus aside. This enabled him to rediscover delicacy, to get back his famed lightness of touch.

He shows that his poise has returned at the very start, poking fun at the construction of a ballot box. It was a topical allusion; the first time that an illustration of a ballot box had appeared in a national newspaper had been in February 1837. Sydney turns the notion over in his mind. Perhaps there could be a 'dagger ballot box . . . you stab the card of your favourite candidate with a dagger'. Or, maybe, some voters might prefer the 'mouse-trap ballot box, in which you poke your finger into the trap of the member you prefer, and are caught and detained till the trap-clerk below (who knows by means of a wire when you are caught) marks your vote, pulls the liberator, and releases you.' When he wrote this opening paragraph Sydney entered, for a few fleeting moments, a wondrous and bizarre imaginative world, a world in which Edward Lear would have been entirely at home.

Given the increasingly conservative cast of Sydney's mind, it is not surprising that he was in favour of open voting. What is strking, however, is the novelty of his arguments. If Sydney had thought conventionally, he would have extolled the influence of aristocracy, and then gone on to complain that, were secret balloting to be introduced, aristocratic influence would dwindle and democracy would take its place. He does nothing of the kind. Showing a fine sense of the nature of social relations in the early Victorian countryside, he offers no value judgement on the power of the landlord, merely treating it as a brute, irreducible fact. Writing with all the verve and confidence of a modern historical sociologist, Sydney skilfully dissects the social carcass of the age in which he lived. 'Does Mr Grote imagine, that the men of woods, forests, and rivers – that they who have the strength of the hills – are to be baffled by bumpkins thrusting a little pin into a little card and in a little box? that England is to be governed by political acupuncturation?' Concealing political preferences from landlords was impossible. For a ballot to be truly secret it would be necessary to 'poll in sedan chairs with the curtains closely drawn'. Nor was Sydney able to detect political passions raging in the breasts of most tenants: 'They have no more predilection for whom they vote than the organ pipes have for what tunes they are to play.' Thus does Sydney sum up in a simple analogy what historians of 'deference' have taken whole books to say.

Sydney's strength is that he manages to marry social realism with morality. A man must be prepared to vote openly, to stand up for his beliefs; in his eloquent words, we must not 'seek for liberty by clothing ourselves in the mask of falsehood, and trampling on the cross of truth'. He makes the same point with a military image, put in such a way as to have wide appeal among his chosen constituency, the country gentry. 'An abominable tyranny exercised by the ballot is, that it compels those persons to conceal their votes, who hate all concealment, and who glory in the cause they support . . . It is as if a few cowards, who could only fight behind walls and houses, were to prevent the whole regiment from showing a bold front in the field: what right has the coward to degrade me who am no coward, and put me in the same shameful predicament with himself?' Later in the pamphlet he expresses the doctrine of personal responsibility in a pair of pithy aphorisms. 'The man who performs what he promises needs no box. The man who refuses to do what he is asked to do despises the box'.

Sydney, in *Ballot*, certainly did not let his public down. He performed, with great skill, one of the most difficult of intellectual conjuring tricks: he created the illusion, for illusion it surely was, that a thoroughly corrupt practice, namely open voting, was in fact the bulwark of justice, fairness and truth. He also showed considerable political guile. Those who campaigned for the ballot were anxious to detach the proposal from other, more radical, measures – annual parliaments, universal suffrage and the like – sure in the knowledge that, unless secret voting was seen to stand alone, there would be a drastic loss of parliamentary support. Sydney set about the task of destroying this strategy. Open ballot or secret ballot, elections would still be rigged by 'those who counted'. There was only one way to deal with bribery and corruption: 'universal suffrage would cure both, as a teaspoonful of prussic acid is a certain cure for the most formidable diseases'. George Grote's attempt to detach the secret ballot from more radical reforming measures had been powerfully countered. The finest piece of irony since Pascal? The praise is certainly extravagant, but there is no denying the fact that Sydney's pen had regained its fluency and its fire.

Sydney knew, in his heart of hearts, that he ought to drop cathedral reform. But there was, deep within him, a hard stone of pride; if attacked he always fought back. This time the javelin was thrown by J. H. Monk, the bishop of Gloucester, a conservative but also an ecclesiastical commissioner and a friend of Blomfield. In November 1838 he made some comments on church reform to a gathering of his clergy. During the course of his remarks Monk made oblique reference to Sydney, a personal attack which was intensified when Monk decided to publish what he had said. The offending passage ran: 'A sense of shame and humiliation affects every serious churchman, at beholding places which ought to be the seats of piety, learning, and dignity, occupied by the scoffer and the jester.' This was too much for Sydney. He ruminated on the insult for a few weeks, sat down at his desk in the window of the drawing-room at Combe Florey during the Christmas holidays, sent what he had written off to the printer early in the New Year, and arranged for a *Third Letter to Archdeacon Singleton* to be published around 20 February.

Sydney's answer to Monk was defiant. Cathedral dignitaries must fight to keep their patronage to the last man. 'I think it better to make any sacrifices, and to endure any evil, than to gratify this rapacious spirit of plunder and confiscation.' He also deployed the 'domino' argument, a standard part of anti-reform polemic. Bishops, be on your guard; you will be next. 'I ask the Bishop of London . . . Does he think, after Reformers have tasted the flesh of the church, that they will put up with any other diet? Does he forget that Deans and Chapters are but mock turtle – that more delicious delicacies remain behind?'

Time had passed Sydney by. When he was younger he had been aware of the needs of the age and had campaigned in favour of social change, but now he was blind to the requirements of a new society. The greatest challenge facing the church in the 1830s was to devise some means of serving the spiritual needs of the urban masses. The

Ecclesiastical Commission – synonymous in Sydney's mind with C.J. Blomfield – wanted to tackle the problem through a scheme for parochial endowment from a central fund, the money for which would come largely from the proceeds of 'surplus' posts in cathedrals. Sydney was horrified. The Commission wanted to create a 'ptochogony – a generation of beggars'. There would be 1000 new vicars and rectors, each with £130 a year. £130 a year! The very idea was absurd – Sydney, we should remember, now earned nearly £2900 a year. The Commission had blood on its hands; it was proposing to 'call into existence a thousand of the most unhappy men on the face of the earth'.[14] Nothing here about the spiritual destitution of the masses; nothing about the problems of urban pastoral ministry. Everything about the material preoccupations of a wealthy canon of St Paul's, the cares and concerns of a rich old man in search of a soft bed and plenty of repose. What was it that old Lord Carlisle had warned Sydney of in 1824? 'Then comes the hour of vengeance for slaps and bruises which timid & patient sufferers have bonded, like corn, and let out of the storehouse upon the sick Lion, who may not then be a match for a Jackass.' The lion was not yet sick but he was definitely ageing.

The spring and early summer of 1839 were without incident. In mid-July Sydney, as was his custom, went down to Combe Florey, staying unusually long, right through, in fact, until November. Domestic life was enlivened by a visit from Saba. Sydney was very fond of his grandchildren, especially of Saba's eldest daughter Caroline, known affectionately as 'Coo'. Now approaching five, Coo was a thoughtful child with a poetic streak. Like many precocious children she quickly became angry with herself, kicking and screaming over difficulties. One morning during this visit Sydney was walking in the garden, in meditative mood and with his arms behind his back, clutching his faithful black crutch-stick, when he heard Coo roaring in an upstairs bedroom. Saba explained that the child was unable to grasp some detail about the lives of the ancient Hebrews. Sydney smiled to himself and continued on his walk. Two hours later Saba found him in his library, surrounded by maps and books, with Coo perched on one knee. The difficulty about the Hebrews was being resolved.

It may well have been during this same visit that another amusing incident involving Coo occurred. There was, at this time, a fashion for keeping giant turtles. Some friends of Sydney had one. He went over to see them, taking Coo with him. While the grown-ups were talking,

Coo went out into the garden and began eagerly stroking the turtle. Sydney followed her out, bent down and whispered in her ear, 'Why are you doing that?' 'Oh, to please the turtle', was Coo's reply. Sydney's face was wreathed in smiles. 'Why, child, you might as well stroke the dome of St Paul's to please the Dean and Chapter.'

Sydney was at his best with children. He spoke to them at their own level, teased them unmercifully and was able to enter their imaginative world, sharing with them his own delicious sense of the ludicrous. This closeness to the young was well understood by Sydney's elder daughter. 'He was', she wrote, 'very fond of children and liked to have them with him in his walks, often joined in their pursuits and plays, and delighted in their happiness, a happiness which, he often touchingly said, he had never known in childhood.' One of his grandchildren once sent him a letter that was overweight. His answer reads as though it had been written by Lewis Carroll:

> Oh, you little wretch! your letter cost me fourpence. I will pull all the plums out of your puddings; I will undress your dolls and steal their under petticoats; you shall have no currant-jelly to your rice; I will kiss you till you cannot see out of your eyes; when nobody else whips you, I will do so; I will fill you so full of sugar-plums that they shall run out of your nose and ears; lastly, your frocks shall be so short that they shall not come below your knees.
> Your loving grandfather,
> SYDNEY SMITH

After his return to London Sydney moved from 33 Charles Street. He was still inside the 'sacred parallelogram' but a little further north: 56 Green Street, a hundred yards south of Oxford Street and just off Park Lane. 'It is everything I want or Wish', he told Lady Grey, the words of a man in search of contentment, not of further fights. And yet the literary pugilist within Sydney would not quite lie down. He wrote a pamphlet – his comment on it is gnomic, but it seems to have ridiculed his friend Lord Lansdowne – which he thought about publishing. Then, surprisingly, he flung the manuscript in the fire. Torn between satisfaction at a job well done and loyalty to friends, loyalty won out: 'This is very funny, and very well written, but it will give great pain to people who have been very kind and good to me through life.' This pyrotechnic scene took place in December 1839. In the New Year he again opted for peace, telling Lady Grey he had given up a projected fourth letter to the venerable archdeacon Singleton. This is a new Sydney, an irenic Sydney, a Sydney tired of combat and wearied by war.

Almost, anyway. In the summer of 1840 the Deans and Chapters Bill, against which Sydney had fought for four years, finally reached the statute book. In the crucial debate in the House of Lords, Blomfield made the finest speech of his life. Describing Sydney, *en passant*, as his 'facetious friend', he alluded to the great wealth enjoyed by the dean and three canons of St Paul's and then invited their lordships to take a stroll through some of the streets a little way from the cathedral:

> I traverse the streets of this crowded city with deep and solemn thoughts of the spiritual condition of its inhabitants. I pass the magnificent church which crowns the metropolis, and is consecrated to the noblest of objects, the glory of God, and I ask of myself, in what degree it answers that object. I see there a dean and three residentiaries, with incomes amounting in the aggregate to between £10,000 and £12,000 a year . . . I proceed a mile or two to the E. and N.E., and find myself in the midst of an immense population in the most wretched state of destitution and neglect, artisans, mechanics, labourers, beggars, thieves, to the number of at least 300,000.

Sydney's answer came on 5 September 1840, in a letter to *The Times*. 'I was sorry' to be forced to give Blomfield 'such a beating', he told a correspondent, 'but he was very saucy and deserved it.' If Sydney had confronted Blomfield's argument head on, his self-satisfaction might have been sufferable. As it was he was unable to rise above petty polemic, making the obvious and not at all strong point that a walk westward from St Paul's would have led towards the episcopal opulence of Lambeth and Fulham palaces. After years of controversy his *tu quoque* was looking threadbare. He ended his letter by shaking his fist at Blomfield, in the best manner of an enraged country squire: 'You have shaken the laws of property, and prepared the ruin of the church by lowering the character of its members, and encouraging the aggressions of its enemies.'[15] Sydney bellicose was not, in old age, an endearing sight.

15

THE BREATHLESS LION ROARS

'Can you ask of the Dead Oak to put forth of its Leaves again? Can you supplicate the deceased Donkey to Bray? Or the breathless Lion to roar?'

SYDNEY SMITH TO JANE HICKS BEACH, May 1841

Sydney had been fortunate with death. Although, by 1840, he was close on seventy, he had only tasted the full bitterness of grief on three occasions: after the death of his mother in 1801, of Francis Horner in 1817, and of Douglas in 1829. This, for someone living in late Georgian England, is not a long list. Sydney enjoyed the blessed privilege of growing old with his friends. As the nineteenth century entered its fifth decade, those who most loved Sydney – his wife Catharine, his brother Bobus, Earl and Lady Grey, Lord and Lady Holland, Georgiana, Lady Carlisle, Samuel Rogers, Francis Jeffrey, John Allen – were all in good health.

Perhaps it was a record that was too good to last. On Wednesday, 21 October 1840, Henry Fox, third Baron Holland, woke up feeling unwell. Three doctors, including Sydney's son-in-law Henry Holland, were sent for. Holland came back at 6 PM to find that the baron's pulse was feeble and his mind was wandering: he was muttering about the Crusades in the Holy Land. Holland sat up with him throughout Wednesday night and he died about six on Thursday morning.[1]

'Milady', always willing to put on a display of histrionics at the drop of a hat, was extremely distraught. Her entries in the Dinner Books are heavy with the scent of melodrama, an emotional response which did not at all surprise those who knew her well. On Wednesday there are just two words: 'illness, illness'. The next day, her beloved husband already in his grave, she gives full vent to her feelings: 'This wretched day closes all the happiness, refinement and hospitality within the walls of Holland House.' Lady Holland was as good as her word. She went to live in her little 'nutshell', as she called it, at 33 South Street in London's Mayfair. Desultory efforts were made to occupy Holland House but these never lasted long and, after the death of John Allen in April 1843, were abandoned entirely. Lady Holland was not as emotionally strong as she made out.

Lord Holland's death was not only a personal loss for Sydney (although, of course, it was that quite profoundly), it was an important social event. Charles Greville caught the sense of things very well: 'Never was popularity so great and so general, and his death will produce a social revolution, utterly extinguishing not only the most brilliant, but the only great house of reception and constant society in England.' Sydney still visited Lady Holland, he still met Rogers and Luttrell, and he still sometimes went to dinner at Holland House, but the atmosphere of happy domesticity that had made the great Jacobean mansion what it was, that had given social life there its special and irreplaceable charm, had vanished, never to return.

There was little risk of Sydney following, with any celerity, in the footsteps of Lord Holland: Sydney's constitution was as robust as his prose. There is no mention of any serious illness in childhood. After he left Winchester, the picture is one of continuous and glowing good health. During his years at Foston he never even emulated his clerical contemporary, Parson Woodforde, by paying a visit to the local farrier to have a tooth pulled out. The first hint of any trouble at all is in Sydney's late fifties, when he began to suffer from periodic attacks of gout, an illness which also afflicted Bobus and Lord Holland. Sydney's description of the excruciating pain of gout has never been bettered. 'I feel', he said, 'as though I were walking on my eye-balls.' He professed himself afraid of the illness and constantly counselled his friends to leave off alcohol in order to combat it, but his attitude towards his own bouts was jocular and dismissive. In 1834, aged sixty-three, he had had to endure a quite savage episode which lasted a month. But he braved the storm, telling Mrs Meynell that he was 'making a slow recovery; hardly yet able to walk across the room, nor to put on a christian shoe'. In his mid-sixties the frequency and variety of his illnesses increased – he suffered from, among other things, lumbago, occasional palpitations and ophthalmia – but he still managed to come through this period without succumbing to a severe complaint.

As from the autumn of 1840, Sydney's letters are peppered with references to aches and agues, and the dreaded subject of his own death begins to come up for frequent discussion. 'I am pretty well,' he told Lady Carlisle on 5 September, 'except gout, asthma, and pains in all the bones, and all the flesh, of my body.' Three months later, writing to Harriet Grote, he tells her that 'life goes on very well, except that I am often reminded I am too near the end of it'. This preoccupation with mortality, Sydney was the first to acknowledge, was a healthy sign in someone, such as himself, who had reached old age. Although he had always loved life, although he had lived it to the full, there had always been within him an element of restraint, a holding back, a hidden resignation to the will of God. This contemplative side of his personality surfaces from time to time. In 1819, for instance, he wrote a poignant letter to Lady Holland, following the death at the age of ten of her favourite daughter, Gina. 'The World is full of all sorts of sorrows and miseries . . . I think it is better never to have been born . . . remember that these renovations of sorrows are almost the charter and condition under which life is held. God Almighty bless you dear Lady Holland.'[2]

Sydney's ill-health and weariness with life intensified during the next two years. In February 1841 he was suffering from inflamed eyes, in May he had a mild attack of gout, and in July he was finding it hard to walk upstairs. The Christmas and New Year of 1841–2 were spent as usual at Combe Florey. It was not a happy time. 'I have suffered a great deal this winter from dullness and ennui', he told his old friend, Sir George Philips. Power no longer matched desire. 'I want very much to write something, but cannot bring myself to do it – principally from the great number of topics which offer themselves, all of which would be equally agreeable to me.' He felt listless and was in desperate need, as always, of stimulation. 'I have no news to send you as I have not seen nor spoken to an human creature for two months', he wrote to one of Lady Holland's daughters-in-law. 'I am,' he went on, 'actually bursting from *besoin de parler*.'[3]

Sydney was a man who wanted to share, to communicate, to join in. His humour had always been spontaneous, never pre-planned or forced. 'I never saw a man so formed to float down the stream of conversation, and, without seeming to have any direct influence upon it, to give it his own hue and charm' is the judgement of George Ticknor, the Harvard professor who so admired Sydney's sermons. But what if, as at Combe Florey that winter, there was no stream down which to float?

Sydney's principal problem in his winters at Combe Florey was loneliness, and in the summer it was heat. Being of 'the family of

Falstaff', he could not bear hot weather. 'Heat ma'am', he once said: 'it was so dreadful here that I found there was nothing left for it but to take off my flesh and sit in my bones.' In the fine summer of 1842, Sydney felt no more than 'half alive'. 'You will die of smallness', he told Sir George Philips in August; 'we shall perish from diameter.' Sydney no longer had the willpower to make the complex arrangements required if people were to come and visit Combe Florey. In consequence, the flow of friends to his West Country retreat almost dried up. Henry Luttrell was the only one who made the effort this year, coming in September.

Once he had seen Luttrell off Sydney began, once more, to harp on about his feelings of desolation. He was living, he told a female friend, 'in the most profound solitude. I saw a crow yesterday, and had a distant view of a rabbit today.' The themes in his correspondence are sombre: loneliness, disease and death. All three come together in a letter to Mrs Sarah Austin, written from Combe Florey on 13 October: 'I am nearly seventy-two' (his seventy-first birthday had passed in fact quite recently, in June) 'and I confess myself afraid of the very disagreeable methods by which we leave this world; the long death of palsy, or the degraded spectacle of aged idiotism.' (Was he thinking of his father, perhaps?) 'As for the *pleasures* of the world – it is a very ordinary, middling sort of place. Pray be my tombstone, and say a good word for me when I am dead!'[4]

He then went up to London but his mood did not improve. At the end of November 1842 he stayed for a few days at the Hampshire home of the Mildmays – Jane Mildmay had been a good friend since childhood – from where he wrote a despairing letter to Lady Ashburton, whose husband had recently negotiated the important Ashburton Boundary Treaty with the USA. 'My health', Sydney told her, 'is so indifferent, and my spirits so low, and I am so old and half-dead, that I am mere lumber.' Sydney was beginning to suffer for the first time in his life from a severe attack of a most debilitating malady: self-pity.

Sydney's literary output in 1842 was meagre: three letters to the *Morning Chronicle*, written in May and June. He chose a topical subject and also one about which his mind was, at this time, much exercised: railways. Construction of the Great Western was proceeding apace in the direction of Combe Florey. In February 1841 Sydney went up to town, taking for part of the journey eighty miles of the Bath railroad; by September 1842 the track had reached Taunton and he was able to get to Bath in two hours and London in six. Sydney was delighted. 'Man is become a bird; he can fly longer and quicker than a Solan goose.' In these early days of rail travel passengers sometimes panicked; the nervous or the drunk would alight between stations, occasionally with fatal consequences to themselves. The directors of the Great Western hit upon a foolproof plan to prevent these needless accidents; staff were instructed to lock the carriage doors on both sides of the train.

Sydney was furious. Loving speed, he hated the feeling of being hemmed in. His whole life had been, in a sense, a protest against constriction. 'Man', he complained to the readers of the *Morning Chronicle*, 'is universally the master of his own body, except he chooses to go from Paddington to Bridgewater: there only the Habeas Corpus is refused.' The loss of freedom was not only physical, it was mental: 'these excellent directors . . . seem to require that the imagination should be sent by some other conveyance, and that only loads of unimpassioned, unintellecutal flesh and blood should be darted along on the Western rail.'

This was just the kind of controversy that Sydney most enjoyed, pitting his wits against the big battalions on ground of his own choosing, carefully selecting an issue which he was sure he would win. The directors of the Great Western were running a monopoly, whose success depended upon securing the psychological ease of the passengers, the company's customers. This ease Sydney set out to destroy. The formula he used was simple and devastating. He painted in words the outline of a spectre, the spectre of 'What if'. Fire and rumour of fire. 'The first person of rank who is killed will put every thing in order, and produce a code of the most careful rules. I hope it will not be one of the bench of bishops; but should it be so destined, let the burnt bishop – the unwilling Latimer – remember that, however painful gradual concoction by fire may be, his death will produce unspeakable benefit to the public.'

The directors took the hint and gave in. Perhaps this was just as well because Sydney was intending to write a fourth letter in which he would have depicted them looking with satisfaction at a whole trainload of incinerated passengers: 'a stewed Duke . . . two Bishops done in their own Gravy . . . two Scotchmen dead but raw, sulphuric acid perceptible'.[5] Sydney was a superb journalist who had learnt, over many years, how to take on the establishment and beat it: he appealed directly to the public and he did not scruple to arouse, in those who were in positions of power, the queasy emotion of fear.

Early in 1843, following Courtney's death from a heart attack, there was more unpleasantness in the Smith family. Courtney had returned home, ostensibly for only three years, in the spring of 1828. The reason for his coming back to England serves as an epitaph upon a brilliant, but chequered, career: he had been temporarily suspended from his judgeship because he had refused to accept the surety of the East India Company. There is no doubting Courtney's gifts (Bobus, no mean linguist himself, reckoned that his youngest brother's practical grasp of Persian and Hindi was ahead of that of anyone else in the English expatriate community) but, equally, there is no gainsaying his defects of character. Courtney was tetchy, arrogant and rude. He had been suspended as a judge once before, in 1817, for being 'saucy' towards the judges of a higher court; he had a large chip on both shoulders; and he was a sullen loner who was deeply suspicious of mankind. After his return to England he settled in Park Street, close to Sydney's house in Charles Street and even closer to his elder brother's final residence in Green Street, but efforts to socialize were rebuffed.

Courtney was as wealthy as Robert Smith's younger brother, John – his estate was valued at £120,000. He had created a great deal of conflict during life, and was set upon doing the same in death. He left an autobiographical fragment, which has not survived, in which he roundly abused both Sydney and Bobus,[6] and he made two wills, neither of which he bothered to sign. Such behaviour, cantankerous in a normal person, was culpable in a judge. Not only were Courtney's wills legally flawed, they were also flagrantly unfair: in one of them he left Sydney out entirely but gave £5000 to Windham and £2500 each to Saba and Emily; there was also an extremely large bequest to Bobus. Knowing Courtney's strange and thoroughly disagreeable personality, he may well have been deliberately trying to sow discord between his brothers. Whatever his motives, he certainly succeeded. 'Bobus', wrote Catharine, 'is upon velvet'; whereas 'to *us* especially, who are to have *nothing*, it does make a marvellous difference.'[7] Sydney was beside himself with rage. 'I am determined,' he told his clerical nephew Cecil, 'to have what the Law gives me.'

Sydney put Bobus under severe pressure, and he agreed to challenge Courtney's wills by applying for joint letters of administration. The hearing to decide the matter was scheduled for Doctors' Commons on Tuesday, 14 March. Sydney went with Saba and Emily, arriving a quarter of an hour before the doors opened; Bobus, more relaxed, was on time. Sydney was prepared for every eventuality, taking with him in his pocket two sealed letters, one marked 'G' ('Good') and the other marked 'B' ('Bad'), to be sent to Cecil as soon as the case was over.

Such elaborate plans were unnecessary. The granting of letters of administration was a formality and he was back at Green Street by twelve o'clock. Sydney still would not rest; he was afraid that the letters of administration might somehow be overturned. Bobus vented his exasperation upon Cecil. Sydney, he complained, has been 'harping on the question whether it might not be expedient to file a bill in Chancery to perpetuate the evidence. I will not go into that question now, but merely say that I think the expence, delay and inconveni- ence . . . so utterly out of proportion to any good that could be got by it, that I should, as at present advised, refuse to be a voluntary party to such a proceeding.' It took all of Bobus's strength of character, and all of his legal training, to calm Sydney down.

Sydney had no reason to be nervous; the letters of administration held. Under them Courtney's estate of £120,000 was divided equally between the three branches of the Smith family - Bobus, Sydney and Cecil. This did not quite resolve matters; there was still the tricky question of what was to be done about making *ex gratia* payments to those who would otherwise have benefited under Courtney's wills. The sums given to most of the claimants were settled amicably but there was sharp disagreement over the amount that should be offered to Miss Henrietta Lee, a young actress to whom Courtney had given many gifts and with whom he had corresponded daily right up until his death. According to Catharine, rumour was rife at the Garrick Club that Henrietta was a 'most accommodating personage'.[8] Cecil, as niggardly as his own father had been open-handed, wanted to give her nothing at all, but Sydney silenced him: 'It is too late to lift up the Petticoats of Miss Lee.' Sydney made enquiries about her character and found that it was 'not bad'; she had, he told his nephew, contributed much to Courtney's happiness; and, in both wills, Courtney had made a point of emphasizing his great affection for her. Sydney was in favour of a payment of £2000 and Bobus wanted to give her even more; she had been bequeathed £16,000 in one will and £6000 in the other. With Cecil opposed to any payment on principle, Sydney's lower sum was agreed upon. Even this encountered opposi- tion. Cecil's moralistic stance was supported by the other lawyer in the family, Nathaniel Hibbert. Windham was speechless. 'That two sensible men of the world should sit down and deliberately vote £2000 to a designing strumpet is beyond belief, and only to be accounted for by temporary insanity brought about by the sudden influx of wealth' are his final words on the subject, addressed to Cecil.⁹ Generosity of spirit was not an emotion with which some of the male members of the Smith family were acquainted.

Sydney's final controversy started a little while after Courtney's death. His choice of subject was both sad and inapt. Sad because it involved Sydney in doing something he was good at, which he had done ever since he was curate of Netheravon, and which brought to the fore the self-seeking strand in his personality: furthering his own financial interests. Inapt because he became embroiled in a dispute with parties in America, the country whose uprightness in the conduct of public affairs he had always praised, and in whose defence he had fought manfully in the past, even though it had cost him dear, being the initial cause of his rupture with old Lord Carlisle in 1824. That the sum in dispute, £1000 in bonds issued on the security of the state of Pennsylvania, was trifling serves to render the conflict still less appetizing.

In financial dealings Sydney always felt sorry for himself whenever he believed he had been done down. This sense of grievance comes through all too clearly in the petition which he presented to Congress in May 1843. The temptation to overstress the significance of his financial loss was not resisted. 'Your petitioner lent to the State of Pennsylvania a sum of money, for the purpose of some public improvement. The amount, though small, is to him important, and is a saving from a life income, made with difficulty and privation.' This was not quite correct: a lot of Sydney's wealth had been made with ease and without privation, as the recent dealings over Courtney's will amply testify.

Self-pleading apart, Sydney's petition was sensible and restrained. Many States in America were in financial difficulty. Debts calculated at $200 million had been run up as a result of extensive programmes of capital expenditure on public works. Pennsylvania's share was $40 million, 20 per cent of the total. The speculative bubble had burst early in 1842; in February of that year Pennsylvania had joined Maryland, Indiana, Illinois and Michigan in defaulting on interest payments. Recession worsened and, when Sydney presented his petition, interest payments on Pennsylvania's debt remained in limbo. It was not, Sydney argued, a situation that should be tolerated. Pennsylvania's perfidy did not result from war or civil commotion; the state was not poor, nor was it struggling against the barrenness of nature; on the contrary, it was the richest state in the Union and was living in profound peace. Sydney's other main argument also had a firm ethical base; he was alarmed by 'that total want of shame with which these things have been done . . . that deadness of the moral sense which seems to preclude all return to honesty'. Sydney's intervention was well received in America. Most American papers carried copies of his petition, usually without comment. There was hostility from the *Boston Courier* and the *New York Post*, but both papers were ably answered by Sydney's friend George Ticknor.

Sydney returned to the attack in two letters to the *Morning Chronicle*, both published in November. He had given up hope that Pennsylvania would ever resume interest payments (unduly pessimistic, as it happened, because the state started making them again in February 1845) and had sold his stock, losing 40 per cent of the purchasable value. No longer having a financial interest himself, he had lost the motive to hold himself in check. All his pent-up bitterness came pouring out, as he forsook argument about principles and personalized the issue:

> I never meet a Pennsylvanian at a London dinner without feeling a disposition to seize and divide him; to allot his beaver [hat] to one sufferer and his coat to another – to appropriate his pocket-handkerchief to the orphan, and to comfort the widow with his silver watch . . . How such a man can set himself down at an English table without feeling that he owes two or three pounds to every man in his company I am at a loss to conceive; he has no more right to eat with honest men than a leper has to eat with clean men.

There was quite a lot more in this vein. The public works of Pennsylvania were given unflattering names – 'Larcenous Lake', 'Swindling Swamp', 'Crafty Canal', 'Rogues' Railway'. This was humiliating enough but Sydney went further. He was a man who really knew how to hurt. 'I am astonished that the honest States of America do not draw a *cordon sanitaire* round their unpaying brethren – that the truly mercantile New Yorkers, and the thoroughly honest people of Massachusetts, do not in their European visits wear an uniform with "S.S., or Solvent States", worked in gold letters upon the coat, and receipts in full of all demands tamboured on their waistcoats, and "our own property" figured on their pantaloons.'[10]

Sydney's American friends were incensed. George Ticknor felt he had been stabbed in the back. In a letter to an English friend, he gives full expression to his pained anger. 'Nobody in this country can be glad' of what Sydney 'has written, unless it be the few who wish to build up their political fortunes on the doctrines of repudiation. He is on their side, and the best ally they now have, so far as I know.'[11] This missed the point; Sydney was no longer trying to persuade, he was striving to aggravate. Ticknor's letter, ironically, is evidence of Sydney's success. Although Ticknor was being a trifle naïve, it is hard not to sympathize with him. Sydney's two letters to the *Morning Chronicle* in November 1843 are a powerful, but extremely sour, ending to a long and often brilliant satirical career.

'The fact is', Sydney told Tom Moore in June 1843, 'it is time for me to die.' He had times when the sense of lassitude was less acute, but his physical deterioration had now reached the point where it was seriously interfering with his life. In the spring and summer of 1843, he began doing something previously unknown: he started turning down dinner invitations. Gout was the main reason; both during and after a severe attack, he was in such discomfort that he was unable to sit down for any length of time. 'I could not', he told Lord Mahon on 4 July, 'bear the confinement of dinner, without getting up and walking between courses, or thrusting my foot on somebody else's chair.'

It did not help that many of those who loved Sydney were ill as well. The health of Lord Grey, in this summer of 1843, gave cause for grave concern. His speech became slurred and his eyesight was impaired, symptoms indicative of a mild stroke. (Very ill in 1843, he was still worse in 1844; first the circulation faltered, then the flesh on the foot became decayed, and finally the bone was exposed.) Next it was the turn of Francis Jeffrey; his health, Sydney told John Murray towards the end of September, was 'very feeble'. In October, Catharine, almost as overweight as Sydney, was 'very ill'. Finally there was Bobus. His own description, in a letter written in August, speaks strongly of sadness and of weariness with life: 'I am an old, stag-headed stump, lame and blind, and beginning to be forgetful.' As always, promises to visit Combe Florey were not fulfilled, but the two brothers did have dinner together in London in early November. Sydney was shocked by the extent of his brother's physical decline: 'I was forced to lead him in, and out of the room, and to assist him at table.' Sydney's world was beginning to fall apart.

He had done little in 1842 and 1843, and he did even less in 1844. With part of himself he was preparing for the end, and with another part he was striving to fight on. Writing to Saba from Combe Florey at the end of January, he makes no effort at concealment. 'I look as strong as a Cart Horse', he began, 'but I cannot get round the garden without resting once or twice, so deficient am I in nervous energy.' Then, interestingly, Sydney corrects himself: 'I believe if I was at Ramsgate or Brighton I should be strong.'[12]

There was little enough in Sydney's life to bring him joy. He followed his usual routine, leaving Combe Florey for London in mid-February and remaining until mid-July. His only new initiative in these months was striking up a friendship with the prime minister. Sir Robert Peel, when young, had attended some of Sydney's lectures on moral philosophy at the Royal Institution, and the two men had corresponded occasionally later on, but they had never been close. It was an act of charity on Sydney's part that brought them together. He befriended a family by the name of Kingston, once opulent but now experiencing hard times. Their son, Albert, was looking for a job. Early in May, Sydney wrote to Peel explaining the family's predicament and pointing out that there would soon be a vacant clerkship in the Record Office. It was a menial post, only £80 a year, but would be ideal for Albert. Peel wrote back, warmly, by return. He would be delighted to be of service: 'All the return I shall ask from you is the privilege of renewing when we meet the honour of your acquaintance.' Ten days later he wrote again, confirming Albert's appointment.

Sydney's answer is extremely touching. 'I hope', he began, 'a man is not a fool because he cries sometimes over human miseries. If he is I must . . . acknowledge that such was the effect your letter produced on me.'[13] Naturalness was the key to Sydney's charm; his ebullitions of feeling came easily from within him and were never forced. The two men quickly became good friends, Sydney sending the prime minister a copy of his *Collected Works* and receiving in return some speeches on currency reform. There was also an invitation to a dinner at Downing Street in mid-June in honour of the king of Saxony. Sydney, who had a prior engagement, showed old-fashioned courtesy and politely refused: 'I have looked in vain for excuses and escapes. I am cut off and made prisoner.' Samuel Rogers had to take him on one side and explain to him that invitations to meet royalty took precedence. So along Sydney went and quite enjoyed himself, although he was not much taken with the king, finding him 'like a cheesemonger'.

Sydney, once again, found the summer at Combe Florey quite intolerable ('It would unstring the limbs of a Giant, and demoralise the Soul of Cato'), but, despite the heat, his spirits perked up. He was feeling fitter and Catharine, he thought, was 'better than I have seen her for years'. It helped that Sydney had company: the Kingstons, thankful for Sydney's support, paid a visit lasting three weeks. They were a musical family and the entertainment they offered pleased Sydney enormously. Although he hated the artificiality of opera, there was nothing he liked more than sitting by the fireside surrounded by his family, singing songs. By the middle of August he was feeling so well that he was even thinking of writing a pamphlet on one of his pet subjects, state payment of the Irish Catholic clergy. The project, however, came to nothing: 'The ideas are all so trite and the arguments so plain and easy that I gape at the thought of such a production.'

In late August he took Catharine to the seaside, going to Sidmouth in Devon, 'that paradise of the waves'. The trip did not work out well. It was Sydney's age-old problem: there was not enough going on. 'I have nothing to do but to look out of the Window and am ennuied . . . I say to every one who sits near me on the Marine Benches, that it is a fine day and that the prospect is beautiful but we get no farther – I can get no Water out of the hard rock.' Back at Combe Florey his mood did not improve; he was brooding now, thinking constantly of death. Yet even in these declining days, he still had fire and poetic force. It was Lady Holland, his favourite and most intimate correspondent, to whom he opened his heart:

> It is a sad scene the last . . . the last act of life. To see beauty and eloquence, sense, mouldering away in pain and agony under terrible diseases, and hastening to the grave with sundry kinds of death. To witness the barren silence of him who charmed us with his exuberant fancy and gaiety never to be exhausted. To gaze upon wrinkles and yellowness and incurvations, where we remember beautiful forms and smiles and smoothness and the blush of health and the bloom of desire. To see . . . but here I recollect I am not in the pulpit, so I stop.[14]

Sydney had to face a life-threatening day early in October. 'The seizure', Catharine told Lady Carlisle, 'was very sudden . . . great giddiness, most acute & intolerable pain all over the chest & such a stream of Perspiration as I never before witnessed.' The heart attack – the same illness as had carried off Courtney in February 1843 – lasted, on and off, for twenty-two hours. With supreme lack of perspicacity Dr Liddon, Sydney's local doctor in Taunton, put the symptoms down to indigestion. Sydney knew better. 'I rather think that last week they wanted to kill me, but I was too sharp for them', he wrote to Lady Grey on 11 October. Henry Holland hurried down to Combe Florey, found his father-in-law much worse than he had expected, and strongly advised that he be moved to London where he could be under his own care. The journey to Green Street, which Sydney found terribly fatiguing, was undertaken on 23 October. Once ensconced in his London home, his health improved quite dramatically. About a week after the move, he wrote a typically open and pleasantly familiar letter to Georgiana, Lady Carlisle:

> From your ancient goodness to me, I am sure you will be glad to receive a bulletin from myself, informing you that I am making a good progress; in fact, I am in a regular train of promotion: from gruel, vermicelli, and sago, I was promoted to panada' (bread boiled in water, sometimes flavoured) 'from thence to minced meat, and (such is the effect of good conduct) I was elevated to a mutton-chop. My breathlessness and giddiness are gone – chased away by the gout. If you hear of sixteen or eighteen pounds of human flesh, they belong to me. I look as if a curate had been taken out of me.

This optimism was not shared by Henry Holland, who was well placed to know; he gave his father-in-law the best possible medical care, visiting him at least twice a day. The more he saw of Sydney's condition the less he liked the look of it. Progress, he told Catharine tactfully, would be slow.[15]

With the passing of each November day, the way in which the illness developed seemed to confirm Sydney's highest hopes. Peel enquired about his health at the end of the third week of the month. Catharine, acting as amanuensis, wrote back by return: 'I believe', she told the Prime Minister on Sydney's behalf, 'I am getting better.' On the 26th Sydney had an unusually good day, laughing and joking with Lord Lansdowne who paid him a long visit. A full report on Sydney's progress was sent to Castle Howard the next day. 'Thank God', said

Catharine, 'he suffers no pain; extreme weakness seems to be the evil, arising perhaps from the length of time that the enemy had him in possession. But his breathlessness is gone, his appetite is returning, all faintness & giddiness has ceased.' Sydney was now allowed fish, broth, sweetbreads and turtle soup. 'If', thought Catharine, 'the stomach could but recover somewhat of its healthy tone, I do think he would soon be almost well.'[16]

During the first two weeks of December the rally petered out and Sydney started to go, slowly but surely, downhill. There is a touch of desperation in a note written by Catharine to Lady Holland in mid-December. 'He has had a good night & and his cough seems gone for the present but he still has an oppression on his breathing which makes any solid food in the stomach an evil. He has just eaten half of a very small light boil'd pudding & and even that he seems to feel as oppressing him. Dr Holland says this weather is very much against his making progress.' Gone is the earlier ring of confidence, the hope of rapid recovery. Catharine had been forced back upon the minutiae of life: 'He has just eaten half of a very small light boil'd pudding.' From such minor triumphs little that is good can ever come.

Christmas was spent at 56 Green Street. Confined to his bed, Sydney suffered from violent oscillations in mood. The days were hard but the nights were harder, a restless night always leaving him feeling weak and miserably tired. On the other hand, if he slept well, he was able to build up a store of strength. Catharine sent a further report to Castle Howard on 20 January. Sydney was trying to get his life going again, dictating notes, making outlines of comic scenes which he could elaborate upon at leisure when he was up, about and fully well, but his wife was not taken in. 'He last night had a tolerably good one & bid me this morning take a pen & and write down "the remarks of an Invalid confined to his sofa from asthma on the passers by seen from his window". There follow'd a few comical remarks upon an old woman, a Baker's boy etc . . . But there is nothing in all this very promising dear Lady Carlisle.'[17]

Thus was the pattern set: up one day and down the next. It was consoling to receive many visits from friends and there was also a large number of messages of support. Sydney was especially touched by a letter from Lady Grey to Catharine. 'Lord Grey is intensely anxious about him. There is nobody of whom he so constantly thinks; nobody whom, in the course of his long illness, he so ardently wishes to see. Need I add, dear Mrs Sydney, that, excepting only our children, there is nobody for whom we both feel so sincere an affection.' Gratifying, this, coming from the former leader of the Whigs. Lady Holland went to see him. She realized that he did not have long to live and was impressed by his efforts at liveliness in the face of death. 'Poor Sydney. When he has breath to utter, he dictates a sprightly story. Four nights ago, his poor wife wrote down a very witty, imaginary scene between a traveller visiting a madhouse and Harriet Martineau.' Sydney's zaniness never deserted him, even when he had but a few weeks left.

There was, in these last days, a gradual slipping away from life. One evening Saba was sitting with him, his room in semi-darkness, when Sydney suddenly startled her, bursting out in a flood of impassioned speech. He was quoting to her from one of his own sermons:

> We talk of human life as a journey, but how variously is that journey performed! There are some who come forth girt, and shod, and mantled, to walk on velvet lawns and smooth terraces, where every gale is arrested, and every beam is tempered. There are others who walk on the Alpine paths of life, against driving misery, and through stormy sorrows, over sharp afflictions; walk with bare feet, and naked breast, jaded, mangled, and chilled.

'The Alpine paths'. His father's overbearingness and cruelty . . . his beloved mother's epileptic fits . . . the harshness of Winchester . . . potatoes and mushroom ketchup at Netheravon . . . Dr Andrewes's rejection of him as a preacher at the York Street chapel . . . being forced by Vernon-Harcourt to go and reside in Yorkshire . . . building the parsonage at Foston with his own hands . . . bad harvests . . . the vitriol poured upon him by old Lord Carlisle in 1824 . . . Earl Grey making Edward Maltby, 'idiot Maltby', bishop of Chichester . . . the row with Lord Holland in 1834 . . . Melbourne's impertinence . . . failure of the Whigs to keep faith with Peter Plymley. Sydney took with him to the grave the image of himself as a fearless but persecuted seeker after freedom and truth.

He faced death well. He sent messages of kindness and forgiveness to the few he felt had wronged him in life. Expressing supreme confidence in his oldest and most trusted servant, he drew Annie Kaye close to him one evening, telling her that he would soon die and asking her to make sure he was buried next to Douglas in Kensal Green cemetery. Then he spoke to her of his children, and of his wife, saying that he hoped they would all strive to keep his spirits up if he lingered long. With his own family, though, he was taciturn about great matters, discussing inconsequential things and always striving to look on the bright side.

One of his last visitors was Bobus. The compact which Sydney had suggested in May 1813, a few months before typhus killed Bobus's daughter Henrietta, had held. 'Pray take care of yourself' had been Sydney's words. 'Let us contrive to last out for the same or nearly the same time: weary will be the latter half of my pilgrimage, if you leave me in the lurch!' It was an emotional meeting: two brothers who revered each other and who were both on the edge of the precipice of death. Bobus, who was quite blind, was even more Stoic than Sydney, not clinging to life but wishing for it to end. Like his younger brother, he had heart trouble and he was also afflicted with the same secondary complaint: hydrothorax, dropsy of the chest.[18] Bobus died two weeks or so after Sydney, early in March.

The family gathered around Sydney at the end. Even Windham, cause of so much pain and disappointment, was there. He had had his own establishment since 1843 and, in his will, Sydney made continuation of this arrangement the condition of Windham's annuity, reduced from £500 to £400 a year. Sydney expressed the emotional verities when, in his final mental wanderings, he took Windham by the hand and said to him softly: 'Douglas, Douglas!'[19] Yet it was Windham who, on 22 February 1845, stepped up to the bed and closed his father's eyes.

NOTES

In these notes I use the following abbreviations:

ER   *Edinburgh Review*
IOL   India Office Library
Memoir   Saba Holland, *A Memoir of the Reverend Sydney Smith . . . with
          a Selection from his Letters,* edited by Mrs Austin, 2 vols, 1855
NCS   Nowell C. Smith, ed., *The Letters of Sydney Smith,* 2 vols, 1953
PP   *Parliamentary Papers*
PRO   Public Record Office
Works   *The Collected Works of Sydney Smith,* 3 vols, new edn, 1845

INTRODUCTION

1 NCS, i, p. 24; Saba Holland, 'Manuscript Notes', p. 12; Charles and
Frances Brookfield, *Mrs Brookfield and her Circle,* i, p. 122; Memoir, p.
368; G.W.E. Russell, *Sydney Smith,* p. 193.
2 Chester W. New, *The Life of Henry Brougham to 1830,* p. 16; Stuart J.
Reid, *The Life and Times of Sydney Smith,* p. 74; NCS, ii, p. 606; ER, ii, p.
131.
3 John Clive, *Scotch Reviewers,* pp. 30, 134–5; NCS, i, p. 332.
4 Memoir, pp. 403–4; *Works,* i, pp. 203, 216.

1 FABER MEAE FORTUNAE

1 NCS, i, pp. 327, 431n., 447–8, 455; Memoir, pp. 2, 293; Saba Holland,
'Manuscript Notes', p. 306E; Sydney Smith to Cecil Smith, 30 August
1827, Bodleian; Catharine Smith, 'First Narrative' (transcript), p. 3.
The marriage registers of St George's, Bloomsbury, are at the Greater
London Record Office.
2 Reid, *Sydney Smith,* p. 148; Memoir, p. 165; William Burrows to Robert
Smith, January 1781, IOL; Catharine Smith, 'First Narrative' (trans-
cript), p. 1; 'Second Narrative' (transcript), p. 2.
3 Saba Holland, 'Manuscript Notes', p. 250; Catharine Smith, 'First
Narrative' (transcript), p. 4; NCS, ii, p. 765; Memoir, p. 2; Robert Smith

to William Burrows, 26 April 1781, IOL.

4 Memoir, pp. 2–5, 162; Catharine Smith, 'First Narrative' (transcript), pp. 3–4; Bobus Smith to Lady Holland, 30 October 1801, Add. Mss. 51801, f. 42, British Library.

5 Sydney Smith to E.L. Bulwer, 21 November 1843, Lytton Add. Mss., Letters and Papers, iii, no. 15, Hertfordshire Record Office; Memoir, pp. 430, 473; NCS, i, p. 36; Catharine Smith, 'First Narrative' (transcript), p. 2.

6 Memoir, p. 4; NCS, i, p. 218; Leonard Horner, *Memoirs and Correspondence of Francis Horner*, i, pp. 192–3; Cecil Smith to Maria Smith, 17 October 1803, IOL.

7 Catharine Smith, 'First Narrative' (transcript), pp. 5, 18; Bobus Smith to Lord Holland, 23 August 1809, Add. Mss. 51801, f. 57, British Library; Courtney Smith to Robert Smith, 21 March 1807, IOL.

8 Maria Smith to Robert Smith, undated, IOL; NCS, i, p. 259; Memoir, p. 6, wrongly states the name of the master as Marsh.

2 JOSEPH WARTON AND THE BIBLING ROD

1 T.F. Kirby, *Winchester Scholars*, pp. 274–5; Catharine Smith, 'First Narrative' (transcript), pp. 6, 14.

2 A.K. Cook, *About Winchester College*, pp. 174–5, 270–71; Memoir, p. 171.

3 Cook, op. cit., p. 180 [An Old Wykehamist], *Recollections of the two St Mary Winton Colleges*, p. 8; Catharine Smith, 'Second Narrative' (transcript), p. 8.

4 Cook, op. cit., p. 227; *Works*, i, p. 229.

5 *Works*, i, pp. 190, 192, 194; Cook, op. cit., pp. 322n., 323, 327; [An Old Wykehamist], op. cit., p. 9

6 H.C. Adams, *Wykehamica*, p. 267; John Wooll, *Biographical Memoirs of the late Revd Joseph Warton*, p. 101.

7 Charlotte Barnett, ed., *Diary and Letters of Madame D'Arblay*, ii, p. 181; Madame D'Arblay, *Memoirs of Dr Burney*, ii, pp. 82–3.

8 Memoir, p. 7; Arthur F. Leach, *A History of Winchester College*, p. 401; Alan Bell, 'Warden Huntingford and the Old Conservatism', in Roger Custance, ed., *Winchester College: Sixth-centenary Essays*, p. 354; Philip Ziegler, *Addington*, pp. 19–24.

9 Custance, op. cit., pp. 360–61; Memoir, p. 6; *Works*, i, p. 225.

10 Memoir, pp. 412–13; *Works*, i, pp. 224, 227–8, 231–2.

11 *Works*, i, p. 232; iii, p. 156.

12 Gertrude Lyster, *A Family Chronicle*, p. 255; NCS, i, p. 482; *Microcosm*, p. 379.

13 Memoir, p. 403; Lord Holland to Caroline Holland, 30 September 1803, Add. Mss. 51737, f. 250, British Library.

14 George Canning to Mary Anne Canning, 2 February 1787, Private Correspondence, Packet 2, West Yorkshire Archives; *Microcosm*, p. 27.

3 A PRETTY FEATURE IN A PLAIN FACE

1 J.E. Sewell, 'Register of Scholars, New College, Oxford', New College, Oxford; Admissions Book, Archive 965, New College; John Buxton and Penry Williams, eds., *New College Oxford 1379–1979*, pp. 31–2.
2 Admissions Book, f. 269, Archive 965, New College, Oxford. I am indebted to my good friend Hannah Stubbs for this reference.
3 Hastings Rashdall and Robert S. Rait, *New College*, p. 211; Buxton and Williams, op. cit., pp. 59, 62; L.S. Sutherland and L.G. Mitchell, eds., *The History of the University of Oxford: The Eighteenth Century*, p. 183. There is a new biography of William Jones, *The Life and Mind of Oriental Jones*, by Garland Cannon (CUP, 1991).
4 Sutherland and Mitchell, op. cit., p. 185; Buxton and Williams, op. cit., p. 165; A.H. Smith, *New College Oxford and its Buildings*, pp. 48, 92, 94, 96; Dinner Book, Archive 8727, New College, Oxford; Buxton and Williams, op. cit., p. 185.
5 Buxton and Williams, op. cit., pp. 66–7, 275; Sutherland and Mitchell, op. cit., pp. 480–81; *Works*, i, p. 196.
6 'The Orders of the Warden and the Thirteen, 1788–1813', New College, Oxford; Sutherland and Mitchell, op. cit., pp. 328, 333, 337; NCS, i. p. 56; Catharine Smith, 'Second Narrative' (manuscript), p. 9.
7 'Junior Common Room Rules and Accounts', Archive 14336, New College, Oxford; Memoir, p. 10; Catharine Smith, 'First Narrative' (transcript), p. 17.
8 Memoir, pp. 11–12; Catharine Smith, 'First Narrative' (transcript), p. 17; NCS, i, pp. 1, 3–4.
9 'List of the Poor of Netheravon, drawn up by Mr Verrey, steward to Michael Hicks Beach, in March 1793', Pierpont Morgan Library; NCS, i, pp. 3–6.
10 Sydney Smith to Robert Smith, 26 June 1796, HM 30411, Huntington Library; 5 November 1797, HM 30414, Huntington Library; 25 November 1797, HM 30415, Huntington Library.
11 NCS, i, pp. 11–12; Sydney Smith to Robert Smith, 25 November 1797, HM 30415, Huntington Library.
12 Memoir, pp. 14, 123.
13 Caroline Fox to Lady Holland, 4 March 1798, Add. Mss. 51744, f. 52, British Library; 8 May 1798, Add. Mss. 51744, f. 64, British Library.
14 John Sparrow, 'Jane Austen and Sydney Smith', *Independent Essays*, pp. 88–96; Sydney Smith to Robert Smith, 29 December 1797, HM 30416, Huntington Library; 31 May 1798, HM 30418, Huntington Library; Sydney Smith to Mr Hicks Beach, 3 December 1800, St John, pp. 116–

117, Pierpont Morgan Library; Anand C. Chitnis, *The Scottish Enlightenment and Early Victorian English Society*, pp. 28, 45, 49.

4 THE ATHENS OF THE NORTH

1 NCS, i, pp. 14–17.
2 NCS, i, p. 18; Sydney Smith to J.G. Clarke, 5 December 1798, Add. Mss. 38650, ff. 93–4, British Library; G.M. Trevelyan, *Ramillies and the Union with Scotland*, pp. 199–200; Henry Cockburn, *Memorials of His Time*, pp. 322–3: Memoir, pp. 15, 17.
3 NCS, i, pp. 18–19, 21–3, 33, 35, 42; S.E. Christian, *A Cotswold Family: Hicks and Hicks Beach*, p. 318.
4 Sydney Smith to Mrs Hicks Beach, 3 August 1798, 12 August 1798, Mss. 11, 981E, National Library of Wales; Works, i, p. iii; Holden Furber, *Henry Dundas First Viscount Melville 1742–1811*, pp. 84–5, 90, 264, 270–71; Cockburn, op. cit., p. 201.
5 NCS, i, p. 20; Cockburn, op. cit., pp. 20–23; William K. Dickson, *The History of the Speculative Society, 1764–1845*, pp. 7–13, 16–17; Davis D. McElroy, 'A Century of Scottish Clubs 1700–1800', i, pp. 188–99, 254–312.
6 McElroy, op. cit., i, pp. 213–14; Henry Brougham to James Reddie, 17 December 1796, Mss. 3704, f. 1–3, National Library of Scotland; New, *Life of Henry Brougham to 1830*, p. 6; S.H. Romilly, *Letters to 'Ivy' from the First Earl of Dudley*, p. 357; Harriet Martineau, *Autobiography*, i. pp. 311–12; Horner, *Francis Horner*, i, pp. 2–3; Cockburn, op. cit., pp. 8–9; NCS, i, p. 87.
7 James A. Greig, *Francis Jeffrey of the Edinburgh Review*, p. 59; George S. Hillard, *Life, Letters, and Journal of George Ticknor*, i, pp. 43–7; NCS, i, p. 65; ii, p. 511; Chitnis, *The Scottish Enlightenment*, pp. 62–6.
8 NCS, i. p. 24: *Works*, ii, p. 91; Sydney Smith to Robert Smith, late 1798, HM 30420, Huntington Library; Henry Cockburn, *Journal*, ii, p. 245; *Sermons* (1801), ii, pp. xix–xxi; Bell, *Sydney Smith*, pp. 27–9.
9 Sydney Smith to Robert Smith, late 1798, HM 30420, Huntington Library; 29 December 1797, HM 30416, Huntington Library. In late June 1800, Sydney told his father that all his difficulties over his future wife's marriage settlement were over 'after a battle of two years', from which it is reasonable to infer that Sydney and Catharine decided to get married in the summer of 1798.
10 Stuart J. Reid, *Sydney Smith*, pp. 51–2; Bell, op. cit., p. 22; Catharine Pybus to Robert Smith, 4 March 1800, IOL.
11 Martha Pybus to Robert Smith, 3 January 1799, IOL; Sydney Smith to Robert Smith, January 1800, HM 30421, Huntington Library; Catharine Smith, 'First Narrative' (transcript), pp. 21–4.

12 Catharine Pybus to Robert Smith, 30 May 1800, IOL; 9 June 1800, IOL; Reid, op. cit., pp. 52–3; Catharine Smith, 'First Narrative' (transcript), p. 22.
13 Memoir, p. 314; NCS, i, p. 295; ii, p. 630.
14 *Works*, i, p. 201; Catharine Smith, 'First Narrative' (transcript), pp. 25–6.
15 Sydney Smith to Robert Smith, 15 April 1803, HM 30432, Huntington Library; note by Mrs St John, St John, p. 100, Pierpont Morgan Library; Sydney Smith to Mrs Hicks Beach, autumn 1800, St John, pp. 101–5, Pierpont Morgan Library.
16 Sydney Smith to Mrs Hicks Beach, October 1800, St John, pp. 110–11, Pierpont Morgan Library.

5 BEYOND THE FRINGE

1 Sydney Smith to J.G. Clarke, 27 October 1799, Add. Mss. 38650, ff. 99–100, British Library; Sydney Smith to Robert Smith, January 1800, HM 30421, Huntington Library; NCS, i, p. 57.
2 NCS, i, pp. 38, 57, 60, 66, 68; Sydney Smith to Mr Hicks Beach, 21 April 1801, St John, p. 131, Pierpont Morgan Library.
3 Sydney Smith to Mrs Hicks Beach, 9 November 1800, St John, pp. 114–15, Pierpont Morgan Library; 3 December 1800, St John, pp. 116–17, Pierpont Morgan Library; Mrs Hicks Beach to Sydney Smith, December 1800, Pierpont Morgan Library; Sydney Smith to Mrs Hicks Beach, 28 December 1800, St John, pp. 118–20, Pierpont Morgan Library.
4 Robert Smith to Mrs Hicks Beach, 7 February 1801, St John, pp. 125–6, Pierpont Morgan Library; Catharine Smith, 'First Narrative' (transcript), p. 24; Sydney Smith to Mrs Hicks Beach, 21 February 1801, St John, p. 127, Pierpont Morgan Library.
5 NCS, i, p. 67; Sydney Smith to Robert Smith, 7 November 1801, HM 30428, Huntington Library; 25 October 1801, bundle 4432, New College, Oxford; William Hicks Beach to Mrs Hicks Beach, 30 October 1801, 12 January 1802, D 2455, Acc. 3049, Box 25, F, Gloucestershire Record Office.
6 NCS, i, pp. 62, 69; Sydney Smith to Mr Hicks Beach, 31 May 1802, St John, pp. 144–5, Pierpont Morgan Library.
7 Sydney Smith to Robert Smith, 5 November 1797, HM 30414, Huntington Library; Bobus Smith to Lady Holland, 30 October 1801, Add. Mss. 51801, f. 42, British Library; NCS, i, p. 66; Sydney Smith to Robert Smith, 29 October 1801, HM 30427, Huntington Library; 7 November 1801, HM 30428, Huntington Library.
8 Catharine Smith, 'First Narrative' (transcript), p. 37; Sydney Smith to Robert Smith, 25 December 1801, HM 30430, Huntington Library; Sydney Smith to James Mackintosh, 13 January 1802, Keele University

Library; Cockburn, *Memorials*, pp. 170–71, 246; Chitnis, *The Scottish Enlightenment*, p. 170.

9 NCS, i, p. 199; Horner, *Francis Horner*, i, p. 186; Clive, *Scotch Reviewers*, p. 61.

10 I am indebted for this insight to my good friend Gavyn Davies.

11 Clive, op. cit, p. 29; Greig, *Francis Jeffrey*, p. 58; Horner, op. cit., i, p. 135; NCS, i, p. 70.

12 Clive, op. cit., p. 24; Cockburn, *Life of Lord Jeffrey*, i, p. 136; ER, i, pp. 90, 237; *Works*, i, p. 29; Bell, *Sydney Smith*, pp. 29–30, 38–9.

13 ER, i, p. 113; Clive, op. cit., pp. 30, 33–41, 134–5; Thomas Constable, *Archibald Constable and his Literary Correspondents*, i, pp. 55–6; NCS, i, pp. 79–80.

14 Reid, *Sydney Smith*, pp. 83–6; Memoir, p. 378; *Works*, i, pp. 59–69; ii, pp. 271, 298.

15 *Works*, i, p. 41; ii, pp. 141, 145–7; iii, p. 14; Julia Blackburn, *Charles Waterton*, pp. 1, 86.

16 NCS, i, pp. 68–9, 71–4; Sydney Smith to Mrs Hicks Beach, February 1802, St John, p. 143, Pierpont Morgan Library; Sydney Smith to Mr Hicks Beach, 31 May 1802, St John, pp. 144–5, Pierpont Morgan Library; Sydney Smith to Mrs Hicks Beach, July 1802, St John, pp. 148–9, Pierpont Morgan Library.

17 Sydney Smith to Mrs Hicks Beach, autumn 1802, St John, pp. 148–9, Pierpont Morgan Library; 8 November 1802, St John, p. 150, Pierpont Morgan Library; Caroline Fox to Lady Holland, 12 September 1799, Add. Mss. 51744, f. 117, British Library; Caroline Fox to Lord Holland, 8 February 1803, Add. Mss. 51736, f. 119, British Library; Bobus Smith to Robert Smith, 23 November 1802, IOL; 25 November 1802, IOL; Caroline Smith to Maria Smith, 23 October 1802, IOL; duke of Northumberland to Robert Smith, 28 October 1802, IOL.

18 Sydney Smith to Mrs Hicks Beach, 22 February 1803, St John, p. 140, Pierpont Morgan Library; Caroline Fox to Lord Holland, 12 April 1803, Add. Mss. 51736, f. 158, British Library.

19 Bobus Smith to Robert Smith, early 1803, IOL; Caroline Smith to Robert Smith, early 1803, IOL; Sydney Smith to Robert Smith, 28 March 1803, HM 30431, Huntington Library.

20 Sydney Smith to Robert Smith, 15 April 1803, HM 30432, Huntington Library.

21 Cecil Smith to Robert Smith, 5 August 1801, IOL. This letter refers to the 'secret' – presumably the illegitimacy – of Eliza's birth.

22 Cecil Smith to Robert Smith, 24 January 1800, 14 April 1800, 9 October 1800, IOL.

23 Cecil Smith to Robert Smith, 1 August 1801, IOL; unnamed correspondent to Cecil Smith, 6 November 1802, IOL; John Kemp to Cecil Smith, 4 December 1802, IOL; Cecil Smith to Robert Smith, autumn 1803, IOL.

24 Unnamed correspondent to Cecil Smith, 6 November 1802, IOL; Cecil

Smith to Robert Smith, late 1802, 22 January 1803, IOL; NCS, i, pp. 77–8.

25 Sydney Smith to Richard Heber, 27 November 1802, Eng. lett. d. 215, f. 147, Bodleian; Catharine Smith, 'First Narrative' (transcript), p. 38; NCS i, p. 75; Sydney Smith to Mrs Hicks Beach, 15 March 1803, St John, p. 157, Pierpont Morgan Library.

6 THE SACRED PARALLELOGRAM

1 Peter Ackroyd, *Dickens*, p. 221; NCS, i, pp. 82, 87–9, 91–2; Catharine Smith, 'First Narrative' (transcript), pp. 39–40; 'Second Narrative' (transcript), pp. 28–9; R.J. Mackintosh, *Memoirs of the Life of Sir James Mackintosh*, ii, pp. 492–3, 499; Horner, *Francis Horner*, i, p. 243.

2 Memoir, p. 139; Sydney Smith to James Mackintosh, March 1805, Mss. Adv. 36. 1. 7b, ff. 5–6, National Library of Scotland; C.G. Oakes, *Sir Samuel Romilly*, pp. xiv, 1; Mackintosh, op. cit., i, pp. 137–8; Records of the King of Clubs, Add. Mss. 37337, ff. 4, 6, British Library; Chitnis, *The Scottish Enlightenment*, p. 83.

3 Memoir, p. 123; Catharine Smith, 'Second Narrative' (transcript), pp. 28–9; Bell, *Sydney Smith*, p. 43.

4 NCS, i, pp. 94–5; Reid, *Sydney Smith*, p. 117; Catharine Smith, 'First Narrative (transcript), p. 41; 'Second Narrative' (manuscript), p. 24.

5 NCS, i, p. 114; Catharine Smith, 'Second Narrative' (manuscript), pp. 25–7; Gerrard Andrewes to Sydney Smith, 17 December 1805, D.C.L. Holland.

6 Augustus J.C. Hare, *The Story of my Life*, ii, pp. 310, 316–17; Memoir, pp. 139–40; *Sermons* (1809), i, pp. 17–18, 361; ii, pp. 80–81, 84–5; 171–2, 302; R.H.D. Barham, *The Life and Letters of the Rev. R.H. Barham*, ii, p. 168; Memoir, p. 161.

7 *Sermons* (1809), i, pp. 73–4, 102; ii, pp. 252, 270, 396; *Sermons preached at St Paul's Cathedral*, pp. 59, 61; Richard Edgcumbe, *The Diary of Frances Lady Shelley*, i, p. 15; Peter Virgin, *The Church in an Age of Negligence*, pp. 5–6, 155–6.

8 James Baker, *The Life of Sir Thomas Bernard*, pp. 45–6; Bell, op. cit., p. 55; Horner, op. cit., i, pp. 181–2, 298–9; Memoir, p. 128n.; Catharine Smith, 'Second Narrative' (transcript), p. 33.

9 James Greig, ed., *The Farington Diary*, iii, p. 238; Bell, op. cit., pp. 55–6; Catharine Smith, 'First Narrative' (transcript), p. 41; 'Second Narrative' (transcript), p. 33.

10 NCS, i. pp. 100–2; Memoir, p. 378; Horner, op. cit., i, pp. 298–9; *Elementary Sketches of Moral Philosophy*, pp. 54, 114, 298–9, 315, 320; Robert Peel to Catharine Smith (letter no. 31), D.C.L. Holland; Jane Marcet to Catharine Smith (letter no. 16), D.C.L. Holland.

11 *Elementary Sketches*, pp. 111, 126, 195–6, 245, 263, 284, 319.

12 Robert Smith to Cecil Smith, 7 June 1804, IOL; Sydney Smith to Maria Smith, 12–16 November 1804, HM 30433, Huntington Library; Sydney Smith to Robert Smith, late 1804, HM 30435, Huntington Library.

13 NCS, i, p. 103; Cecil Smith to Robert Smith, 9 September 1805, IOL; Sydney Smith to Robert Smith, 31 December 1805, HM 30440, Huntington Library; Maria Smith to Sydney Smith, 9 January 1807, HM 30442, Huntington Library.

14 Courtney Smith to Bobus Smith, 6 September 1806, IOL; Sydney Smith to Maria Smith, 19 January 1807, HM 30448, Huntington Library; Sydney Smith to Maria Smith, 11 February 1807, HM 30453, Huntington Library.

15 Cecil Smith to Robert Smith, 3 March 1806, IOL; Sydney Smith to Maria Smith, 13 January 1807, HM 30444, Huntington Library; Sydney Smith to Robert Smith, 14 January 1807, HM 30445, Huntington Library; 'Paper explaining the decision of the committee of finance at Madras', IOL.

16 Sydney Smith to Maria Smith, 19 January 1807, HM 30448, Huntington Library; 14 February 1807, HM 30454, Huntington Library; John Roberts to Robert Smith, 17 January 1807, IOL

17 Cecil Smith to Robert Smith, 21 October 1807; IOL; Sydney Smith to Maria Smith, 24 December 1807, Pierpont Morgan Library.

7 HOLLAND HOUSE

1 Holland House Dinner Books, Add. Mss. 51950, ff. 4–7, 36–7, 64, 75, 98, 103, British Library.

2 Memoir, pp. 273–4, 312; Princess Marie Liechtenstein, *Holland House*, i, pp. 24, 199; ii, pp. 13–23, 101–6.

3 Holland House Dinner Books, Add. Mss. 51950, ff. 104, 112, and 51951, f. 44, British Library; Hugh Stokes, *The Devonshire House Circle*, pp. 90–91, 200.

4 The Commonplace Book of Samuel Rogers, Add. Mss. 51649, f. 2, British Library; C.E. Macfarlane, 'Reminiscences', Add. Mss. 39776, f. 114, British Library; P.W. Clayden, *Rogers and his Contemporaries*, ii, pp. 130, 152; NCS, i, pp. 327, 451.

5 NCS, i, p. 252; Clayden, op. cit., i, p. 208; Alexander Dyce, ed., *Table Talk of Samuel Rogers*, p. 1.

6 Derek Hudson, *Holland House in Kensington*, p. xiv; Henry Luttrell to Lord and Lady Holland, Add. Mss. 51594, ff. 75, 78, 98, 106, 109, 120, British Library; Earl of Ilchester, *Chronicles of Holland House*, p. 19; Hesketh Pearson, *The Smith of Smiths*, p. 194.

7 Lord John Russell, ed., *Memoirs, Journal, and Correspondence of Thomas Moore*, v, p. 280; NCS, ii, p. 503; Alan Bell, *Sydney Smith*, pp. 198–9.

8 Earl of Ilchester, *The Home of the Hollands*, pp. 250–51; Holland House Dinner Books, Add. Mss. 51953, f. 175, British Library; Lady Seymour, *The 'Pope' of Holland House*, pp. 119–20.

9 NCS, i, p. 312; Abraham D. Kriegel, ed., *The Holland House Diaries 1831–1840*, p. xv; Clayden, op. cit., i, p. 282.

10 David Cecil, *The Young Melbourne*, p. 60; Wilmarth Lewis, *Collector's Progress*, p. 17; NCS, i, p. 108; ii, p. 624; [Caroline Holland], *The Notebooks of a Spinster Lady*, p. 254; Memoir, p. 125.

11 NCS, i, pp. 105, 479–80; Memoir, p. 57; John Gore, *Creevey's Life and Times*, p. 405.

12 Earl of Ilchester, *Chronicles of Holland House*, p. 310; Sir Henry Holland, *Recollections*, p. 233; Henry Reeve, ed., *The Greville Memoirs: A Journal of the reign of Queen Victoria from 1837 to 1852*, ii, p. 154; Francis Bickley, ed., *The Diaries of Sylvester Douglas, Lord Glenbervie*, ii, pp. 71–3.

13 NCS, i, p. 108; ii, pp. 723, 743; Sonia Keppel, *The Sovereign Lady*, p. 3; Marcel Proust, *In Search of Lost Time*, ii, p. 42

14 Osbert Burdett, *The Rev. Sydney Smith*, p. 157; Earl of Ilchester, *The Home of the Hollands*, pp. 140–41; idem., *Chronicles of Holland House*, p. 326; Keppel, op. cit., pp. 8–10, 66–7, 74.

15 Keppel, op. cit., pp. 32, 34, 40, 43; Liechtenstein, op. cit., i, p. 158.

16 Sir Henry Holland, op. cit., pp. 228–30; Keppel, op. cit., p. 294; NCS, i, p. 173.

17 Romilly, *Letters to 'Ivy'*, p. 58; Henry Reeve, ed., *The Greville Memoirs: A Journal of the reigns of King George IV, King William IV and Queen Victoria*, ii, pp. 340–41; NCS, i, pp. 107, 256.

18 NCS, i, pp. 181, 207, 252, 302, 413; ii, pp. 532, 599, 601, 693–4, 727, 847.

19 NCS, i, pp. 128, 212; ii, p. 763; Russell, op. cit., iv, p. 53.

20 E.V. Duychinck, *Wit and Wisdom of the Rev. Sydney Smith*, p. 446; Walter Jerrold, ed., *Bon-mots of Sydney Smith and R. Brinsley Sheridan*, pp. 49, 55; Stuart M. Tave, *The Amiable Humorist*, p. 83; Russell, op. cit., v, p. 75; vi, pp. 263–4.

21 Romilly, op. cit., pp. 131–2; *The Spectator* 4 July 1713; Martineau, *Autobiography*, i, p. 325.

22 Memoir, p. 417; Jerrold, op. cit., pp. 34, 81; W.H. Auden, ed., *Selected Writings of Sydney Smith*, p. xiv.

23 Pearson, op. cit., p. 11; *Works*, i, p. 322; iii, p. 350; Jerrold, op. cit., pp. 24, 26, 108.

24 Ford K. Brown, *Fathers of the Victorians*, pp. 18–19, 326. The quotation is from Colossians 3:2.

25 Sydney Smith to Revd. Cecil Smith, 4 June 1827 and 1 December 1828, Bodleian.

26 T. Wemyss Reid, *The Life, Letters, and Friendships of Richard Monckton Milnes, first Lord Houghton*, ii, p. 471. The biblical reference

is to St Mark 11:1–11.

27 Matthew 8:12.

28 Bell, *Sydney Smith*, pp. 197–8; Brookfield, *Mrs Brookfield and her Circle*, ii, p. 479; Dyce, op. cit., p. 289. The biblical reference is to 2 Kings 8:13.

8 APOSTLE OF LIBERTY

1 Dyce, *Table Talk of Samuel Rogers*, p. 98; Reid, *Sydney Smith*, pp. 130–31.

2 Memoir, p. 147; Catharine Smith, 'First Narrative' (transcript), pp. 44–5; Dyce, op. cit., p. 288.

3 Greig, *The Farington Diary*, iv, p. 76; Michael Roberts, *The Whig Party 1807–1812*, p. 18; E.A. Smith, *Lord Grey 1764–1845*, pp. 77, 120–25.

4 NCS, i, p. 124; Memoir, pp. 140–41; *Sermons* (1809), ii, pp. 98–9.

5 Memoir, pp. 148, 151; NCS, i, p. 124.

6 *Works*, i, p. v; 'P. Plymley' to Mr Budd, 26 May 1808, Bodleian.

7 *Works*, iii, pp. 328, 355, 361–2, 365, 372–3, 381, 383; NCS, ii, p. 772.

8 *Works*, iii, pp. 333, 336, 351, 403, 411, 413; F.M. Cornford, *Microcosmographia Academica*, p. 32.

9 *Works*, iii, pp. 347, 379, 390–92, 399, 402–3; Roberts, op. cit., p. 39.

10 *Works*, iii, pp. 332, 342n., 350–51, 400–1; Mitchell, *Holland House*, p. 128; Tave, *The Amiable Humorist*, p. 31; NCS, i, pp. 144–5, 169–70; Pearson, *The Smith of Smiths*, pp. 154–5.

11 NCS, i, pp. 90–91, 96, 99, 101, 131; Clive, *Scotch Reviewers*, pp. 12–13, 149; Lochhead, *Lockhart*, p. 291; Catharine Smith, 'Second Narrative' (manuscript), pp. 25–7.

12 *Works*, i, p. 84; iii, pp. 348–9.

13 *Works*, i, pp. 84, 89, 97, 141, 168–9; ii, pp. 331–2, 337.

14 *Works*, ii, pp. 334–6.

15 Chandos, *Boys Together* p. 278.

9 PRINT IN THE SAND

1 Virgin, *The Church in an Age of Negligence*, pp. 198–200, Table xix, p. 293; Sydney Smith to Robert Smith, 4 February 1808, Huntington Library.

2 NCS, i, pp. 122–3, 137, 139, 143–5, 154, 158; Memoir, p. 123; Catharine Smith, 'First Narrative' (transcript), p. 45.

3 *Yorkshire Weekly Post*, 22 September 1906; PP, 1812, xi, 393; Memoir, p. 312; 'Material relating to Sydney Smith', pp. 225, 228, York Reference Library; *Yorkshire Observer*, February 1909.

---

4 Memoir, p. 154; York Diocesan Archives, Fos. 16/3, Borthwick; Catharine Smith, 'First Narrative' (transcript), p. 53; 'Second Narrative' (transcript), p. 38.

5 NCS, i, pp. 161, 164; *A Sermon preached . . . at Malton, at the Visitation, August 1809*, p. 9; Memoir, pp. 158–60, 422.

6 Memoir, pp. 145, 161, 201, 473, 476; *Works*, ii, pp. 181, 196–7; Catharine Smith to Francis Cholmeley, 9 May 1818, North Yorkshire Record Office.

7 L.P. Wenham, ed., *Letters of James Tate*, Yorkshire Archaeological Society, cxxviii (1966), 58; Sydney Smith to Richard York, 15 December 1835, Major Christopher York; NCS, i, pp. 194, 259–60, 273, 324; *Works*, ii, pp. 150–1; Blackburn, *Charles Waterton*, pp. 88–90; Memoir, p. 262.

8 Henry Brougham, *My Life and Times*, i, p. 472; Sydney Smith to Earl Grey, 25 December 1809, Durham University.

9 G.M. Trevelyan, *Lord Grey of the Reform Bill*, p. 185; NCS, i, pp. 176 181, 202, 371, 374; E.A. Smith, *Lord Grey*, pp. 12, 135, 138, 146–7, 150.

10 Brougham Mss. 31, 298–9, University College London; NCS, i, pp. 166, 183, 186; Material relating to Cecil Smith, Mss. 1072, ff. 191–4, National Library of Scotland; Bobus Smith to Lord Holland, 10 January 1813, Add. Mss. 51801, ff. 56–7, British Library; Saba Holland, 'Manuscript Notes', p. 184; Catharine Smith to Lady Georgiana Morpeth, 23 October 1819, Castle Howard.

11 Bickley, *The Diaries of Lord Glenbervie*, ii, pp. 65–6; Romilly, *Letters to 'Ivy'*, p. 99; NCS, i, pp. 190, 194; ER, xvii, p. 336.

12 Catharine Smith, 'First Narrative' (transcript), pp. 32–3.

13 NCS, i, pp. 191, 194, 207, 214, 229; Memoir, p. 202; York Diocesan Archives, MGA 1813/1, Borthwick; Catharine Smith, 'First Narrative' (transcript), pp. 48, 54.

14 Catharine Smith, 'First Narrative' (transcript), pp. 48, 50; NCS, i, pp. 226, 228, 231–2.

15 York Diocesan Archives, Fos. 17/1, Borthwick; NCS, i, 236; Catharine Smith, 'First Narrative' (transcript), pp. 50–51; Catharine Smith to Maria Smith, 17 May 1809, IOL; Romilly, op. cit., pp. 185–6; Sir Lewis Namier and John Brooke, eds., *The History of Parliament: The House of Commons, 1754–1800*, p. 202; House of Commons, 11 February 1813, *Hansard*, xxiv, 482.

16 NCS, i, p. 236.

17 Memoir, p. 200; Catharine Smith 'First Narrative' (transcript), p. 49.

18 Memoir, p. 200; NCS, i, p. 242; George Canning to Joan Canning, 14 July 1814, Private Correspondence, Packet 25, West Yorkshire Archive Service; Namier and Brooke, op. cit., pp. 202–3.

19 Catharine Smith, 'First Narrative' (transcript), pp. 51–3; Memoir, pp. 206, 209–10; NCS, i, p. 246.

---

10 A CLOSE PRISONER

1 Unnamed correspondent to Robert Smith, 10 December 1813, IOL; NCS, i, p. 248, 251–2, 255; Saba Holland, 'Manuscript Notes', pp. 306f.; Memoir, pp. 259–60.

2 NCS, i, p. 363; Russell, *Sydney Smith*, p. 193n.; Thomas Sadler, ed., *Diary, Reminiscences and Correspondence of Henry Crabb Robinson*, ii, p. 175; Memoir, pp. 167–70, 207, 210–11, 226, 235–6, 259.

3 Memoir, pp. 166, 207–8, 212, 261; Reid, *Sydney Smith*, pp. 167–8; G. Kitson Clark, *Churchmen and the Condition of England*, pp. 168–75.

4 Catharine Smith, 'First Narrative' (transcript), pp. 29–31; NCS, i, p. 246, 345; Memoir, pp. 220, 260, 408; Parish Records of Foston, Fos. 9, Burials, 1813–1965, Borthwick.

5 Reid, op. cit., pp. 170–72; NCS, i, p. 243; Saba Holland, 'Manuscript Notes', pp. 238–42; Memoir, pp. 212–13.

6 ER, xliv, pp. 442, 447, 449; Memoir, pp. 250–51; Sydney Smith to Francis Cholmeley, 1816, North Yorkshire Record Office.

7 Virgin, *The Church in an Age of Negligence*, pp. 119–21, 124–5, Table xiv, pp. 285–6; *Works*, i, p. 278; Anne Digby, *Madness, Morality and Medicine*, pp. 30–32, 42–3, 122, 127; Andrew Scull, *The Most Solitary of Afflictions*, pp. 70–71, 73, 103, 148.

8 Phebe Doncaster, *J.S. Rowntree, His Life and Work*, p. 216; Bell, *Sydney Smith*, p. 105; *Works*, i, pp. 268–9, 278–9.

9 ER, xxviii, pp. 433–4; Digby, op. cit., pp. 9, 239–56; PP, 1814–15, iv, 805–14; Scull, op. cit., pp. 111–14.

10 Memoir, pp. 215–16; A.I.M. Duncan, 'A Study of the Life and Public Career of Frederick Howard, Fifth Earl of Carlisle 1748–1825', pp. 200, 244; fifth earl of Carlisle to Lord Morpeth, 15–16 August 1814, J17/1/298, Castle Howard.

11 NCS, i, pp. 142, 253; Sydney Smith to fifth earl of Carlisle, 1 September 1819, J14/1/476, Castle Howard; Diaries of Georgiana, Lady Morpeth, J18/62/4, J18/62/7, J18/59/18, Castle Howard; Sydney Smith to Georgiana, Lady Morpeth, 16 February 1820, Castle Howard.

12 Catharine Smith, 'Second Narrative' (manuscript), pp. 35–6; Memoir, p. 254.

13 Catharine Smith, 'Second Narrative' (transcript), p. 53; NCS, i, pp. 268, 350, 358, 362; Parish Records of Foston, MGA, 1813/1, Borthwick; Memoir, pp. 165, 262.

14 Sydney Smith to Francis Cholmeley, 21 September 1817, North Yorkshire Record Office; Sydney Smith to William Vernon, 29 March 1818, Halifax Papers, Borthwick; NCS, i, p. 333.

15 Sydney Smith to Caroline Fox, 4 October 1815, Add. Mss. 51968, f. 87, British Library; NCS, i, pp. 264–5, 270; Memoir, p. 219; Horner, *Francis Horner*, ii, pp. 329, 344–6, 363.

16 Bobus Smith to Lady Holland, 14? October 1816, Add. Mss. 51801, f.

69, British Library; NCS, i, pp. 275, 288, 294, 299, 301.
17 NCS, i, pp. 331, 335, 359, 365, 379; Virgin, op. cit., Table vi, p. 277.

11 A STRANGE REFORMER

1 NCS, i, pp. 103, 206, 268–70, 323.
2 NCS, i, pp. 286, 293, 302–3, 392; Catharine Smith, 'First Narrative' (transcript), pp. 60–66; 'Second Narrative' (manuscript), p. 38; 'Second Narrative' (transcript), p. 43; Chandos, *Boys Together*, pp. 87–8; John Field, *The King's Nurseries*, pp. 62–5; PP, 1817, vi, 173–221; *Works*, iii, pp. 346, 349.
3 *Works*, iii, p. 359; NCS, ii, p. 828; William Thomas, *The Philosophic Radicals*, pp. 47–57.
4 Memoir, p. 241; Sydney Smith to Lady Georgiana Morpeth, 31 October 1821, J18/59/29, Castle Howard; NCS, i, p. 383; will of Mary Smith, probate 11, microfilm 1649, sheet 572, PRO.
5 Catharine Smith to Lady Georgiana Morpeth, 31 October 1821, J18/59, f. 30, Castle Howard.
6 Catharine Smith, 'First Narrative' (transcript), p. 57; Sydney Smith to Francis Jeffrey, 7 April 1823, Mss. Adv. 2.1.15., f. 75–6, National Library of Scotland; Sydney Smith to duke of Devonshire, 10 March 1823, Archive 770, Chatsworth; Virgin, *The Church in an Age of Negligence*, Table v, p. 276.
7 Sydney Smith to Mrs Hicks Beach, 24 January 1824, St John, pp. 171–2, Pierpont Morgan Library; Sydney Smith to Lord Carlisle, 6 October 1828, Castle Howard; Virgin, op. cit., pp. 185–8.
8 *York Herald*, 29 March 1823; *Yorkshire Gazette*, 12 April 1823; 1823 Prison Act – 4 Geo IV, c. 64; *Works*, ii, pp. 64–7, 70, 76, 78.
9 Reid, *Sydney Smith*, p. 191; *Works*, i, pp. 414, 433, 440, 446; Sydney Smith to Sir Robert Peel, 13 March 1826, Add. Mss. 40386, f. 11–12, British Library.
10 *Works*, i, pp. 304–5, 308–9, 311, 314, 317.
11 *Works*, i, pp. 402, 405, 413; ii, p. 165; NCS, i, p. 382.

12 AT THE RISK OF MY LIFE

1 T.C.R. Read to Lord Carlisle, 25 October 1824, J14/1/491, Castle Howard; Lord Carlisle, undated notes, J14/1/492, Castle Howard.
2 Lord Carlisle to T.C.R. Read, 23 September 1824, J14/1/485, Castle Howard; Sydney Smith to Lord Carlisle, 20 September 1824, J14/1/483, Castle Howard; Lord Carlisle, undated notes, J14/1/484, Castle Howard; T.C.R. Read to Sydney Smith, 7 October 1824, J14/1/489, Castle Howard.

3 G. Cholmley to T.C.R. Read, undated, J14/1/481, Castle Howard; Lord
   Carlisle, undated notes, J14/1/493, Castle Howard; J.C.D. Clark, *English
   Society 1688–1832*, pp. 109–15.
4 *Works*, ii, pp. 93, 102; Ackroyd, *Dickens*, p. 355; Lord Carlisle to Sydney
   Smith, October 1824, J14/1/496, Castle Howard.
5 Sydney Smith to Lord Carlisle, 30 October 1824, J14/1/496, Castle
   Howard.
6 Sydney Smith to Lord Carlisle, 10 January 1825, J14/1/498, Castle
   Howard.
7 Sydney Smith to Francis Wrangham, April 1825, Fondren; *Yorkshire
   Gazette*, 16 April 1825; *York Herald*, 16 April 1825; *Works*, ii, p. 478;
   iii, p. 52; NCS, i, p. 417.
8 NCS, i, p. 425; *Works*, iii, p. 284; Sydney Smith to Lord Carlisle, 11
   February 1826, Castle Howard.
9 *Works*, iii, pp. 281, 284.
10 NCS, i, pp. 349, 429, 431.
11 NCS, i, pp. 426–8; Duff Cooper, *Talleyrand*, pp. 292, 299; Bobus Smith
   to Lord Morpeth, 13 August 1797, J17/1/26, Castle Howard.
12 NCS, i, p. 378; Sydney Smith to Bobus Smith, July 1826, IOL; Courtney
   Smith to Bobus Smith, 11 August 1817, IOL; Bobus Smith to Revd Cecil
   Smith, August 1826, IOL; Sydney Smith to Bobus Smith, 30 June 1826,
   IOL; will of Robert Smith, probate 11, microfilm 1732, sheet 613, PRO.
   The codicil is dated 2 October 1825, surely a misprint for 2 October
   1826.
13 Sydney Smith to Revd Cecil Smith, 13 August 1826, Bodleian; 27 August
   1826, Pierpont Morgan Library; Jemima Pyke to Revd Cecil Smith, 9
   October 1837, IOL.
14 NCS, i, pp. 370, 457–61; Sydney Smith to Basil Hall, 25 January 1827,
   A.S. Bell; Sydney Smith to Sir Walter Scott, 7 March 1827, Mss. 3904, f.
   90, National Library of Scotland; Catharine Smith, 'First Narrative'
   (transcript), p. 2.
15 E.A. Smith, *Lord Grey*, p. 241; *Works*, ii, pp. 229, 231–2, 239–40, 243–
   4; Sydney Smith to duke of Devonshire, 5 November 1827, Archive 1592,
   Chatsworth.

13 THE OAK WILL SPRING UP

1 Sydney Smith to Francis Wrangham, 24 December 1825, Fondren; E.A.
   Smith, *Lord Grey*, p. 260; Mitchell, *Holland House*, p. 128; NCS, ii, p.
   596.
2 Sydney Smith to Revd Cecil Smith, 30 August 1827, 6 October 1827,
   Bodleian; Robert Smith to unnamed correspondent, 16 April 1826, IOL.
3 Sydney Smith to Dr Headlam, 20 August 1827, St Paul's Cathedral
   Library; Lord Lyndhurst to Sydney Smith, 9 or 16 September 1827,

archive 4437, no. 12, New College, Oxford; Lord Fitzwilliam to Sydney Smith, 3 December 1827, archive 4429, no. 72, New College, Oxford; Romilly, *Letters to 'Ivy'*, p. 330.

4 NCS, i, pp. 469–70n., 477; Romilly, op. cit., pp. 331–2; PP, 1835, xxii, 37.

5 NCS, i, p. 481; Memoir, p. 266; Virgin, *The Church in an Age of Negligence*, Table xv, p. 287; *Sermons* (1809), ii, p. 288.

6 Sydney Smith to Lady Carlisle, 18 February 1828, Castle Howard; October? 1828, J18/59, f. 57, Castle Howard.

7 Sydney Smith to E. J. Littleton, 7 November 1828, Hatherton Papers, Staffordshire Record Office.

8 NCS, i, pp. 392, 476, 480, 483, 487; Sydney Smith to Maria Smith, April 1805, HM 30439, Huntington Library; Catharine Smith, 'First Narrative' (transcript), p. 66.

9 NCS, i, p. 489; ii, pp. 494, 496; Sydney Smith to Lady Carlisle, 7 January 1829, Castle Howard; Catharine Smith, 'First Narrative' (transcript), p. 69.

10 Catharine Smith, 'Second Narrative' (transcript), pp. 51–2; Sydney Smith to Revd Cecil Smith, 20 October 1828, Bodleian.

11 Sydney Smith to Lord Lyndhurst, 25 March 1829, Mss. O.16.3859, Trinity College, Cambridge; Sydney Smith to Lord Carlisle, 17 April 1829, J18/59 f. 9, Castle Howard; Sydney Smith to Richard York, 12 March 1841, Major Christopher York; NCS, i, p. 491.

12 Sydney Smith to Mrs Austin, 28 August 1835, D.R. Bentham; *Country Life*, 3 June 1971; Sydney Smith to Richard York, 18 December 1829, Major Christopher York; NCS, ii, p. 498; Memoir, pp. 240, 289, 307, 383–4.

13 Memoir, pp. 294–6, 397; Saba Holland, 'Manuscript Notes', pp. 331, 333; Catharine Smith, 'Second Narrative' (manuscript), pp. 22–3.

14 NCS, ii, pp. 515, 523–4, 552–3, 797; Memoir, pp. 392, 394; Smith, op. cit., pp. 255, 258; *Works*, iii, pp. 65, 69, 78–9.

15 Virgin, op. cit., p. 19; *Works*, iii, p. 76; Read, *Sydney Smith*, pp. 273–9.

16 Sydney Smith to Sir Robert Wilmot Horton, 3 November 1833, Catton Papers, Derby Public Library; Catharine Smith, 'First Narrative' (transcript), p. 69; Smith, op. cit., pp. 144, 261; Mitchell, op. cit., p. 104; Memoir, p. 258.

17 NCS, ii, p. 528; Kriegel, *Holland House Diaries*, pp. 52, 174; R.A. Soloway, *Prelates and People*, pp. 11–12.

18 Henry Cockburn, 'An Account of the Friday Club', *The Book of the Old Edinburgh Club*, iii (1910), p. 108; John Jolliffe, ed., *Neglected Genius; The Diaries of Benjamin Robert Haydon 1808–1846*, p. 223; NCS, ii, pp. 542, 611; Memoir, p. 294; Catharine Smith, 'First Narrative' (transcript), p. 70; Saba Holland, 'Manuscript Notes', p. 324; PP, 1835, xxii, 55; Virgin, op. cit., p. 90.

19 NCS, ii, pp. 558, 562, 868; G.L. Prestige, *St Paul's in its Glory*, pp. 26–7;

Dean Milman to Catharine Smith, 1 January 1850, D.C.L. Holland.

20 Lord John Russell to Dean and Chapter of St Paul's, 6 July 1837, 20 September 1837, 27 November 1837, Chapter Minute Book, 1833–1860, St Paul's Cathedral Library; NCS, ii, pp. 863–4, 867.

21 Memoir, pp. 360–61; Reeve, *The Greville Memoirs: A Journal of the reigns of King George IV, King William IV and Queen Victoria*, iii, p. 170; Hillard, *George Ticknor*, i, p. 414.

22 Sydney Smith to Richard York, 9 April 1840, Major Christopher York; Read, op. cit., pp. 305–6; NCS, ii, pp. 671, 687, 776; Martineau, *Autobiography*, i, pp. 276, 369; Lord Houghton, *Monographs, Personal and Social*, p. 267; Sir Henry Holland, *Recollections*, pp. 221–5; Earl of Ilchester, *Chronicles of Holland House*, p. 241; Memoir, p. 138; *The Letters of Charles Dickens*, i, p. 24; Reeve, *The Greville Memoirs: A Journal of the reign of Queen Victoria*, ii, p. 273.

23 Memoir, p. 415; NCS, ii, p. 755; John Ruskin, *Praeterita*, ii, p. 296; T. Wemyss Reid, *The Life, Letters and Friendships of Richard Monckton Milnes*, i, p. 215.

14 PUT ON THE DRAG

1 Catharine Smith, 'Second Narrative' (transcript), p. 56; Sydney Smith to Miss White, 29 June 1822, Haverford College Library; Sir Henry Holland, *Recollections*, pp. 80f., 111; Sydney Smith to Richard York, 7 February 1834, Major Christopher York.

2 Holland, op. cit., pp. 5–6, 151, 179, 184, 278; NCS, ii, pp. 596–8, 601, 608, 741, 818; G.F.A. Best, *Temporal Pillars*, pp. 297–8, Appendix vi, p. 545; Minute Book of the Ecclesiastical Duties and Revenues Commission, Church of England Record Office.

3 NCS, i, pp. 240, 252; ii, pp. 594, 616–19, 626–32, 759, 814; Reid, *The Life, Letters and Friendships of Richard Monckton Milnes*, ii, pp. 476–7; Sydney Smith to earl of Carlisle, July 1835, J18/59, f.7., Castle Howard; Sydney Smith to Richard York, 27 October 1835, 15 December 1835, Major Christopher York.

4 NCS, ii, pp. 611, 633, 637, 639.

5 *Ibid.*, ii, pp. 614, 624, 639, 748; [Caroline Holland], *Notebooks of a Spinster Lady*, p. 254.

6 Owen Chadwick, *The Victorian Church*, i, pp. 112–21; David Cecil, *Lord M.*, pp. 137–44; Lord Houghton, *Monographs, Personal and Social*, p. 278; Saba Holland, 'Manuscript Notes', p. 320; Kriegel, *Holland House Diaries*, p. 344.

7 Sydney Smith to Lord John Russell, 14 January 1836, Mss. 30/22/2A, ff. 85–6, PRO.

8 Sydney Smith to Lord John Russell, 19 July 1836, Mss. 30/22/2B, ff. 254–5, PRO; Sydney Smith to Lady Ashburton, 9 January 1837, Harvard

College Library; *Works*, iii, p. 122; Sydney Smith to Richard York, 7 February 1834, Major Christopher York; R.H. Barham to Mrs Hughes, 7 June 1836, in Barham, *The Life and Letters of the Rev R.H. Barham*, i, pp. 286–7.

9 NCS, ii, pp. 665, 669, 838; *Works*, ii, p. 303; iii, pp. 124–5, 149, 157.

10 Sir Robert Peel to William Howley, 22 March 1835, Add. Mss. 40418, f. 14, British Library; Howley to Peel, 25 March 1835, Add. Mss. 40418, f. 83, British Library; *Works*, iii, pp. 122, 146–8, 153–4.

11 *Works*, iii, p. 154; Sydney Smith to Lord Palmerston, 7 April 1836, Osborn College, Yale University Library; C.J. Blomfield to Sydney Smith, 24 January 1837, St Paul's Cathedral Library; Sydney Smith to Revd Cecil Smith, 18 May 1837, A.S. Bell; Sydney Smith to Humphrey Mildmay, 5–6 May 1837, formerly Mildmay-White Trust; NCS, ii, p. 657.

12 Sydney Smith to Lord Melbourne, 18 April 1837, and Sydney Smith to William Cowper, 7 June 1837, Melbourne Papers, Box 80, Royal Archives, Windsor.

13 Sydney Smith to Lord John Russell, 28 June 1837, P.R. Glazebrook; *Works*, iii, pp. 164, 166, 168, 176; Lord Carlisle to Sydney Smith, May 1838, Castle Howard; Sydney Smith to Lord Carlisle, 22 May 1838, J18/59/f.4, Castle Howard.

14 E.A. Smith, *Lord Grey*, pp. 263–4; Catharine Smith, 'Second Narrative' (manuscript), p. 50; Thomas, *The Philosophic Radicals*, p. 414; *Works*, iii, pp. 93, 95, 98–9, 105, 109–10, 113; J.H. Monk, *Charge*, pp. 23–4.

15 Memoir, pp. 331–2; Saba Holland, 'Manuscript Notes', pp. 174, 340; [Caroline Holland], op. cit., p. 180; Jerrold, *Bon-Mots*, p. 34; NCS, ii, pp. 694, 696, 699, 707, 709, 711, 812.

15 THE BREATHLESS LION ROARS

1 Ilchester, *Chronicles of Holland House*, p. 283.

2 Keppel, *Sovereign Lady*, pp. 350, 353, 358, 365; Reeve, *The Greville Memoirs: A Journal of the reign of Queen Victoria*, i, p. 341; NCS, i, pp. 340–1; ii, pp. 591, 715; *Sermons* (1809), ii, p. 294.

3 NCS, ii, pp. 719, 725–6, 730, 748–9, 751.

4 Hillard, *Ticknor*, i, p. 265; NCS, ii, pp. 721, 758, 765, 767, 769, 771.

5 *Works*, iii, pp. 423, 425, 427–8; Sydney Smith to Miss Fox, June 1842, *Miscellanies of the Philobiblon Society*, xv (1877–84), vii, pp. 17–18.

6 NCS, i, p. 475; Letters of Administration relating to the will of Courtney Smith, Probate 6, microfilm 219, sheet 318, PRO; Sydney Smith to Revd Cecil Smith, 10 February 1843, Bodleian.

7 Catharine Smith to Mary Smith, 6 March 1843, IOL; Sydney Smith to Revd Cecil Smith, 10 February 1843, Bodleian. One of Courtney's wills is at the India Office Library.

8 Sydney Smith to Revd Cecil Smith, 14 March 1843, 15 March 1843, 29 March 1843, Bodleian; Catharine Smith to Mary Smith, 6 March 1843, 14 March 1843, IOL; Bobus Smith to Revd Cecil Smith, 14 March 1843, IOL.

9 Sydney Smith to Revd Cecil Smith, 16 March 1843, 19 March 1843, 5 April 1843, Bodleian; Windham Smith to Revd Cecil Smith, 16 March 1843, IOL.

10 J.B. McMaster, *A History of the People of the United States*, vii, pp. 6–7, 14–15, 29, 34, 42; *Works*, iii, pp. 441–2, 446–7, 451, 453; Memoir, pp. 349–55; Hillard, op. cit., ii, p. 214.

11 Hillard, op. cit., ii, pp. 215–16.

12 Sydney Smith to Thomas Moore, 10 June 1843, Iowa University Library; NCS, ii, pp. 786, 796, 799, 803, 807, 821–2; E.A. Smith, *Lord Grey*, pp. 323–4; Lyster, *A Family Chronicle*, p. 186.

13 Sydney Smith to Sir Robert Peel, 5 May 1844, Add. Mss. 40544, f. 54, British Library; Sir Robert Peel to Sydney Smith, 6 May 1844, 17 May 1844, Add. Mss. 40544, f. 56, 63, British Library; Sydney Smith to Sir Robert Peel, 18? May 1844, Add. Mss. 40544, f. 64, British Library.

14 Sydney Smith to Sir Robert Peel, before 15 June 1844, Add. Mss. 40546, f. 367, British Library; NCS, ii, pp. 838, 845–6, 849–50; Sydney Smith to Lady Holland, 15 September 1844, *Miscellanies of the Philobiblon Society*, xv (1877–84), vii, pp. 22–3.

15 Catharine Smith to Lady Carlisle, 1 November 1844, J18/59/f.82, Castle Howard; Memoir, pp. 172, 459; NCS, ii, pp. 856, 858; Sydney Smith to Revd Cecil Smith, 5 November 1844, Bodleian.

16 Sydney Smith to Sir Robert Peel, 22 November 1844, Add. Mss. 40554, ff. 298–9, British Library; Catharine Smith to Lady Carlisle, 27 November 1844, J18/59/f.80, Castle Howard.

17 Catharine Smith to Lady Holland, *c*. mid-December 1844, Add. Mss. 51645, f. 57, British Library; Catharine Smith to Lady Carlisle, 20 January 1845, J18/59/f.81, Castle Howard.

18 Memoir, pp. 460–61, 464; Ilchester, *Chronicles of Holland House*, p. 341; Clayden, *Rogers*, ii, pp. 268–9.

19 NCS, ii, p. 814; Catharine Smith, 'First Narrative' (transcript), p. 67; Memoir, p. 464; Will of Sydney Smith, Probate 11, microfilm 2016, sheet 341, PRO.

BIBLIOGRAPHY

MANUSCRIPTS

A.S. Bell, Oxford: Letters between Sydney Smith and Basil Hall; and between Sydney Smith and Revd Cecil Smith.

D.R. Bentham, Loughborough, Leicestershire: Letter from Sydney Smith to Mrs Austin.

Bodleian Library, Broad St, Oxford: Letters between Sydney Smith and Revd Cecil Smith; between Sydney Smith and Richard Heber; and between 'P. Plymley' and Mr Budd.

Borthwick Institute of Historical Research, St Anthony's Hill, Peasholme Green, York: Archives of the Diocese of York, including those of the parish of Foston; letter from Sydney Smith to William Vernon (Halifax papers).

British Library, Great Russell St, London WC1: Commonplace Book of Samuel Rogers; Holland House Dinner Books; C.E. Macfarlane, 'Reminiscences'; records of the King of Clubs; letters between Earl Grey and Mr Willoughby-Gordon; between Lord Holland and Caroline Fox; between Lady Holland and Caroline Fox; between Henry Luttrell and Lord and Lady Holland; between Sir Robert Peel and William Howley; between Bobus Smith and Lord Holland; between Bobus Smith and Lady Holland; between Catharine Smith and Lady Holland; between Sydney Smith and J.G. Clarke; between Sydney Smith and Caroline Fox; and between Sydney Smith and Sir Robert Peel.

Castle Howard, Yorkshire: Diaries of Georgiana, Lady Morpeth; letters between G. Cholmley and Revd T.C.R. Read; between the fifth Earl of Carlisle and Lord Morpeth; between the fifth Earl of Carlisle and Revd T.C.R. Read; between the fifth Earl of Carlisle and Sydney Smith; between the sixth Earl of Carlisle and Sydney Smith; between Georgiana, Lady Morpeth and Catharine Smith; between Georgiana, Lady Morpeth and Sydney Smith; between Revd T.C.R. Read and Sydney Smith; and between Bobus Smith and Lord Morpeth.

Church of England Record Office, Galleywall Rd, London SE16: Minute Book of the Ecclesiastical Duties and Revenues Commission.

Derbyshire Record Office, New St, Matlock: Letter from Sydney Smith to Sir Robert Wilmot Horton (Catton Papers).

Duke of Devonshire, Chatsworth House, Bakewell, Derbyshire: Letters between the duke of Devonshire and Sydney Smith.

Durham University Library, Palace Green, Durham: Letter from Sydney Smith to Earl Grey.

Fondren Library, Rice University, Houston, Texas, USA: Letters between Sydney Smith and Francis Wrangham.

P.R. Glazebrook, Cambridge: Letter from Sydney Smith to Lord John Russell.

Gloucestershire Record Office, Clarence Row, Gloucester: Letter from William Hicks Beach to Mrs Hicks Beach (St Aldwyn Papers).

Greater London Record Office, Northampton Rd, London EC1:   Records of the parish of St George's, Bloomsbury.

Haverford College Library, Haverford, Pennsylvania, USA: Letter from Sydney Smith to Lydia White.

Hertfordshire Record Office, County Hall, Hertford: Letter from Sydney Smith to E.L. Bulwer (Lytton Papers).

D.C.L. Holland, Polegate, East Sussex: Saba Holland, Manuscript Notes forming the basis of a Memoir of Sydney Smith (undated); *idem*, Commonplace Book (undated); Catharine Smith, Narrative (undated); *idem*, Transcript of Narrative (undated); *idem*, Second Narrative (undated); *idem*, Transcript of Second Narrative (undated); letters relating to publication of Sydney Smith's *Elementary Sketches of Moral Philosophy* in 1850; letters between Sydney Smith and Dr Gerrard Andrewes.

Houghton Library, Harvard University, Cambridge, Massachusetts, USA: Letter from Sydney Smith to Lady Ashburton.

Henry E. Huntington Library, San Marino, California, USA: Letters between Sydney Smith and Robert Smith; and between Sydney Smith and Maria Smith.

India Office Library, Blackfriars Rd, London SE1:   Paper explaining the decision of the committee of finance at Madras; Will of Courtney Smith; Letters between William Burrows and Robert Smith; between Catharine Pybus and Robert Smith; between Martha Pybus and Robert Smith; between an unnamed correspondent and Robert Smith; between Bobus Smith and Robert Smith; between Caroline Smith and Robert Smith; between Cecil Smith and Robert Smith; between Bobus Smith and Courtney Smith; between Bobus Smith and Revd Cecil Smith; between Bobus Smith and Sydney Smith; between Caroline Smith and Maria Smith; between Catharine Smith and Maria Smith; between Catharine Smith and Mary Smith; between an unnamed correspondent and Cecil Smith; between Maria Smith and Cecil Smith; between Revd Cecil Smith and Jemima Pyke; and between Revd Cecil Smith and Windham Smith.

Iowa University Library, Iowa City, Iowa, USA: Letter from Sydney Smith to Tom Moore.

Keele University Library, Keele, Staffordshire: Letter from Sydney Smith to James Mackintosh.

National Library of Wales, Aberystwyth: Letter from Sydney Smith to

Mrs Hicks Beach.

National Library of Scotland, George IV Bridge, Edinburgh: Davis D. McElroy, 'A Century of Scottish Clubs 1700–1800', 2 vols, 1969; material relating to Cecil Smith; Letters between Henry Brougham and James Reddie; between Sydney Smith and Francis Jeffrey; between Sydney Smith and James Mackintosh; and between Sydney Smith and Sir Walter Scott.

New College, Oxford: Admissions Book; Dinner Book; Junior Common Room Rules and Accounts; J.E. Sewell, Register of Scholars; The Orders of the Warden and the Thirteen, 1788–1813; Letters between Sydney Smith and Robert Smith; between Sydney Smith and Lord Lyndhurst; and between Sydney Smith and Lord Fitzwilliam.

James M. and Marie-Louise Osborn Collection, Yale University Library, New Haven, Connecticut, USA: Letter from Sydney Smith to Lord Palmerston.

Pierpont Morgan Library, East 36th St, New York, USA: Letters between Sydney Smith and Maria Smith; between Sydney Smith and Revd Cecil Smith; and between Sydney Smith and Mr and Mrs Hicks Beach; list of the Poor of Netheravon, drawn up by Mr Verrey, steward to Michael Hicks Beach, in March 1793.

Public Record Office, Chancery Lane, London WC2:   Letters of Administration relating to the Will of Courtney Smith; Wills of Mary Smith, Robert Smith and Sydney Smith.

Public Record Office, Ruskin Avenue, Kew: Letters between Sydney Smith and Lord John Russell.

Royal Library, Windsor Castle, Berkshire: Letters between Sydney Smith and Lord Melbourne; and between Sydney Smith and William Cowper.

St Paul's Cathedral Library, Ludgate Hill, London EC4:   Chapter Minute Book, 1833–1860; Letters between Sydney Smith and Bishop Blomfield of London; and between Sydney Smith and Dr Headlam.

Staffordshire Record Office, Eastgate St, Stafford: Letter from Sydney Smith to E.J. Littleton (Hatherton Papers).

Trinity College, Cambridge: Letter from Sydney Smith to Lord Lyndhurst.

University College London, Gower St, London WC1:   Letters between Sydney Smith and Henry Brougham.

Major Christopher York, Long Marston, Yorkshire: Letters between Sydney Smith and Richard York.

North Yorkshire County Record Office, Malpas Road, Northallerton: Letters between Catharine Smith and Francis Cholmeley; and between Sydney Smith and Francis Cholmeley.

West Yorkshire Archive Service, Chapeltown Road, Sheepscar, Leeds: Letters between George Canning and Mary Anne Canning; and between George Canning and Joan Canning.

York Reference Library, Museum St, York: Material relating to Sydney Smith.

DISSERTATIONS

A.I.M. Duncan, 'A Study of the Life and Public Career of Frederick Howard, Fifth Earl of Carlisle 1748–1825', Oxford University D.Phil., 1981.

MAGAZINES, NEWSPAPERS, OFFICIAL DOCUMENTS AND PERIODICALS

Country Life
Edinburgh Review
Hansard
Miscellanies of the Philobiblon Society
The Microcosm
Notes and Queries
Parliamentary Papers
Proceedings of the Yorkshire Archaeological Society
Quarterly Review
Spectator
York Herald
Yorkshire Gazette
Yorkshire Observer
Yorkshire Weekly Post

SECONDARY WORKS

Ackroyd, Peter, *Dickens*, Sinclair-Stevenson, 1990.

Adams, H.C., *Wykehamica*, 1878.

[An Old Wykehamist], *Recollections of the two St Mary Winton Colleges*, 1883.

Auden, W.H., *Selected Writings of Sydney Smith*, 1957.

Baker, James, *The Life of Sir Thomas Bernard*, 1819.

Barham, R.H.D., *The Life and Letters of the Rev Richard Harris Barham*, 2 vols, 1870.

Barnett, Charlotte, ed., *Diary and Letters of Madame D'Arblay*, 6 vols, 1904.

Bell, Alan, *Sydney Smith: A Biography*, OUP, 1980.

Best, G.F.A., *Temporal Pillars*, 1964.

Bickley, Francis, ed., *The Diaries of Sylvester Douglas, Lord Glenbervie*, 1928.

Blackburn, Julia, *Charles Waterton*, Bodley Head, 1989.

Brookfield, Charles and Frances, *Mrs Brookfield and her Circle*, 2 vols, 1905.

Brougham, Henry, *My Life and Times*, 3 vols, 1871.

Brown, Ford K., *Fathers of the Victorians*, 1961.

Burdett, Osbert, *The Rev. Smith, Sydney*, 1934.

Buxton, John, and Williams, Penry, eds., *New College Oxford 1379–1979*, New College, Oxford, 1979.

Cecil, David, *Lord M.*, 1954.

—— *The Young Melbourne*, new edn, 1960.

Chadwick, Owen, *The Victorian Church*, I, 1966.

Chandos, John, *Boys Together: English Public Schools 1800–1864*, Hutchinson, 1984.

Chitnis, Anand C., *The Scottish Enlightenment and Early Victorian English Society*, Croom Helm, 1986.

Christian, Susan Emily, *A Cotswold Family: Hicks and Hicks Beach*, 1909.

Clark, J.C.D., *English Society 1688–1832*, OUP, 1985.

Clayden, P.W., *Rogers and his Contemporaries*, 2 vols, 1899.

Clive, John, *Scotch Reviewers*, 1957.

Cockburn, Henry, *Life of Lord Jeffrey*, 2 vols, 1852.

—— *Journal, 1831–1854*, 2 vols, 1874.

—— *Memorials of His Time*, new edn, 1910.

Constable, Thomas, *Archibald Constable and his Literary Correspondents*, 3 vols, 1873.

Cook, A.K., *About Winchester College*, 1917.

Cooper, Duff, *Talleyrand*, Cassell, 1987.

Cornford, F.M., *Microcosmographia Academica*, 3rd edn, 1933.

Custance, Roger, ed., *Winchester College: Sixth-centenary Essays*, OUP, 1982.

D'Arblay, Madame, *Memoirs of Dr Burney*, 3 vols, 1832.

The Letters of Charles Dickens, 3 vols, 1880.

Dickson, William K., *The History of the Speculative Society, 1764–1845*, Edinburgh, *c.* 1903.

Digby, Anne, *Madness, Morality and Medicine*, CUP, 1985.

Doncaster, Phebe, *J.S. Rowntree, His Life and Work*, 1908.

Duychinck, E.A., *Wit and Wisdom of the Rev. Sydney Smith*, 1858.

Dyce, A., ed., *Recollections of the Table Talk of Samuel Rogers*, 1856.

Edgcumbe, Richard, ed., *The Diary of Frances Lady Shelley*, 2 vols, 1912–13.

Field, John, *The King's Nurseries*, James and James, 1987.

Furber, Holden, *Henry Dundas First Viscount Melville 1742–1811*, 1931.

Gore, John, *Creevey's Life and Times*, 1934.

Greig, James, ed., *The Farington Diary*, 8 vols, 1928.

Greig, James A., *Francis Jeffrey of the Edinburgh Review*, 1948.

Hare, Augustus J.C., *The Story of my Life*, 6 vols, 1896–1900.

Hillard, George S., *Life, Letters, and Journal of George Ticknor*, 2 vols, 1876.

[Holland, Caroline], *The Notebooks of a Spinster Lady, 1878–1903*, 1919.

Holland, Sir Henry, *Recollections of Past Life*, 1872.

Holland, Saba, *A Memoir of the Reverend Sydney Smith . . . with a Selection from his Letters*, edited by Mrs Austin, 2 vols, 1855.

Horner, Leonard, ed., *Memoirs and Correspondence of Francis Horner*, 2 vols, 1843.

Houghton, Lord, *Monographs, Personal and Social*, 1873.

Hudson, Derek, *Holland House in Kensington*, 1967.

Ilchester, Earl of, *Chronicles of Holland House 1820–1900*, 1937.

—— *The Home of the Hollands 1605–1820*, 1937.

—— *The Journal of Elizabeth, Lady Holland, 1791–1811*, 2 vols, 1908.

Jerrold, Walter, ed., *Bon-Mots of Sydney Smith and R. Brinsley Sheridan*, 1893.

Jolliffe, John, ed., *Neglected Genius; The Diaries of Benjamin Robert Haydon 1808–1846*, Hutchinson 1990.

Keppel, Sonia, *The Sovereign Lady: A Life of Elizabeth Vassall, third Lady Holland, with her family*, Hamish Hamilton, 1974.

Kirby, T.F., *Annals of Winchester College*, 1892.

—— *Winchester Scholars*, 1888.

Kitson Clark, G.S.R., *Churchmen and the Condition of England 1832–1885*, Methuen, 1973.

Kriegel, Abraham D., ed., *The Holland House Diaries 1831–1840*, Routledge and Kegan Paul, 1977.

Leach, Arthur F., *A History of Winchester College*, 1899.

Lewis, Wilmarth, *Collector's Progress*, 1952.

Liechtenstein, Princess Marie, *Holland House*, 2 vols, 1874.

Lochhead, Marion, *John Gibson Lockhart*, 1954.

Lyster, Gertrude, *A Family Chronicle*, 1908.

Mackintosh, R.J., ed., *Memoirs of the Life of Sir James Mackintosh*, 2 vols, 1836.

McMaster, J.B., *A History of the People of the United States*, 7 vols, 1910.

Martineau, Harriet, *Autobiography*, 3 vols, 1877.

Mitchell, Leslie, *Holland House*, Duckworth, 1980.

Monk, J.H., *Charge*, 1838.

Namier, Sir Lewis, and Brooke, John, eds., *The History of Parliament: The House of Commons 1754–1800*, 1964.

New, Chester W., *The Life of Henry Brougham to 1830*, 1961.

Oakes, C.G., *Sir Samuel Romilly 1757–1818*, 1935.

Pearson, Hesketh, *The Smith of Smiths*, 1934.

Prestige, G.L., *St Paul's in its Glory*, 1955.

Proust, Marcel, *In Search of Lost Time*, 6 vols, Chatto and Windus, 1992.

Rashdall, Hastings, and Rait, Robert S., *New College*, 1901.

Reeve, Henry, ed., *The Greville Memoirs: A Journal of the Reigns of King George IV, King William IV and Queen Victoria*, 3 vols, 1874–87.

—— *The Greville Memoirs: A Journal of the Reign of Queen Victoria from 1837–1852*, 3 vols, 1874–87.

Reid, Stuart J., *The Life and Times of Sydney Smith*, 4th edn, 1896.

Reid, T. Wemyss, *The Life, Letters and Friendships of Richard Monckton Milnes, First Lord Houghton*, 2 vols, 1890.

Roberts, Michael, *The Whig Party 1807–1812*, 1939.

Romilly, S.H., *Letters to 'Ivy', from the First Earl of Dudley*, 1905.

Ruskin, John, *Praeterita*, 3 vols, 1885.

Russell, G.W.E., *Sydney Smith*, 1905.

Russell, Lord John, *Memoirs, Journal, and Correspondence of Thomas Moore*, 8 vols, 1853–6.

Sadler, Thomas, ed., *Diary, Reminiscences and Correspondence of Henry Crabb Robinson*, 3rd edn, 2 vols, 1872.

Scull, Andrew, *The Most Solitary of Afflictions*, Yale University Press, 1993.

Seymour, Lady, *The 'Pope' of Holland House*, 1906.

Smith, A.H., *New College Oxford and its Buildings*, 1952.

Smith, E.A., *Lord Grey 1764–1845*, OUP, 1990.

Smith, Nowell, C., ed., *The Letters of Sydney Smith*, 2 vols, 1953.

Smith, Sydney, *Collected Works*, 3 vols, new edn, 1845.

—— *Elementary Sketches of Moral Philosophy*, 1850.

—— *Six Sermons, preached at Charlotte Chapel, Edinburgh*, Edinburgh, 1800.

—— *Sermons*, 2 vols, Edinburgh, 1801.

—— *Sermons*, 2 vols, 1809.

—— *A Sermon preached . . . at Malton, at the Visitation, August 1809*, York, 1809.

—— *Sermons preached at St Paul's Cathedral*, 1846.

Soloway, R.A., *Prelates and People*, 1969.

Sparrow, John, *Independent Essays*, 1963.

Stokes, Hugh, *The Devonshire House Circle*, 1917.

Sutherland, L.S., and Mitchell, L.G., eds., *The History of the University of Oxford: The Eighteenth Century*, OUP, 1986.

Tave, Stuart M., *The Amiable Humorist*, 1960.

Thomas, William E.S., *The Philosophic Radicals*, OUP, 1979.

Trevelyan, G.M., *Lord Grey of the Reform Bill*, 1929.

—— *Ramillies and the Union with Scotland*, 1932.

Trollope, Thomas Augustus, *What I Remember*, 2 vols, 1887.

Virgin, Peter, *The Church in an Age of Negligence*, James Clarke, 1989.

Wooll, John, *Biographical Memoirs of the late Revd Joseph Warton*, 1806.

Ziegler, Philip, *Addington*, 1965.

INDEX